Mail this card TODAY for John T. Reed's **Football Coaching Lessons Learned booklet**

Yes, please senc
and any other pro

Name ______________

Address ______________

City ______________ State __ Zip ______________

sent to buyers of this book who send in this card.

Football Clock Management	**$19.95**	______
Coaching Youth Football, 2nd ed.	**$21.95**	______
Coaching Youth Football Defense	**$19.95**	______

Prices effective August 1997 and are subject to change.

Subtotal ______

CA residents add sales tax ______

Shipping: $4 for first item, $2 for EACH additional item ______

Total ______

☐ Check enclosed ☐ Visa ☐ MasterCard

Card # ______________ Exp. ______

Signature ______________ Tel. ______________

Fax: ______________ E-mail: ______________

Mail to: John T. Reed, 342 Bryan Drive, Alamo, CA 94507 Call **510-820-6292 or fax 510-820-1259 E-mail**:johnreed@johntreed.com
Web site http://www.johntreed.com

Place
Stamp
Here

John T. Reed
342 Bryan Drive
Alamo, CA 94507

Football Clock Management

by

John T. "Jack" Reed

342 Bryan Drive, Danville, CA 94526 (City and ZIP scheduled to change to Alamo 94507 on 9/27/97)
E-mail: johnreed@johntreed.com, Web site: www.johntreed.com
Voice: 510-820-6292 Fax: 510-820-1259

To my players

About the author

John T. "Jack" Reed is a professional writer and publisher. He has coached freshman, junior varsity, and varsity high school football and all ages of youth football. Reed also coached youth soccer, high school volleyball, and baseball from the tee ball to semi-pro levels. He is a member of the American Football Coaches Association, the California Coaches Association, the National Federation Interscholastic Coaches Association, National Youth Sports Coaches Association, and the American Baseball Coaches Association.

He holds a bachelor of science degree from the United States Military Academy at West Point and a master of business administration degree form Harvard Business School.

Thanks to

My sons, Daniel, Steven, and Mike for agreeing to my recommendation that they try football for a year before deciding whether they wanted to play soccer or football...my wife for being a football widow to an extent during coaches meetings, scouting trips, practice, and games...the San Ramon Bears for taking my oldest son in after he was cut by another team and for giving me the opportunity to coach...Pat Elliott for selecting me as defensive coach for the 1991 season...Steve Noon for selecting me as assistant head coach and defense/special teams coach in the 1992 season...Jim Monroe for helping me design my defensive system...Kathryn Steele, Bears trainer and Shannon Pablo, Miramonte trainer for their counsel on injury prevention and treatment...my fellow coaches for putting up with my foibles and faults...our cameramen without whose videotaping of games we coaches wouldn't know what the heck happened out there...my players, who also put up with my faults and foibles as we struggled together through their early years as players and my early years as coach...Miramonte High School coaches Richard Blaisdell, Floyd Burnsed, Paul Yriberri, Vince Dell'Aquilla and Granada High School coaches Aaron Gingery, Bob Turnbeaugh, Ken Nelson, Brad Morosoli, Hank Stephens, T.J. Thomas, John Glover, and Doug Pederson for their instruction and encouragement...Roger Theder, NFL and college coach, for his advice and encouragement...Dana Bible, Stanford offensive coordinator for sharing his thoughts and experiences on clock management with me...Holly Newman, referee for reading the book and straightening me out on high school rules...Ace Cacchiotti of NFL Films for his generous assistance...Victor Vitorelli of ABC Sports for his help...NFL team public relations men: Bob Moore of the Chiefs, Harvey Greene and Neal Gulkis of the Dolphins, Frank Ramos of the Jets, Greg Gladysiewski of the Cardinals, Rich Dalrymple of the Cowboys, Lee Remmel ofthe Packers, Pat Hanlon of the Giants, Todd Starowitz of the Eagles.

Cover design: John T. Reed

Published by John T. Reed, 342 Bryan Drive, Danville, CA 94526 (City and ZIP scheduled to change to Alamo 94507 on 9/27/97) 510-820-6292, fax 510-820-1259, e-mail: johnreed@johntreed.com, Web site: www.johntreed.com
Library of Congress Catalog Card Number: 97-091682
ISBN: 0-939224-39-9

Other football books by John T. Reed

- Coaching Youth Football, 2nd edition
- Coaching Youth Football Defense, 2nd edition

For more information, contact John T. Reed, 342 Bryan Drive, Danville, CA 94526 (City and ZIP scheduled to change to Alamo 94507 on 9/27/97). Telephone 510-820-6292 or fax 510-820-1259 or E-mail: johnreed@johntreed.com. Web site: www.johntreed.com

Table of contents

1

Overview

On October 19, 1996, Wisconsin was beating Northwestern 30-27 with 1:33 left in the game. They had the ball first and ten at their own 38-yard line after a missed field goal. Northwestern had one timeout remaining. Wisconsin Head Coach Barry Alvarez called two handoff plays. His running back fumbled the exchange on the second-down play, Northwestern recovered at the Wisconsin 41 with 47 seconds left. Two plays later, Northwestern scored a touchdown and won the game 34-30.

Three ESPN announcers: Brad Nessler, Gary Danielson, and Lee Corso, were highly critical of Alvarez for not having his quarterback just take a knee four times. Corso, who had been a college coach at Louisville, Indiana, and Northern Illinois, went so far as to say, half seriously, that Alvarez should resign because of the blunder.

In fact, the ESPN experts were wrong, not Alvarez. Nessler formally apologized.

Confusing subject

The fact that three national football analysts, including one former coach, could be so wrong, in spite of the fact that they had a lot less to deal with at the time than Wisconsin Coach Barry Alvarez did, shows how confusing football clock management can be.

In fact, the offense can**not** take a knee for the rest of the game in the situation Alvarez confronted: winning 30-27, first and 10 on your own 38, opponent has one timeout, 1:33 remaining. There was too much time remaining given the other aspects of the situation. Although there is a play I have never seen that might have won the game for Wisconsin.

I'll discuss the '96 Wisconsin-Northwestern game in great detail in the chapter on taking a knee, including the play I think might have won them the game.

Clock-management mistake ends NFL coach's career overnight

On November 19, 1978, Bob Gibson was the offensive coordinator of the New York Giants. The next day, his coaching career was over. What happened? He made a clock-management mistake in a game against the Eagles. His team reached the take-a-knee point and began to take a knee. But for reasons he has refused to explain, (apparently to retaliate against an Eagles linebacker who hit the Giants quarterback on the take-a-knee play),

Gibson had his offense run two handoff plays **after** the take-a-knee play. The second was fumbled, the Eagles picked it up and ran it in for the game-winning touchdown.

New Yorkers call the play "The Fumble." Others refer to it as the "Miracle of the Meadowlands." The Giants head coach and director of operations were fired the day after the season ended, because they were unable to turn the team around after "The Fumble."

'Butchering the clock'

In his book *The New Thinking Man's Guide to Pro Football, Sports Illustrated* football writer Paul Zimmerman says,

> *How many times have I seen a coach butcher the clock at the end of the first half, or make some obviously stupid call? Oh, only about every week. The players know it, and I wonder how they feel when he comes into the locker room and claps his hands and says, 'OK, now we'll get 'em!'*
>
> *If I'd have to point to the one area of greatest coaching screw-ups it would be the management of the clock. Some of them don't seem to understand the most basic clock fact, that when you're behind and you're fighting the clock, you call timeouts on the other team's plays, not your own. Those are things a quarterback and a coach have to know, but you'd be surprised how many of them don't.*
>
> *...in the '84 NFC championship game against the Redskins the 49ers butchered the clock at the end, losing 15 vital seconds before they called timeout with 54 seconds left to play. It happens to everyone.*

Former San Francisco coach Bill Walsh said,

> *In college, so few coaches get to know the clock. You can hear it at the clinics. They always want to talk about some drill they run, not about how to work the clock.*

Little written about it

I have a large library of football books, periodicals, and catalogs of football books. I have compiled a large bibliography of out-of-print football books. I did a computer search for articles or doctoral theses, whatever, on the subject of football clock management.

As far as I can tell, no one has ever written a book on football clock management. In fact, no one has ever written an **article** on football clock management. Sure, there are many articles on the two-minute drill and some mentions of the four-minute drill and onside kick. But no one has ever addressed football clock management in its entirety. The closest anyone ever came is a chapter in the book *The Hidden Game of Football* by Pete Palmer, John Thorn, and Bob Carroll. And they only touch on a couple of issues.

Is it important?

Some coaches may figure no book has ever been written before because clock management is only important occasionally. Week by week, fundamentals are what matters. I agree that fundamentals are important. So are a lot of other aspects of the game. Clock management is **not** the most important thing in football. However, it is **more** important than most laymen and coaches realize. As I'll explain below, perhaps as many as **half** of all football games would have ended with a **different winner** had the clock management been different.

Basic principles

The '96 Wisconsin-Northwestern game only illustrates one clock-management principle: knowing the point at which you can take a knee. There are many other football clock-management principles.

Most people are reasonably familiar with the most famous football clock management routine—the so-called **two-minute drill**, which is used when you are on offense and behind. But there's a lot more to clock management. For example, there's the **four-minute drill**. Most laymen and many football coaches do not know what the four-minute drill is. (It's the opposite of the two-minute drill—a slowdown to use up the clock.)

There are four different possession-lead clock-management situations:

• you are ahead on offense
• you are ahead on defense
• you are behind on offense
• you are behind on defense

You can also be **tied**, as always at the start of a game or overtime, but you can't manage the clock until you see who leads or until you're in your last possession of a half.

Laymen and many football coaches are probably least familiar with clock-management aspects of **special-teams plays**. Everybody knows about onside kicks. But less well-known are such special teams plays as the fake-punt, deliberate taking of a safety or, in high school and the NFL, the fair catch free kick field goal after a safety free kick.

This book covers **all** the various clock-management situations for not only offense and defense, but also special teams. It also covers in detail every clock-management play known to man—plays like spiking the ball to stop the clock, taking a knee, and the Hail Mary pass. You will learn how to use your timeouts to maximum advantage.

When do you start?

Perhaps the most basic principle is **when do you start clock management**? Most laymen think it's in the last two minutes of a game. They interpret the phrase "two-minute drill" literally. Many people might cite the times at which the NFL rules change: the last **two** minutes of the **first half** and the last **five** minutes of the **game**. Other coaches would probably say that clock management starts in the last four minutes or so of a half. Also wrong. I would have said that myself before I started writing this book.

But when I sat down and thought through the question and analyzed hundreds of games, I came to a surprising conclusion: *you start clock management when either team takes a lead or on the last possession of the first half, whichever comes first.* In other words, in the vast majority of games, **both** teams should start clock management in the **first quarter**.

Any game that was decided by eight points or less might have been won by the other team had they done a better job of **whole-game** clock management, or if the winning team had done a poorer job of whole-game clock management.

What percent of games are decided by eight points or less? **More than half** in the NFL, which has the most readily accessible statistics. So it's possible that the application of the principles in this book could turn more than half of a team's losses into victories.

Whenever I state a principle of clock management, I will put it in italics, *like this*. The main one is the principle of ***more versus enough***.

More versus enough

Football coaches are generally in a "more" mindset. That is, they want more yards and more points and they want them as fast as possible. Most clock-management blunders that result in a leading team losing in the last seconds of a game stem from the leading coach pursuing **more** when he should have been pursuing **enough**. For example, in that '96 Wisconsin-Northwestern game, it appeared to Barry Alvarez's ESPN critics that he had tried to gain **more** yards and one more first down than was **enough** to win.

When you get into a clock-management situation, you must switch mental gears to gaining **enough** yards, getting **enough** first downs, and scoring **enough** points to win. Furthermore, you get that enough at whatever speed is **enough** to win before time runs out. In other words, you should advance the ball according to a clock-conscious schedule. That schedule is determined by

• whether you need a field goal or a touchdown
• distance to goal line or field-goal kicking spot if you need three or less points
• time remaining.

You score in 'clumps'

The difference between two teams' scores in a game can be **any** number from zero on up. But you can only score in three "clumps:"

play	points
• safety or college PAT runback	2
• field goal	3
• touchdown and PAT	6-8.

That means some margins which appear **different**, like four or five points, are really the **same**, because they both require the trailing team to score a touchdown to take the lead. If the trailing team is willing to settle for a temporary **tie**, which they often are, the clumps get bigger. Four-, five-, six-, and seven-point margins are essentially all the same because each requires a touchdown to score or tie. An eight-point margin can be added to that clump, athough the success rate on two-point conversions is generally down around 40% so a seven-point margin is not quite the same as an eight-point margin.

Points are not a meaningful concept when making football decisions. Only score clumps are. The question is not how many **points** the leader is ahead by, but how many **scores** they ahead by.

Army-Navy 1995

On December 2, 1995, my alma mater, Army, was losing 13-6 to Navy in the Army-Navy Game at Veterans Stadium in Philadelphia. With fourth and goal at the Army 1-foot line, Navy's 40-year-old, first-year coach, Charlie Weatherbie, had a decision to make.

He could have kicked what would have been an 18-yard field goal—which is actually **two yards shorter than an extra-point kick**. Had they made it, the score would have been 16-6 with 8:26 remaining in the game—enough to **force Army to score twice** to tie or win.

He chose, instead, to throw a **pass**. The receiver was wide open, but the pass was low and fell incomplete. Army then drove 99 2/3 yards in the ensuing 7:20 to score a touchdown and a two-point conversion, taking the lead 14-13.

It is possible that a Navy field goal attempt might have failed—bad snap, block, wide right, whatever—and that Army might have then mounted an 80-yard winning drive. It is also possible that a fake field goal pass might have succeeded, where the pass from a normal scrimmage formation did not. It is even possible that Army might have won even if Navy had successfully kicked a field goal—on say, an Army kick-return touchdown, two-point conversion, onside-kick recovery, and field goal.

Few would dispute that Weatherbie's decision to throw a pass was very dumb and cost his team the game. Weatherbie, himself, did not dispute it. Here are his own words.

> *...I made a stupid tactical error...I was the one that screwed up and lost [the game].*

Weatherbie went for **more** when he should have settled for **enough**.

The stuff of Hollywood

The more-versus-enough mistake was the subject of a Hollywood film. The '83 film *All the Right Moves* starring Tom Cruise, as player Stefan Georgevich, and Craig T. Nelson, as head coach Nickerson, told of a high school football team. The heroes' team was Ampipe, a poor Rust Belt mill town; the villains, the undefeated, ranked-third-in-the-state, Walnut Heights Knights—a school so affluent it had "both boys and girls golf teams."

In the big game scene, Ampipe miraculously is about to beat the perennially superior Knights. Ampipe takes the lead, 14-10, on Georgevich's interception runback for a touchdown with 3:47 left in the game. It is now pouring rain.

'I strong right 42'

After the ensuing kickoff, Walnut Heights drives to Ampipe's one-yard line where a heroic goal-line stand forces them to turn the ball over on downs. With 12 seconds left, Ampipe's offense takes the field. Coach tells his quarterback, "I strong right 42." The play was apparently an isolation or blast play through the right center-guard gap.

The quarterback-tailback exchange was fumbled, Walnut Heights fell on the ball in Ampipe's end zone. Touchdown. Final score: Walnut Heights, 16, Ampipe, 14.

The coach chews out the tailback for losing the game. Cornerback Georgevich points out the coach called the unnecessary handoff. "If youda had Rifleman [the quarterback] hold onto the ball, we woulda won the game."

Angry at Georgevich's criticism, Coach throws him off the team and bans him from the team bus. Bosco, the head of a group of local redneck boosters wonders, "Why he didn't just take a safety and then punt it outta there?" The boosters then trash the coach's house while giving Georgevich a ride home. Georgevich is spotted. Coach badmouths Georgevich to recruiters, apparently ending his chances for a scholarship. (I won't tell you how it ends. Rent the video.)

Suffice it to say, Coach Nickerson was guilty of poor clock management. Both player Georgevich and booster Bosco were right. Either a no-handoff quarterback sneak or taking a safety would have been more likely to preserve the victory. The best call would have been take-a-knee (unless Walnut Heights had three timeouts, the movie didn't say). Although on your own one-yard line, taking a knee outside the goalline is a tight fit. Deliberately taking a safety with 12 seconds left would probably not take all 12 seconds off the clock, so a free kick after the safety would be required. That could be run back for a touchdown or a last play from scrimmage could be run after a fair-catch of the free kick after the safety.

Arkansas vs. Texas, 1969

In the late '60s, quarterbacks still called their own plays on most teams. So it was Arkansas quarterback Bill Montgomery who made the more-versus-enough mistake in the 1969 Arkansas-Texas game.

Arkansas was leading 14-8 with 14:47 left to play. Although they had the lead, Montgomery decided to be very aggressive throwing passes right and left. For a while, it worked. They drove from their own 20-yard line after the kickoff to Texas's 9-yard line.

After a two-yard gain to the seven, Arkansas threw an incompletion. With third down, they could have just run a sneak or some such to set up a field goal from the seven or closer. A successful field goal would make the score Arkansas 17 Texas 8, a nine-point margin that would require Texas to score twice in the remaining 10:45. In other words, the field goal probably would have been successful and probably would have been **enough** to win the game. Montgomery decided to go for **more** than enough. He threw an **interception** which was returned to the Texas 20.

Later in the game, with fourth and three at the Texas 43 and 4:47 left, with the national championship on the line, Texas coach Darrell Royal made one of the gutsiest, most famous play calls in football history. (The coach called the play during a **timeout**.) He called "86 throwback pass to the tight end." It had failed every time they had tried it in previous games. It gained 44 yards to the Arkansas 13. Two plays later, Texas scored a touchdown and Happy Feller's extra point kick gave them the winning margin, 15-14.

The game ended with Montgomery throwing yet another interception. Texas went on to win the national championship.

There are points and there are points

Another way to think of the more versus enough issue is to recognize that **all points are not created equal**. In *The Hidden Game of Football*, the authors say that they analyzed two NFL seasons in detail in a computer and thereby came up with win probabilities for all sorts of game situations.

For example, they analyzed a Jets-Patriots game in which the Jets were trailing by 14-0 with 7:30 left in the half with first and ten at the Patriot 42. That situation gave the Jets a .145 probability of winning the game. The Jets then scored seven points with 4:56 left in the first half, thereby increasing their win probability from .145 to .266. That means the value of those seven points is .266 - .145 = .121. Later in the game, the Jets scored their final touchdown with 1:05 left in the game to make the final score Jets 48 Patriots 17. The Jets' win probability both before and after they scored that last touchdown was 100%. So the win-probability value of those seven points was **zero**.

By the same token, in the 1995 Army-Navy game, Navy would have increased their win probability dramatically had they kicked a field goal to put themselves up 16-6 with 8:26 left in the game. But the **incremental** win-probability value of the additional four or five points they would have gotten for scoring a **touchdown** and conversion would be very close to zero. So Navy's Coach Weatherbie traded a **significant** incremental **risk** for a **zero** incremental **win-probability**. Dumb move.

Statistically, Navy would still be the most likely winner even after throwing their incomplete fourth-down pass. But the computer cannot discern the momentum shift from Navy to Army as a result of Navy's snatching a chance of defeat from the jaws of almost certain victory. By taking a blatantly stupid gamble, and losing it, Navy handed Army a totally unexpected reprieve and incalculable psychological uplift in what is always an extremely emotional game.

Clock-management plays are more important

Football clinic speakers and authors often talk about how special teams plays are more important than offensive and defensive plays because they involve big chunks of yards and changes of possession as well as disproportionate scoring. I can make a similar argument about clock-management plays.

In *The Hidden Game of Football*, they calculate the value of a drive early in the **first** quarter and compare it to the same drive late in the **fourth** quarter. Three minutes into a 0-0 game you take over first and ten at your own 35. Your win probability then is .518. If you drive to a first down at the other team's 35 three minutes later, your win probability goes up to .576, so the drive was worth .576 - .518 = .058.

Now there are two minutes left in the game, the margin between the two teams is almost the same, only now you are trailing by one point. If you get the ball first and ten at your own 35, your win probability is .066. If you drive to the opponent's 35 for another first down with one minute left, your win probability goes up to .279. In each case you went from first and ten at your 35 to first and ten at your opponent's 35. But when you do it in the last two minutes of a close game, the drive is worth .279 - .066 = .213 win-probability points compared to just .058 win-probability points when done in the first quarter—about four times as much.

Not enough practice on clock management

When you look at it in that light, most football coaches are spending too little time on their clock-management skills. In terms of the number of times a team runs their two-minute drill or four-minute drill in games, clock management seems minor. But when you look at the **importance** of clock management plays, it becomes apparent that they are far more important and therefore deserve far more practice time than they usually get.

Actually, I say in this book that teams should be in a clock management mode for **most of the game**. But even if that were not true, coaches should still devote more practice time to clock management because of its greater **importance** and **difficulty**.

This book is about the part of a football game when everything matters two, three, or four times as much as normal.

'You never give up points'

Deliberately taking a safety is another example of the "enough" mindset replacing the "more" mindset. If you are ahead by three or more points, and the safety you take will be the last score of the game, you win. The safety will give your opponent two points. But you have **enough** of a margin, three points, that you can give up two and still win.

Every season brings examples of teams winning by deliberately taking a safety at all levels of football including the NFL. Yet in 1994, an experienced high school football coach told me, "You never give up points" when I mentioned deliberately taking a safety. That's further evidence that football clock-management principles are not widely understood, even among football coaches.

When the winner took the lead in 25 Army–Navy games

I have a book by Bill Cromartie on the history of the Army-Navy Game. (He has also written football books on six other famous rivalries.) The Army-Navy book has the virtue of having detailed accounts of each game so it is a useful reference source for clock-management research. The Army-Navy Game is generally a pretty even match. As of the 1996 game, the series was Army, 47 wins; Navy, 43 wins (7 ties). The following table shows **when** the winner took the final lead, as well as the score and margin of victory. Where there is a time rather than a quarter, it is the time remaining in the fourth quarter.

Year	Time of last go-ahead score	final score	margin
1995	1:06 left in game	14-13	1
1994	6:19 left in game	22-20	2
1993	first quarter	16-14	2
1992	0:12 left in game	25-24	1
1991	first quarter	24-3	21
1990	first quarter	30-20	10
1989	0:15 left in game	19-17	2
1988	second quarter	20-15	5
1987	first quarter	17-3	14
1986	first quarter	27-7	20
1985	8:23 left in game	17-7	10
1984	first quarter	28-11	17
1983	first quarter	42-13	29
1982	first quarter	24-7	17
1981	tied in the third quarter	3-3	0
1980	first quarter	33-6	27
1979	first quarter	31-7	24
1978	first quarter	28-0	28
1977	first quarter	17-14	3
1976	first quarter	38-10	28
1975	first quarter	30-6	24
1974	first quarter	19-0	19
1973	first quarter	51-0	51
1972	third quarter	23-15	8
1971	first quarter	24-23	1

According to this table, you could start clock management (leading team, use the entire play clock, prefer the run; trailing team, hurry up) in the **first quarter** in the vast majority of games. In 18 of the 25, the team that was ahead in the first quarter stayed ahead until the end of the game. Some of those 18 games were exciting, close games, but **the lead still never changed hands after the first quarter**.

Would have won

If the **loser** in the 1989 and 1992 games had started their slowdown offense just a little earlier, they would have **won** those games. In fact, the winner won with only 15 and 12 seconds left respectively. If the loser had run **just two more slowdown plays**—that is, stay-in-bounds running plays where the snap was done at the end of the play clock—the game would likely have ended **before** the come-from-behind scores. There were only three games in the 25—1985, 1994, and 1995—where it might have been a mistake for the team that was ahead to go to a slowdown offense at the beginning of the fourth quarter.

Of course, you would not want to totally abandon a successful offensive game plan long before the end of the game. Rather, you would simply **use the entire play clock and try to stay in bounds**. In play calling, you would still call the play you need to get your next first down or to score when you are in a "blank and goal." But given a choice between two equally effective plays, you should, when you are ahead, prefer running plays.

Close games

Note that nine of the 25 games were decided by seven points or less. The winners did an adequate job of clock management. But what about the losers? Could they have won any of those games if they had conserved a little more time as the game went along?

Year	loser's final possession
1995	spike ball to stop clock on third down, snap at winner's 37, threw into end zone, intercepted
1994	fourth & four at loser's 30 with 5:03 left, punted
1993	spiked ball to stop clock at 0:06, fourth & goal at winner's two, missed field goal
1992	kick-return play, tackled short of end zone
1989	winner spiked ball to stop clock then kicked a field goal leaving about 0:11
1988	onside kicked failed with 1:35 left
1981	tie—Army missed 55-yard field goal as time ran out
1977	fourth & two at winner's nine, timeout, 1:07 left, overthrew receiver
1971	turned over on downs at winner's seven with eight seconds left

In the 1993 and 1995 games, the loser had to spike the ball at the end because they had no timeouts left and because the game clock was running out. Had they conserved time on just one or two plays earlier in the game, they could have run another play instead of wasting a down to spike the ball. In 1993, Navy would have had third & goal at Army's two if they had not needed to spike the ball. Surely they would have tried to run or pass for a touchdown. They might have failed and still missed the field goal.

In 1989, the winner scored by kicking a 31-yard field goal with 15 seconds left. The loser could have won, had they run maybe another 20 seconds off the clock when they had the ball earlier in the game. That would have forced their opponent to kick from farther out or to abandon hope of a field goal and try to complete a Hail Mary pass on their last play.

In the 1971 game, the loser threw two incomplete passes from their opponent's 7 on third and fourth downs leaving 8 seconds on the clock. With more time, they might have been more successful with a more varied, more time-consuming attack.

First scorer wins 84% of the time in the NFL

In the 1994 NFL season, the team that scored first won 84% of the games. That is a very important statistic for coaches to know. It answers one of the main clock-management questions: when do you start clock management?

First scorer wins 70% of the time in Pac 10

In 1996, the team that scored first won 70% of the time in games involving Pac 10 teams. I checked a bunch of Division IAA games and found the following:

- First scorer won 72% of the time
- Halftime leader won 92% of the time
- Third quarter leader won 86% of the time

I do not have the first-scorer-wins percentages on lower level teams. But I strongly suspect it's **higher** than in the NFL and college because younger, less-experienced players tend to get **more discouraged** when they fall behind.

I coached the San Ramon Bears 8-10 year olds from 1990 to 1993. The San Ramon Bears organization was founded and began play in 1988. My 1993 team was the first San Ramon Bear 8-10 team to ever come from behind to take the lead. That's about five and a half years of the team that scored first winning **100%** of the time.

In another game, one of our opponents beat us after we were up 14-0 in 1993. That's the first time I ever saw a team come from behind to win at that level.

First-quarter clock management

Let's say you score first at 9:30 left in the first quarter. Should you then start a slowdown? Yes. There is around a 70% to 84% probability that you will win. That means there is a 70% to 84% probability that your **opponent**, not you, will be in need of time at the end of the half.

True, there is as much as a 16% to 30% chance that by slowing down, the team you screw will be your own. But when you cannot forecast the future for sure, you have play the percentages. Often, the percentages are not very comforting. For example, the 1995 NFC two-point conversion rate was .451. So do you go for two? It's a toss-up.

But 70% to 84% is not 45%. When one side is 70% to 84%, you gotta go with it.

Make no mistake about it, doing a slowdown whenever you are ahead or in your last possession of the half will be the **wrong** thing to do 16% to 30% of the time. You will find yourself trailing toward the end of 16% to 30% of the games, frantically trying to score, and wishing you had back the time you wasted earlier in the game. But the percentages say that for every 20 times you do the slowdown, you will be right 14 to 17 times and wrong only three to six. (84% of 20 = 16.8)

LSU vs. Mississippi, 1959

Here's an example of one of the exception-proves-the-rule games. Ole Miss took the lead 3-0 on a field goal 7:45 into the first quarter of their game with LSU. It was still 3-0 at halftime. Mississippi coach John Vaught decided to get conservative in the third quarter. He stopped passing unless absolutely necessary.

He punted twice on **first down**! Although that was a more common strategy in previous generations. The field was wet and he figured his defense could prevent LSU from scoring during the rest of the game and his excellent punter (48-yard average in that game) could keep LSU bottled up in their own end of the field.

With third and seventeen, Ole Miss lined up in punt formation and punted—to Billy Cannon—at the 11-yard line. LSU Coach Paul Dietzel prohibited fielding a punt inside the 15-yard line. Most coaches apply that rule to punts behind the **ten**. Cannon decided to follow the rule most coaches use, and ran 89 yards for the game-winning touchdown.

Punting to Billy Cannon was not a great idea in 1959. That was the year he won the Heisman Trophy. Two years later, he led the AFL in rushing.

Coach Vaught's conservative approach in the second half may have been a factor leading to his becoming one of the 16% to 30% of teams who score first but go on to lose.

The Ice Bowl, 12/31/67

One of the most famous clock-management stories in football was the 1967 New Year's Eve Ice Bowl between Vince Lombardi's Green Bay Packers and Tom Landry's Dallas Cowboys. Given that Green Bay scored the winning touchdown with 16 seconds left, you might think that a longer slowdown, might have won it for Dallas.

Maybe not. It was a see-saw battle. Green Bay was ahead until 4:54 was left in the fourth quarter. If Lombardi had followed sound clock-management principles, he would have run a slowdown for those first three and two-thirds quarters, thereby preventing his team from having enough time to make their dramatic last-minute scoring drive.

Dallas, on the other hand, did not have the lead very long—just 4:54. If they did not run an all-out slowdown during that time, failure to follow the slowdown-when-you-are-ahead-prunciple may have cost them the game. The question is could the Cowboys have run another 20 seconds or so off the game clock during the time that they were ahead?

Halftime about the same

The probability of winning because you are ahead does not increase much in the first half in the NFL games I looked at. But in college Division IAA games, it went up from 72% to 92% at halftime.

In the 1995 NFL season, 31 games were tied at halftime. Of the other 220, the team that was ahead won 183 or 83%—about the same win probability as the first scoring team.

Higher after third quarter

The probability of the leading team winning **does** increase in the **third** quarter. Fifteen NFL games were tied at the end of three quarters in 1995. The winning team won 205 of the other 236 games. That's 87%.

To state it succinctly, the team that is currently ahead has a 70% to 90% or higher chance of winning the game. That's a strong enough indication *to warrant switching to a clock-management mode whenever either team is in the lead. You also should switch to a slowdown, regardless of whether you are ahead or not, in your last possession of the first half, if the distance to go for a score and the time remaining so indicate. In the second half, you would switch to a slowdown when indicated by distance and time, even if you were trailing, if the possession in question was likely to be your last one of the game and you were within one score of winning or tying.*

Why 'last possession of the half?'

You may wonder why I say you may want to slow down, even if you are trailing, during your "last possession of the half." That's to take into account the **need to score slowly** at the end of a half. In one of his books, Joe Namath said he felt he became a pro quarterback the day he was leading his team to a come-from behind score, but had the presence of mind to do it slowly, so the other team would not have much time to come back. He did just that and his Jets won.

Patriots at Miami, 1986

Late in the 1986 season, the Patriots had to beat Miami to make the playoffs. Miami was a 3 1/2 point favorite.

The score was tied at 27 when the Pats took over first and ten at their own 14 with 6:55 left. Starting quarterback Tony Eason had been knocked out of the game in the second quarter. New England's win probability at that point was .456. In other words, they would likely lose the game because of their lousy field position.

But Patriot backup Steve Grogan led his team 86 yards for the go-ahead touchdown, which is great, but he also had the smarts to do it **slowly**. By the time Miami got the ball back, there were only 44 seconds left on the clock. Too few as it turned out. New England's win probability at that point was .994, partly because of the score, but also because of the little time they had left for Miami to come back. That one drive had a win-probability value of .994 - .456 = .538.

Contrast that with a similar drive in the first quarter. New England drove 75 yards to break a 0-0 tie with a touchdown and PAT kick. That drive only changed the win probability by .718 - .502 = .216. Scoring to take the lead when you are tied or behind at the end of a half is nice, but it's even nicer to do it slowly.

I mentioned this to my son's varsity high school football coach, Floyd Burnsed of Miramonte High School in Orinda, CA. He said he did it in the 1996 season playoffs.

Beating El Cerrito—sloowly

Miramonte was trailing heavily favored El Cerrito 13-10 with four minutes plus left in the fourth quarter. As they drove from their own 40-yard line for what they hoped would be the go-ahead score, Floyd deliberately slowed the pace. His thinking was that this would be Miramonte's last possession one way or the other. If they were going to win the game, they would have to score on this possession. So why not do it slowly to prevent the potent El Cerrito offense from having much chance to mount their own last-minute comeback? Miramonte did just that, scoring with just eleven seconds left, upsetting El Cerrito 17-13 and advancing in the playoffs.

1997 Rose Bowl

Jake Plummer and his Arizona State team had to score late in the fourth quarter of the 1997 Rose Bowl to beat Ohio State and preserve their undefeated season. But they did not have to score as fast as they did. Since they had to score the go-ahead points, they should have assumed that they **would** and paced their scoring drive accordingly. But they scored somewhat quickly, and Ohio State was able to mount its own dramatic and successful drive in the time ASU left on the clock, thereby destroying ASU's hopes for Rose Bowl and national championships.

Do not accuse me of exercising "20-20 hindsight" about the '97 Rose Bowl. Rather I am saying that *coaches in that situation should* ***always*** *score slowly because there is no need to score faster than the time left and scoring faster than the time left requires is dangerous.* Monday morning quarterbacks add nothing to the knowledge of football unless they turn the lessons of the previous weekend's games into principles which apply to all future games. That's what I'm trying to do in this book.

If ahead, slow up; if behind,...

If you are ahead, or you are behind but on the way to taking the lead, slow up so as to use as much of the remaining time in the half as possible to score.

Roughly speaking, you should be in a slowdown mode whenever you are ahead and in a speed-up mode whenever you are behind, regardless of what quarter it is—because the team that is currently ahead wins 70% to 90% of the time.

Tie or win

Coaches frequently confront situations where they have to decide whether to go for the win or the tie. I don't have a definitive all-purpose answer. But I do have some thoughts on how you ought to evaluate the decision in the chapter devoted to that subject.

Coach looks really bad

Experts, like fellow coaches, can watch a football game and tell if the coach of the losing team did a lousy job. But in most games, laymen can only suspect the losing coach did a poor job. They cannot tell when the players are at fault or the team is hopelessly outmatched. But when the mistake is in the realm of late-game clock management, everybody knows the coach screwed up.

In the "Behind on defense" chapter, you'll read about the "Miracle of the Meadowlands," a clock-management blunder that instantly ended the coaching career of the New York Giants offensive coordinator and got the head coach and operations director fired the day after the season ended. Many berelieve it started a multi-year bad spell for the Giants. (They were 26-46 in the next five years.)

The last play of the game

The last play of the game is a far more interesting issue than most laymen and even coaches think. Here's an example. You are ahead and on defense. You intercept the opponent's desperation pass. What should your interceptor do? *He should not try to run the ball back for a touchdown. Rather he must run around wasting time until the clock runs out if he can. He must avoid being tackled. As soon as the final gun sounds, he must take a knee or run out of bounds.* Remember the game does **not** end on the **gun**, it ends on the **whistle**. Taking a knee, sliding, or running out of bounds causes a referee to blow the whistle. There are many different last-play-of-the-game situations, and they call for many different special plays.

Turnover avoidance

In researching this book, I read a zillion accounts of great comebacks and turnabouts. In general, dramatic come-from-behind victories require **turnovers**. That, in turn, means that preserving a lead in a clock-management situation requires **avoiding** turnovers. I will not discuss the standard turnover avoidance measures, like carrying the ball correctly, in this book. But I will discuss the play-calling variety of turnover avoidance.

Practicing clock management

You have to **practice** clock management. You need at least **one repetition of everything**. And you need many repetitions of skills like the two-minute drill, the four-minute drill, and the onside kick.

Many coaches, especially at the junior varsity and lower levels, **never** practice clock management on the grounds that such things are too advanced for their level. That's nonsense. I have practiced clock management at every level from junior pee wee (8- to 10-year olds) to freshman to junior varsity. And my teams have won games as a result.

In 1996, my freshman team practiced clock management especially hard the next-to-last week of the season. The game that week saw us trailing for the entire game. We got the ball late in the fourth quarter in the game around our own 38-yard line. We had no timeouts. We were down 13-11.

Wednesday practice yields Thursday victory

But we simply ran the two-minute drill which we had just practiced the day before. Down the field we went with quick out passes, running out of bounds. With about five seconds left, our head coach, not I, signaled to spike the ball. I had practiced spiking the ball, but at that point, I did not think we had time even to line up and do that. The spike stopped the clock with **one second left**. We had moved to the opponent's nine-yard line.

Our opponents were kind enough to use one of their timeouts so we could get organized. We then tried our **first field goal attempt of the season**. The final gun sounded while our snap was on its way to the holder. The kick was good. We won 14-13. The poor guys we played had not won a game all season. One week later, our devastated opponents played a team we had tied earlier in the season—and lost by 40-some points.

You could practice ONLY clock management

The notion that junior varsity and lower level coaches don't have time for clock-management practice apparently stems from the notion that they have more important things to practice. Baloney. To take an extreme example, you could **practice nothing but clock management** and it would not adversely affect your team. I did that in 1993. We always ran either what I called the "Warp-Speed No-huddle" or a slowdown offense. We **never** ran a medium speed offense either in practice or in games.

How did it work? We were the most successful offense in the 32-team history of our organization. The correct approach is to spend almost all your time practicing clock-conscious plays and only a little practicing things like normal kickoffs. The reason is that the medium-speed stuff generally requires no special skills. A medium-speed offense is just a slower version of a hurry-up offense.

Another argument is that there really is almost **never a need for a medium-speed offense**. Roughly speaking, when you are ahead, you should be in a slowdown and when you are behind, you should be in a speed-up. You should **never** go at a **medium** speed, with the possible exception of when the game is **tied**. Yet most coaches spend nearly all their time practicing that medium-speed offense and spend little or no time on their two-minute drill or four-minute drill.

Coach practice, too

Practice generally means practice for the players. But clock management is the one exception to that rule. Clock management is something **coaches can practice all by themselves**—and they should.

When he first became head coach of the Oakland Raiders, John Madden used to go to Foothill High School (in Pleasanton, CA near Madden's home) games to practice calling plays from up in the stands. You can practice using TV games, high school games, youth games, and even computer football games.

Can't wait until game

You cannot wait until the game to worry about what play you're going to call. Coaches almost all have play lists which tell them what plays to call in various common situations like first and ten or third and two. But they **rarely have clock-management play sheets**. In fact, they need clock-management play sheets **more** than they need regular play sheets because clock-management decisions are made under extreme time pressure.

Special knowledge

Coaching football in general requires special knowledge. For example, coaches have to know how far their place kicker can kick. They need to know how many downs you get to obtain a first down.

Most coaches have the basic knowledge regarding offense and defense. But I suspect many, if not most, might flunk a quiz on clock-management special knowledge like pertinent rules and how long it takes to do the various things a clock-conscious team has to do. For example, how many seconds does the average play take? How many plays can a well-trained team run in one minute going at maximum hurry-up speed?

Clock rules

Competent clock management requires that you and your players know the rules that apply to clock-management situations. Not everyone does. For example, the clock does not start if the first touching of a kick is an illegal touch. There is a chapter in this book devoted to the clock-related rules at the high school, college, and NFL levels.

For now, I'll just give you a crude rule that Brian Billick uses at the Minnesota Vikings:

What stops the clock, starts the clock.

By that he means, if the **official stopped** the clock, say for a measurement or official's timeout, the **official** will **start** the clock with a ready-to-play signal. If the **ball stopped** the clock, by going out of bounds or falling incomplete, the ball, that is the **snap**, will **start** the clock.

Scoring rates

Football teams score points at a certain rate. Most coaches, players, and fans have a vague sense of that rate. For example, if you are behind by 30 points with two minutes left to play, you don't need clock management, you need to give some playing time to your bench. Why? Because we all know it's all but impossible for a team to score 30 points in two minutes. Here are some numbers to make sure you have an accurate idea of the number of points football teams score in short periods:

High school scoring

In the high-school league where I coached freshman offense in 1996, the Tri-County Athletic League, South Division, the total number of points scored in five league games by six teams was 833. That's 27.77 points per team per 48-minute game or **6.94 points per 12-minute quarter**.

Of course, the rate varies by team. The **most successful** offensive team, Foothill, scored 204 points or 204 ÷ 5 games ÷ 4 quarters per game = **10.2 points per quarter**. The **least successful** offensive team, Miramonte, where I coached in 1994 and 1995, scored 108 points or 108 ÷ 5 ÷ 4 = **5.4 points per quarter**.

It should be noted that Miramonte finished in second place. They adopted a defensive-emphasis policy in 1996 and were the **most successful defensive team** in the league, allowing only 63 points or 63 ÷ 5 ÷ 4 = **3.15 points per quarter**. The scoring rate varies not only from team to team, but from match-up to match-up.

The clock-management portion of your game plan must make assumptions about the scoring rate of your team and your opponent in the game you are preparing for. Furthermore, you need to be ready to change those assumptions as the game goes along if things are not going as expected.

Some might point out that the scoring rate can be as high as eight points divided by the time it takes a pass to fly through the air from just behind the line of scrimmage to the end zone. True. But you cannot use such best-case or worst-case performances to make decisions. Rather, you must play the percentages.

College scoring

Here are a few numbers chosen at random to give you the idea of the scoring rates in college. In 1994, **Penn State** led Division I-A (big name football schools) with 47.8

points per 60-minute game or **11.95 points per quarter**. That same year, **Miami** led Division I-A in **fewest points allowed** at 10.8 per game or **2.70 per quarter**.

Pro scoring

In 1994, the **49ers** led the NFL in points scored with 505 in 16 games. That's 505 ÷ 16 = 31.56 per 60-minute game and **7.89 per 15-minute quarter**. The **best defense** in the NFL in 1994 was **Cleveland** with 204 points allowed. That's 204 ÷ 16 = 12.75 per game and **3.19 per quarter**.

Recapping:

Level	**Maximum rate**	**Minimum rate**
H.S.	7/quarter	3/quarter
college	12/quarter	3/quarter
pro	8/quarter	3/quarter

The biggest comeback in NFL history

You might wonder what the scoring rate was in the biggest comebacks ever. The greatest comeback in NFL history was the 1/3/93 AFC wild card playoff game involving Houston at Buffalo. At halftime, the score was Houston, 28; Buffalo, 3. It got worse for Buffalo. Early in the third quarter, Bubba McDowell picked off a tipped Frank Reich pass and ran it back for a touchdown: Houston 35; Buffalo, 3.

At that point, one of the announcers said, "The lights have been on in Rich Stadium since noon today but they may as well turn them out now."

But Houston managed only a field goal during the rest of the game. Meanwhile, aided by an onside kick recovery, an interception, and a bobbled field goal snap, Buffalo scored 35 points in the second half, tying the game at 38. They went on to win it with a field goal in overtime. What was the scoring rate in that greatest NFL comeback ever? 35 points per half or **17.5 points per quarter**.

By the way, the Buffalo quarterback that day was backup **Frank Reich**. Believe it or not, he **also** holds the record for the **greatest comeback in NCAA Division I-A history**. He brought Maryland to a 42-40 victory over Miami, after being down 31-0 at the half. How did he let Miami get that far ahead to begin with? He didn't. He didn't go into the game until the third quarter. He was a backup there, too. The Maryland scoring rate in the second half of that game? 42 points in two quarters or **21 points per quarter.**

Greatest fourth quarter comeback in NFL history

The greatest **fourth quarter** comeback in NFL history happened 11/8/87. Entering the fourth quarter, St. Louis was down 28-3 to Tampa. With the help of a **fumble** that was picked up and ran for a touchdown, the Cardinals scored 28 unanswered points to win 31-28. That's a scoring rate of **28 points per quarter**.

Legendary coach Vince Lombardi said that a 28-point lead in the fourth quarter was insurmountable. St. Louis revealed that he was at least one point off.

Minnesota also scored 28 points in the fourth quarter of a 12/1/85 game, including a **picked-up fumble touchdown**, to beat Philadelphia 28-23.

High school and college records

Because there are so many high schools and colleges, the records at those levels are extreme. Here they are in case you're interested.

High school:	Most points per game: **256** Haven, KS 11/16/27 (64 per quarter)
College IA:	Most points in **one quarter: 49** (three times)
College IAA:	Most points in **one quarter: 50** AL State 10/26/91
College II:	Most points scored in a **brief period of time: 21 points in 1:20** Winona State 10/15/94

If you happen to be in one of those extreme situations, you'll have to come up with your own scoring-rate predictions.

How long a play takes

To manage the clock, you need to know durations. Each play has three phases:

- snap to end-of-play whistle
- end-of-play whistle to ready-to-play whistle
- ready-to play whistle to snap.

In his book, *Developing an Offensive Game Plan*, Viking offensive coordinater Brian Billick says "a running clock is worth 35 seconds." In their book *The Hidden Game of Football*, authors Carroll, Palmer, and Thorn say a team trying to run out the clock can take about 36 seconds per play. With an official play clock in each end zone, I would have though they could get the time per play up to 38 or 39 seconds.

The Hidden Game of Football also says hurry-up offenses use about **18 seconds per play** on plays where they **do not stop the clock** by going out of bounds or some such.

They also peg the **minimum time per play** in a no-timeouts-left hurry-up offense at about **six seconds per play** assuming a steady series of eight-yard out passes that are followed by the receiver getting out of bounds. Coach Howard Schnellenberger, whose resume includes a national championship at Miami in 1983, says he tries to get each play off in 15 seconds when he's running the no-huddle.

In the *1994 National Interscholastic Coaching Affiliates Football Manual*, Lavern Pottinger, head coach of Belvidere High School (IL) said his no-huddle offense took 10 to 24 seconds per play depending on the situation. He further said that he averaged over 60 plays per game every year and that his team set a national high school record of 925 plays in a season and 66.1 plays per game (48-minute games) in 1988. (The 925 record still stands, but the plays-per-game record was broken by Hemingford, NE in 1989. They ran 68.9 plays per game.)

The NCAA records are as follows:

Level	most plays in one game	highest average plays per game
I-A	112 (Montana 11/1/52)	92.4 (Notre Dame 1970)
I-AA	113 (Villanova 10/7/89)	89.6 (Weber State 1991)
II	117 (Texas A&M Kinsville 10/30/82)	88.7 (Cal. St. Chico 1967)
III	112 (Gustavus Adolphus 11/2/85)	85.6 (Hampden-Sydney 1978)

Different plays take different amounts of time. Here are some rules of thumb based on my analysis of a tape of the 1996 Liberty Bowl between Syracuse and Houston:

Dive	2-4 seconds
Off tackle	3-4 seconds
QB draw	5 seconds
Option pitch	6 seconds
Sweep	7 seconds
Reverse	9 seconds
Pass	4-6 seconds
Kick return to own 37	6 seconds
Uncaught punt	7 seconds

Of course, the more yards a run gains or the more yards a pass travels, the more seconds the play takes. For example, a dive that gains ten yards takes about five seconds, not three. And you should know that each of these plays actually consumed almost twice as much clock time as I'm showing because the clock operator was slow to stop the clock.

Slow clock operator

I thought the Liberty Bowl clock operator had awfully slow reactions. He or she would almost always let several extra seconds run off when the clock should have been stopped. For example, on a QB draw, the ball was snapped at 12:29 of the second quarter. The ball carrier was tackled at 12:24. A first down had been gained, which should stop the clock to move the chains. But the clock did not stop until 12:21, wasting three extra seconds.

A dive play started at 10:39 and the ball carrier was tackled at 10:36 after gaining a first down, but the clock continued to run until 10:33, again wasting three seconds. Snap at 9:34, dive, tackle at 9:29, first down, clock not stopped until 9:26. That's a 5-second dive (big gain) and three seconds of clock operator slow reaction.

On the six-second kick return, the clock operator let the clock run an extra second for a total runoff of seven seconds. On an uncaught punt which was downed after seven seconds, the clock operator allowed a total of 12 seconds to run off.

As a rule of thumb, you can figure that a clock operator will take one to three seconds to react to the referee's signal to stop the clock after a play.

Four speeds

There are four speeds you can go at, in terms of seconds per play:

Speed	approximate time per play	how run
top speed	6 seconds per play	no-huddle, stop clock after every play by going out of bounds, timeout, or incomplete pass
inbounds hurry-up	20 seconds per play	no-huddle, keep clock going by staying in bounds and on the ground
regular speed	40 seconds per play	huddle, about 5 seconds for the play, 16 for the referee's housekeeping, and 19 from ready-to-play whistle to snap
slowdown	40 seconds per play	Huddle, wait until 23 seconds have run off the play clock in high school and college and 38 seconds have run off the play clock in the NFL. The slowdown may be no slower than the average regular speed because of the nature of the play calling—running plays—and, in high school and college, the officials hurrying their housekeeping chores to avoid favoring the leading team.

Top speed no-huddle

The **top-speed, no-huddle** is what most people think of when you mention clock management. In it, the offense goes as fast as possible. They do not huddle. They hurry to the line after each play and call the play by audible or signal from the sideline. And they try to stop the game clock after each play.

Inbounds hurry-up

The **inbounds hurry-up**, which I have never seen discussed by any name anywhere other than this book, is a no-huddle except that you do **not** try to stop the clock after each play. The idea here is that you want to **run as many plays as possible**, but you also want to run about twenty seconds off the clock per play because that is the appropriate schedule for the situation you are in.

You use the inbounds hurry-up in certain field-position-and-time-remaining situations when you need to score, but also need to leave the minimum amount of time on the clock for your opponent to score after you do. *That would **always** apply to your last possession of the **first half**. It also applies if you are **behind by eight or less points** in what is likely to be your **last possession of a game**.*

You do not always do the inbounds hurry-up in those situations. You only use it when your field position and time-remaining in the half dictate a 20-second-per-play pace. Often, at the end of the first half or game, you will find that you have to run a slowdown or top-speed hurry-up because of the distance you must go and the time you have to do it in, **not** an inbounds hurry-up. The closest thing to the inbounds hurry-up in modern football is the **whole-game, no-huddle** used by such teams as the Buffalo Bills and late-'80s Cincinnati Bengals.

'Regular' speed

Regular speed is what most coaches do the vast majority of the time and spend almost all their practice time on. An argument could be made that you **never** should run or practice the regular speed. About the only time you would run it is when the game is **tied**.

Slowdown

The **slowdown** is what you run when you are **ahead** or when you are **behind by eight or less**, but in your last possession of the half. I have a table in the slowdown chapter to show you when that is.

When you are behind, you use the slowdown to make sure little time is left for your opponent to come back after you score.

'Decision making under conditions of uncertainty'

Most football coaches studied physical education in college. My background, West Point and Harvard Business School, is not the usual one for a football coach. [Actually, a number of West Pointers have done well at coaching. Twenty-one-year Tennessee coach Bob Neyland (Army '16) has the sixth highest winning percentage in NCAA Division IA history (.829). Dartmouth and Army coach Red Blaik (Army '20) has the 27th highest winning percentage (.759). Bill Yeoman (Army '49) went 160-108-8 at the University of Houston with his veer offense. Duke basketball coach Mike Krzyzewski was in the class behind me at West Point.]

As far as I know, Harvard Business School has not produced any great football coaches, but we studied some stuff there that should interest football coaches.

I recall an article written by one of our professors. The title was something like *Decision Making Under Conditions of Uncertainty*. Football coaches can relate to that.

One Harvard Business School trick for analyzing decisions under conditions of uncertainty was the **decision tree**. Here's how it works.

Decisions are represented by boxes, like this: □

Events which are beyond your control are represented by circle, like this: ○

At each brach of an event, you write the probability of that branch. The total probability at each event branch must equal 100%. Here's a simple example: You've just scored a touchdown which puts you **behind by six** points. Should you go for one or two?

I know there are standard guides to answer that question. You'll find one later in this book, along with a detailed discussion of each point differential. For this example, suffice it to say that the standard guide says "either" when the point differential after the touchdown is six points.

Let's futher say that you are head coach of the San Francisco 49ers in 1995 (I have the stats handy for that year).

Here's your decision:

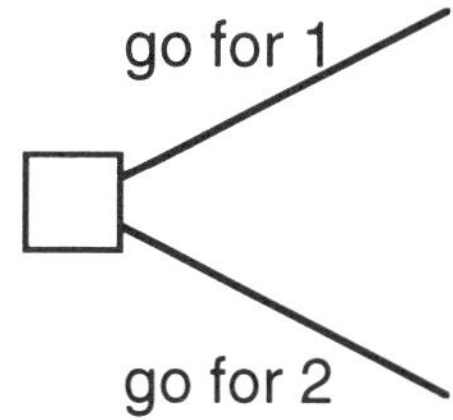

Now let's add the event nodes:

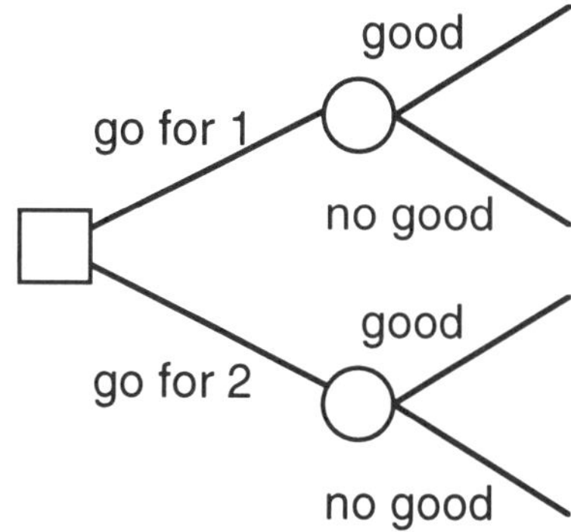

Now add the probabilities which I take from 49er 1995 statsistics:

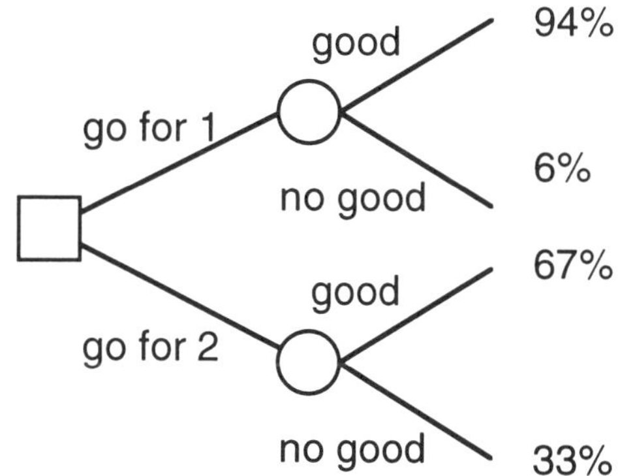

Next you add the **value** of each outcome. In this case, you would put the points scored.

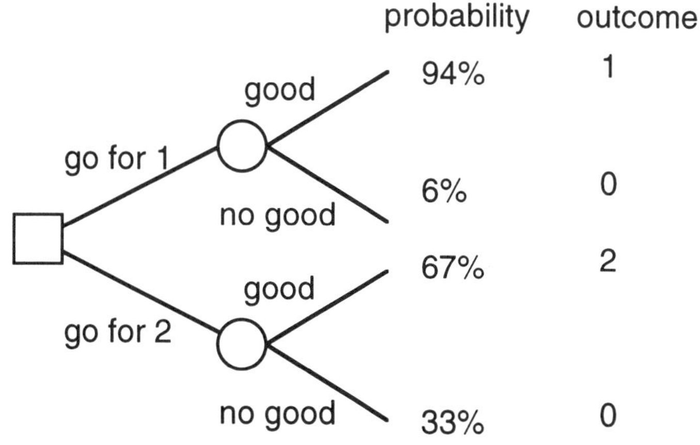

Next you multiply the probability by the outcome to get the weighted average for each event node:

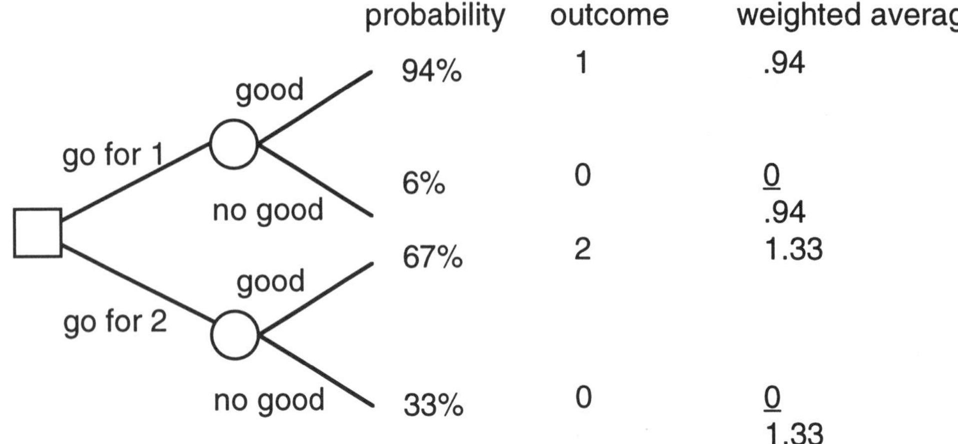

Now you have your answer. The expected value of going for one point is .94 and the expected value of going for two is 1.33. So going for two is the right decision for the 49ers in 1995.

Some might point out it's impossible to score 1.33 points. True. But if you make this decision a hundred times, you will find that you score 133 points if you always go for two and you will score 94 points if you always go for one. Law of Averages.

Different teams would get different results from this calculation because they have different success rates for their one-and two-point conversions plays. Also, the actual numbers were that the 49ers went 51 for 54 when they kicked and only 2 for 3 when they went for two. Some would point out that 54 attempts establish the success rate much better than three. Fine. Try three more and see if the success rate changes.

You should apply this concept to any decision where the best course of action is not obvious. You actually have been doing decision trees in your head all your life. You just never thought of them in such a formalized way.

Some might complain that you cannot do a decision tree during a game. I know. Decision trees are something you use **off the field** to create **rules of thumb** and **quick-reference tables and charts** which you take onto the field on game day. Decision trees are also things you work out in the **off-season**. And they are a technique you use when you are writing a book like this one.

'I don't need no fancy book learning'

Whenever someone advocates the use of sophisticated analytical tools, like decision trees, to an area of endeavor where numerous successful people get along without them, you hear militant dismissals of the tools.

In many cases, the speaker is ignorant or incompetent and is trying to bluff his way by the issue because he does not understand it. Some sincerely reject sophisticated tools because they believe that "it's a people business" and all that.

"Don't knock it if you ain't tried it," is another of those militant "My daddy done told me" sort of lines, and it applies to rejection or acceptance of sophisticated analysis. Coaches who have tried both seat-of-the-pants and sophisticated analytical approaches are in a sound position to reject one or both in whole or in part. But it is not sound for a coach who has not tried sophisticated analysis to reject it.

The Rule of Thirds

I long ago discovered a principle I call the Rule of Thirds. I often sit down and do a detailed analysis of something. It may be a business question or a legal question. Or a coaching question in football or another of the sports I have coached, or almost any area of life. Virtually every time I have done that, I have found:

- about one third was as I expected

• about one third was different than I expected and was a pleasant surprise
• about one third was different and was an unpleasant surprise.

For example, before I studied it, I assumed the team that scored first in a football game won about 60% of the time. But when I studied it, I found it was 70% to 84%.

Neglected aspect of football

Clearly, clock management is a neglected aspect of football, like special teams used to be in the NFL (actually, they still are somewhat neglected). Clock management is much **talked about** by observers of close games. Even then, there are many situations where virtually all observers failed to understand the clock-management aspects of a game.

Coaches and players generally do not understand clock management as well as they should. They do not spend enough time on it in practice nor do they switch to a clock-management mode as early as they should in games.

Clock-management skills range from extremely easy to acquire, like spiking the ball correctly, to somewhat difficult, like completing an out pass when the defense is expecting it. But the skills required to manage the clock well are also needed in **all** aspects of football. Even a team that never has to manage the clock will want to have an out pass.

As many as half of all football games could have been won by the loser had the loser done a better, or the winner a worse, job of clock management. Clock management will never replace the more prominent aspects of football—fundamentals, sound offensive and defensive systems, the right player at each position, conditioning. But poor clock management has often nullified everything else. If the scoreboards or officials at your games have clocks, you must become proficient in football clock management. Some may consider my saying clock management is neglected as a vague, general criticism. But there are many specific things you can cite to prove the case.

Clock management coordinator?

Special teams were not taken seriously until George Allen invented the special teams coordinator. Can we cite the lack of clock-management coordinators as evidence that clock management is not taken seriously enough?

A coordinator would probably be overkill and conflict with the other coordinators. But coaches could probably benefit from a **clock-management assistant coach**. As far as I know, no one has such an assistant. A clock-management assistant could plan the clock-management aspect of practices for both players and for coaches-only practice. He could analyze clock-management statistics and the clock-management aspects of the scouting report. During games, he would stand next to the coordinators and remind them of the clock-management ramifications of the current situation.

Where's the clock?

When football teams practice **passing**, they have a bag of **balls**. When they practice **blocking**, they have a **sled**. When they practice **field goals**, they have a **goal post**.

By the same token, in order to practice clock management, you need certain equipment, namely:

• a game clock
• a play clock
• a chain gang
• a 100-yard field
• a referee
• a score.

In fact, most teams at the high school and lower levels go entire seasons without ever having any of these things on the practice field. I attended a two-day clinic at Stanford when Bill Walsh was coach in 1994. He had real referees working the scrimmage. I called Stanford in 1997 and asked about equipment for clock-management practice and offensive corodinator Dana Bible said that although they practice clock management daily and use real or fake referees and a chain gang, they do **not** have a scoreboard or clock other than the head coach's stop watch. Seems to me that any team that wants to really get good at clock management needs to have a scoreboard on their practice field or practice on their game field with the scoreboard turned on.

Where are the stats?

As football has become more sophisticated, the number of stats has increased. Special teams stats are the most recent to arrive on the scene. But if clock management is important, how come there are no stats on it? The only clock-related stat I know of is time of possession. In fact, one could devise various measures of the clock-management proficiency of a coach or team. How many seconds were left on the play clock at each snap when the team was ahead? How many when they were behind? How well were timeouts used? How many seconds were left on the clock for the team's last play? How many seconds did each play take when they were operating at various speeds? And more.

Where is the video?

High school coaches typically tell their videotapers to turn the camera off right after a play is blown dead until the offense breaks the huddle for the next play. How can you get better at clock management if you have no video that **shows** your clock management?

Where are the goals?

Football teams typically have goals—goals for offense, defense, and, recently, special teams. But where are the clock-management goals? If you have none, how can you say clock management is important to your team?

Not an either-or decision

Coaches have to make many **either-or decisions** like whether to focus on the option or the pass. They tend to treat clock management versus regular game management as a similar either-or decision. And clock management usually **loses** because of the perception that it is only used in **rare** end-of-close game situations.

In fact, much of what you have to practice for clock management is **not** time taken away from needed "regular" practice. Rather it is **just speeded-up regular practice**. You do **not** have to **give up** regular practice time, just **speed** it up.

Much of clock-management practice can be achieved in one- or two-rep-per-season drills. Coaches can even practice their clock management skills without the presence of the players to a large extent.

In short, much improvement is needed to bring football clock management up the standard that coaches have set in other aspects of the game. That's the **bad** news. The **good** news is that, in the clock-management area, much can be accomplished with little effort or with only slight modification of efforts that are already taking place.

Errata

The referee who read the book said it was extremely ambitious of me to try to write about the rules at three different levels of football. So I would not be surprised if this book contained an error. If you find one, please tell me. I'll post a correction on my Website.

I work at home and answer my own phone. Here's how to get in touch with me:

Voice: 510-820-6292, fax: 510-820-1259, E-mail: johnreed@johntreed.com, Web site: www.johntreed.com. Please check that site periodically to see if there are any errors to correct.

Controversial stuff

This book contains much controversial advice. **All** fourteen of the books I've written are controversial. I would not **write** a book that was not controversial. If a writer is just going to agree with conventional wisdom, why bother?

My sole criteria in this book is what course of action is most likely to lead to victory on the playing field. One might think, "What's controversial about that? That's exactly what all football coaches want."

No, it's not. It should be, but it's not. What most football coaches want is to **keep their job**. True, coaches who lose too many games at the high-school varsity and higher levels generally lose their jobs because of their lack of winning. That undeniable fact has given rise to the myth that football coach employment is based solely on coaching competence. Losing **will** cost you your job in football coaching above the junior-varsity high school level. But the implied corollary, that **winning** will enable you to **keep** your job, is **not** true.

Witness George Seifert, the coach with the highest winning percentage in NFL history, out of his 49er head coaching job. Or Lou Holtz, who was on the verge of surpassing Knute Rockne as Notre Dame's winningest coach when he resigned, apparently because the athletic director did not like him. Or the late NFL Hall of Fame coach George Allen, who had trouble holding a coaching job even though he has the third highest winning percentage among coaches with over 100 career victories. Or Bobby Ross or Bill Parcells. From 1974 to 1983, three NFL Coaches of the Year were subsequently fired.

Coaches can be fired at the whim of the principal, athletic director, or owner. Often, the only thing that keeps a coach in his job is the boss's fear of outcry among the press, parents, alumni, or fans. The fact that those groups have enormous power regarding the coach's employment, causes coaches to be very eager to please them.

In general, those groups are **not** going to read this book. So a coach may read something here, agree that it makes sense, then do it in a game, resulting in questions about his competence from the incompetent. If he loses the game for some other reason, the rabble may nevertheless blame the controverisal clock-management decision. Or maybe the controversial decision was actually what the lost the game, but only because it was a Law-of-Averages thing that will pay off in the long run.

So I fear that some will agree with stuff in this book, but not use it in games because of job insecurity. And others may think, stuff that's in this book must be wrong because they don't see it in very many games. In fact, there is enormous reluctance in football coaching to use **anything** new until it has been well established by others. One of the reasons I continued to coach youth football even after I became a high school coach was the great freedom to innovate that exists at the youth level.

Coaching versus being a coach

When it comes down to it, there are a lot of football coaches who are more interested in **being** a coach than they are in **coaching**. Coaching is making the hard decisions so as to maximize the probability of victory. Being a coach is having a title, a position.

In the business world, we dismiss some people as "empty suits." It is sad but true that the football coaching world has a counterpart, the "empty polo shirt," coaches who walk on eggs every day of their career devoting more energy to reading the mood of their bosses than to trying to give their players and fans the best coaching they are capable of. Their unspoken motto is, "If it's not what everybody else is doing, I won't do it either."

Henry Clay said,

I would rather be right than president.

I'm with Henry. I would rather be right than coach in a way I knew was wrong to pander to the ignorant but powerful.

Coach your team the way that makes the most sense to **you**. If that results in your losing the job, so be it. Don't live your life for other people. And don't get fired because you chickened out of doing it **your** way, only to find that doing it someone **else's** way got you just as fired.

2

Before halftime

The dominant fact about pre-halftime clock management is that you don't **have to** do anything. Unlike end-of-game situations, you never **have to** score before halftime to win. Also, the score or even who's leading does not matter just before halftime.

You should try to score before halftime if you can do it without too much risk of the other team scoring as a result of a chance you took. The distance and time-remaining combination that fits that description varies year to year and opponent to opponent. *If you decide to try to score, you should do so at a pace which leaves no more than 20 seconds on the clock for the opponent.*

Psychological effect?

Radio and TV football announcers constantly say that coaches "...don't want to go into the locker room at halftime on a down note." Excuse me, but why not? Has anyone ever done a study of how often a team that scored just before halftime ended up winning the game? Here's my own little study, based on every NFL game played in the 1994 season.

Date	Team that scored before half	Points	Halftime score	Winning team
9/4/94	Eagles	7	NY 21-10	Giants
9/4/94	Chargers	8	SD 27-24	Chargers
9/11/94	Cowboys	3	Dallas 13-10	Cowboys
9/11/94	Dolphins	7	Miami 17-0	Dolphins
9/11/94	Giants	7	NY 20-10	Giants
9/18/94	Saints	3	NO 9-7	Saints
9/18/94	49ers	7	SF 17-10	49ers
9/25/94	Dolphins	6	Minn 28-6	Twins
9/25/94	Patriots	7	NE 17-7	Patriots
9/25/95	Bears	3	Chicago 10-7	Bears

9/26/94	Bills	7	Buffalo 17-7	Bills
10/2/94	Saints	7	NO 17-13	Saints
10/9/94	Chargers	7	SD 13-3	Chargers
10/9/94	Raiders	7	NE 17-14	Raiders
10/9/94	Saints	7	NO 7-0	Bears
10/9/94	Falcons	7	Atlanta 24-3	Falcons
10/10/94	Giants	7	10-10	Vikings
10/13/94	Browns	3	Cleveland 11-0	Browns
10/16/94	Steelers	7	Pitt. 14-0	Steelers
10/16/94	Jets	7	NY 21-7	Jets
10/16/94	Cowboys	7	Dallas 14-7	Cowboys
10/20/94	Packers	7	GB 10-7	Packers
10/23/94	Cowboys	7	14-14	Cowboys
10/23/94	Redskins	7	Ind. 17-13	Redskins
10/30/94	Cowboys	7	Cinn. 17-14	Cowboys
10/30/94	Dolphins	7	Miami 13-3	Dolphins
10/30/94	Chargers	8	SD 14-7	Chargers
10/30/94	Cardinals	7	Arizona 17-14	Cardinals
11/6/94	Jets	7	Buffalo 14-10	Jets
11/6/94	Bengals	3	Cinn. 8-7	Bengals
11/6/94	49ers	7	SF 17-3	49ers
11/13/94	Browns	3	Cleveland 13-7	Browns
11/13/94	Raiders	7	LA 14-7	Raiders
11/13/94	Patriots	3	Minn. 20-3	Patriots
11/20/94	Packers	6	Buffalo 27-6	Bills
11/20/94	Bengals	3	Cinn. 7-6	Colts
11/20/94	Dolphins	7	Miami 7-6	Steelers
11/20/94	Raiders	3	LA 10-0	Raiders
11/27/94	Vikings	3	Tampa 14-9	Buccaneers
12/4/94	49ers	3	SF 27-14	49ers
12/4/94	Redskins	7	DC 21-17	Buccaneers
12/5/94	Chargers	7	14-14	Raiders
12/10/94	Jets	7	Detroit 9-6	Lions
12/11/94	Patriots	7	Ind. 10-7	Patriots
12/18/94	Seahawks	7	10-10	Raiders
12/24/94	Packers	7	GB 28-6	Packers
12/24/94	Chiefs	7	KC 14-3	Chiefs
12/24/94	Chargers	7	SD 17-13	Chargers
12/24/94	Rams	7	LA 21-17	Redskins
Super Bowl	Chargers	3	SF 28-10	49ers

Conclusions

If scoring just before half were fatal, the team that did it would **always** win the game. That does not happen. It's better to be **ahead** at the half, **no matter when** you scored, than to score just before the half. 78% of the time, the team that **led** at half won the 1994 NFL games in which someone scored just before the half. The team that **scored** just before the half won 72% of the time.

Did scoring just before half demoralize the leading team so much that they ended up losing the game? We don't know the **reasons** for the loss, but when the team that was trailing at half scored just before half, they ended up winning just 6 of the 50 games or 12%. But on the other hand, it went the opposite way almost as many times. Five times, the team that was leading at half and which scored just before half, ended up losing the game in spite of their big "psychological lift."

The games that were **tied** at half are especially interesting. In three of the four halftime ties, the team that scored just before the half to tie it up ended up **losing** the game in spite of their great "psychological lift" at halftime.

Second half is a different game

Have the announcers forgotten what it's like in a football locker room at halftime? Players aren't sitting around feeling sorry for themselves. They are busier than a one-armed paperhanger in a windstorm. Injuries and equipment are attended to. Players go to the bathroom. Position coaches, coordinators, and the head coach are interrogating players as to problems and opportunities, instructing them as to adjustments to make for the second half, and trying to get them into the right mental frame of mind.

My impression is that the second half is another game. I have seen teams that were ahead at halftime come out and get beat in the second half and had the feeling that if there had been no halftime break, the early leader would have won the game. It is further my impression that who scored just before half probably matters little other than the fact that **all** scores help the scoring team.

Case in point: 1996 Aloha Bowl

On Christmas Day, 1996, Cal played Navy in the Aloha Bowl. With 34 seconds left in the first half, Cal had three timeouts left and the ball, first and 10 at their own 39. They stopped the clock at 0:28 by getting a first down at the Navy 45. Then they completed an out pass and the runner stopped the clock at 0:20 by going out of bounds at the Navy 30.

*Since that was another **first down**, he should **not** have gone out of bounds. Rather he should have gotten a few more yards.* No matter. The next play was a pass complete to the 20 where the receiver was immediately tackled. Timeout Cal. 0:11 left. Then Cal threw a post pass for a touchdown. The extra point kick was good: Cal, 35; Navy, 28. Time remaining: 0:05. Cal pooched the kickoff to about the 25 and the returner was tackled soon after he got the ball. Time expired during the runback. Halftime.

Wonderful. Cal executed their two-minute drill almost to perfection and scored seven points in a 61-yard, 29-second drive. They went into halftime with both the lead and the fresh memory of that just-before-the-half score.

Different ball game

Big psychological advantage? Apparently not. The second half was a somewhat different ball game. Cal loaded up to stop Navy's run. Navy brought in their passing quarterback and often ran a stack trips formation. Navy won 42-38 in dramatic come-from-behind fashion. So if there's a big psychological advantage to scoring just below the half, it was not apparent in the '96 Aloha Bowl.

It should be noted that Navy's coach for the '96 Aloha Bowl was Charlie Weatherbie, the same guy who blew the 1995 Army-Navy game by going for six when three would have been enough, then doing a poor job of clock management on their final possession. I am not a Navy fan, but I must say that Weatherbie did a heck of a job in the Aloha Bowl.

1997 Cotton Bowl

With one second before the half, Kansas State's threw a Hail Mary pass to the end zone. It was caught after a tip in spectacular fashion for a touchdown. But BYU still came from behind to win the game in the fourth quarter.

On the other hand...

Of course, it sometimes goes the other way. On 10/15/95 the Jets were leading the Panthers 12-6 in Carolina. There were 22 seconds left in the half and New York had the ball with second down on their own 36. Bubby Brister dropped back then threw a weak shovel pass to running back Adrian Murell. It was intercepted by blitzing linebacker Sam Mills, who ran it in for the tying score. The extra point was good, giving Carolina the lead, 13-12, 13 seconds before halftime. The 1996 *Pro Football Revealed* says "...they ultimately defeated the disheartened Jets 26-15 for their first victory ever."

Good to score

My position is that scoring when the game is still in doubt is **always** good for the team that scores and always bad for the team that is scored upon. But I see no special psychological advantage to scoring just before the half. On the other hand, the team in possession of the ball should use the clock to their advantage at the end of either half.

Go for it or run out the clock

Your basic pre-halftime decision is whether to try to score or to just run out the clock or both. I am inclined to go for it. One of my more satisfying coaching moments in 1996 came in my freshman team's game against Benicia.

As halftime approached, we were on defense, but I could see that we might get the ball back with enough time for one or two plays. On the sideline, I gathered the first-string offensive players who were not playing defense and discussed the situation with them. One player suggested we run our tailback pass. "Good idea," I said.

I told the kids to get ready to hustle out and run that play as soon as we got the ball. Sure enough, we got the ball back, at the other team's 40-yard line, turned over on downs, with seven seconds left. The change of possession stopped the clock until the snap. We huddled so the two-way players could get the play. Then we ran it. The buzzer sounded while the pass was in the air. The receiver caught the ball, broke two tackles, and scored.

We did it again in our Miramonte game. In that case, we just ran a two-minute drill and drove the length of the field. The buzzer sounded with our touchdown pass in the air.

Unfortunately, Dublin did it to **us** during another game. We won the Benicia game 34-8, tied Miramonte, and lost to Dublin 34-0. As you can see, we needed the touchdown in the **Miramonte** game to escape with a tie. But I don't think the fact that it came just before halftime accomplished any more than if we had scored early in the second quarter instead.

If you go for it, going SLOWLY may be appropriate

Believe it or not, if you decide to try to score before halftime, doing so slowly may be the correct pace. See the chapter on slowdown offense for a table which shows the situation when it is appropriate run your scoring drive at a slow pace.

When do you NOT go for it?

Going for a score, in a short period of time, when you are out of scoring range, is risky. You generally have to engage is *dangerous ball handling* like passing and pitches. If you try hard to score from a long distance out, you may turn the ball over and enable the **opponent** to score instead.

If you have an explosive team that can score in one play from anywhere on the field, you should probably try to score from anywhere no matter how much time is remaining in the half. On the other hand, if your team speed is such that your receivers and running backs normally get tackled from behind on long runs, it will take you a number of plays to score. When time is short and you probably don't have enough time to drive down the field and score, run out the clock. If you cannot score in the time remaining, you are taking a stupid risk to try. At the **end of the game**, you'd try to score in the same situation. But just before half, why risk giving **up** a score when there is little chance of your getting one?

Play until the whistle

On 12/17/95, the Kansas City Chiefs offensive line quit before the whistle just before halftime, apparently thinking the play was dead. It was not. Denver cornerback Ray Crockett frew in untouched and blasted Chiefs quarterback Steve Bono knocking the ball loose. Crockett picked it up and ran 50 yards for a touchdown with three seconds left in the half making the score 14-7 Chiefs. However, that big psychological lift didn't have much effect.The Chiefs won 20-17.

Decide before the game

The decision as to what you are going to do an the end of the half if you have the ball should be made before the game starts, **not** in the heat of battle.

Field position	Time left	Decision
Inside own 25	4:00+	Score touchdown
	<4:00	Run out clock
Own 26 to 50	3:00 +	Score touchdown
	<3:00	Run out clock
50 to opp. 26	2:00 +	Score touchdown
	<2:00	Run out clock or kick field goal if in range
opp. 25 to goal	Any	Score touchdown

This table is simply based on the crude formula that your team can gain about 20 yards a minute. Your field-goal kicker's range is a factor and varies from team to team and especially from level to level. Accordingly, this is a chart **you** must make up each week based on the **scouting report** and your expectation as to **how the game will go**. For example, if you are handling the opponent well, you will probably be willing to gamble more and will expect to gain more yards per carry. In a tight game against a tough opponent, you will probably want to be more conservative and try to run out the clock when there is more time left and/or fewer yards to go to score than in a game against a weak opponent.

My main message is that you have to decide **before the game** what you will do at the end of the half.

3

End of game

End of game is now-or-never time if you're behind. It's be-smart time if you're ahead.

Last play of the game

Let's work backwards from the last play of the game.

Situation	Last play
Ahead on offense	Take a knee
Ahead on defense	Hail Mary or other desperate scoring play. Take a knee if you intercept, which is common in this situation.
Behind on offense	Hail Mary or other desperate scoring play. Lateral rather than be tackled
Behind on defense	Take a knee. Try to recover fumbled snap.

Next-to-last play

Situation	Next-to-last play
Ahead on offense	Take a knee
Ahead on defense	When behind by three points or fewer, offense may try to get ball into field-goal position and stop the clock so they can get their field goal team onto the field for one last play. Keep them inbounds and out of field-goal range. When behind by four or more points, offense should go for six.
Behind on offense	Maneuver to get into field goal kicking position if three points are enough. Either stop clock on play or leave enough time to get field-goal team on the field. Ball carrier may have to take a knee or get out of bounds before being tackled to prevent the game from ending during his run if he cannot score the winning TD.

Behind on defense	Take a knee. Try to recover fumbled snap. Use timeout if you have any.

Last series

Situation	Last series
Ahead on offense	Take a knee
Ahead on defense	Offense will maneuver to try field goal if down by three or fewer or will try to score touchdown if they need four or more.
Behind on offense	Advance on whatever schedule you need to get into field-goal range or end zone. Leave time to get field-goal team onto field or have a way to stop the clock for the field-goal team to get onto the field.
Behind on defense	Take a knee. Try to recover fumbled snap.

Next-to-last series

Situation	Next-to-last series
Ahead on offense	If you are ahead by three or more, and within the quarterback-keep-sweep-slide period, run plays that go backwards toward your own goal so that you end up on your own ten or so for fourth down, then take a safety killing the remaining time on the clock. If you are ahead by three or more, and not within the quarterback-keep-sweep-slide period, get one more first down. Call plays that avoid turnovers. Maybe one or more quarterback keepers. If you are ahead by one or two, get one more first down. You may **not** want to score a touchdown if you are ahead by just one point because it only puts you up by seven or eight and forces you to kickoff to the other team. You only need to get a first down to win. You do not need to score any more points.
Ahead on defense	Stop offense from getting first down. Be conscious of drive schedule dictated to offense by game situation.
Behind on offense	Score or get a first down at the pace indicated in the pace graph in the slowdown chapter.
Behind on defense	Strip the ball. Must stop the offense from getting the first down. This is the ball game. Once they get to take-a-knee point, it's over. May be smart to deliberately allow a touchdown if you are just down by one point.

Special teams last plays

Situation	Last play
Ahead	Kickoff—onside kick is least likely to be returned for a TD Kick return—take a knee after getting possession of opponent's onside kick Field goal—do not kick a field goal for the last play of the game if you are ahead—take a knee Field goal defense—Watch the fake if the ball is near the limit of the kicker's range or if you are ahead by 3. Punt—If you are ahead by eight or fewer, a blocked punt could cost you the game in one play. Leading teams

should generally not punt on the last play of the game unless they are backed up to their own end zone, leading by less than three, and cannot use all the remaining game-clock time with their fourth-down play. If you are leading by three or more, deliberately take a safety.

Free kick after a safety—If you are ahead by three or less, you must **kick the ball out of field-goal range**. You should also kick so that there is no chance of a fair catch, which would stop the clock if it had not run out during the kick. You avoid a fair catch by kicking a grounder. If you are ahead by four or more, you should probably do an **onside kick**. That has the least probability of a return and causes the most time to run off the clock, which starts when the receiving team touches the ball.

Free kick return after a safety—The trailing team will undoubtedly try an **onside kick**. Put your hands team in if you have one.

Punt defense—If you are ahead, the opponent should not punt in this situation, although my head coach did once. The offense should not even line up in punt formation. Count on a fake punt if they do. More likely, they will go for the score on the last play of the game.

PAT—If in college and ahead by one point, do not try for the extra point. It could be blocked, stripped, o intercepted and run back for the winning score. Take a knee. In high school and NFL, there will be no PAT if your touchdown leaves you ahead and time has run out.

PAT defense—If ahead by one, block that kick but watch the fake. If ahead by 2, stop the 2-point conversion play.

Behind

Kickoff—onside kick, also applies to free kick after a safety

Kick return—trick return if you have one—ball carrier **must lateral** rather than be tackled after time has run out, also applies to free kick after a safety.

Field goal—Protect the kicker. Fake may be better choice.

Field goal defense—Offense will not kick a field goal on the last play of the game if they are ahead. If they are dumb enough to try, make all-out block attempt and run it back for a touchdown.

Punt—You don't punt on the last play of the game when you are behind. You probably should not even line up in a punt formation to run a fake. No one would believe there is any chance of a punt.

Punt defense—If you are behind on the last play of the game, the offense generally will not punt even on fourth down unless they are inside their own two- or three-yard line and leading by just one or two points. If they do punt, with so little time left on the clock that the punt play will use it all up, you must either block it or return it all the way. If you can fair catch before the end of regulation, do so. It stops the clock

and, in high school and the NFL, you can try a free-kick field goal on the next play if three points is enough to win or tie.
If they are leading by three or more points, they should take a safety. You should try to **strip** the ball and score by falling on it in the end zone or picking it up and running it into the end zone.

PAT—If in college and behind by one point, go for the tie or win based on which has the greatest probability of leading to ultimate victory. See the tie-game discussion below.

PAT defense—If behind by one in college, block that kick and run it back for a touchdown. College teams should not kick if ahead by one, but you can demand that they at least snap the ball for the point after touchdown. If they are smart, they will take a knee. But if they are dumb enough to kick, block it and run it back. In high school and the NFL, there should be no last play PAT if the offense is already ahead.

You should do at least one repetition of practice for each of these situations. More importantly, the coach must have a quick reference sheet at the game so he can make the correct decision in the heat of battle.

End of a tie game

If the game ends in a tie, it will go to overtime in most cases. Although pre-league high school games in my area are allowed to end in a tie.

In a tie game, each team needs to decide whether they are more likely to win during regulation or during overtime. The question is mainly one of field position and possession. As regulation winds down, you knew which team has the ball and their field position. You should also know your overtime rules.

NFL: Coin flip decides who receives kickoff. First team to score wins. Logic on deciding whether to go for it at the end of regulation: *If you have **possession** now, you'd better go for it. You may never get possession in overtime.*

College: Each team takes two turns driving for a score from its opponent's **25-yard line**. The team that scores the most points in overtime wins. The 25-yard line is, itself, the line of scrimmage for a 25 + 17 = 42-yard field goal. A lot of college kickers can make that. *The question becomes which team has the best **red zone offense** in this game. If it's not you, you'd better win in regulation. If it **is** you, no point in taking a chance of losing in regulation. Run out the clock in regulation.*

High school: Each team takes one shot from the opponent's **ten-yard line**. *The question in high school is which team has the better **goal-line offense** in this game. If it's you, let the regulation game end in a tie.*

Nine or more point margin

If one team is ahead by nine points or more, the trailing team has to score twice to win. As I said in the overview chapter, high school teams generally score at a rate of **seven points a quarter**. In the NFL in 1995, the average team scored 343.8 points in 16.73 games for a game average of 20.55, which is **5.14 points per quarter**. In 1994, the average major college game saw the two teams score 49.1 points which translates to 49.1 ÷ 2 = 24.55 per team per game or 24.55 ÷ 4 = **6.14 points per team per quarter**.

So if a team needs to score nine or more points, they generally need either more than one quarter to do it or a takeaway. In the slowdown chapter, I talk about running your final drive according to a schedule. *If you need to score twice in the fourth quarter, you need to get at least the first score at top speed.* Depending on how much time is left, you get the ball back by forcing the other team to punt or by an onside kick. Then you can check the final-drive table to see what pace to use for your second score.

The outcome-no-longer-in-doubt point

You should decide before the game or before the season, the combination of time remaining and margin at which you will conclude that the outcome is no longer in doubt and give your bench some playing time. This would apply to both leading and trailing teams.

Two NFL teams have since scored 28 points in the fourth quarter, thereby coming from behind to win.

The greatest NCAA Division IA comeback was 42 points in the second half.

The California Youth Football League requires the game turn into a controlled scrimmage if either team has a 28-point margin after halftime. Oregon has the "Don Markham Rule," which says high school games there are over when either team has a 45-point margin. (Markham runs a double-wing offense which tore up the state when he was there.) It's also called the "Bandon Rule" because he did it at Bandon High School.

Putting your subs in with less than a 28-point margin is really a philosophical question. It has a **political** element. Playing time pleases the bench warmers and their parents. Lack of playing time angers them, especially when they perceive the outcome is no longer in doubt.

On the other hand, running up the white flag when there is still time left will anger the **starters** and their parents. At higher levels or at highly competitive high schools, it could get you fired.

There is also a training consideration. Game experience helps your bench warmers become better players. Game experience is hard to come by. You don't want to define your no-longer-in-doubt point so narrowly that your bench has less game experience than your opponents' benches.

Finally, there is a **competitive** issue. If you are ahead, you don't want to put your subs in before the opposing team does. One year when I coached varsity high school volleyball, our arch rival Campolindo showed their disdain for our team by putting their subs into the second game of a match. They had beaten us by a large margin in the first game. And our school had never beaten Campo in the eight-year history of volleyball in that area.

We won the second game, beating Campo's subs by a large margin. Campo put its first-string back in, but my kids played as if they were possessed. They were angry about Campo's subs coming in so early. They were also tired of losing to them. We won the five-game match tying Campo for second place in the league for the season.

Football ain't volleyball. Because of the nature of volleyball, you really **never** reach a point where you can put in the second string and remain confident of victory. There **is** a point when you can do it in football. But you'd better be careful you don't do it too soon if you are ahead.

Come up with a number-of-touchdowns-margin-and-time-remaining rule. You might state that *you will substitute at such-and-such point when you are* ***ahead*** *as long as the opponent keeps their first string in, or when the opponent puts* ***its*** *subs in, whichever is sooner. When you are* ***behind****, you should put your subs in when you are behind by four touchdowns in the second half or three touchdowns in the fourth quarter.* If you are only behind by **two** touchdowns, you probably have a chance to win no matter how late it is in the fourth quarter.

4

Using timeouts

Timeouts are a key tactic in football clock management. But coaches are sometimes unclear on when to use them.

Advantages and disadvantages

First consider their advantages and disadvantages:

Advantages

- stops both game and play clocks when you are trying to **conserve** time
- permits coach-player **conference**
- gives your team 40 to 110 seconds (varies at different levels and in different situations) which can be used to:
    - make **substitutions**
    - **consider** options
    - **explain** tactics
    - catch **breath** and drink **water**
    - **gather thoughts** (or in the case of "icing" a kicker, inspire too much thought)
    - **line up** properly
    - **change play** or defense
- lets you run or pass in the middle of the field and still stop the clock after the play

Disadvantages

- stops both game and play clocks when you are trying to **waste** time
- **reduces** the number of **timeouts** you have **left**
- **saves** one of your **opponent's timeouts** in some cases
- permits **opponent** to have a coach-player conference
- Gives your **opponent** 40 to 110 seconds which **they** can use to:
    - make substitutions

- consider options
- explain tactics
- catch breath and drink water
- gather thoughts
- line up properly
- change play or defense

Purpose hierarchy

Some purposes are better than others. For example, in one game, my team discovered before our first offensive play of the game that we only had 10 men on the field. We had to call timeout to figure out who was missing and get him out there. (Just before the game, we had told every player who was first and second-string on each team and actually had each of the eight units—offense, defense, kickoff, kick return, punt, punt return, FG, FG defense—line up to make doubly sure everyone knew which teams he was supposed to be on.) The guy who was missing **forgot**—in the space of 15 minutes—that he was on first-string offense. I would have thought that being named to first-string would be a more memorable event to the player.

Generally speaking, you should try to use your timeouts **only to stop the clock**. The other good purpose is to get your field goal team in at the end of a half or at the end of a game when you are behind by three points or less. Colorado's Rick Neuheisel says,

> *The only reason for a timeout is to get more plays. We don't use a timeout to make decisions or think about what we are going to do.*

All the other purposes timeouts are used for can and should be accomplished with**out** using a timeout. *If your team uses a timeout for any purpose other than stopping the clock or getting your field goal team on the field, you screwed up.*

Wasting a timeout shortens the usable game clock time by about 12 to 40 seconds depending on your level. If you are behind and close at the end of a game, wasting a timeout earlier in the game can cost you the game. At the time they are wasted, the timeout does not seem important. Wasted timeouts are generally forgotten by the time the end of the game rolls around. But coaches should point out to players in post-game film study how the wasted timeout could have been used to win the game.

Wasting a timeout versus ending a possession prematurely

Quarterbacks frequently call a timeout because they "don't like what they see," to use the announcers' favorite phrase. Should coaches instead teach quarterbacks to run a keeper when they don't like what they see?

Maybe not. Teams get about seven to 14 possessions per game, depending on the level. Lower levels use 8- to 10-minute quarters; high school varsities, 12-minute quarters; and college and pro, 15-minute quarters. Wasting a down typically forces you to punt in a close game, thereby ending one of your precious possessions.

Only ten men on the field but seven on the line

There are other ways than timeouts to fix problems. For example, Denver only had 10 men on the field for an offensive play in a game against Kansas City. They first made sure at least seven were on the line of scrimmage as required by the rules. The missing player was a split end. Then John Elway ran a quarterback draw for a touchdown to take the lead, 28-24 with 1:22 left in the game. (Unfortunately, KC's quarterback was Joe Montana and he then led his team to a go-ahead touchdown with 0:08 left to win 31-28.)

Which is worse: wasting a timeout or ending a possession prematurely because you went ahead with a play even though something was wrong? Actually, it's not that simple. The play that was called may work in spite of the quarterback's misgivings. A quarterback keeper instead of the play that was called or a timeout may keep the drive alive. A play called after a timeout may fail as bad or worse than the play that was called originally.

It's going to have to be a judgment call. But quarterbacks should be less cavalier about calling timeouts whenever they "don't like what they see." Each timeout can enable the team that owns it to run an extra two or more plays at the end of a half. It doesn't make sense to eliminate **two** plays to **possibly** improve **one** play's chances of success. On the other hand, if the timeout can keep a drive alive, it may be worth two plays. I suggest the following rule:

> *Don't call a "don't-like-what-you-see" timeout unless it is pretty certain that failure to do so will mean the difference between punting or turning the ball over on downs, and continuing to drive toward a score.*

The solution is **prevention**. Get your act together so you have the right people on the field, can make good decisions quickly, communicate without face-to-face conferences, are cardiovascularly fit, and can adjust quickly on the field.

Defense different

Defense is different. If the defensive captain doesn't like what he sees, and fails to take a timeout to correct it, the opponent could score as a result. The stakes are higher on defense. Is it worth it to give up a timeout to prevent a score? You bet.

But again, the defense should be trained and managed so that they can adjust to whatever the offense does with**out** wasting timeouts. Using a timeout to make a defensive adjustment may be the best thing to do at the time, but it still indicates a big-time screw-up in **preparation** by the defensive coordinator.

When NOT to call a timeout

Generally, you should **not** call a timeout when:

- the clock is stopped anyway, namely (parenthese shows when clock restarts):
    - the **other** team has called a timeout (until snap)
    - the ball has gone **out of bounds** (until snap)
    - an **incomplete pass** has been thrown (until snap)
    - **chains are being moved** (until ready-to-play whistle)
    - after a **fair catch** (until snap)
    - during **penalty** decisions and enforcement (until ready-to-play whistle)
    - within 20 seconds before the two-minute warning in the NFL (until snap)
    - after a **score** (on subsequent kickoff)
    - **change of possession** (until snap)
    - **referee's timeout** (until ready-to-play whistle).
- it will not save you from having to punt or turn the ball over on downs
- when it will help the **other** team more than yours.

This may seem obvious, but in the heat of battle, coaches and players often call timeouts when time is already out. In the 1996 Aloha Bowl between Cal and Navy, Cal called a timeout during their final unsuccessful attempt to retake the lead. They threw an incomplete pass with 1:05 left, **stopping the clock**. Then they called a timeout! Maybe they meant to do that. If so, it's a poor use of a timeout when you are on your own 14 and losing 42-38.

Ask for a measurement

There is one situation where you may be able to **create** a referee's timeout. If either team runs a play that is close to a first down, and the officials indicate a result which is adverse to your team (either **you** did **not** make it or your **opponent did** make it), you can request a measurement. If your request is granted, the officials will stop the clock to measure. Once they are finished, if a first-down was **not** achieved, they will immediately signal for the clock to **start**.

Don't help your opponent with your own timeouts

In a 1996 freshman game where I was offensive and special team coordinator, we were behind by two points near the end of the game. We had used all our timeouts on defense forcing the other team to get a first down or punt. They had to punt. We managed to stop the clock with one second left by spiking the ball. We were on their nine-yard line and decided to try to kick a field goal.

Unfortunately, we had never even **attempted** a field goal all season, and had not even attempted a PAT kick since the beginning of our first game. The game in question was our next-to-last one. We had **practiced** kicking a field goal every week and had practiced getting our field goal team onto the field the day before every game. But I still was not confident we could get the right eleven guys out there, lined up properly in the heat of battle with one second on the clock, and only the 25-second play clock's time in which to do it.

Fortunately, our opponent had a timeout and they decided to use it to discuss field-goal defense with their players. That gave us an additional 35 seconds or so, and enabled our head coach to go out on to the field to get our players organized. We kicked the field goal and won the game by one point. The timeout obviously was not enough to enable our opponent to block the kick. But it was very helpful to us.

There is a tendency in war and in athletic contests to be so preoccupied with **your own** problems that you forget that the **opponent** has problems, too. All timeouts help both teams. Consider whether you want to help your opponent in the situation in question before you call the timeout.

There's also a tendency to want to use **all** your timeouts. Baloney. Just use them if you need to stop the clock; never because they are "burning a hole in your pocket."

When to call timeout

If you are trying to **conserve** time, you want to call timeout *as soon as the play is dead.* If you are trying to **waste** time, but still have to take a timeout, *wait until the last second to do it.* Arizona State made the mistake of calling a timeout too fast in the 1997 Rose Bowl and I believe it cost them the game.

If you are on offense, wait until the play clock hits 1 second left to call it. If you are on defense, wait until just before the quarterback is ready to receive the snap. If the offense is in a shotgun formation, you have to call your timeout no later than when the center has hold of the ball and six other men are on the line and set. If the offense is snapping the ball to a quarterback under center, you have to call timeout ***before*** *the quarterback puts his hands under the center because they can snap as soon as the quarterback's hands are in place.*

Use the universal timeout signal (forming a "T" with your hands) for a **conserve-time timeout**. I suggest that for a **last-second, waste-time timeout** you make a plus sign with your **forearms**. Practice calling these two different timeouts.

When to call a timeout on offense

You generally should not call timeouts on offense. But sometimes, through no fault of your own, you are unable to use them on defense.

Colorado's Rick Neuheisel says to call your first offensive timeout at around 1:30 but not until you run a play that does not get a first down, go out of bounds or involve an incomplete pass. I agree with the notion that you don't call it on a play that stops the clock anyway and that you call it early rather than late. But I suspect 1:30 is too late. I have seen many drives, most notably Ohio State's winning final drive in the 1997 Rose Bowl, where they got the ball at 1:40, ran twelve plays, and used no timeouts at all. In other words, the situation when Neuheisel says to call the timeout never came up. Ohio State ended up using their timeout for the PAT—which they missed anyway.

Getting the other team to call a timeout

Sometimes, when you have no time-outs left, but need to take one, you can get the other team to use one of theirs. They will typically take an emergency time-out if you line up in an **unexpected formation**. That could be either a crazy formation for running a scrimmage play or a normal formation that is different from what the defense expected: like a slot I when the defense expected a field goal.

Since you are running out of time, you need to be able to run a play from the formation in question if the defense does **not** *take the bait and call time out.* You don't have time to bluff it then shift to another formation. So the stunt in question should be one that works **either** as an opponent-time-out inducer or as a play itself. Here are some suggestions:

- Line up in field-goal formation but with passing play personnel then shift to regular formation.
- Line up in passing formation but with field-goal personnel then shift to field-goal formation and kick. It would be prudent to send the kicker in **after** the shift if he is not a regular offensive player.
- Lonesome polecat or swinging-gate formation (center is by himself and eligible, rest of line is way off to one side, quarterback is in 12-yard deep shotgun)

You may also be able to get the other team to call timeouts for your benefit at the **end of the first half** by playing possum until the opponent has used all their timeouts. That is, behave as though you plan to let the clock run out. Run draw plays and sweeps. Then when they have exhausted their timeouts, switch to a top-speed hurry-up or whatever pace as appropriate given your distance and time remaining.

Best to use timeouts when your opponent is in a slowdown

Most coaches who are behind, try to save their timeouts until they are on **offense**. I said above that it's generally dumb to use timeouts on defense, **if the purpose of the timeout is to get your defense organized**.

But it's **better** to use your timeouts when you are on **defense** to stop the opponent from wasting time. Think about it. Late in a game, the leading team will be in a slowdown mode. And the trailing team will be in a hurry-up mode.

What does a timeout do? It eliminates the time wasted between the dead-ball whistle and the next snap. Which team uses the **most time** between the end of the last play and the snap for the next one? Obviously, it's the team which is on **offense** and ahead near the end of the game. Which team uses the **least** time between the end of the last play and the snap for the next one? Obviously the trailing team which has the ball and is running their two-minute drill to try to catch up.

So if you use a timeout when the leading **opponent is on offense** and running their **slowdown**, you save around **25 to 39 seconds per timeout**. Remember the leading offense can use almost the entire 25-second play clock, (40-second play clock in the NFL) plus the time the referee takes between the dead-ball whistle and the ready-to-play whistle (in high school and college and some NFL situations).

But if you wait until **you** are on **offense**, and in your **hurry-up** mode, your timeouts will only save about 12 seconds. A team running a hurry-up takes about 18 seconds per play if the play does not stop the clock. And about six of those seconds are the play itself. You can't call timeout until the play is over. Furthermore, it is normal for the clock to stop frequently with**out** a timeout when you are running your two-minute drill. In the 1997 Rose Bowl, Ohio State executed a brilliant 12-play winning drive in 1:21 without ever using the timeout they had.

Remember it stops every time you go out of bounds or throw an incomplete pass. It also stops for penalties, referee's timeouts, all sorts of stuff. You cannot know in advance how your plays will go or whether the opposing defense will draw penalty flags or call their own timeout. It may be that you save all three timeouts for your final offensive drive only to find there were not three plays where timeouts were needed to stop the clock.

The New Thinking Man's Guide to Pro Football author Paul Zimmerman says:

> *Some [NFL coaches] don't seem to understand the most basic clock fact, that when you're behind and you're fighting the clock, you call timeouts on the other team's plays, not your own. Three running plays can eat up two minutes. But call time after each one and you've only lost 20 to 30 seconds.*

When you *use the timeouts during your leading opponent's final offensive possession*, you are sure you can use **all** of them and that you will get full value for each.

No parochial bickering

On some football teams, I have seen parochial bickering between offense and defense. In theory, the head coach has the joint overall team perspective. But, as with a military Chairman of the Joint Chiefs, he came up on "one side of the ball or the other." For example, former 49ers head coach Bill Walsh was an offensive guy; his successor George Seifert, a defensive guy. Many head coaches tend to favor the side of the ball from whence they came. You can't do that. *Timeouts are best used on defense when the opponent is in their slowdown mode.* Saving them for offense is dumb.

'Nice to have'

Many offensive coaches will say, "I don't know. It's awfully nice to have those timeouts on offense at the end of a game when you're behind." I don't doubt it. But it's still a bad idea to save them for the offense. Grand Valley State's Tom Beck says,

> *I like to save the timeouts until the last two minutes. I want the insurance that we have the timeouts at the end of the game.*

I respect the records and years of experience of coaches like Tom Beck. But I still find the logic **against** Beck's position compelling. There is no doubt that using the timeouts during your opponent's slowdown saves **more** time than using them during your own hurry-up. Saving timeouts for "insurance" costs you about 13 to 27 seconds per timeout. It's the only "insurance policy" I know of where the "premium" is twice as much as the maximum "benefit."

A coach who uses his timeouts during his opponent's slowdown will be able to run **more plays** during his two-minute drill than a coach who saves timeouts until the two-minute drill. This is arithmetic, not opinion.

Hardly any observers of a particular game will be knowledgeable enough to recognize that the team that used its timeouts while on defense made the better decision. The benefits are hidden and counterintuitive. But the logic of the use-timeouts-during-the-slowdown policy is irrefutable.

Having a timeout available lets the offense run, say, a pass play over the middle. If it's complete, the offense can call timeout to stop the clock. True. But how much time will that save? As I said above, about 12 seconds. The play itself takes about six seconds. And in the absence of a timeout, the clock would keep running during the additional twelve seconds it would take for the team to get lined up and run another play.

But if you use the same timeout earlier, when the opponent is taking up to 39 seconds after the dead-ball whistle to get a play off, you can save 25 to 39 seconds for your offense. Twenty-five to 39 seconds is enough to run **two completed** pass plays over the middle in a two-minute drill.

Timeouts are nice to have. So are Heisman Trophy winners. But nobody ever won the league championship by wasting time and energy whining about the "nice to have" stuff that you **don't** have. Head coaches need to tell their offensive coordinators, "You will probably **NOT** have any timeouts for your two-minute drill at the end of the game. Deal with it. Plan on it. Practice for it."

When should a trailing team START calling timeouts on defense?

OK, you're convinced that you should use your timeouts when you are on defense and trailing late in the game. When do you start? You must obviously use them before the game ends. But when does a football game end? If the leading team has the ball, it ends for all practical purposes when the **take-a-knee point** is reached. So you have to use your timeouts **before** the other team reaches the take-a-knee point.

For that, I refer you to the table in the Take-a-knee chapter. Basically, you want to use the **last** one *no later than about 1:40 left* in the game in high school and college; 2:20 in the NFL. In my worst-case take-a-knee table, the leading offensive team in high school or college can start taking a knee at 1:35 if they have first down and the trailing defense has no timeouts left. In the NFL, they can start taking a knee at 2:02 at the earliest.

Working backwards on the assumption that each play (snap to dead-ball whistle) can take as much as ten seconds, you would have to *use your next-to-last timeout no later than 1:50 and your first timeout no later than 2:40 in the NFL or 2:00 at the lower levels.*

The NFL is different because the clock stops anyway when it reaches two minutes. If you call a timeout at, say, 2:06 in the NFL, you only save six seconds because the clock would have stopped at 2:00 anyway. In college and lower levels, the clock does not stop for the two-minute warning.

Do you have to cut it that close? How big is the window when you can use the timeouts while your are trailing and on defense? There really is *no disadvantage to using them early,* **except** that you *don't want to use them* ***before*** *the other team gets in their slowdown mode*. Remember they are **wasting the maximum time** when they are in their slowdown offense, you save the most time per timeout by waiting **until** they get into that slowdown pace. Recapping:

When you are trailing and on defense in high school or college

- *Use your* ***first*** *timeout* ***after*** *the opposing offense begins its* ***slowdown*** *pace but* ***no later than 2:00*** *left in the game.*
- *Use your* ***second*** *timeout* ***no later than 1:50 left*** *in the game.*
- *Use your* ***third*** *timeout* ***no later than 1:40 left*** *in the game.*

When you are trailing and on defense in the NFL

- *Use your* ***first*** *timeout* ***after*** *the opposing offense begins its* ***slowdown*** *pace but* ***no later than 2:40*** *left in the game.*
- *Use your* ***second*** *timeout* ***no later than 2:30 left*** *in the game.*
- *Use your* ***third*** *timeout* ***no later than 2:20 left*** *in the game.*

Is a field goal timeout an exception?

You might think there is one exception to the timeouts-are-best-used-during-the-opponent's-slowdown-offense rule: using a timeout to get your field goal unit onto the field for a last-second kick.

The authors of *Hidden Game of Football* figure it takes about 27 seconds between when you yell "Field goal team!" and when that unit can run out onto the field, line up, and snap the ball. Stanford offensive coordinater Dana Bible says that, after much practice, his team can get their field goal unit on the field in about **seventeen seconds**. If you do **not** have 27 seconds or ten seconds left for your final play, and the clock is not stopped, you have to go for **six**, even though you only **need** three.

If you are only behind by three points or less, and you are within field-goal range, you want to have the time to try a field goal. Should you save a timeout until you are on offense for a possible field-goal attempt if the opponent is only three points or less ahead? **No**.

Zimmerman quotes Raider managing partner Al Davis,

> *I have seen teams call time and line up for a field goal with 10 seconds left, when they could have run another play. If I'm on the other guy's two-yard line with five seconds to go, I can throw a pass in four seconds and still get my field goal team on the field, if the pass is incomplete.*

Saints–Jets 1983

Paul Zimmerman said Ken Stabler was a great clock manager when he was with the Raiders, but not so hot during his subsequent stint with the Saints. In a 1993 game in the Superdome in New Orleans, the Saints got the ball at their own twenty. They were down by three points, had 2:05 remaining, and had all three timeouts left as well as the ref's timeout for the two-minute warning.

> *They lah-de-dahed out of their huddle, they called timeouts late (they blew 19 seconds on one of them alone), they took 1:46 to run off eight plays to reach the Jets 34, where they called their final timeout and sent in Morton Anderson to try a 51-yard field goal, which he missed.*

Anderson's longest for the year had been 50 yards. When the ball was snapped for the field-goal attempt,

> *They had 19 seconds left, time to call two more plays and get closer.*

The Saints lost 31-28.

If you consult the table in the slowdown chapter, you will find that the Saints were in a **top-speed hurry-up situation** with 80 yards to go and 2:05 to do it in. That means they needed to operate at a **six-seconds-per-play pace** to score a touchdown and win. In fact, they ran eight plays in 1:46 which is a play every **13.25 seconds**, an inbounds hurry-up pace which would only have been appropriate if they had **eight** minutes left.

In a top-speed hurry-up situation, if you have timeouts, you call them as soon as the previous play ends, not 19 seconds later. Had the Saints done that they would have had 19 seconds more on the one timeout and I'll guess about 10 seconds each more on the other two. That's a total of 39 additional seconds.

I also agree with Zimmerman's statement that they could have run two more plays before the field goal attempt with the 19 seconds they had left. (Assuming it was first or second down. Zimmerman did not say what down it was.)

Stop the clock another way

The problem is you simply cannot **tell** two minutes in advance if you are going to be within field-goal range for the last play of the game. And you must use all your timeouts to prevent the opponent from getting to the take-a-knee point. Once the opponent reaches take-a-knee, any possible field goal is irrelevant.

You'll just have to use a **non-timeout method** of stopping the clock, like spiking the ball, for your last-second field goal. And *if you are* ***out of downs****, which means you cannot spike the ball, you'll just have to go for six, even though you only need three.*

Is that a violation of the more-versus-enough principle? No. If a field goal takes 27 seconds, and you don't **have** 27 seconds, or a timeout, the field goal is **not** one of your options. If your only way to win is to score a touchdown, you have to go for the touchdown. Remember using a timeout on defense when your opponent is in a slowdown mode saves 25 to 39 seconds, about what you need to get your field-goal team onto the field. And it's a **sure thing** on defense. *Letting the opposing offense waste 25 to 39* *seconds so you can save a timeout for a* ***possible*** *need on offense violates the a-bird-in-the-hand-is-worth-two-in-the-bush principle.*

More Zimmerman:

> *I once saw a practice at which Walsh and Montana worked for a half an hour on the deliberate incomplete to stop the clack...throw the ball on the ground, don't sail it out of bounds because it takes the official five seconds longer to get the clock stopped when he's watching the fight of the ball.*

'The Fainting Irish'

In the 1954 Notre Dame-Iowa game, Notre Dame drove to the Iowa 14 with two seconds left in the half and no timeouts left. All-American Notre Dame lineman Frank Varrichione suddenly groaned and collapsed. The officials called an injury timeout, during which Varrichione was taken from the field and Notre Dame lined up for the next play. It was a touchdown pass which tied the game at seven going into halftime.

Late in the fourth quarter, Notre Dame did it again. The Irish were losing 14-7 with only six seconds left on the clock and had no timeouts left. Varrichione went down again, this time accompanied by the entire Notre Dame line. The officials called another injury timeout. Notre Dame again was able to line up for one last play and completed a touchdown pass on the last play of the game. The PAT tied the game preserving Notre Dame's unbeaten record.

Newspapers dubbed them the "Fainting Irish." NCAA authorities immediately put an end to the practice. Faking injuries, which also occurred in the NFL games involving the Cincinnati Bengals when they ran their whole-game no-huddle, has always been unethical. Paragraph h of the NCAA Football Code says,

> *Feigning an injury for the purpose of gaining additional, undeserved time for one's team. An injured player must be given full protection under the rules, but feigning injury is dishonest, unsportsmanlike, and contrary to the spirit of the rules. Such tactics cannot be tolerated among sportsmen of integrity.*

Because of the safety aspects of the situation, it is difficult to outlaw faking injury. But the rules do require that the player leave for at least one down in high school. (NFICA 3-5-10, NCAA 3-3-5).

In the NFL, this rule applies to the last two minutes of each half. All NFL injury timeouts above four are penalized five yards. In addition, when the score is tied or the offense is behind, an injury timeout by the offense results in ten seconds being taken off the clock. (NFL 4-3-6)

What about FIRST HALF timeouts?

The team in possession near the end of the **first** half often does not start a slowdown until **very late** in the half—**after** the point at which I said to start using your timeouts.

Using your timeouts when you are on **defense** may enable the **other** team to score more points. That applies to **both** halves. But in the **second** half, you have **no choice** but to **assume** that you will regain possession of the ball and drive for the winning score. In the **first** half, however, you **do** have a choice.

If you are convinced the other team will not try to score before the end of the first half, and you are on defense, you should use your timeouts then. But if you are not convinced they will not try to score, you should save them for offense.

Don't worry if you don't use them. The best purpose of timeouts is to help you score. If you can use them for that purpose in the first half, do so. But do **not** use them in a way that may help the **other** team score, that is, when you are an defense and the other team is still trying to score before the half.

Paul Zimmerman, author of *The New Thinking Man's Guide to Pro Football* disagreed:

> *[In the 1983 Jets-Saints game], the Jets had butchered the clock at the end of the first half. This is where most clock butcheries take place, and largely go unreported, because the sense of urgency isn't as great. The Jets could have had the ball with a minute and a half left, but they let the clock run and got it on their own 20 with 30 seconds to go, whereupon they ran the clock out.*

This sounds like **hindsight** to me. At the time the Jets would have called the timeouts, on defense, they had no way of knowing whether the Saints would get a first down or not. If they call timeout, which helps **both** teams remember, and the Saints **do** get a first down, who is helped by the conservation of time? The opposing team—the Saints—who are still on offense.

Remember you can only manage the clock when you have a good idea **who** will be needing time at the end of the half. In the case of the Jets versus the Saints in 1983, no one knew who would be in possession with enough time to score at the end of the half.

I disagree with Zimmerman's statement about this game in particular and about first half "butcheries" in general. At the end of the first half, you do not know whose time you are conserving when you call timeout on defense.

I called Zimmerman and discussed this with him. He said he no longer agrees with that paragraph, although he thinks it was correct when he wrote it in 1984. He says now NFL coaches are more sophisticated. Now, when they have possession, they often play possum near the end of the first half. When they are deep in their own territory, they may run a draw or other running play which does not stop the clock. They are trying to get the defense to conclude that they are trying to run out the clock so the defense will help the offense by using its timeouts. Then after the defense has used all their timeouts, the offense switches to a top-speed hurry-up, or whatever they need based on field position and time remaining.

I asked Zimmerman what the rule should be for calling a timeout when you are on defense in the first half. He said, "The rule is there are no rules." In other words, you need to go by **feel of the game**, **knowledge of the opposing coach**, and all that stuff that's impossible to write about in a book like this. All I can do is alert you that calling timeouts when you are on defense at the end of the first half is a **tricky business** in the NFL. At lower levels, it is probably easier to read the intentions of the opponent.

Even NFL coaches screw up timeout usage

The Hidden Game of Football authors analyzed the use of timeouts by the trailing team in 59 close (seven points or less) 1986 games where the trailing team had possession at least once during the final three minutes of the game and found the following:

- 177 timeouts total were available (59 games x 3 timeouts per second half = 177)
- 10 had been used before the final three minutes
- 39 were called just before the two-minute warning
- 33 of those were used while on defense
- 95 were called after the two-minute warning
- 61 were used after two-minute warning by the trailing team when they were on offense
- 5 were used in a manner that eluded the scorekeepers
- 28 were left over when the game was finished

They say 39 were called "just before the two-minute warning." I hope they were used long before the two-minute warning because the two-minute warning itself stops the clock.

They say 33 were used while on **defense**. That's good. But why weren't all 167 used on defense? They **should** have been.

Sixty-one were used while on **offense**. That's dumb. Remember the trailing team will be running its **hurry-up** when they are on offense near the end of the game. They could have saved about twice as much game-clock time if they had used the timeouts on **defense** during the opponent's slowdown.

And 28 timeouts were left over at end of the game. That's crazy! Remember these are **trailing** teams who ran out of time in a close game! They ran out of time even though they had time "in their pockets" in the form of timeouts they could have used to save about 25 to 39 seconds each. That further proves the point about not knowing in advance whether you will **need** any timeouts to stop the clock when you go on offense.

Colorado's Rick Neuheisel says,

> *[Referring to a second and two with 1:27 left example] You have an opportunity to use a timeout right there and you don't know if that opportunity is going to come again. The worst sin is to die at the end of the game with timeouts in your pocket.*

Neuheisel says if you only have two timeouts and you need a touchdown, use the first one around 1:00 and if you only have one, use it around :30. If you need a field goal, he says to save one timeout to get the field goal team onto the field.

Again, I disagree. I think you should use timeouts when you are **on defense**. And if that's no longer possible, *use them at the first opportunity, that is, the first play when the clock does not stop for another reason, when you are in your last possession.*

Neuheisel also says to call a timeout after a sack if you have one. That's what Arizona State coach Bruce Snyder did in the 1997 Rose Bowl and I believe it cost him the game. Actually, it wasn't that he called the timeout. Calling it really didn't matter. The problem was that he called it as if he were in a **top-speed hurry-up mode, immediately after the sack**, when he should have been in a maximum slowdown mode, and called the timeout at the **end of the play-clock period**.

Neuheisel apparently likes what Snyder did because he says not to worry about scoring fast. I'll discuss that at length in the slowdown chapter. For now, my position is that you should call your timeouts when you are **defense**. If you have any left on **offense**, you should call them only when necessary to stay on schedule (see the slowdown chapter). If you are on a maximum-slowdown schedule, you should either not call them at all or wait until the **end** of the play clock to call the timeout.

I see no big difference between a sack and a play that gains, say, one yard. Neuheisel says you need to call time because your team is demoralized after a sack during a two-minute drill. Seems to me that is better dealt with by putting sacks into your two-minute drill **practices**. If you have done that many times in practice, your players should respond calmly to the occasional sack in a game. Calling timeout just because you had a sack strikes me as coach panic, which can be contagious and infect the players.

Another reason to not rely on timeouts to undemoralize your team after a sack is that you may have a sack when you are out of timeouts. If your standard response to a sack is a timeout, and you have no timeouts left, your players may panic.

I am not totally against calling a timeout after a sack. Just make sure you don't call it too **fast** if you are in a situation where you should be driving **slowly** down the field. And make sure it's not your only way to respond to a two-minute-drill sack.

Practice your two-minute drill assuming you have no timeouts, because that's the way you should end up doing it when you get to your actual games.

Use 'em if you got 'em

From strictly a time-saved standpoint, it's better to use timeouts when you are on defense and your opponent is in their slowdown mode. But time is not the only advantage of a timeout. Having timeouts available when you are running your two-minute drill gives you some **additional flexibility**. You can run plays that do not stop the clock like running plays that do not go out of bounds or passes over the middle and still maintain a top-speed hurry-up pace.

You should **not** get into a situation where you have timeouts available on offense when you are behind at the end of a game, but if you do, remember the added flexibility they give you and take advantage of it when appropriate.

When you are ahead

This chapter has been entirely about using timeouts when you are **behind** at the end of a half in a close game. How do you use timeouts when you are **ahead**?

You don't, except for "icing" the other team's kicker or when the opposing offense goes into a maximum slowdown in spite of the fact that they are behind. For example, in the 1997 Rose Bowl, Arizona State was behind and doing a hurry-up until they completed a pass to the Ohio State eight-yard line with almost three minutes left. They then shifted into a slowdown. Ohio State had a timeout and should have used it to prevent Arizona State from wasting time. If your opponent should want to waste time, you should want to conserve it. That sometimes happens even when you are ahead.

The ideal situation is that you are always ahead, in which case you should end each half with three timeouts in your pocket. *When you are **ahead**, don't prolong your "enemy's" life by using timeouts on offense*. Timeouts help the trailing team. Don't help the trailing team when you are ahead.

'Icing' the place kicker

In the 1993 Army-Navy game, Navy spiked the ball at the Army two-yard line with six seconds left in the game. Army was ahead 16-14. Navy was closer to the goal line than they would be for a PAT kick.

Navy sent in their freshman place kicker, Ryan Bucchianeri. He was two for two on the season. But he was only a freshman playing in front of 67,852 at Giants Stadium and an international TV audience of millions. Army had a couple of timeouts left. They used them to "ice" Navy's plebe kicker.

He missed. Army won.

Did "icing" work in this case? Maybe so. The unique status of plebes at service academies puts extra pressure on them. Giving Bucchianeri more time to think about that pressure may well have made the difference. It's impossible to know for sure.

The following year, Bucchianeri again missed a relatively easy field goal from the Army 20, a field goal which would have won the game as it turned out. Bucchianeri's 1994 field goal attempt came in the first quarter, not the fourth, so there was no "icing." Navy lost 22-20 on senior Kurt Heiss's 52-yard field goal, the longest in Army-Navy history.

"Icing" did not work for Army in the 1989 Army-Navy game. Navy was trailing 17--16 with fifteen seconds left in the game. The ball was at the Army 14-yard line. Army used a timeout to "ice" Navy kicker Frank Schenk. It didn't work. Army lost 19-17.

Should you use timeouts to make the opponent's place kicker think longer about his kick? If it's the last play of the game and the other team has no problem getting lined up to kick, why not? Can't hurt. At that point, what else are you going to use them for? Of course, if the other team is rushed by a running clock or inexperienced, the way my freshman team was in 1996, calling a timeout **helps** the opponent get lined up and get their subs in. Don't help them by calling timeout.

Should you **save** a timeout for that purpose? No way.

Place kickers are a strange bunch. But they are generally competent and their competence includes ignoring opponents' psychological war games.

5

Penalties

In basketball, teams often deliberately foul the opponent when they are behind and running out of time. Are there any situations is football where you behave differently regarding penalties when time is running out? Yes.

Deliberately taking a delay-of-game penalty

We have all seen teams deliberately take a delay-of-game penalty. The benefit of that is you use the **full** 25 seconds of the play clock (40 in the NFL). Since the typical slowdown uses 23 seconds, that's only a **two-second benefit**.

When do you take a delay penalty? When you need the extra two seconds and losing five yards does not matter to you. You could add one two-second block of time to all the times in the take-a-knee tables if you take one delay-of-game penalty in the final series.

There is no point in taking **two** successive delay-of-the-game penalties without a snap in between. The game clock will not start until the snap after a delay penalty.

When you don't care about penalties

Normally, you don't want penalties when you are on offense because they cost you yards. Is there ever a time when you don't care about field position? Yes. When you are ahead and you no longer need a first down to retain possession for the rest of the game, that is, during take-a-knee.

Also, when you're behind and your opponent has fourth down inside your territory. They often take a deliberate delay-of-game penalty so they can waste clock time and get a better angle to kick. You can't stop the waste of time. But you **can** decline the yardage penalty (NFL 4-3-10 Supplemental Note 1).

The only sensible reason to decline the yardage penalty for a kicking play is to avoid snapping or kicking from a bad spot on the field, like a puddle, patch of mud, or patch of ice.

Another school of thought is even though the other team does not really **get** a benefit from the "better" angle, they **think** they do, so why not refuse the penalty and thereby mess with their minds—the punting equivalent of "icing" the place-kicker. OK. I'm not enthusiastic about it, but I can go along with that.

Eliminate 'housekeeping' time

In high school and college games, one of the things that wastes time between plays is the officials spotting the ball and getting lined up for the next play. On average, that takes 16 seconds per play. When I ran my warp-speed hurry-up, I found that the refs reduced their housekeeping time to about **eleven seconds per play**.

However, if there is a **penalty** on the play, the refs will stop the game clock to discuss the penalty with the innocent team's captain. In the NFL, a penalty on the play will change the play-clock period from a 40 seconds to a 25 seconds, an effect similar to what happens in high school and college. This is true whether the penalty is accepted or declined.

Consequently, the eleven to 16 seconds in high school and college, and the extra 15 seconds available in the NFL, that is normally wasted, will remain on the game clock. That will screw up the take-a-knee table which you will find in the take-a-knee chapter.

Incentive for trailing team to commit penalty?

If a penalty saves the trailing team eleven to 16 seconds, should they deliberately commit penalties in that situation, the way trailing basketball teams commit deliberate fouls?

Remember that **defensive penalties advance the ball and repeat a down**. When you get to the take-a-knee chapter, you will find that the point at which a leading team can take a knee depends on the down, time remaining, and number of timeouts possessed by their opponents. The earlier the down, the earlier the leading team can take a knee. Committing a penalty may give the opponent a first down, which makes their take-a-knee point arrive sooner. Committing a penalty also lets the leading team get **two** play-clock periods for the same down, which wastes about 25 seconds.

So *you are worse off committing a penalty when you are on defense.*

Incentive for leading team to commit penalty?

How about the **leading** team? If they commit a penalty, will they thereby get two play-clock periods for one down, which enables them to waste an extra 25 seconds?

If they are still in the situation where they need first downs, the penalty will push them back and may force them to punt or turn the ball over on downs. So it's hard to justify deliberately committing a penalty when you need a first down.

When you are in a take-a-knee period, the refs will generally not allow the leading team to gain an advantage by deliberately committing a penalty. (NFICA 3-6-3, NCAA 3-4-3, NFL 4-3-9)

In the NFL, which has the most advanced rules, in the last two minutes of a half, you are not only penalized five yards for delay, they change the clock. If the **offense** committed the penalty to conserve time, they take **ten seconds off the clock**. If the **defense** committed the penalty, they **restart the play clock at 40 seconds** and start the game clock at the same time. Also in the NFL, more than two successive penalties during the same down, after a warning, is unsportsmanlike conduct.

Useful for getting field goal team onto the field

It takes considerable time to get a field goal team onto the field. One estimate is 27 seconds. Suppose you have the following situation:

- fourth down
- need to kick a field goal to tie or win
- ten seconds or less are left in the game
- you are in field goal range
- a five-yard penalty will not significantly change your kicker's success probability.

Should you deliberately commit a penalty on the next-to-last play to generate a referee's timeout to give you time to get your field goal team onto the field? **No**. It's unethical.

Since it's **fourth down**, you **cannot spike** the ball to stop the clock. It would go over on downs if you did. Same is true for an incomplete pass.

You probably cannot get your field goal team onto the field and snap the ball within ten seconds.

You **must** practice getting your field goal team onto the field quickly. And if a game situation arises where a last play field goal is likely, you must gather your field goal team on the sideline in advance so they are "in the starting blocks" when their time arrives.

Everything's more important, including penalties

As I said in the overview chapter, everything becomes more important in the closing minutes of a close football game. That includes penalties.

A penalty can move a team into game-winning field goal range—or back out of it. A penalty can nullify the winning score—or give a trailing team a second shot. A penalty can give the trailing team an extra untimed play after time runs out. A penalty can take away a crucial first down—or deliver a crucial first down to a team that failed to gain one.

My experience is that *when you draw a flag, you punt*. There are exceptions, but **a flag is almost the equivalent of a turnover in that it raises your yards to a first down by 50% or more, which is generally enough to prevent you from getting the first down**.

In the 1997 Rose Bowl, Arizona State committed two interference penalties which were crucial to Ohio State's come-from-behind winning drive.

1991 Orange Bowl

In the 1991 Orange Bowl, Notre Dame's Rocket Ismail scored what appeared to be the game-winning kick return touchdown in the final minute. But the touchdown was called back on a clipping penalty. Notre Dame was unable to score during the rest of the game and lost to number-one-rated Colorado 10-9.

1992 Army-Navy Game

In the 1992 Army-Navy Game, a penalty almost cost Army the game. Patmon Malcolm kicked what appeared to be the game-winning field goal from 44 yards out to go ahead 25-24 with twelve seconds left in the game.

But there was a flag on the play. Delay against Army.

He had to do it all over only this time from five yards farther out—a 49-yard field goal. Fortunately, he made it again. But that little lapse by Army could have cost them the game.

1993 Notre Dame-Boston College

A devastating penalty contributed to Notre Dame losing the national championship in 1993. Notre Dame had taken the lead 39-38 with 1:09 left in the game. On the ensuing kickoff, BC's returner went out of bounds at **his own ten-yard line**, but Notre Dame's Jeremy Sample was flagged for hitting him out of bounds. That moved the ball out to the **BC 25**. Boston College then drove down the field and kicked a 41-yard field goal with no time left on the clock. Notre Dame came into that game 10-0 with national championship hopes.

'Penalty killed the threat'

In the 1981 Army-Navy Game, Army drove to the Navy 32 in the final seconds of the game "but a penalty killed the threat" says Bill Cromartie in his book on the Army-Navy series. Army had to settle for a 55-yard field goal attempt which failed as time ran out. The final score was 3-3.

Navy had been favored to win but barely kicked the tying field goal from Army's 18 after stopping the clock with one second left just before halftime.

How to avoid penalties

When my oldest boy was eight, I attended his first football game against Napa at Napa Community college. It was a penalty flag fest. Virtually every play, it seemed, was stopped for illegal procedure or some other dumb penalty. As the season wore on, seemingly half the touchdowns scored by our opponents were called back on clipping penalties.

I was traumatized.

When I became a coach the following year, I bought a penalty flag and still carry it to practice every day. In general, my teams have been among the least penalized in the league. I have heard many coaches discuss penalties as if they were an external factor, like the weather. I had an argument with a football parent once. He said lack of penalties indicated lack of aggressiveness. Baloney. That's a rationalization—an excuse.

Avoiding penalties requires a three-pronged effort:

- keep "penalty slobs" off the field
- emphasize penalty avoidance in practice
- avoid play calls likely to generate penalties.

Penalty 'slobs'

Some people are late slobs. They are chronically late. They don't understand what the big deal is. Football has players who have a similar attitude about penalties. A typical penalty slob will draw one penalty flag per week. I tell those players to knock it off if they want to continue to play. The first one I bench is usually flabbergasted. They just don't get it. They see lots of penalties on TV. What's the big deal? However, the other penalty slobs on the team usually are mightily impressed by the first slob's loss of his job.

I had the following discussion with a couple of linemen after a game halfway through the 1996 season where we lost the lead and had to settle for a tie.

How many possessions do you guys think we get in the average game?

15?

Eight. We averaged 5.62 yards a carry is last night's game. Is that enough to gain ten yards for a first down in three plays?

Yes.

Suppose you get a holding penalty like you did last night. How many yards do we have to gain for a first down then?

Twenty.

Right. Is three times 5.62 twenty yards?

No.

But 5.62 yards a carry is pretty darned good isn't it?

What do we do when we don't get a first down?

Punt.

Right. So we're having a great day on offense but you two force us to give away two of our eight possessions—twenty-five percent of our possessions for the day—because of holding. Can you see why I make such a big deal about penalties?

They could. Neither of those players drew a penalty flag during the rest of the season.

What you tolerate, you encourage.

If you permit a penalty slob to remain in your starting lineup, don't come running to me when he does his penalty-of-the-day at a crucial moment in a big game.

Don't depend on the undependable.

Penalty avoidance

You need to teach penalty avoidance in practice just like you teach blocking or tackling. The players must know the rules.

I do a 10-minute unsportsmanlike conduct clinic the first day of practice whenever I am head coach. I have been head coach of two youth teams and was acting head coach of a high school freshman team. I did my clinic and **no one on those three teams ever committed an unsportsmanlike conduct penalty**. Those are the only teams I have been involved with which did **not** commit an unsportsmanlike conduct penalty.

Teaching is not enough. You also have to motivate the players to do what they have been taught. That means jumping on any infraction in practice. If criticism is not enough, you must penalize the player by sending him to remedial blocking or remedial tackling or whatever he was doing when he broke the rules.

Punishment is a controversial issue in our society today. As a West Point graduate, I am not among those who have lost their bearings trying to be politically correct on the issue of discipline.

At West Point, I saw discipline standards far beyond anything laymen can imagine. You would be amazed at how well-behaved 4,000 young men can be when the people in charge insist on it. For example, we had to be on time, to the second, about eight times a day the whole four years we were at West Point. I was late once, because I had conflicting instructions as to where to be and chose to obey the wrong one. My single instance of lateness in four years was typical of all cadets. Most laymen think that sort of iron discipline would somehow harm the cadets. Wrong. It produces 4,000 solid citizens.

My approach is to do **whatever it takes**, short of unethical conduct, to get my players to do what they are supposed to do.

Today, many adults, maybe most, are so concerned about political correctness that they are **not** willing to do whatever it takes. Kids test them, as they have since the beginning of time, and they soon figure out the adults are bluffing. Then the kids do **not** do what they must to win the football game, and indirectly, what they need to do to become the good citizens that all amateur levels of football are supposed to create.

Draw a flag, leave the game

When I am head coach or coordinator it is generally my policy to remove a player who commits a 15-yard penalty from the game. I repeat that policy every time I see such an infraction in practice. In 1992, my defense committed one fifteen-yard (face-mask) penalty all year. The father of the boy in question was a know-it-all who told his son not to pay much attention to us coaches. I do not recall any 15-yard penalties against us in 1993.

In 1996, with**out** the remove-from-the-game policy because I was not head coach, I believe we were called for clipping once or twice.

My high school varsity volleyball team included several guys who were determined to talk back to referees. They did not stop until I started removing them from games because of it.

In short, I have found the remove-from-the-game policy is the minimum necessary with some players to get them to refrain from committing serious penalties.

Penalty-prone plays

Certain plays are more likely to draw flags. Generally, you are more likely to draw a flag when you make things **more complicated** than normal.

One of the ways we all but eliminated false starts was to either snap the ball on the same count every time or to eliminate the snap count altogether and have everyone go on ball movement. That's standard in scrimmage-kick plays.

Some line coaches may feel they cannot give up the advantage of knowing the snap count. But then most of them have never tried not varying the snap count. In my experience, the fact that we are not varying the snap count is impossible to see on the game videos. If you can't **see** it, I wonder how much of an advantage it is. But I **guarantee** you that using the same count every time all but eliminates false starts.

Silent 'cadence'

In 1993, my team went on a silent signal. The tailback signaled for the ball with his thumb, which the center could see. He then snapped when he was ready the way most teams do with punts and place kicks. As with punts and place kicks, the rest of the team went on ball movement.

We jumped offside twice that **season**, both times in response to a defensive player trying to get us to jump.

In 1996, my freshman team used the silent cadence for much of the year. Then we always went on one. We false started two or three times all season as I recall.

I have been tempted to put in a play (play zero?) in which we simply call cadence and never move, to draw the opponent offside. It seems like it would be **especially effective if you always went on the same count**.

Another advantage of the silent "cadence" is that it's **faster**. You save about **two seconds per snap** when you have no cadence. In this "game of seconds," that will, sooner or later, be the difference between your winning and losing.

Someone ought to do a study to see if the benefits (beating the defender to the punch) of varying the snap count really outweigh the disadvantages (false start penalties, which cost you both yards and time, and two extra seconds per play).

Shifts and motion

If you do not use a shift or motion, it is extremely unlikely that you will be penalized for illegal shift or illegal motion. If you shift or motion most of the time, you will probably learn how to do it without drawing a flag. But, shifts and motion **take time**, which is precious if you are behind at the end of a game.

Unusual formation, play

Many's the time I have seen a team that was trailing try something unusual, only to be penalized for too many men on the field or delay of the game. *If you want to try a new formation, play, or person, do it a week in advance and make sure everyone is totally squared away with it in practice the week before the game.* If you dream it up during the game in question, forget it, or you'll be sorry.

Although I must tell you that Granada High School won their toughest playoff game in 1995 with a play which they had never run or even mentioned. They went on to win the North Coast Section championship, which is the highest you can go on the field in our area.

Granada varsity head coach Aaron Gingery has what I call a **modular play-calling system**. It takes six to nine words and numbers to communicate a play. Each word or number tells a player or group of players what they do on the play. As a result, each player only needs to learn ten to twenty tricks. But when you consider all the possible combinations, you can run a **hundred million different plays**, literally, and each player will feel like he is just doing one of the ten or twenty things he has been doing all season.

Actually, it's a little more complicated than that. Football plays often have **timing** aspects which must be specifically practiced. There are also little twists which are not taken into account by the modular system. For example, I had a freshman play in 1996 where the fullback dove to the weak side out of an unbalanced formation with a strong-side backfield alignment. Normally, we open pivoted on all plays. (Quarterback turned toward the side where the handoff would take place.) But to add to the pre-snap impression that we were running strong, I had the quarterback reverse pivot on the weak side dive out of that formation. On one fourth-and-one play, it went 60 yards for a touchdown.

On the other hand, Miramonte varsity head coach Floyd Burnsed, who does **not** use a completely modular play-calling system, told me he once accidentally called a play he had not used in years and had not taught to his current team. Their reaction was, "Say what?"

Injury subs

Subs can kill you. If you have any coaching experience, you can probably remember, painfully, games lost when an injury sub or project went in and screwed up. *If you have to put in an injury sub and know it in advance, spend extra time with him during the week before the game in question.* Your regular players know what to do. But at least half of all failures in football are caused by missed assignments, not getting beat. And injury subs are infinitely more likely to blow their assignment than regulars. In fact, you would probably be better off during a playoff week if you sent the regulars home and spent the entire week trying to get the injury subs whom you knew were going to play up to speed.

Since the injury in question typically happens **in** a game, you do not always know in advance that an injury sub will be called on. So you'd better prepare your injury subs well in general. If you are not confident of an injury sub, the coordinators should make sure they are informed of all injury subs who go in during a game and should adjust their play calling accordingly. For example, you may not want to call your inside trap play if the pulling guard is out hurt and his sub has replaced him.

In 1996, Miramonte played Foothill in the semi-final North Coast Section championship game. In overtime, Foothill scored seven points then Miramonte scored six and lined up to kick the PAT. The regular right guard for Miramonte left the game on his own initiative because his shoulder was hurt. He selected a lineman on the sideline to replace him without telling the coaches. The underclass substitute lineman was unfamiliar with the PAT-block rules and let a linebacker through to block the kick, ending Miramonte's playoff hopes. Viewing the replay, I thought the substitute also committed an illegal-use-of-the-hands penalty, reaching out sideways with his arm fully extended to try to stop the linebacker, but it was not flagged.

Subs are also highly likely to trigger penalties for **twelve men on the field or improper alignment or motion** or some such. They also have a tendency to forget they are supposed to be on the field. If they are supposed to be on the line of scrimmage, their not going into the game can cost you a penalty for not having seven men on the line.

When I coordinate special teams, I have cards showing the formation and jersey numbers of each special teams player on each team. When a player is injured during the game, I immediately circle his number on **each** card where he appears. Then when that team goes in, I start yelling the sub's name as soon as the circle on the card reminds me. Here's an actual card I used in 1996:

Punt

2-foot splits
except 14" at left A gap
step outward 5" on snap, block
the area where you stand

85 73 54 55 56 64 40
20/35 24

32

22

Subs: End 80
Long snapper 52, 53
Flanker 40
Lineman 70
Punter 40, 56

Do NOT kick a returnable ball.
Fan out. Full speed.

Frequently he is standing on the sideline oblivious to the need to go in on punt team for so-and-so. In the typical case, the injury occurs during **offense** or **defense**. The injury sub goes in, then when a special team goes onto the field, he comes **off** because he is not normally on that special team. He has to be reminded that he is the injury sub for the player in question on both offense or defense **and** on certain special teams.

Accepting or declining penalties

Should you make decisions as to whether to accept or decline penalties **differently** when time is running out? Yes.

Generally, in penalty-acceptance decisions you prefer the decision that will give you

1. points or take points away from your opponent

2. possession
3. the most favorable field position

in that order.

But remember the **more-versus-enough principle**. The normal guideline on whether to accept or decline a penalty is to get more of the most valuable thing at stake: points, possession, or yards. But when the time is running out, you must switch gears to seeking **enough**, not more.

You score

Suppose you scored. Is there ever a time when you would accept a penalty that took those points off the board? Sure, notwithstanding the fact that announcers like to say, "You never take points off the board."

In general, you would **not** accept a penalty that took points off the board if those points put you **ahead**. However, if those points gave you a **tie** or left you **needing to score again**, you might want to take the penalty and give up the points.

For example, suppose you kicked a **field goal** on fourth down with three minutes left to bring you within two points of your opponent. But they roughed the kicker.

That's 15 yards and an automatic first down. You have to score more than three points. If you decline the penalty and keep the points, you have to do a successful onside kick to get possession again. So you should **accept** the penalty. Your probability of winning is **higher** if you have first and ten and thereby a chance to score a go-ahead **touchdown**.

It's the more-versus-enough principle. The three points you would get if you declined the penalty and kept the field goal are **more** points than you have but they are **not enough**. Furthermore, they give you a lower probability of scoring the remaining points you need to win than accepting the penalty.

Your opponent scores

Turn it around. Let's say your **opponent** scores, specifically, you deliberately take a safety in a game where you were ahead by three points and only eight seconds remained in the game when the ball was snapped. The clock ran out during the play. But there's a flag on the play. They committed unnecessary roughness during the play, angry about being behind or maybe about a comment or gesture from one of your players.

If you **decline** the penalty, **they** get **two more points**, but **you win** the game. If you **accept** the penalty, they **lose** the **points** but you **must play one more untimed down**. You should *decline the penalty*. It is unlikely, but you could fumble the snap on the untimed down, they could pick it up and run it in for a touchdown. There is no need to risk it.

So the old analysts' adage that you never take points off the board or leave opponent points on the board is ***incorrect*** *in an end-of-game situation where leaving the points on the board violates the more-versus-enough principle.*

Obsession with possession

Teams generally prefer possession. For example, the penalty for kicking a kickoff out of bounds is often declined, especially when the kickoff team is in an **onside-kick** mode, because the receiving team wants possession.

You also see teams decline penalties when doing so leaves the offense with **fourth down**. The theory is that this will force a punt, which is correct in most situations.

As the half draws to a close, your normal desire for possession should become an **obsession**. I know of no penalty decision other than those involving points, where you would give up possession or risk losing possession, as in a second onside kick return, at the end of a half. Except for a safety, the opponent cannot score if you have possession.

Loss of down

Some penalties, namely **intentional grounding**, **forward lateral**, **illegal forward pass**, and **offensive pass interference**, carry a **loss of down** in addition to a yardage penalty. But most penalties do not. Rather they let the offense **repeat** the same down.

Remember that the game does not end when the final gun sounds. It ends in almost all cases when the team in possession of the ball reaches their take-a-knee point. Remember further, that the take-a-knee point is a function of the time remaining **and the down**. The lower the down, the earlier the take-a-knee point. If you are **behind**, you do **not** want the take-a-knee point to come earlier. If you are **ahead**, you **do** want it to come earlier.

Automatic first down

By the same token, some penalties award the offense an **automatic first down**, namely **defensive pass interference**, **roughing the passer**, **roughing the long snapper** (HS starting in 1997), **roughing the holder**, and **roughing the kicker**.

Example where you decline the penalty

For example, let's say you are behind with 1:30 left in the game. You have no timeouts left. The clock is stopped for a holding penalty against the offense. If you accept, it will be first down and twenty. If you decline, it will be second and eight.

Normally, that twenty yards would loom large. When you are in your "more" mode, you would take the ten-yard setback for the other team. The more yards you move the ball in your favor, the better. But this is **clock-management time**. You must shift mental gears to the "enough" mode.

The take-a-knee table, which is in the take-a-knee chapter, says you can start taking a knee when the clock gets below 1:35, if it's first down and your opponent has no timeouts. If you accept the penalty, that will be the situation. Twenty yards, fifty yards, it doesn't matter. If you **accept** that penalty, you throw the offense into take-a-knee time and you have **instantly lost** the game.

But if you **decline** the penalty, it's **second** down with 1:30 left, still **outside** the take-a-knee point. The offense has to get one more first down. You still have a chance.

True, it would be harder to get the first down if they were pushed back ten yards by the penalty. But if you keep the down at first down by accepting the penalty, **THEY NO LONGER HAVE TO GET ANOTHER FIRST DOWN!** The game's over right now!

Whenever the penalty gives you a choice of one down or another, and you are inside three minutes left in the game, you must consult the take-a-knee table before you make the penalty-acceptance decision.

*If you are **ahead**, the lower-numbered down may put you into the take-a-knee period. If so, take the lower-numbered down.* In other words, accept the penalty. *If the lower-numbered down does **not** put you into the take-a-knee period, you **may** want to **decline** the penalty and take the result of the play if it gives you a better chance of gaining another first down.* In that case, the best decision will depend on the **result of the play**, like normal. In other words, *the down does not take on any abnormal meaning until it takes you across the take-a-knee point.*

*If you are the guilty team, you must consult the take-a-knee chapter after the penalty is enforced if the opponent accepts it, to see if you have gone **into** or back **out of** the take-a-knee period.*

Recheck your tables after penalties

There are a couple of tables in this book which you should have with you during games. They are based on

- field position
- time remaining
- opponent timeouts left
- down.

Since penalties change **field position, down,** and **time remaining (they stop the clock)**, you must recheck the tables **after** penalty enforcement to see if you need to change your approach.

During your final possession of a half, a significant change in field position will probably mean you should change to a **different pace**. That's true whether the field-position change comes from a long pass completion or a big penalty.

For example, if you had 4:10 left, you were six points behind, and you were at the other team's 30 yard line, you should be running a **maximum slowdown** so that you leave little time on the clock after you score the go ahead conversion.

But suppose one of your players commits **offensive pass interference** and you are penalized back to the 45-yard line. The **pace table** in the slowdown chapter says when you are at the 45 and have 4:00 left in the game, you should operate at an **inbounds hurry-up** pace.

I gave you an example of rechecking the **take-a-knee table** just above under the "Example where you decline the penalty" subheading. In that case, if you were the team ahead and on offense, and your opponent were dumb enough to accept that holding penalty, you would immediately signal to start taking a knee. **Before** the opponent accepted the penalty, you still needed to get one more first down.

Quarters, including the fourth, are extended for most penalties

You could win the game in regulation, only to have the issue reopened because one of your players committed a penalty on the last play.

Penalties can prolong a quarter or a game beyond the end of regulation time. The **high school rule** says each quarter will be extended by one untimed down if any of the following occur:

- foul and accepted **penalty by either team** (unsportsmanlike conduct and non-player fouls are not included in this rule)
- **double foul**
- **inadvertent whistle**
- **touchdown** was scored on the last play of the period. (NFICA 3-3-3)

If any of the above occur again during the untimed down, there will be yet another untimed down, and so forth. College has the same rule (NCAA 3-2-3).

In the NFL, the rule is similar but somewhat different.

If the **defense** fouls at the end of a period, and the offense accepts the penalty, there is an untimed down at the end of either **half**. At the end of the **first or third quarters**, the offense may accept the penalty but **pass up the untimed down**. In that case, the penalty is enforced before the first play of the following quarter.

Wind direction may be a consideration

You would *pass up the untimed down if you were ahead* so you could use the down to run time off the clock. *If you were behind, you would accept the untimed down* to conserve time. (NFL 4-3-11a) The exception to that principle is if there is a **strong wind** and you plan to kick or pass on the play. *You may want to accept or reject the untimed down depending on which would put the wind at your back.* In the NFL, at the end of the first and third periods, after you make a fair catch, you can either kick a fair-catch field goal in a play which is an extension of the period just ended or you can kick the same fair catch field goal as the first play of the new quarter. In other words, at the end of the first or third quarter, you can select the quarter which gives you the best wind direction. (NFL 4-3-11e) At the end of either half, you are stuck with whatever wind direction you had before the half ended.

Offensive fouls on last play in NFL

If the offense commits the foul, there is no untimed down. (NFL 4-3-11b) However, there are several exceptions for offensive fouls on the last play of the quarter in the NFL.

Offensive score on last play of half does not count if offensive penalty

If the offense scores on the last play of the **half**, and the offense committed a foul on the play, the score does not count and the half or game is over. No decision need be made by the defense. At the end of the **first or third quarter**, however, the defense would **have to accept the penalty** to nullify a score. (NFL 4-3-11b)

Illegal touching of a kick on the last play of the quarter

If the offense illegally touches a kick on the last play of the quarter, the defense may choose to have the quarter extended by an untimed down. One such play is immortalized in an *NFL Films* segment involving the Kansas City Chiefs. *NFL Films* asked sixteen NFL head coaches about the rule [NFL 4-3-11 Exception (1)]. Only six knew the rule.

What is illegal touching? The **kicking team may not touch** the ball **before the receiving team** on a scrimmage kick, that is, a punt or field goal, unless the ball has stopped rolling. This is illegal, but few fans know it because no flag is thrown and no yardage penalty is marked off. The penalty is that the receiving team gets the ball at the spot of the touching by the kicking team. Illegal touching also **stops the clock**, in the NFL, which is important to know if either team is behind or it's near the end of a half. It also gives the receiving team the option of an untimed down after time has run out.

*Because illegal touching stops the clock, you should **not** do it when you are tying to waste time. That would be when you are **ahead**. When you are **behind**, and have to punt you **should** illegally touch the ball so you can stop the clock and conserve time.*

This is an NFL-only rule.

Fair catch interference

Another way the kicking team can give the receiving team an untimed down at the end of a half is fair catch interference. [NFL 4-3-11 Exception (2)] I would add that even with**out** the interference, the receiving team can elect to do an untimed-down free kick after a fair catch in the NFL.

'Palpably unfair act'

Exception (3) of NFL Rule 4-3-11 says a "palpably unfair act" by the offense extends the quarter by an untimed down if the defense wishes. The only example of a "palpably unfair act" which I could find in the NFL rule book was a substitute interfering with a play. A substitute is a player who is on the sidelines and not in the game at the moment. Officials have great discretion in the case of a "palpably unfair act." They can eject the player, make up any penalty they feel is equitable, and even award a score! (NFL 12-3-3)

Foul followed by change of possession

Exception (4) of NFL Rule 4-3-11 says the quarter is extended by an untimed down if there is a foul followed by a change of possession. That would be the case on any kicking play. That could also occur on a non-kicking play if the ball was fumbled or passed to a defender.

Double foul only extends HALVES in NFL

In high school, a double foul extends all four quarters for one untimed down. But in the NFL, only the end of the first half and of the game are extended for an untimed down by a double foul. (NFL 4-3-11c) Also, if the **defensive** foul carries a **five**-yard penalty and the **offensive** foul carries a **15**-yard penalty, there is **no extra play** after the end of the half. (NFL 4-3-11c2) Continuous action fouls, that is fouls that occur after the down ends, don't extend the half either. (NFL 4-3-11c1)

Free kick after a safety optional if offensive foul during safety

When a team scores a safety, the other team has to kick off to them from their own 20 on the next play. But what if time runs out on the half during the safety play, a common occurrence since deliberately taking a safety is often done on the last play of the game?

In the NFL, there are two kinds of safeties:

- safeties that occur **without fouls**
- safeties that are **accompanied by or caused by offensive fouls**.

When there is an offensive foul on the safety, the team that got the two points can demand a free kick even if time had run out on the half on the safety play. (NFL 4-3-11h)

That's kind of a big deal, isn't it? You are up by three. You shrewdly take a safety on the last play of the game, only to learn than one of your players held on the play, thereby forcing you to do an untimed-down free kick to your opponents. If they run it back for a touchdown, they win the game you thought was over.

What are examples of offensive fouls that cause a safety?

- clip by a defender in the end zone after his teammate intercepted a ball in the end zone
- forward lateral by a defensive interceptor or kick returner in the end zone
- offensive player bats or kicks the ball out the side or back of the end zone
- an offensive player holds during a play in which his teammate is tackled or takes a knee or steps out the back or side of the end zone or throws a backward pass out of the end zone
- an offensive player holds in the end zone on a play in which his teammate throws a forward pass out of the end zone.

In each of these foul-accompanied or foul-caused safeties on the last play of the half, the team that received the two points has the option to make the other team do an untimed free kick. *During the first half, such a team should make the opponent free kick. In the second half, do* ***not*** *make the opponent free kick if you are ahead.* The kicking team could gain possession of the free kick and score a touchdown on the play if their possession came after a fumble, not a muff, by the receiving team. *If you somehow forgot this rule and insisted on the free kick, none of your team members should attempt to gain possession unless it went into your end zone.* Remember it's an untimed down. The kicking team can gain possession but they cannot advance a kick. On an untimed last down of the game, possession outside the end zone is meaningless.

If you are behind at the end of the game, force the other team to free kick to you. It's a reprieve of your loss. You must return the free kick for a touchdown or, in high school or the NFL, fair catch it and free kick the game-winning field goal.

6

Ahead on offense

Whenever you are ahead, you should use as much clock time as possible. How much is that? In theory, you can use 25 seconds per play, plus play time and referee TIME if the game clock is running when the play clock starts. As a practical matter, you cannot cut it that close because you'll draw delay-of-game penalties, which will prevent you from getting your first downs. If you don't get your first downs, you are not going to be on offense anymore.

Rules for wasting clock time

There are a dozen rules you and your players should follow if you want to waste clock time:

- use as much play clock time as possible if the game clock is running
- avoid calling timeout
- stay in bounds
- throw no incomplete passes
- run outside the hashes
- leave the ball on the ground after the run
- avoid hurrying when you get up from the pile after a tackle
- when you take a knee, do not kneel down until you are about to be tackled
- use as many plays as possible to get each first down
- make sure kicks hit the ground so no fair catch
- do not touch punts (Note: A new high school rule for 1997 will permit a kicking team member to catch a punt in the air if no receiving team member is attempting to catch it. Previously, that was interference.)
- keep punts in bounds

Time-consuming drives

Here are some drives that sports writers thought were of noteworthy slowness:

• 70-yard drive that took 10 minutes	7yds/min.	
• 89-yd, 19-play, 11 minutes	8 yds/min.	1.73 plays/min.
• 69-yd, 16-play, nine minutes	7.67 yds/min	1.78 plays/min
• 98-yd, 17-play, 10:25	9.56 yds/min.	1.66 plays/min.
• 74-yd, 15-play, 7:33	10.1 yds/min.	2.05 plays/min.

How much you are ahead by

How much you are ahead by determines your options. Obviously, the more points the better. But there are some less-than-obvious break points.

One point

If you are ahead by one point, you may find that the **other team deliberately lets you score a touchdown** to get the ball back. If you score a touchdown then kick the extra point, you are up by **eight points**. But you have to kickoff. If the opponent can score and do a two-point conversion, they tie the game.

All you need in this situation is a **first down**. You are ahead. A first down will put you into take-a-knee period or close to it. Improved field position is nice, but not very important in this situation. *If your ball carrier senses that he is being allowed to score a touchdown, he should run past the first-down line, but* ***not*** *into the end zone. He should stand at the other team's two-yard line or so until he is about to be tackled. Then take a knee as the tacklers approach.* Remember the enough-versus-more principle.

Granted, this is wierd and rare. Clock-management situations justify strange behavior.

In ***college****, you should* ***not*** *do the PAT at all if you are ahead by one or two points and the touchdown was the last play of the game. If the opponent insists that you do the PAT play, take a knee.*

Two points

If you are ahead by one or two points, you generally would not take a **safety**.

That happened to Division I-AA Illinois State on 10/20/84. They were ahead of Central Florida, but only by two points, 24-22. On the last play of the game, they had fourth down, apparently right in front of their own goal. Normally, you would take a safety in that down-and-distance-and-time-remaining situation. But it's **not** such a great idea when you are only ahead by two. They punted. They had to. It was caught at Illinois State's 30-yard line (not much of a punt) and run back for the winning touchdown by Jeff Farmer.

Illinois State might have been able to win if they had done a slightly better job of running time off the clock earlier in the game. Time ran out **during** the punt return. So there could not have been more than about ten seconds left when the fourth down snap was made. If they could have found a way to run off an additional ten or whatever seconds earlier in the second half, the game would have ended on the third down or, if there was only one or two seconds left, could have been run off on fourth down with a quarterback sneak or wider quarterback keep play.

Again, if you score a touchdown on the last play of the game in college and you are up by two, do not run a PAT play.

No passes

You do not throw a pass when you are ahead, unless you have to to get a first down, because incomplete passes stop the clock. Of course, having to punt the ball away is worse than stopping the clock.

Take a sack—before fourth down

If you are ahead, and have called a pass play, and it's not fourth down, your quarterback should prefer a sack to an incompletion or interception. That's the opposite of the two-minute drill situation where you **never** want a sack. But then being **ahead** is also the opposite of the two-minute drill situation.

On ***fourth down****, you don't mind an incompletion because the clock is going to stop anyway due to the change of possession. In that case, you should get better field position by incompleting the ball back to the line of scrimmage.*

The congratulatory-handshake touchdown

Remember that the last play of the game does **not** end when the **horn** sounds. Rather it ends when the officials **whistle** the last play dead. They will do that when the ball carrier is **down** or the ball goes **out of bounds**.

A small-town quarterback learned this to his chagrin in a game I read about somewhere.

His team was ahead. On the final play, the horn sounded. The quarterback was still upright at the time and stayed that way. One of his opponents walked up and extended his hand as if to shake and congratulate the quarterback on his team's victory. As the quarterback shifted the ball to his left hand, the defender suddenly grabbed the ball, ran the length of the field and scored the winning touchdown. The game-ending **whistle** did not sound until the defender crossed the goal line.

That quarterback, now a grown man, still gets cursed by some of the diehard fans in that small town when they run into him.

7

Taking a safety

Howard Cosell needed to read this book

During a *Monday Night Football* game late in 1973, the Dolphins were beating the Steelers 30-24. On his own 15 with about :45 left, Dolphins quarterback Bob Griese ran back out of his own end zone. The Steelers got a safety making the score 30-26. *Monday Night Football's* Howard Cosell went nuts. "What are they doing?" That's not so surprising. He wrote a book titled, *I Never Played the Game.*

But his broadcast partner, "Dandy" Don Meredith, played plenty, including quarterbacking the Dallas Cowboys. He, too, expressed mystification at Griese's lining up to "go for it" on fourth down so deep in their own territory.

Such is the degree of ignorance of the clock-management tactic of deliberately taking a safety. By the way, the Dolphins won the game 30-26.

1971 Army–Navy Game

At the end of the 1971 Army-Navy, Navy could have kicked a field goal, which would have tied the game. There was no overtime rule in college football then. If you "kissed your sister," she stayed kissed in the record books for the rest of time.

With 00:08 left in the game, Army was ahead 24-21 and had the ball with fourth down at their own seven-yard line. The clock was stopped awaiting the snap. Army's punter Ron Damhof took the snap and scrambled around in his own end zone until the clock ran out, at which time he ran out the back of the zone. That's a safety. But safeties are only two points. Final score: Army, 24; Navy, 23.

Two youth football victories

In 1994, the San Ramon Bears youth football team on which I was the special teams coordinator won two games by deliberately taking safeties.

On September 17, 1994, our team was playing the Fairfield Suisun Indians, the defending league champions. With 1:42 left on the clock, we were ahead 6-0 on the strength of an interception runback. We had fourth and fourteen at our own four-yard line.

Suisun had been moving the ball in spite of their inability to score. Our previous punt had been blocked. Kids that age (9-11) generally cannot kick PATs (which are worth two points in youth football versus one point for running or passing for the conversion), let alone field goals. We concluded that there was too great a chance of a blocked punt or a punt run back or, at best, a short scoring drive after a successful punt. So we told the quarerback to take a safety.

You have to practice taking a safety

Fortunately, we had practiced taking a safety the previous year. Otherwise, the players would probably have concluded we had lost our minds after we explained what we wanted them to do and would have punted instead.

When our quarterback got tackled in the end zone (he should have stepped out instead), a strange thing happened. The Suisun sideline and fans **and** our coaching staff all cheered.

Our free kick was hard to handle and the Suisun player fell on it at our 40-yard line. When the game ended, they had only managed to get to our 20. Final score: Bears, 6; Indians, 2.

Later in the same season, on October 1st, we were ahead of the Bencica Cougars 15-12. With 14 seconds left in the game, we had fourth down and long at our own 15-yard line. Our previous punt had almost been blocked. We took a safety and managed to run about ten seconds off the clock. Benicia cheered, joined by our coaching staff and, this time, our newly sophisticated parents and players.

We free kicked and the final buzzer sounded during the run back. We tackled the Benicia ball carrier at our two after the final horn. And there was also a clipping penalty against Benicia. Penalty declined. Game over. Final score: Bears, 15; Cougars, 14.

We almost certainly would have lost both these games had we not taken safeties.

1994 NFC Wild Card game

In a 1994 Wild Card playoff game between Green Bay and Detroit, Green Bay was winning 16-10 with 5:35 left in the game. The Lions marched to Green Bay's 17-yard line then threw incomplete on 4th and 14 with 1:45 to play. The Packers took over and ran out the clock, deliberately taking a safety on the last play. Final score: Green Bay, 16; Detroit, 12.

Benefits of a safety

Taking a safety has several benefits:

- It uses up about five to ten seconds.
- It gives you the right to free kick from your own 20-yard line.
- It lets you avoid the possibility of a blocked punt or bad snap.

Of course, it also has the **disadvantage** of giving the other team two points. But two points are meaningless if you are ahead by more than two and the safety is likely to be the last score of the game.

Two points are also meaningless if they do not change the number of scores the trailing team needs to tie or win. If the game is **tied** or one team is **behind by one, four, or five** points, giving up a safety does not change the number of scores they need to tie or win.

When the trailing team might want to take a safety

Behind by	Scores needed to tie or win	Scores needed to tie or win after trailing team takes safety
0	**field goal**	**field goal**
1	**field goal**	**field goal**
2	field goal	touchdown
3	field goal	touchdown
4	**touchdown**	**touchdown**
5	**touchdown**	**touchdown**
6	touchdown	touchdown and two-point PAT
7	touchdown	touchdown and field goal

I know that this table seems to equate a tie with a win. Normally, I would not do that. But when you are considering taking a safety, you are worried about **losing** right now. Compared to losing, a tie ain't bad. And as you'll read below, in 1994, Arizona Cardinal coach Buddy Ryan gambled on taking a safety, when he was already **behind**, which left him in a position to tie, which he did, then his team won in overtime. A tie is sometimes the best path to a win.

Note that in the table above, margins 0, 1, 4, and 5 are such that the **losing** team can give up a safety and still have the same number of scores required to tie or win. I am assuming that kicking the extra point is pretty much a sure thing. I did not include the **six-point** margin because after you took a safety and increased that to **eight**, you would have to do a successful **two-point conversion**. Two-point conversions are **not** a sure thing. They only succeed about 40% of the time in the NFL and NCAA Division IA.

Ahead by less than three

You may also want to take a safety when you are **ahead but by less than three**. If you are ahead by two, and you take a safety, you tie the game and now need to score a field goal to win. Plus you get to free kick the ball out of your own end of the field. But if you do **not** take a safety, when you are deep in your own territory, the other team may get such good field position after your punt that they can easily kick a field goal. That would leave you in the same position, in terms of number of scores needed, as if you took a safety. But taking a safety has the advantage of reducing the probability of the other team getting a touchdown, which would leave you in a **worse** position. Punting from deep in your own end zone risks a blocked punt which is a touchdown if the opponent falls on it in the end zone or runs it in.

Taking a safety is probably the best course of action more in **high school** and **youth** football than in college or the NFL, because the difference between punt distance and free-kick distance is greater and the incidence of blocked punts and bad snaps is higher.

When the leading team might want to take a safety even though they are ahead by less than three

Ahead by	Scores needed to tie or win	Scores needed to tie or win after leading team takes safety
0	field goal	field goal
1	none	field goal
2	none	field goal
3	Taking a safety still leaves you ahead	

Wyoming takes a safety—and loses

The Wyoming Cowboys deliberately took a safety in the inaugural Western Athletic Conference championship game against the BYU Cougars on December 7, 1996. Their coach, Joe Tiller, said it was "A brilliant call."

Maybe not.

Wyoming stopped BYU at the Cowboys' two-yard line with 2:57 left in the game. The score was Wyoming, 25; BYU, 20.

Wyoming was unable to move the ball. On fourth down, they faced a choice of punting out of their own end zone to BYU's James Dye, a dangerous kick returner, or taking a safety. They decided to take the safety. Wyoming, 25; BYU, 22.

BYU returned the ensuing free kick to their own 40-yard line. In the next seven plays, they drove to Wyoming's three-yard line. They almost lost the game when they failed to notice that an apparent incomplete pass was actually caught. Lesson: *watch the referee, not the ball.* Literally at the last second, BYU's captain called a time out. BYU kicked a 20-yard field goal to tie the game—and kicked 32-yarder in overtime to win: 28-25.

Had Wyoming **not** taken the safety, BYU would have had to score a **touchdown** to win. They would have had about **ten seconds more** if Wyoming had punted instead of taking the safety. And they would have fielded the punt about **20 yards closer** to Wyoming's goal line because punts from scrimmage go about 40 yards in college, while kickoffs go about 60 yards.

I think Wyoming did the right thing. They killed some clock. They avoided the possibility of a blocked kick. The field position advantage gained by the free kick was pretty much canceled out by the fact that BYU only needed a field goal after the safety. Wyoming made the **right** call. But it was a **close** call, not "a brilliant call."

*A **sure-thing safety**, that is, one where the safety play will **end the game**, is a no brainer. You do it whenever the situation presents itself.* But if you cannot make the safety play last until the final horn sounds, there is a risk the opponent may score a touchdown on the kick return or on a subsequent snap or kick a field goal.

Cardinals early safety in 1994

Phoenix took a safety **much earlier** than the last play of the game in their 10/16/94 game with the Redskins. They were also **behind** at the time!

On fourth down with 4:47 left in the game, Arizona was losing 14-9 and facing a punt out of their own end zone. Arizona coach Buddy Ryan decided his best couse of action was to take a safety. After the safety, the score was Redskins, 16; Cardinals, 9.

I called the Cardinals to ask why. Public relations man Greg Gladysiewski explained that the Redskins had been having a horrible day on offense. Only three of their drives lasted six plays that day. Half of their 14 points came from a 27-yard interception runback for a touchdown.

The Cardinals defense, on the other hand, ended up second in the NFC (behind Dallas) that year in average yards allowed per game. Ryan was confident that giving the ball to the Redskins that day meant only a short delay before they punted or otherwise turned it over. But he did **not** want them to start out first and ten inside Cardinal territory.

Arizona had the ball fourth and eight on their own four-yard line. If they punted, the punter would be right at the back of the end zone to receive the snap. Arizona's average punt that year was 40.8 Yards. And the average generally masks a **wide variation** when it comes to punting.

On the other hand, if they took a **safety**, they could kickoff from the 20-yard line. NFL kickoffs typically travel 65 yards in the air and they are very consistent.

Ryan also took note of the **score**. Before the safety, his team needed a **touchdown to take the lead**. After the safety, they only needed a **touchdown and a kicked extra point to tie**. Ryan figured he was likely to get his seven points, throw the game into overtime and win it then with his superior defense.

As it turned out, the Cardinals **did** get the ball back at their own 28 with 3:03 left in regulation and managed to tie the game with a touchdown drive and PAT kick at :19. The Cardinals kicked a field goal to win in overtime.

Buddy Ryan was not your usual NFL coach. He took an unusual gamble in this case and managed to squeak out a victory. This was a case where your feel for the game helps you decide.

Free kick after a safety

After giving up a safety, you free kick from your own 20-yard line. Free kick means the opposing team has to stay ten yards away from your kicking point. Essentially, a free kick after a safety is the same as a kickoff except that it's from your **20** and you have three choices as to how to kick:

- punt
- place kick
- drop kick.

Few people can drop kick anymore. And I know of no advantage of drop kicking in this situation. So forget that.

Punting may have a **hang-time advantage**. No snap is required if you punt. The punter just stands around where the kicking tee would be and punts. But punters shank punts. Place kicks may be wide right or left, but they are rarely shanked. In the NFL, you may **not** use a tee for the place kick after a safety. Therefore place kicking in the NFL after a safety requires a holder, which diminishes the kick coverage somewhat.

You need to practice the free kick after a safety at least once or twice to avoid confusion if you have to do it in a game.

Free kick after a fair catch

In **high school** and the **pros**, the receiving team can **fair catch** a free kick and then do its own free kick. In **college**, the receiving team can only snap the ball on the next play.

If a high school or pro player can fair catch the free kick **within their field goal kicker's range**, they may then try to kick a **free kick field goal**. That lets them place the ball **anywhere they want between the hashes** on the yard line where they fair caught the kick. They can then try to kick the field goal by teeing the ball up on that yard line—or having a holder hold it in the NFL. The defense must stay ten yards away like on a kickoff. There is no snap and no time runs off the clock during the free kick after a fair catch.

It would take a line-drive kick or short shank that was fair caught to be inside the typical kicker's field goal range. Remember that the ball will not be kicked from seven yards behind the line of scrimmage as with a normal field goal. Rather it will be kicked from right **on** the "line of scrimmage," that is, the yard line where the ball was fair caught.

How to take a safety

You take a safety by running to the corner of the end zone and stepping out the back or side of the end zone just before you are to be tackled or immediately after the final horn sounds, whichever comes first. You do NOT allow yourself to be tackled, because of the danger of fumbling the ball.

In an emergency, you can take a safety by kicking or throwing (**backward pass only**) the ball out the back or side of the end zone. Practice that once or twice to make sure it's in your players' minds. But remember it is a foul which entitles the opponent to an untimed free-kick play if time ran out during on the safety.

Disasters in taking a safety

You must make sure you completely explain taking a safety to your ball carriers and give them opportunities to practice the play. It would be a disaster if they:

- **fumbled** the ball
- ran **out of the end zone** into fair territory and got tackled
- threw a pass that was **incomplete** or **intercepted**
- **tripped** and fell in fair territory.

Do **not** try to explain it for the first time in the heat of battle.

Yard line for taking a safety

How far out can you be and still take a safety? When you take a safety, you are essentially running a sprint race to the back of the end zone. Your guy **must** win the race. But he has a couple of handicaps:

- He has to start with his **back** to the goal line. His opponents **face** it.
- He has to take a **snap**. His opponents do not.
- He has to **carry a football**. His opponents do not.

Marty Glickman was an Olympic sprinter and a halfback for Syracuse. He once was timed in the hundred-yard dash **with** and with**out** a football. That is, he ran the hundred without a football in his arm, then he ran it again with a football. He was **one or two seconds slower when carrying the football**. That's why another Olympic sprinter and football player, Dallas recevier Bob Hayes, sometimes got caught from behind and tackled, even though he was the "World's Fastest Human."

When you think of it that way, you begin to see that this is not equally advisable from just any yard line. The farther out you are, the greater the probability that the defenders coming around the end will catch your quarterback before he gets to the end zone—a disaster. The probability that disaster will occur enroute to the end zone is small, but the farther out you are, the greater the danger.

Experiment in practice to see how far out you can get and still get safely to the end line. I would expect you would have trouble being sure of success if the line of scrimmage were beyond the **twenty**. Of course, outside the twenty, you also have a better chance to punt the ball out of field-goal range.

Go backwards

Suppose you are **beyond** your twenty yard line, ahead by three or more, but you are just outside of worst-case take-a-knee time. If you could take a safety on the fourth-down play, the extra time that play takes would eat up the remaining time after your three take-a-knees. You could schedule your first three downs as **go-backwards plays** to get you back to the twenty-yard line for your take-a-safety fourth-down play.

One "play" should certainly be the deliberate taking of a **delay-of-game penalty**. That moves you back five yards, if the other team accepts. A smart team might decline the yardage. Deliberately taking a delay-of-game penalty will get you about two more seconds than are assumed in the take-a-knee table.

The other plays should be quarterback-keep-sweep slides that lose an appropriate number of yards per play and do not risk a tackle. You want to end up at your twenty for fourth down. Then, on fourth down, you deliberately take a safety, running as much time off the clock as you can, again without risking a tackle.

Formation for taking a safety

The formation and techniques used to take a safety should minimize the possibility of the above disasters.

The safest snap is the quarterback-under-center style. Use your normal center and quarterback if possible. A **long snap** is dangerous because of the possibility of a fumble in fair territory. If the line of scrimmage is so close to the goal line that the long snap would be very unlikely to be fumbled in fair territory or in the end zone, the only danger is that a bad snap may go out the back of the end zone on the fly. That's a safety. But it will use far less than the normal time. The result may be that there is time for a free kick return and another play after the safety.

The best formation is a double-tight, field-goal type formation with tight splits. The linemen would be in two-point stances as is normal in field goal plays. Guards should overlap their inside foot with the center's foot in high school and college. In the NFL, **all** linemen can lock legs if the line coach so desires. Backs other than the quarterback should be at wing, also in two-point stances, two on one side and one on the other. Here's the play diagram.

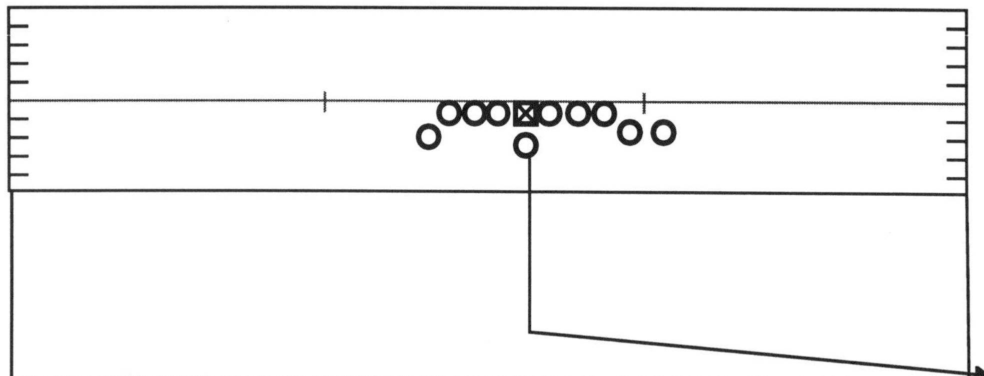

Loose ball in the end zone

You sometimes see a punter kick a loose ball out the back or side of the end zone. That's generally smart. Such a kicked ball is a safety. But if the offensive player had left the ball in the end zone, tried to recover it, and failed, a recovery by the defense would be a defensive **touchdown**. But remember that kicking or batting out is a foul in the NFL and entitles the opponent to an untimed free kick. The only time you do it is to avoid a touchdown.

Intentional grounding from the end zone is a safety

It is also a safety if the offensive team intentionally grounds the ball from the end zone. In theory, you could avoid being tackled on your safety play by throwing an intentional-grounding pass just before you were tackled. But do **not** do that.

For one thing, it could **slip** out of the passer's hand and be intercepted or recovered for a defensive touchdown.

For another, the officials might call your intentional grounding a simple **incomplete pass**, in which case the ball would go over on downs to the opponent at the previous line of scrimmage if it were fourth down, the usual take-a-safety down.

Stepping out of bounds just before you are hit is the best way to take a safety.

8

Slowdown offense

A slowdown consists of the following:

- use all the play clock
- stay in bounds
- prefer the run to the pass
- run outside the hashes
- walk to the line of scrimmage after the play in high school and college
- leave the ball on the ground in high school and college
- if you must call a timeout, wait until the end of the play clock

You use the slowdown offense whenever you are ahead. You also use it when you are behind by eight or fewer points on your last possession of the game if slowing down is necessary to leave no more than 20 seconds on the clock after you score. You also use the slowdown on your last possession of the first half, regardless of the score, if slowing down is necessary to leave no more than 20 seconds on the clock after you score.

You're already in a slowdown

The notion that you start a slowdown as soon as you take the lead, even in the first quarter, is probably the most controversial idea in this book. But it's less controversial when you realize that most teams are **already almost doing the slowdown**. Most teams run a "normal" speed offense, except at the end of a game. "Normal" speed is actually pretty close to a slowdown speed.

The slowdown pace is as few as 31 seconds per play, assuming the refs take at least six seconds between blowing the last play dead and blowing the ready-to-play whistle for the next play (in high school and college). You can wait until about 23 seconds of the play clock have run before you call for the snap (38 seconds in the NFL) and the play itself takes at least two seconds.

Film analysis I have done revealed that teams operating at the "normal" pace take about 16 seconds between the ready-to-play whistle and their snap. A slowdown would require them to wait **just seven more seconds**. On the other hand, a hurry-up requires that the play clock only run a second or two before the snap. So the 16-seconds most teams normally take is almost the same as the maximum time they could take and is far from the hurry-up pace.

In other words, you can probably adopt my suggestion that you begin your slowdown as soon as you take the lead **without anyone knowing** that you have done so.

Every second you fail to waste could be the one that costs you the game

Every time you snap the ball when you are ahead, you have the opportunity to use the full play clock, or at least 23 seconds of it.

In the first half, even though you are ahead, you may still be trying to extend your lead late in the first half. Wasting time after you take the lead in the first half has no effect on the second-half game clock. And it may prevent you from scoring yet another field goal or touchdown near the end of the half. But in general, it is the **trailing** team that **needs** to score, not the leading team. So you should start wasting time as soon as you take the lead in the first half.

In the second half, every second you snap the ball before the clock hits 23 is a gift to the team which is behind near the end of the game. If you are **currently ahead**, the team which is most likely to be behind near the end of the game is your **opponent**. So every second you could have wasted by using the whole play clock, but failed to, when you had the ball and were ahead in the second half, is very probably a gift to your opponent.

How much of a gift? In the typical NFL game, each team runs 31 plays per half. If you snap the ball seven seconds before you have to, every play during the course of the second half, you give your opponent 31 x 7 = 217 extra seconds or 3:37 more time to beat you. How would you like to have back every game you lost in the last 3:37?

Stay in bounds

How much time does staying in bounds save? Going out of bounds typically stops a play at around six seconds duration. Running a slowdown typically uses at least 31 seconds in high school and college and around 40 seconds in the NFL. So going out of bounds when you are ahead or on your last drive of the half makes a gift to the team that is behind near the end of the game of about 25 to 34 seconds per play. An incomplete pass does about the same. That's about enough time for a top-speed hurry-up offense to run four to six more plays.

Avoid passing if you can

In 1995, the 49ers threw about 12 **incomplete passes** per game or six per half. If you were ahead in the second half, and still threw your usual six incompletions, you would thereby make another gift to the team that's trailing near the end of the game of 6 x 34 = 204 seconds or 3:24.

I don't know how many times a team goes **out of bounds** when they are not trying to do so. Let's say that's also six times.

So the total amount of time you are unnecessarily giving to the trailing team in the second half alone, if you do **not** follow my advice to go to a slowdown when you are ahead is:

• not using all the play clock	3:37
• incomplete passes	3:24
• going out of bounds unnecessarily	3:24
Total	**10:25**

That's not precise. Most teams do go into a slowdown in the last four minutes so they do not waste the whole 10:25. And it will be somewhat less at lower levels. But it's still a heck of a lot of time. Roughly speaking, that is the amount of time per half that the leading team unnecessarily gives the trailing team if they do not switch to a slowdown as soon as they take the lead.

I've had resistance from several coaches who discussed this book with me regarding the issue of starting a slowdown as soon as you take the lead. But no one had any substantive criticisms. One said, "I'd hate to see it." So would I. But under current rules, the wisdom of slowing down as soon as you take the lead is essentially a mathematical fact, not a matter of opinion. And coaches are losing games their players played well enough to win solely because they violated this principle of sound clock management.

Conceal it

You can run a "hidden slowdown" by **just breaking the huddle later**. Your team needs to ascertain from practice how long it takes from huddle break to snap. It varies from team to team according to

- how far from the line of scrimmage you huddle
- how fast your players move to the line
- how wide your receivers line up
- whether you use shifts or motion.

In a slowdown, you want to snap at about 23 on the play clock in high school and college, 38 seconds in the NFL. In a "hidden slowdown," you do the same, but you do most of your waiting **in the huddle** rather than at the line of scrimmage.

If you cannot master the "hidden slowdown," run a more obvious slowdown. In the obvious slowdown, you get to the line of scrimmage early but do not start cadence until the play clock hits about 20 seconds. This will be less likely to get you a delay-of-game penalty.

How long a slowdown play takes

In the NFL, a slowdown play takes about 38 seconds plus the amount of time the play itself takes. That's the result of the NFL's 40-second clock. In the event of a penalty or other referee timeout, which triggers the NFL's 25-second play clock, a slowdown play only takes about 23 seconds plus the amount of time the play itself takes plus any time between the dead ball whistle and the stop-the-clock signal. When you consider that the play itself can take between two and nine seconds, figure an NFL slowdown play will take from 23 + 2 = **25** seconds to 23 + 9 = **32** seconds or from 38 + 2 = **40** seconds to 38 + 9 = **47** seconds.

In high school and college, the length of time a slowdown play takes is very much a function of how much time the referees take. Take the NFL 25-second clock slowdown and add to it the referee's "housekeeping" time to spot the ball, get into position to officiate the next play, and give the ready-to-play signal.

In my experience, referees take from ten to about twenty seconds to give the ready-to-play signal after they blow the last play dead. So a high school or college slowdown play takes 25 + 10 = **35** seconds to 32 + 20 = **52** seconds. The longest referee-housekeeping time will probably occur during a hidden slowdown early in the game when nobody is aware that you are taking a long time to huddle. The shortest would be when the offense is running a hurry-up or when the offense is running a slowdown at the end of a half. The refs will hurry to avoid seeming to help the team which is trying to waste time.

Play clock

In college and the NFL, using all of the play clock is easy, because there is a big play clock at each end of the stadium. In high school, however, there is almost never a play clock. I suggest you hang one out your press box window at home games and turn one of your sideline players into a **human play clock** at away games. That is, he uses his right arm like an old-fashioned second hand. He starts with it straight down in the "six o'clock" position when the play clock hits seven seconds left.

A coach with a countdown timer stand next to him and counts out loud and the human play clock moves his right arm like a second hand to five o'clock, four o'clock, and so forth. By the time he has it straight up, the quarterback must call for the snap.

Human play clock **Clock-management assistant coach**

Have the clock-management assistant coach on the sideline start his stopwatch, preferably a countdown timer (that goes backward to zero), when the referee blows the ready-to-play whistle. I once started my sideline stopwatch at the **end** of the ref's ready-to-play whistle blast—and got flagged for delay of game. Start your stopwatch at the **beginning** of the ready-to-play whistle blast.

Inconsistent refs

But I cannot guarantee you that even that will prevent delay-of-game. I once started my stopwatch at the beginning of the ref's ready-to-play whistle blast, and announced out loud each five second mark:

"Five"

"Ten"

"Fifteen."

But at 15 seconds we were shocked when the ref threw a flag and charged us with delay of game. All the coaches on my sideline erupted in outrage. (They were normally well trained that only the head coach could talk to the officials.)

Apparently the ref had used the **game** clock as his 25-second timer, and had fouled up his math. We protested in vain, even though a line judge had been standing a few feet away from us and heard my marking the elapsed time. If I had that situation to do over, I'd have fought harder to get the penalty canceled. When you're right, and it's not a judgment call, you have a duty to your team to protest strenuously. Don't get an unsportsmanlike penalty, though.

Miramonte High School (Orinda, CA) head coach Floyd Burnsed says that, in his 25 plus years of coaching, he has seen many instances of officials giving the offense less than 25 seconds toward the end of a close game. I don't know what to tell you to do about it except to complain to the refs. You are not supposed to complain about judgment calls. But this is no judgment issue.

When to begin the slowdown

As I said in the Overview chapter, you should start clock management, either slowdown or speed-up whenever one team takes the lead. The reason is the team that's currently ahead wins about 85% of the time. And most of those teams probably did not start slowing down when they took the lead. When you consider that more than half of all NFL games were decided by eight points or less in 1994, it appears likely that adherence to the slowdown-as-soon-as-you-take-the-lead rule would increase the percentage of first scoring teams winning up to **90%** or so.

Illinois vs. Minnesota, 1916

A book called *Against All Odds* by Bill Shanklin tells the stories of football's greatest upsets and come-from-behind victories. The first game in the book, told of Illinois' upset victory over heavily-favored Minnesota in 1916.

Illinois scored on their first possession taking the lead 7-0. My rule says Illinois coach Robert Zupke should have started a slowdown at that point. There is no indication that he did. Illinois intercepted a pass during Minnesota's possession after the first Illini touchdown, and ran it back for a second touchdown making the score 14-0. However, at **halftime**, Zupke told his Illini players to run a slowdown for the **whole second half**.

In the third quarter, Minnesota scored a touchdown and a safety, making the score 14-9. But further they scoreth not. The Illini got a delay-of-game penalty in the fourth quarter and were forced to punt as a result.

Author Shanklin says, "Coach Zupke's halftime instructions to his team to stall as much as possible worked." Shanklin also quotes a newspaper account of the day:

> *With his team in the lead...[Illinois quarterback] Captain Macomber deemed discretion much the better part of valor and used his brains to delay the game, drag things along and maintain his lead. Often he chose to make line plays straight into the center, each occasion developing a pile of men which had to be unpiled before play could be resumed. This took time and time was what Macomber was after. He used all his double shifts, complicated formations and ring-arounds, and then called the men back and did it over. He used all the minutes possible and only once was his team penalized for unnecessarily delaying the game.*

Younger readers should be informed that prior to the seventies, quarterbacks called the plays, not coaches.

Miramonte versus Alhambra, 1992

Miramonte High School (Orinda, CA) played Alhambra H.S. (Martinez, CA) in 1992. Alhambra was a heavy favorite. Miramonte managed to go into halftime with a 10-7 lead. Miramonte ran a slowdown the whole second half. They scored one more touchdown but did not get the PAT. Miramonte 16, Alhambra 7. Their defense also played well and managed to hold Alhambra to two field goals in the second half. Miramonte was ahead 16-13 and Alhambra was driving when the game ended. The second-half slowdown probably saved about seven minutes, seven minutes which may have made the difference in the game.

How to run the slowdown

On my 1993 youth team, we found that our warp-speed no-huddle also gave us an easy way to run our slowdown. In the hurry-up mode, we selected a play, wrote it on our white board and **immediately** showed it to our players. By the time the referee blew the ready-to-play whistle, our guys had the play and got set on the referee's whistle and ran the play one or two seconds later.

To run the slowdown, we simply started a stop watch on the sideline when the ref blew the ready-to-play whistle and delayed showing the white board to the players. By trial and error, we found the correct time to show it was after **15 seconds** had elapsed. When we did that, our players got the play off at around the 23-second mark. That's about as close as you want to cut the 25-second clock.

Belvidere (IL) High School coach Pottinger says he ran his slowdown similarly.

> *After fifteen seconds, we point to the quarterback. Usually we run 21 to 24 seconds off the clock for each play.*

Peter Moe, head coach of Washburn (ND) High School, has a coach watch the play clock and signal the quarterback when to proceed in their slowdown.

Remember this only relates to the time between the ready-to-play whistle and the snap. You would typically run an additional six seconds off with the play itself and around ten to fifteen more between the dead-ball whistle and the ready-to-play whistle. (In the NFL, the new play clock starts at the end of the previous play and runs for 40 seconds unless the clock was stopped by the officials, In that case, the NFL has a 25-second clock similar to the high school and college rule.)

Green, yellow, red, and checkered panels

I suggest you have an assistant coach act as clock manager. You could have him hold up some sort of speed-limit sign. One method would be colored panels. You could take an old flip-style down marker and paint the four down panels green, yellow, red, and checkered. The meaning of the colors would be:

- green — maximum slowdown—"green" timeout, if called, is at end of play clock
- yellow — inbounds hurry-up
- red — top-speed hurry-up—"red" timeout, if called, is as soon as play ends
- checkered — take a knee

The clock management assistant would watch the clock and field position as well as the down and opponent timeouts. He would refer to field copies of a pace graph like the one later in this chapter and a take-a-knee table like the one in the take-a-knee chapter. Using the colored panels, he would signal both his fellow coaches and the players on the field as to the correct pace to set at the moment.

I considered numbers like 30, 20, and 6 indicating the number of seconds the offense should use per play. But officials or opposing coaches might complain about an extra numbered down-style marker on the sideline.

University of South Carolina head coach Brad Scott uses a colored card system in his shotgun no-huddle. But in his system, the colored cards communicate a formation-personnel package, not a pace. For example, his green card means pro-set formation and pro-set personnel on the field. Players who are **not** part of that package run off the field when they see a green card. The blue card sent the tight end off the field and he was replaced by a wide receiver who is flexed out. The sideline subs hang around the card-carrying coach. Scott practices these substitutions and the accompanying automatics five minutes a day.

Keeping count of the number of timeouts left

It would also be useful for the clock-management assistant to keep track of the number of timeouts each team has left. True, the scoreboard is supposed to do that. But it's dangerous to rely on the scoreboard, especially at the lower levels of football.

He should keep track of the **opponent** timeouts like the officials, with a pencil and paper. He can and should check his number with the officials as the game progresses. The clock-management assistant needs to know the number of opponent timeouts left to figure out when your team reaches the take-a-knee point if you are ahead.

The clock-management assistant needs not only to keep track of your timeouts. He also needs to keep his players and fellow coaches **informed** of the number of timeouts they have left. You could not use a number sign with 0, 1, 2, and 3 on it because it might be confused as the official down marker.

Here's an idea I have not tried. Put three spring clamps near the top of the pole that holds the colored panels. Make the clamps easy to see by attaching a tennis ball or some such to each one. As each timeout is used, take one clamp off the pole and stick it in your pocket. Both the players and the fellow coaches will then be able to tell at a glance how many timeouts they have left.

Possession durations

I said your last possession of each half is special from a clock-management standpoint. One coach asked me, "So how do you tell when you are in your last possession?" You can't be sure, but here are some numbers that will enable you to make an intelligent guess.

A couple of pro games I looked at each had 25 drives. NFL games last 60 minutes so that's 120 minutes and 50 drives or 120 ÷ 50 = 2:24 per drive. At a slowdown pace, about 40 seconds per play, 2:24 is 3.6 plays—three and out. At an inbounds hurry-up pace, about 20 seconds per play, 2:24 is 7.2 plays. At a top-speed hurry-up pace, about six seconds per play, 2:24 is 24 plays.

In 1994 and 1995, the average NFL team ran about 62 plays per game. If you figure twelve drives per game, that's 62 ÷ 12 = 5.17 plays per drive. Of course, how many plays you can run before you have to punt varies from team to team and from game to game. But sticking with the average 5.17, that means you can generally make a drive last 5 x 40 seconds = 200 seconds or 3:20.

You are **guaranteed** at least four plays, as long as you don't fumble or throw an interception. In the absence of opponent timeouts and incomplete passes, you can run about 40 seconds off the clock on each of the first three downs and the duration of the play on the fourth down. That's about 3 x 40 = 5 = 125 seconds or 2:05.

So how long does a drive last? At least two minutes if you go slow, about 3:20 on average. At the other extreme, one drive can, in theory, last the entire half.

Arizona State's fourth-quarter scoring drive in the 1997 Rose Bowl

Let's look at the 1997 Rose Bowl final scoring drive by Jake Plummer and Arizona State. They seemed to score the come-from-behind winning touchdown in spectacular fashion, only to see Ohio State come back in the time left and retake the lead. Could ASU have done a better job of wasting time in that final drive? Yes. In fact, they almost certainly would have won the game if they had managed the clock better.

ASU got the ball at their own 42 with 5:36 and three timeouts left. Ohio State had one timeout left. ASU was behind 14-10 so a field goal would not be enough. They had to go 58 yards. Ideally, they would want to score in the last second. But that's cutting it a bit close. Better they should give themselves about **20 seconds** of slack time. That might give Ohio State 20 seconds to work with. But it's hard to drive the usual 80 yards after a kickoff in 20 seconds.

Run the inbounds hurry-up

So ASU had 5:36 - :20 = 5:16 to work with.

If they use the maximum play-clock time and keep the ball on the ground and inbounds, they will use up at least 35 seconds per play (about 5 for the play, 7 for the ref to set the ball, and 23 of play-clock time). 5:16 ÷ :35 = 9 plays. 58 yards ÷ 9 plays = 6.42 yards per play. It's tough to gain that many yards staying on the ground.

Suppose they run a hurry-up but without trying to stop the clock after every play? That would use about 20 seconds per play. That would give them 5:16 ÷ 20 seconds per play = 16 plays. If they had 16 plays to go 58 yards, they would only have to gain 3.63 yards per carry.

That might be possible **keeping the ball on the ground**. The hurry-up does not necessarily give more time to the other team because it permits you to make fewer yards per play, which, in turn, permits you to keep the ball on the ground. So paradoxical as it might sound, the best way to waste time in some situations is to run the hurry-up, but run a stay-on-the-ground-and-inbounds hurry-up. A sort of **time-conserving play-clock pace** combined with a **time-wasting play-calling style** to produce an overall time-wasting, turnover-avoiding result. Call it the **inbounds hurry-up**.

Play-by-play

Play #1: Did ASU do that? Not quite. Their first-and-ten play was to go for it all—a bomb down the left sideline. It was batted away, incomplete. Second and ten. The play took eleven seconds before the clock was stopped by the incompletion. 5:25 left. Not a play designed to score slowly.

#2: The second play was a run left. It gained six yards, took five seconds, and left the clock running. That's a nice score-slowly play.

#3: Third and four. I could not tell when the refs gave the ready-to-play whistle because ABC cut away to a replay of the forward lateral on the blocked field goal at the beginning of the drive. But the clock was down to 4:55 when Jake Plummer called for the snap. That means 25 seconds elapsed between the dead-ball whistle and the snap. That's an **inbounds hurry-up** pace when you figure the refs probably took about ten seconds to spot the ball.

ASU's third play was a **quick out pass** to the right. Complete. The receiver tried to get out of bounds, but the defender would not let him. He should **not** have been trying to get out of bounds. ASU had enough time to score. Getting out of bounds in that situation would more likely save time for **Ohio State**. The defender should have pushed him out.

The official initially signaled to keep the clock going, then changed his mind when he realized the play was a **first down**. The clock stopped at 4:48. First and ten at the Ohio State 43-yard line.

#4: The game clock stopped to move the chains then was restarted by the referee. The clock was moving and at 4:34 when Plummer got the snap. He dropped back to pass and was almost sacked. He managed to get a short pass off to a running back who gained three yards on a six-second play to the 40. The clock continued to run. ASU huddled. The clock was down to 3:51 when they snapped.

#5: A sweep right (short side) went for only a two-yard gain to the 39 and took four seconds. The clock continued to run.

#6: Third and five at the 38. The ball is snapped at 3:12. Three-step drop. No one open. Plummer scrambles. Tackled at the 37. Fourth and four. Clock at 3:07 and still running. Coach Bruce Snyder calls a **timeout**. The clock stops at 3:00. Announcer Brent Mussberger is saying, "This is the season right here." Coach Snyder is probably not interested in scoring **slowly** at this moment. Rather he desperately wanted the four yards he needed for a first down.

#7: Three-step drop. The blitz is coming. Fade pass down the left sideline. Complete to the eight-yard line. The receiver does not get out of bounds on the diving catch but the clock stops to move the chains. First and goal at the eight.

#8: Snap at 2:32, dive left, gain of one. The play takes three seconds. Clock is running. ASU huddles. Second and goal at the seven.

#9: Snap at 1:57. Three-step drop. Pump fake. Sacked from behind by the defensive right outside linebacker. Play takes three seconds. Third and goal at the eleven. ASU **immediately calls** its second **timeout** at 1:47.

#10: Plummer drops back, heavy blitz, he breaks free and dives into the end zone with 1:40 left in the game. Arizona State 16, Ohio State 14. The kick was good. ASU 17, OSU 14.

Second-guessing Coach Snyder

OK. ASU Coach Bruce Snyder forgot more football than I ever knew. But having acknowledged that, let's now Monday-morning quarterback this drive and see if we can learn any principles we can apply to similar situations.

I said *we should try to leave about 20 seconds on the clock when we score*. ASU violated that by leaving 1:40. Could they have avoided that and still scored? A hurry-up pace combined with keeping the ball on the ground would require gaining an average of 3.63 yards per carry. Could ASU do that against Ohio State? Yes. Their average yards per rush on the day was, in fact, 3.6.

ASU also had **three timeouts**. The best time to use the first one while your opponent is running their slowdown and no later than 2:00. That situation never occurred in this game so there is no basis for criticizing Snyder for still having all three of his timeouts at 5:36 when he got possession.

Use the timeouts on offense

Since this is likely to be his **last** possession, and he must assume he will be ahead when it ends, Snyder should use his timeouts on **offense** during this drive. The three timeouts will give him an additional 36 seconds (12 seconds each x 3 = 36). That will let him run two or three additional plays. With two additional plays, he need only average 58 ÷ 18 plays = 3.**2** yards per play.

All of this suggests that the **optimum plan** for Snyder in this situation would have been the **inbounds hurry-up**, a hurry-up pace and conserve-time use of timeouts, combined with time-wasting play selection, that is, running plays that stay in bounds. What Snyder actually did was **alternate** between time-wasting type plays and a slow or medium pace and hurry-up tactics like the out pass and use of quick timeouts.

Analysis of each play

Play #1: Bad idea. If it had worked for a touchdown, Ohio State would have had about 5:23 to come back. The bat down also suggests the play came very close to an interception. The element of surprise sometimes works. But here a rather large and unnecessary gamble was taken by a team that need only gain 3.2 yards per carry over the next five minutes to win.

#2: Good play selection but too slow a pace. Given the distance, ASU has to run too many of these plays to afford this leisurely pace. Still time to get back on schedule. Could have used a timeout to stop the clock in which case ASU would have stayed right on schedule.

#3: Overly dangerous way to get four yards. Why gamble with a pass when we can stop the clock with a timeout? When this scoring drive was over, ASU still had a timeout left. That should not have been. It should have been used on one of these plays after they fell behind schedule.

#4: Another pass gamble. Almost a sack, which would have knocked us off schedule. Another chance to use a timeout, but it was not used.

#5: OK play call but Snyder was **not** in a hurry-up mode. 30 seconds between plays. Too long to maintain a 3.2-yards-per-play schedule. We are forcing ourselves into situations where we **have to pass**. We started the drive with enough time and timeouts to **avoid** that.

#6: Given the down and distance, 3rd and five, and the fact that ASU was in a **no-more-punts mode**, they only had to average 2.5 yards per carry on the next two carries to get a first down. In view of the fact that they averaged 3.6 yards per carry on the day, it seems like a couple of running plays would have done the job here, while simultaneously running off clock time that might be left lying around for the use of Ohio State. The pass, with its less-than-100% completion rate and danger of interception, seems an unnecessary risk in this situation.

The pass did **not** work and the resulting scramble only gained one yard. Now ASU has a bit of a problem. It's fourth and four. The game is on the line. Snyder wisely called a timeout. Averaging 2.5 yards, which is less than normal for the day, is different from gaining 4, which is **more** than normal for the day. But it's easy to overstate the danger. Four yards is a bit beyond the comfortable range, but only a bit. One would think there were many plays in the ASU play book which had a high probability of gaining four yards.

#7: Either Snyder or his quarterback (Ohio State showed blitz and did indeed blitz) calls for a deep fade pass. The receiver beat the defender by **a step**, not two. And quarterback Jake Plummer laid the ball exactly where it had to be thrown to be completed, but not intercepted.

In a four-yards-to-go situation, one would normally expect a run or a more conservative pass. Apparently, Ohio State expected a pass because they blitzed. You would not expect a fade on fourth and four, unless that was a standard ASU response to a blitz. So one might expect that the element of surprise might make the play work. But the Ohio State defender was **not** very surprised. He was almost right there. The play seemed to work because of the extraordinary skill of the quarterback (who came in third in the Heisman balloting) and the receiver, Lenzie Jackson.

Huge, unnecessary gamble

This play seems like an extreme gamble that was unnecessary but which had the virtue, at least, of succeeding big time. It **changed the clock-management complexion of the remainder of the game entirely**.

Arizona State started out with a good situation. They needed to score a touchdown, but they had enough time that they could do almost all conservative running plays and only needed to average 3.2 yards per carry if they minimized play-clock time by running a hurry-up pace along with an occasional timeout or run out of bounds.

Now, after the completed pass to the eight-yard line, the problem is less how to score—they have four plays to go eight yards. They only need to average two yards per carry. True, this is goal-line. But they also have an undefeated team and the almost-Heisman winner. **The problem is clock management**. We're trying to **both** score **and** leave no more than 20 seconds on the clock.

Now average 35 seconds per play

When the pass was complete, there was 2:54 left. The clock stopped temporarily to move the chains. ASU now needs to average about 35 seconds per play—**maximum slowdown speed**—to score and leave only 20 seconds or so on the clock. They no longer have any choice about **how many** plays to run because they can no longer get any first downs.

Accordingly, Plummer should let the play clock get up to 23 before he calls for the snap. Subtracting :23 from 2:54 we get 2:31. In fact, the clock was down to 2:32 when Plummer got the snap. Nice job of clock management, except for one thing: the play clock did not start the moment the receiver hit the ground. This isn't the NFL.

There must have been a delay while the officials ran upfield from the previous line of scrimmage, which was 30 yards back. I'd guess there was about fifteen seconds of referee-housekeeping time before the play clock was started—to move the chains, bring the ball into the hash, and get the officials into position for the next play. So it would appear that Plummer called for the ball about 15 seconds too early.

#8: This play, a dive, only gains one yard and takes just three seconds. That keeps the clock running. Now ASU has to average $7 \div 3 = 2.33$ yards per carry on its remaining three downs. ASU wisely huddles wasting time. The play took three seconds. If the refs take about ten more to set the ball, and Plummer lets the play clock get to 23, the time for the next snap should be 2:32 - 3 - 10 - 23 = 1:54.

Immediate timeout after sack

#9: In fact, the snap is at 1:57. It may be that the refs did not take ten seconds. It appears that Plummer is wisely trying to both score and take time off the clock while he does it. Plummer pump fakes, apparently a designed part of the play because it looked rather mechanical. That's a somewhat slow-developing play for such close quarters—it's not like the receivers can use the pump-fake time to outrun the defenders. They' start the play only 17 yards from the back of the end zone. It runs additional risk of a sack. And that's what happened. Time elapsed between the snap and sack: 3.00 seconds. That's about when you expect to be sacked.

The play loses four yards to the eleven. The **good** news is the clock is still running. The bad news is ASU now has to average 11 ÷ 2 = 5.5 yards a carry. That will limit play selection.

Another piece of bad news for clock management—**really** bad news: ASU's coach Snyder calls another timeout. He called it **before** the refs even gave the ready-to-play signal and **that may have cost Arizona State the game**. The clock was down to 1:47 when they got the timeout.

How much time would have run off if Snyder had not called that immediate timeout? Assume the referees use eight seconds to spot the ball, then give the ready-to-play whistle which starts the play clock. If Plummer again gets the snap at 23 on the play clock, the clock is down to 1:47 - 8 - 23 = 1:16.

Call your timeout, but **call it at 24 seconds on the play clock**! That way you get the refs' housekeeping time, the play-clock time, and the timeout to discuss your next play.

If ASU had a clock-management assistant coach as I advocate, that assistant would have been showing his **yellow** panel for **plays 1 through 7**. Then he would have flipped to **green** for plays **8, 9, and 10**. That green-colored panel would have reminded Snyder and Plummer that any timeout should be called at the **end** of the play-clock period.

Touchdown—but 1:40 left

#10: The rest, as they say, is history. Plummer took the snap starting the clock at 1:47. He dropped back to pass, no one was open. He scrambled and scored. I don't blame him for not taking all four downs to score. A touchdown in hand is worth two in the bush. But his crossing the goal line stopped the clock **permanently**, as far as ASU's control of clock management was concerned. Next comes the untimed PAT down followed by a kickoff in which the clock does not start until the receiving team touches the ball.

By taking their timeout too fast on the previous play, ASU unnecessarily gave Ohio State a **gift of about 30 seconds**. When Ohio State came back and scored the winning touchdown, there were 19 seconds left on the clock.

Schizophrenic clock management

In general, Arizona State's scoring drive strikes me as a bit schizophrenic regarding clock management. Plays #1, 3, 7 and the timeout after play 9 are run like a team that frantically needs to score **as fast as possible** and only has one minute to do so. In fact, they had much more than one minute.

Plays #2, 4, 5, 8 and 10 are run at a **slowdown pace**. In fact, #2, 4, and 5 should have been run at a inbounds hurry-up pace, not trying to stop the clock after each play. Plays #8 and 10, which came after the completion to the eight-yard line, should have been run at a **slow-as-possible pace**. Two were, but the third was the too-quick-timeout play.

Too many passes

I am biased against the pass—almost certainly because I have never coached a player like Jake Plummer. But even allowing ASU's skill with the pass, it appears that too many passes were called on the final ASU scoring drive.

The passing game on that drive went three for seven. Plummer did not **throw** seven times, but he meant to. He scrambled twice and got sacked once. Two of the passes were for gains so short you wonder why they risked the interception. On the day, Plummer's passing was 19 for 35 for 201 yards with one interception, a 54% completion rate. ASU averaged 5.7 yards per pass in the Rose Bowl. The run game on the final ASU scoring drive, including Plummer running with the ball, went 17 net yards on six carries or 2.83 yards per carry.

It appears to me that Arizona State should have done the inbounds hurry-up, for plays 1 through 6. ASU ranked number 1 in rushing in the Pac-10. If they fell behind schedule, they should have used their timeouts, passes, and getting out of bounds to get back on schedule.

Key on the run?

Some coaches might say that you can't just run the ball play after play in NCAA Division IA. The opposing team will just play the run and stop you cold, these coaches would claim.

First off, if I had been Bruce Snyder I wouldn't have given Ohio State a certified written guarantee that I would not run a pass during that last scoring drive, even if that were my plan. So it would take OSU a while to **figure out** I was sticking with the run.

But even after they began to suspect it during that final scoring drive, what're they going to do? Run a Gap-8 defense—against Jake Plummer who had the second highest passing rating in the Pac-10—against the undefeated Arizona State University team which ranked number 1 in the Pac-10 in offense? As the drive wore on, the time would be running out and Ohio State is still ahead 14-10. Seems to me that in that situation their defensive coordinator would never put his defense in a heavily run-oriented scheme.

Legendary Ohio State coach Woody Hayes said "The threat of the pass is more important than the pass itself."

Ahead of schedule

Once they got to the eight on play #7, there is no question that they were **ahead of schedule** and needed to got to an **all-out slowdown**. Snyder appeared to panic after the sack on play #9, resulting in his calling an **immediate** timeout. True, they lost four yards on the play, but the need to stick to a slow-as-possible pace was **unchanged**. And they could have had even more time to discuss the strategy for the next play had they called the timeout when the play clock had almost run out.

Credit to Ohio State

Give credit to Ohio State. Few would have given much for their chances as they awaited the kickoff with 1:40 left. They ran 12 plays in 1:40 - :19 = 1:21, gaining 65 yards and the winning touchdown. That's an average of almost 5.5 yards per play and just **6.75 seconds per play!** No doubt, Ohio State's comeback was one of the greatest last minute drives in football history. But the fact remains that smarter timing of the 1:47 ASU timeout would probably have prevented even such a great comeback from succeeding.

Coach of the Year

Again, I want to acknowledge that Bruce Snyder's knowledge of football coaching far exceeds mine. He won multiple, well-deserved, Coach-of-the-Year awards for the 1996 season. He also made **his** decisions within seconds at the Rose Bowl surrounded by 100,000 screaming people and under the scrutiny of millions of people listening and watching on radio and TV around the world. I have analyzed this at my leisure in my home office over a period of days.

As I said in the "Using timeouts" chapter, you need to have two modes: the **immediate** timeout which is signaled from the sidelines with the traditional hands in the shape of a T. But there is also the **last-second timeout**, for which I suggested the crossed **forearms** signal.

That needs to be practiced, if only a few times. Snyder should have given that crossed forearm signal at 1:47, in which case Plummer would have told a ref, "I'll be calling timeout when the play clock hits 24 seconds."

Snyder and Plummer could then have discussed their next play while keeping an eye on the play clock. When it hit 20, Plummer would have walked over to a ref and signaled timeout at 24 seconds, then resumed his conversation with Coach Snyder before going out to take the snap with about 1:16 left.

I have also said that coaches should practice their clock management using computer games, televised games of other teams, or local high school or college games. I suspect that if Coach Snyder had practiced dealing with various game-end situations, he would have learned during that coach-only practice that this was clearly a **time-wasting** situation, notwithstanding the fact that his team was **behind**, and he would have handled the calling of the 1:47 timeout better in the 1997 Rose Bowl.

I faxed Coach Snyder a copy of this chapter for his comments. He never replied.

Dolphins-Raiders AFC Divisional Playoff 12/21/74

The 1974 AFC Divisional Playoff game between the Dolphins and Raiders is considered by many to be the greatest NFL game ever played. The Miami Dolphins had to come from behind to take the lead. They did, but in the post-game words of Miami coach Don Shula, "We scored too fast." They left enough time for the Raiders to score a last-minute victory, 28-26, with a Ken Stabler pass to Clarence Davis in front of the Oakland home crowd.

Stabler was being tackled and almost horizontal when he threw the ball. Davis was in a crowd of four defenders when he caught the ball. NFL Films made it Touchdown Number Two (after "The Immaculate Reception") in their *100 Greatest Touchdowns* video.

Reading Shula's "We scored too fast" line, I suspected a series of clock-management mistakes like the '97 Rose Bowl. But when I got the official play-by-play for the 1974 game, I saw no such mistakes. Here it is:

OAKLAND 21 MIAMI 19
Jakowenko kicks off to the Miami 9 Ginn returns to the Miami 32 (Johnson)
MIAMI BALL (4:28)

1-10	M32 Griese pass complete Moore left hash for 23 (Wilson)	FIRST DOWN
1-10	O45 Csonka right end for 7 (Villapiano)	
2-3	O38 Csonka up middle for 15 (Tatum)	FIRST DOWN
1-10	O23 Malone sweep right end for 23 yards and TD (2:08)	

OAKLAND 21 MIAMI 25
Morrall holds Yepremian converts PAT (4 plays 68 yards)
OAKLAND 21 MIAMI 26

If Shula had a clock-management assistant, he would have consulted his pace graph and found that Miami should drive for the come-from-behind score at an **in-bounds hurry-up pace**. He would have shown his **yellow panel** for all plays. Yellow means no huddle, use minimum play-clock time, stay in bounds, prefer the run to the pass. I can't tell about the huddle or play-clock time, but it appears they did stay in bounds and did prefer the run except for the first play. They ran off a total of 4:28 - 2:08 = 2:20 off the clock or **35** seconds per play! The yellow pace is actually about **20** seconds per play. They went much slower than that and it still was not slow enough. They never had first and goal. The speed of the drive appears to be the fault **not** of Miami, but of **Oakland's defense** which gave up **17 yards per play** during this drive! The plays Shula or Griese called were not the kind that normally gain that many yards. One was a dive for Chrissake!

You need a schedule

When you are behind by eight points or less, and you have possession on what is likely to be your last drive of the game, you must *select the best schedule for scoring*. That schedule must first, give you the maximum probability of taking the lead and, second, give you the maximum probability of using all but about 20 seconds off the game clock.

Doing a hurry-up gives you the **maximum number of plays** which, in turn, gives you the **maximum number of choices** for each play. For example, when you need to average **seven** or more yards per play, you generally have to run passes, sweeps, reverses, and such. But if you only need to average **three** yards per play you can choose almost any play in your play book. The more plays you can run the harder it is for the defense to anticipate what you will do and stop it.

Here are some tables:

Time left: 6:20

Distance	# of inbounds hurry-up plays	Needed average yards per play
80	18	4.44
60	18	3.33
40	18	2.22

The number of yards per play can never drop below 2.5 outside the 10-yard line, because that is the minimum needed to get a **first down** when you are a four-down (no punting) situation. *When the number of yards needed per play to reach the needed field-goal field position or touchdown drops below 2.5, you go into a maximum slowdown offense*. Stay in bounds. Avoid passing. Call timeouts at the **end** of the play-clock time.

Time left: 4:20

Distance	# of inbounds hurry-up plays	Needed average yards per play
80	12	6.67
60	12	5.00
40	12	3.33
20	12	1.67

Time left: 2:20

Distance	# of inbounds hurry-up plays	Needed average yards per play
80	6	13.33
60	6	10.00
40	6	6.67
20	6	3.33
10	6	1.67

Now look what happens to the yards per play needed if you do **not** run the hurry-up pace in this situation. Figure each slowdown play takes 30 seconds.

Time left: 6:20

Distance	# of slowdown plays	Needed average yards per play
80	12	6.67
60	12	5.00
40	12	3.33
20	12	1.67

With 6:20 left, the inbounds hurry-up lets you gain just 4.44 yards per play and still score the winning touchdown while leaving just 20 seconds on the clock for your opponent to come back. But if you fail to run the hurry-up, you increase the number of yards per play you have to gain to 6.67. Teams rarely average that many yards per play except on

passes, but if you have to pass every play, there is a high probability of an interception, which, in this situation, means you lose.

Whenever possible, you want to *pick a schedule which lets you go at the lowest possible yards-per-play rate*. That, in turn, tells you what pace to use between plays.

Here's another table:

Distance	6:20	5:20	4:20	3:20	2:20	1:20
80	inbounds	inbounds	inbounds	inbounds	**top**	**top**
60	inbounds	inbounds	inbounds	inbounds	**top**	**top**
50	inbounds	inbounds	inbounds	inbounds	inbounds	**top**
40	**slow**	inbounds	inbounds	inbounds	inbounds	**top**
30	**slow**	**slow**	**slow**	inbounds	inbounds	**top**
20	**slow**	**slow**	**slow**	**slow**	**slow**	**top**
10	**slow**	**slow**	**slow**	**slow**	**slow**	**slow**

What this table does is get you as close as you can get to only needing three and a third yards per play while killing all but 20 seconds of the game clock at the end of the drive. Once the average needed to **score** is **less** than the 2.5-yard average needed to get a **first down**, you go to the **maximum slowdown pace**. Once you reach first and **goal**, and avoid losing ground back behind the 10-yard line, you can average fewer than 2.5 yards per carry because you no longer need a first down.

Remember these distances are to the **scoring point**: a **touchdown** if you need it or a **field-goal kicking field position** if three points is enough.

Here's a graph that better illustrates the three different paces that apply to the various yards to go for a score and time remaining situations. The numbers on the left side are the yards you have to go for a score. The numbers along the bottom are the time remaining in the half. Find the intersection of your current yards to go for a score and time remaining and you learn what pace you need to operate at to score on schedule, that is, with about 20 seconds left in the half.

During the last possession of the **first half**, you would shoot for a touchdown in terms of the pace you set. You would only **settle** for a field goal before halftime if you had fourth down within field goal range.

At the **end of the game**, you would shoot for whichever score was **enough** to win or tie. If you are down by three or less, field goal range would be the number of yards you would use to set your pace. Although if you had plenty of time to either score a touchdown or a field goal, you would not kick the field goal, with its risk of missing or being blocked, until you had fourth down or were almost out of time.

The second graph is a simplified pace graph showing each play of ASU's final scoring drive in the 1997 Rose Bowl. The graph seems to show that ASU should have gone back to an inbounds hurry-up on play 10, the scoring play. Not true.

In fact, once you get a **first down inside the opponent's ten-yard line**, that is, you have first and goal, your pace in terms of time per play is the number of seconds left in the game less ten (about all the time you would need to leave on the clock when you're this close) divided by the number of downs you have left. After the sack on play #9, ASU needed a 1:54 - :10 = 1:44 ÷ 2 = 52-seconds-per-play pace, that is, a maximum slowdown. Here's a table:

First-and-goal table

Down	2:00	1:40	1:20	1:00	0:40	0:20
1	slow	inbounds	inbounds	inbounds	top	top
2	slow	slow	slow	inbounds	top	top
3	slow	slow	slow	slow	inbounds	top
4	slow	slow	slow	slow	slow	inbounds

Pace chart for the last possession of the game when you are behind by 8 or less points and the last possession of the first half regardless of who is ahead or the score.

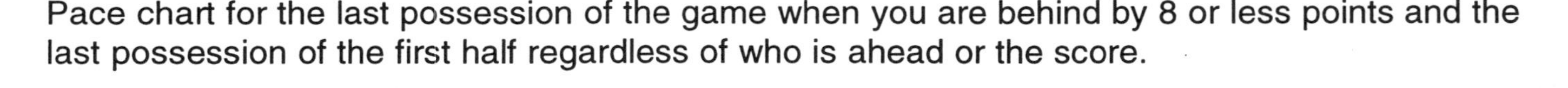

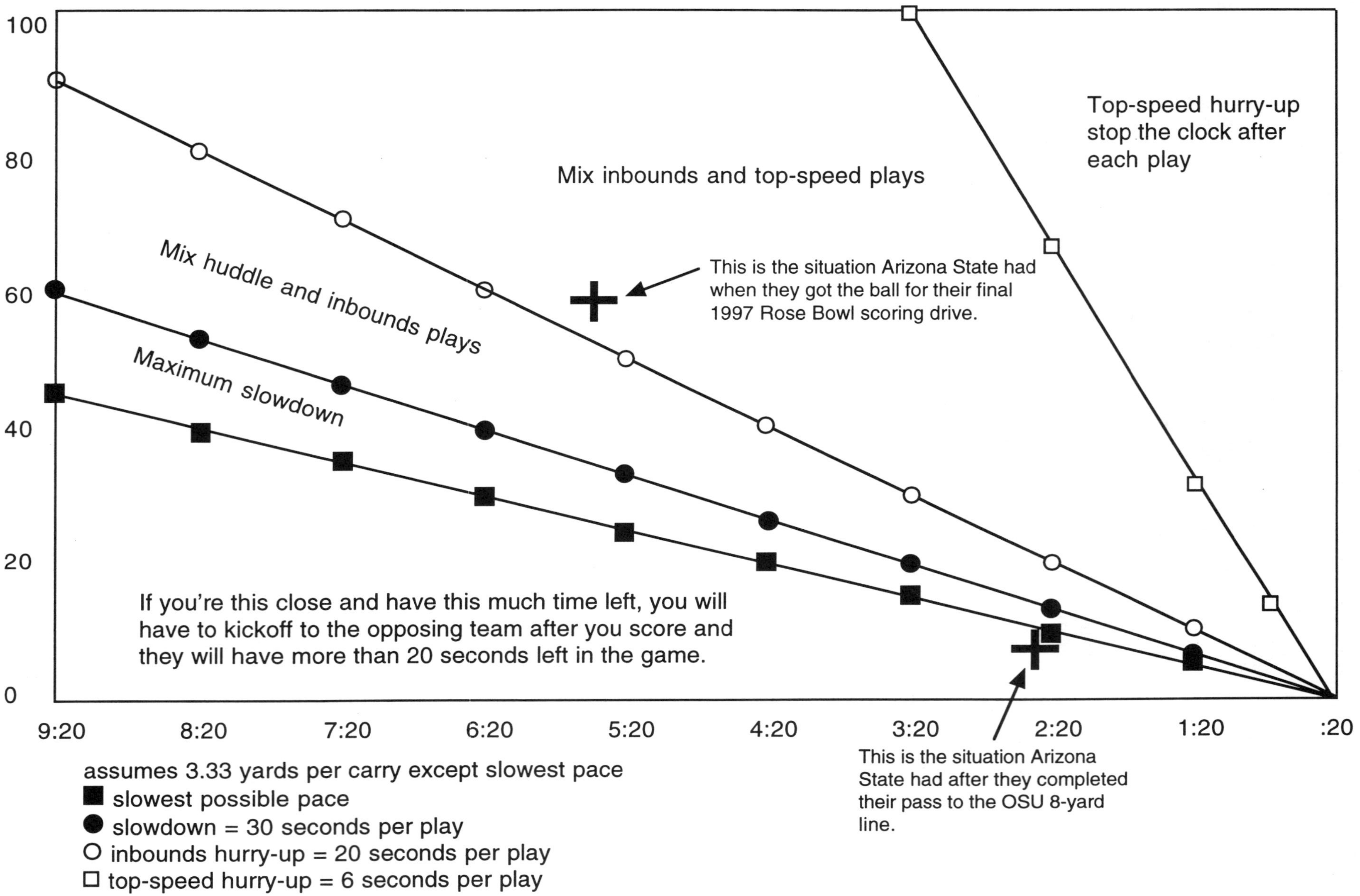

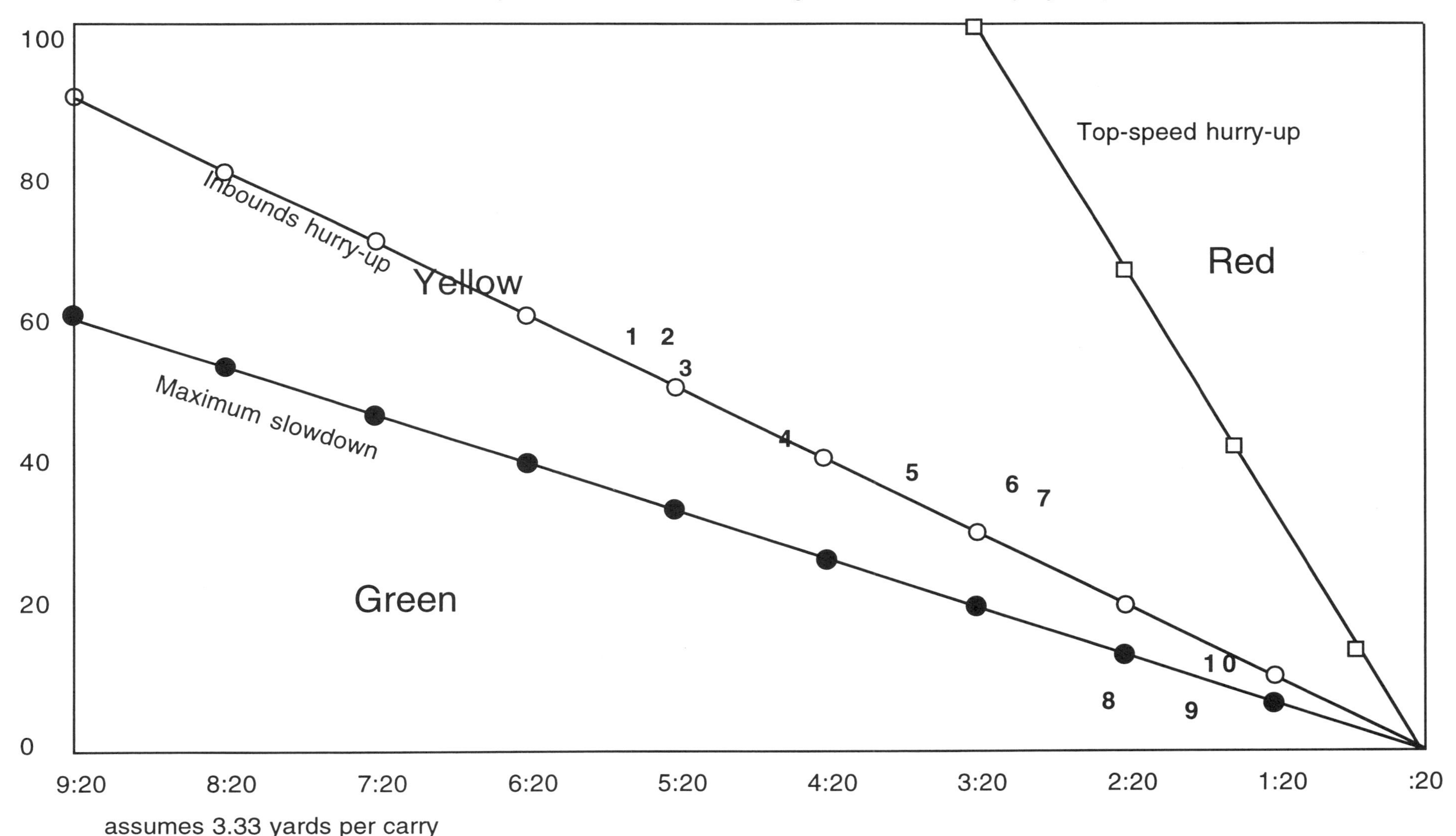
Simplified pace chart showing Arizona State's final scoring drive in the 1997 Rose Bowl.
Numbers show the field position and time remaining at the start of the play in question.
100
80
60
40
20
0
9:20
8:20
7:20
6:20
5:20
4:20
3:20
2:20
1:20
:20
Inbounds hurry-up
Maximum slowdown
Top-speed hurry-up
Red
Yellow
Green
1
2
3
4
5
6
7
8
9
10
assumes 3.33 yards per carry
● slowdown = 30 seconds per play
○ inbounds hurry-up = 20 seconds per play
□ top-speed hurry-up = 6 seconds per play

The longest you can control the ball

The longest you could control the ball would be

- on a 99-yard drive
- maximum use of the play clock (23 seconds)
- minimum yards per carry (2.5 yards)
- inbounds running plays.

In other words, you would take about 43 seconds per play, assuming 23 seconds of play clock, four seconds for the play and sixteen seconds for the referee's housekeeping. At that pace, over that distance, gaining the minimum 2.5 yards per carry on average, it would take you 99 ÷ 2.5 = 40 plays to score and those forty plays would take 40 x 43 seconds = 1,720 seconds or 1,720 ÷ 60 = 28:40. That's an **entire half** in youth and high school football and almost an entire half in college and the NFL!

If there were any **accepted penalties**, the time of possession would be **even longer**, because in most penalties, the down is played over. In 1995, the average NFL team had 103 penalties for the season which is about **six per half**.

I almost consumed an entire half on offense once. In 1993, my youth team's starting tailback did not feel well at one of our games. He sat out the whole first half. A halftime, the score was 6-6. In the second half, he agreed to play offense only and we went to a maximum slowdown for the entire second half to conserve his energy. We won the game 25-6. But the amazing thing was that the opposing team only got to run **six plays in the entire second half**! They ran one play in the third quarter, a pass which we knocked out of the receiver's hands and picked up and ran back about ten yards. And they ran five plays in the fourth quarter. We recovered one onside kick in the second half.

A week later, I had the same referee. He said he had been telling all his football friends what my kids had done in terms of second-half possession time the previous Saturday.

They'll change the rules

Can you control the ball for an entire half? In theory, yes. But if very many NFL teams do it, they'll change the rules and put in the football equivalent of basketball's shot clock. But this book is about increasing your probability of victory under the **current** rules.

When I was a cadet at West Point, our basketball coach was Bobby Knight. West Point had a severe handicap in basketball then. It could not have cadets who were over 6'6". But Knight, who is one of the most successful college basketball coaches ever, did not make excuses. He found a way to win—with **defense**. In 1966, Army's basketball team was ranked third in the nation in defense. In a 1965 game, Army held Penn State to 39 points. It was not pretty or popular, but Coach Knight got the most out of what he had.

Good coaches sometimes cause changes in the rules. The current football rules requiring everyone to be set for one second were passed as a result of Knute Rockne's success with the whole-backfield shift.

Yours is not to reason why when it comes to rules. Yours is but to find a way to win.

It's scoring slowly, not sitting on a lead

In the 1996 season, my freshman team was leading against Miramonte 20-14 with about seven minutes left. We had the ball. I was the offensive coordinator. It occurred to me that we should start our slowdown. I decided **not** to for two reasons:

- The only slowdown I had taught involved lining up at the line of scrimmage then looking to the sideline for a signal. In other words, it was an obvious slowdown, not the hidden variety that results from huddling and taking your time getting to the line of scrimmage.
- I had not explained to my team that scoring slowly, not sitting on a lead, was the purpose.

You have to chalk talk your team on the concept that a slowdown does not mean sitting on a lead. Rather they must play as hard as ever to get the first downs you need and to score. To convince them, you might use a **more varied offense** when you are huddling rather than just a slower version of your hurry-up. You could even avoid calling it the slowdown. Call it the "Multi" offense or some such. Teach your kids, "When we are in the multi, we take our time and make sure everybody has the play and knows their assignment." Do not emphasize the slowdown aspect. Rather treat it as another way to pound the opponent, only now with more complex plays.

'We don't worry about scoring slowly'

Colorado's Rick Neuheisel says,

> *We don't worry about scoring too fast. If you start worrying about that you get too conservative. If you don't score, you'll hate yourself. The idea is to score. If you do, you put the situation back on your defense. When you need a touchdown take it any time you can get it. The field goal is another matter You want to take all the time off the clock before you kick the field goal.*

He's wrong. Number one, there is **no need** to get conservative. You run the best plays you can, you simply adjust your use of the **play clock** and **boundary** according to the distance and time remaining. If you call a timeout, you call it at the end of the play clock. That has nothing to do with being conservative.

I say also to **prefer the running play** when the run and pass plays you have for the situation in question are **equally effective**. If I had **not** said when they are equally effective, Neuheisel's "conservative" remark would be valid. If you need to pass during a green or yellow pace, you pass.

"...put the situation back on your defense" is a common excuse for lousy clock management. It is unconscionable to "put a situation on your defense" when you did not have to. How would the offense like it if the defense let the opposing offense score slowly to take the lead and rationalized the decision to do so by saying, "We're putting the situation on our offense?"

Is it the "situation" that's being put on the defense, or the **blame**? The public is too unsophisticated to recognize a failure to score slowly. To them, games lost because the offense failed to score slowly, like the 1997 Rose Bowl, look like a failure of the **defense**. The offensive coordinator in such games is a hero for coming from behind to score, while the TV camera focuses on the defensive coordinator who "lost the game."

'Leaving money on the table'

In the business world, we have an expression, "Leaving money on the table." It refers to doing something stupid in a deal so that you lose profit you could have easily had. Neuheisel is advocating a football equivalent: "leaving game-clock time on the table." You don't snap the ball at :15 on the game clock when you could just as easily have snapped it at :23. You don't run out of bounds when you could just as easily have turned up field. You don't call an immediate time out when you should be operating at a green pace. The head coach has an obligiation to help his players every way he can.

I agree that you take a touchdown whenever you can get it when you are behind. But it's not a very meaningful statement. In general, your opponent does not leave touchdown opportunities lying around for you to "take" one. However, I would agree in theory that if the defense started doing something **unsound** that opened a clear opportunity to grab a quick long-distance touchdown, you should go for it. A bird in the hand is worth two in the bush and I would rather be ahead and "put the situation on my defense" than be behind.

But that's a false issue, a straw man. The actual problem you confront in a game is a series of down-and-distance situations which generally require you to gain one to ten yards with no obvious opportunities to "take" a touchdown. You constantly compare your distance and time remaining to the pace chart and shift speeds to top-speed as soon as appropriate. In other words, you don't make just one decision per drive on how fast you want to score, you make and remake that decision on every play.

Bias against the defense

Football coaches should try to maximize the percentage of time their offense is on the field and minimize the percentage of time their defense is on the field. Americans love scoring, that is, they love offense. American sports authorities change the rules whenever the defense gets too successful.

In 1968, the Major League Baseball All-Star Game was won by a score of 1-0. Baseball authorities were horrified and immediately lowered the pitcher's mound and shrunk the strike zone.

Defenses used to be great in football. But look at this trend of major college average scores by both teams per game:

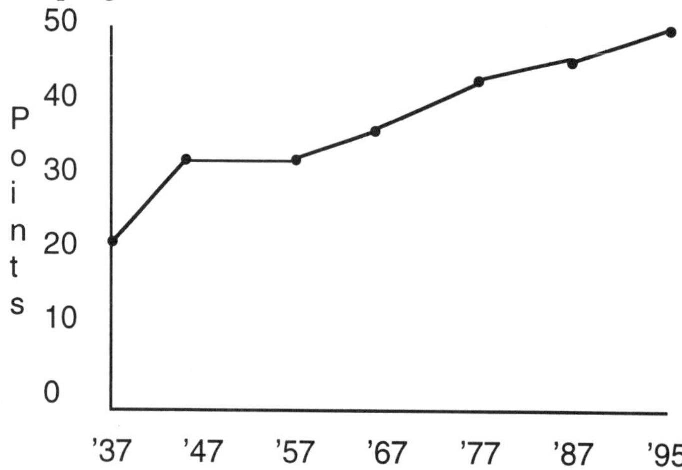

This is, in part, the result of rules changes designed to increase scoring, like the 1976 change permitting offensive blockers to extend arms.

In the fifties and early sixties, there were an average of three scoreless ties per season in major college play. There was only **one** scoreless tie total (Oregon-Oregon State, 1983) in the eighties and nineties before the 1996 tie breaker rule in college.

In the early sixties, the AFL, a separate league from the NFL, had a wide-open, high-scoring style of play. The NFL noticed it was a crowd-pleaser, especially after Super Bowl III, in which the NFL Colts were beaten by the AFL Jets. According to the Official NFL Chronology of Professional Football, in 1974,

> *Sweeping rules changes were adopted to add action and tempo to games...restrictions were placed on members of the punting team to open up return possibilities;...roll blocking and cutting of wide receivers was eliminated; the extent of downfield contact a defender could have with an eligible receiver was restricted; the penalties for offensive holding, illegal use of the hands, and tripping were reduced from 15 to 10 yards...*

In his book, *Football, the Violent Chess Match*, former Super Bowl-winning coach Tom Flores says,

> *With equal material a team should be able to stop the 11 offensive players with 17 men. If the defense ran a gap eight alignment to stop the run*

and had defenders in all six short zones and in all of the three deep passing zones, the offense would be hard pressed to move the ball.

Unfortunately, the defense upon which Rick Neuheisel will "put the situation" after he scores at a pace careless of the clock, is only allowed to have eleven guys.

The rules of football are explicitly designed so that the defense will fail on about 20% of the possessions. To draw a nautical analogy, football defenses have the job of keeping afloat a boat with a 20-gallon-per-minute leak and they are only allowed to use a 16-gallon-per-minute pump. Why? Because **the spectators want the boat to sink**.

If I were a prospective college defensive player or defensive coordinator, I would avoid head coaches who did not worry about scoring too fast.

Army–Auburn in the 1997 Independence Bowl

Army had a chance to run a last-possession-of-the-half slowdown in the 1997 Independence Bowl. They had the ball first and ten with 2:29 left in the first half at their own 44. That is a **top-speed hurry-up situation**. They completed a pass to the Auburn 22 with 1:50. First down. That turned it into an **inbounds hurry-up situation**. That is, Army should have taken about 20 seconds per play on its subsequent plays so as to leave around 20 seconds on the clock for Auburn after Army scored. Let's see how they did.

The completion stopped the clock to move the chains. Army could have let the clock run down to about 1:40 before snapping. In fact, Army snapped the ball at 1:38. Good job of clock management. But Army's quarterback McAda kept on the option and got all the way to the Auburn three-yard line. The clock stopped to move the chains with 1:30 left.

Now, Army is in a **maximum slow down situation**. They should run off almost the entire play clock before snapping. Figure 23 seconds, so they should snap at 1:30 - :23 = 1:07. But Army snapped at 1:21. Too fast. they scored on the play stopping the clock at 1:15. That was a gift to Auburn of 14 seconds—in what is often called "a game of inches" and could just as well be called "a game of seconds." Army was in a mindless hurry-up, unwittingly saving time for their opponent, time which there was almost no way Army could ever use themselves.

Auburn's drive

Auburn ran a **top-speed hurry-up** on their ensuing drive. Auburn got to the Army four with 19 seconds left. They turned the ball over by fumbling a pass reception into the end zone pylon. That gave Army the ball at the spot of the fumble, the four-yard line with 19 seconds left. Army took a knee to end the half.

Army was lucky. With 19 seconds left and first and goal at Army's four, Auburn would probably have taken one or two shots at a touchdown before kicking a field goal. But if Army had taken an additional 14 seconds off the clock before their last play, Auburn would have had just five seconds left when they got to Army's four. Surely they would have just tried a field goal rather than tried for a touchdown.

The four points involved would become extremely important at the end of the fourth quarter. See the Top-speed hurry-up chapter for details.

Surprise pass play

Sometimes, when you are running a slowdown and the opposing team knows it, it just might be appropriate to pop a pass. San Francisco quarterback John Brodie was once ahead by four points in a game against Atlanta with about **six minutes left** when coach Dick Nolan told him to run out the clock.

Brodie felt there was no way he could hang onto the ball for that long. Receiver Gene Washington came into the huddle and said, "The cornerback's cheating up. I can get deep on him." Brodie completed a bomb to Washington for a touchdown and caught hell when he got back to the bench.

9

Take a knee

Take-a-knee formation

You cannot just yell, "Take a knee!" to your team during a game. You must **teach** them the formation and have them do a couple reps of the play.

The formation is **double-tight ends** with **zero line splits**. The guards **interlock** their inside legs with the center's outside legs. That is, they put them behind the center's legs so that the guards inside feet are between the center's feet in high school and college. In the NFL, all linemen can lock legs. All linemen should get as close as possible to the neutral zone.

The quarterback is under center, assuming that's your regular mode of snapping. I ran a **single-wing** offense a couple of seasons. It would **not** have been prudent for us to put a quarterback under center even for one play because we had not practiced that snap. We likely would have fumbled it, which can be disastrous in that situation. So if you never snap with the quarterback under center, don't start on the last play of a close game.

Your **free safety** is behind the quarterback about five yards and he is playing **defense**. Put two **cornerbacks** at **halfback**—behind the guards and about two yards back. Their job is to recover any fumbled snaps—like a kick-return "hands" team. All the backs are in two-point stances focusing on their special responsibilities. There is no need for the backs to look like an offensive formation. The line, of course, must be in a legal formation. The defensive players need practice responding to the snap count and staying motionless before the snap. Here's a diagram of the take-a-knee formation:

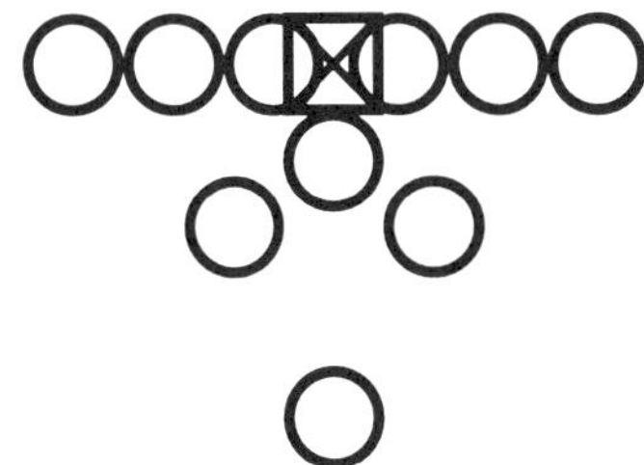

Have the quarterback deliberately fumble the snap so you can practice recovering it in this formation.

When can you start taking a knee?

The **worst-case** time each take-a-knee play takes when the other team has no timeouts is 40 seconds in the pros and 31 seconds in high school and college. That assumes the play itself only takes **one second**, that you run **all but one second off the play clock** before the snap (39 in the NFL and 24 in high school and college), and that the ref takes only **six seconds** to start the play clock for the next down in high school and college. In the NFL, the time the ref takes is irrelevant because the play clock starts on the end of the previous play.

In their excellent book, *The Hidden Game of Football*, authors Carroll, Palmer, and Thorn say an NFL team trying to run out the clock can take about 36 seconds per play.

Note that my times are based on the **worst case**. *The Hidden Game of Football* 36 seconds is based on the **usual** case. The difference between them and me is five seconds and that could be a big deal difference. I don't want to write that you can start taking a knee at three downs x 5 seconds = 15 seconds sooner, only to have you follow my advice in a game and get screwed because the referees gave the ready-to-play signal faster than normal. If you want to assume you can run off 36 seconds per play, be my guest.

Check your video tapes

I suggest that you keep track of the time you are able to run off the clock during practice when you run your two-minute drill. Also, tell your team videotaper to let the camera run instead of turning it off and on after every play during games. That way you can use your game tape to figure out how much time the refs in your conference take between the dead-ball whistle and the ready-to-play signal, as well as how fast the clock operators react after each play. I suspect that the clock operators are much faster at stopping the clock and slower at starting it when **their** team is behind at the non-televised levels.

When you find numbers that you are certain of in your league, modify my worst-case formula to fit your situation.

You actually have to get your knee down

High school referee Holly Newman told me she had a game in which a quarterback meant to take a knee, but only squatted down in a **low crouch**. His side was outraged when he got clobbered by the other team and no flag was thrown. Until part of your body other than your hands or feet touches the ground, you are fair game.

Wisconsin's last-minute 1996 loss to Northwestern

On October 19, 1996, Wisconsin was ahead 30-27 with 1:33 left in the game. As a result of a missed field goal, they got the ball at their own 38 yard line. Northwestern had one timeout left. The ESPN analysts said Wisconsin head coach Barry Alvarez should have told his quarterback to take a knee three times. Let's make a detailed list of the probable sequence if Wisconsin **had** just taken a knee several times:

time	down	distance	event
1:33	1	10	snap and take a knee
1:29	2	11	end-of-play whistle
1:23	2	11	ready-to-play whistle
0:59	2	11	snap and take a knee
0:56	3	12	end-of-play whistle and timeout called by Northwestern
	3	12	snap and take a knee
0:53	4	13	end-of-play whistle
0:47	4	13	ready-to-play whistle
0:23	4	13	take a safety, score now Wisconsin 30, Northwestern 29
0:18			end-of-play whistle, game clock stops
			free kick after safety
			ball touched by Northwestern, clock starts
0:16	1	10	Northwestern begins two-minute drill, probably around midfield, needing only a field goal to win

Too much time

In the actual game, Alvarez decided that he could **not** take a knee because of the time left and the fact that Northwestern had one timeout. On his first play, he called a dive to Ron Dayne which went for seven yards. He then had second down and three to go at the Wisconsin 45. When he snapped the ball for his second-down play, another dive, there must have been about 54 seconds left.

Freshman running back Dayne, who had been having a career day, never got the handoff. He said after the game, "I thought Mike [Samuel, the quarterback] was probably going to keep it and run with it." "Probably!?" Isn't a running back supposed to be **sure** what the play is? The quarterback said he thought the play call was clear.

Strong safety Eric Collier recovered the ball at the Wisconsin 41 with 37 seconds left.

And there were 12 seconds more than they thought

The officials then added 12 seconds to the clock because the clock operator had incorrectly let the clock run after Northwestern's field goal attempt. So Wisconsin would have been in much more trouble if they had taken the knee than even Alvarez thought. But you can't do anything about refs adding time back onto the clock.

Northwestern scored the winning touchdown two plays later. They kicked the extra point making the score Northwestern 34, Wisconsin 30. There were still 37 seconds left in the game, but Wisconsin was unable to score on the kick return or ensuing plays.

One first down THEN take a knee

If there had been no fumble, Dayne probably would have gotten the first down on his second-and-three run. There then would have been about 44 seconds left when the referees blew the ready-to-play whistle starting the play clock. In that first-down situation, even though Northwestern still had one timeout, Wisconsin could have taken a knee on successive snaps to end the game. Each snap consumes at least 31 seconds including the play itself, the refs positioning the ball, and the play-clock time that elapses before the offense has to snap again. Even with a timeout stopping the game clock during one play-clock/position-the-ball time, Wisconsin could still burn about 60 seconds by taking a knee twice, once they got a first down.

The highest percentage play was to try to get a first down. The 260-pound Dayne had just gained seven yards on the previous play. Dayne had gained 139 yards on 28 carries earlier in the game—five yards a carry. With only three yards to go and two downs to do it, Alvarez might have called a quarterback keeper. But then there's the question of who is more likely to have the ball stripped, a running back who is highly experienced at protecting the ball, or a quarterback, who rarely runs with it?

The take-a-knee formula

You can create a formula. K = 40(D -1) in the NFL and K = 31(D -1) in high school and college, where K is game clock time remaining when you can start taking a knee to run out the clock, and D is the number of downs remaining. You have to use D - 1 because the fourth-down play doesn't trigger a fourth play-clock period after the dead-ball whistle. The game clock runs **after** you take a knee. And on fourth down, taking a knee causes a change of possession so the clock **stops** after the knee.

Also, for every **timeout** the opponent has, you subtract a down. To be precise, you can run off about two seconds even when they have and use a timeout. They cannot call timeout until the ref blows your take-a-knee play dead. So the formulas are NFL K = 40(D - 1 - T) and HS/NCAA K = 31(D - 1- T), where T = number of opponent timeouts left.

Actually, we need two more refinements. Although your fourth-down play does not start another play-clock period while the game clock is running, the play **itself** still takes a little time off the clock. Let's figure two seconds and add that to the formula. Also, although the game clock does not run after you take a knee on the downs when your opponent calls timeouts, it does run **during** the play, so we need to add at least two more seconds for each timeout:

NFL	K = 40(D - 1 - T) + 2T + 2
High school and college	K = 31(D - 1 - T) + 2T + 2

This formula gives the time remaining **when you snap** the ball for the down in question. The formula requires that you **ignore the any timeouts in excess of D-1**.

What this formula says is that in the NFL, you can take 40 seconds off the clock by taking a knee on first-, second-, or third-down plays when the defense has no timeouts left and two seconds on each play when they **do** have a timeout left plus two seconds on the fourth-down play. In high school and college, the post-play time consumption depends on the ref's speed at giving the ready-to-play signal.

Let's apply this formula to Barry Alvarez's situation against Northwestern in their 1996 game. When Wisconsin got the ball, there was 1:33 left and Northwestern had one timeout left. So the formula is K = 31(D - 1- T) + 2T + 2 = 31(4 downs - 1 - 1 timeout) + 2 + 2 = 31(2) + 2 + 2 = 66 seconds or 1:06. That is, Wisconsin could take a knee if there were only 1:06 remaining, but not with 1:33 remaining.

Game clock before first-down snap

You can run time off the game clock **before** a first-down snap if the previous play was the **gaining of a first down** by that same team. On a gained first down, the referee gives the ready-to-play signal when the chains have been moved and you can run as much as 24 seconds off the game clock before the first down snap. So in college and the NFL, you can add another 24 seconds to the take-a-knee time if you **gain** a first down as opposed to your first down following a kicking play or turnover on downs or other event that stops the clock until the snap.

No time for algebra

You do not have time to do algebra on the sideline during a game. And sideline computers are prohibited in high school and college (H.S. Rule 1-6-1 and NCAA Rule 1-4-9b). So those coaches need a **table**. You need to make your own when-you-can-take-a-knee table based on your own assumptions about how long your plays will last and how much time the refs will take to give the ready-to-play signal. Here's a table based on **my** worst-case assumptions described above.

When you can take a knee in terms of seconds left in the half

Worst case

H.S.&NCAA

		Opponent timeouts left			
		0	1	2	3
	1	1:35	1:06	:37	:08
Down	2	1:04	:35	:06	:06
	3	:33	:04	:04	:04
	4	:02	:02	:02	:02

NFL

		Opponent timeouts left			
		0	1	2	3
	1	2:02	1:24	:46	:08
Down	2	1:22	:44	:06	:06
	3	:42	:04	:04	:04
	4	:02	:02	:02	:02

Here's the same table using the 36 seconds that *The Hidden Game of Football* authors assume rather than my 31 seconds for high school, college, and NFL stopped-clock plays.

Worst case assuming 36 seconds

		Opponent timeouts left			
		0	1	2	3
	1	1:50	1:16	:42	:08
Down	2	1:14	:40	:06	:06
	3	:38	:04	:04	:04
	4	:02	:02	:02	:02

When NOT to take a knee

Do **not** take a knee on **fourth down** unless you do it **after the horn**. Do **not** take a knee **in your own end zone** unless the horn has sounded and you are ahead by more than two points.

Increasing the time used by the take-a-knee play

Most quarterbacks hurry to the ground when they run a take-a-knee play. If you hurry, the play only takes **one second** off the clock. But hurrying on a take-a-knee play is a contradiction in terms. By definition, you are trying to run out the clock. Why hurry to end the play when you are trying to waste time? *Rather you should stay standing as long as possible. You want to get down* ***before you are tackled****, because you want to avoid being stripped.* But there is no sense to taking the knee long before any defender is about to tackle you. By waiting as long as possible, you can stretch the amount of time run off by a take-a-knee play from one second up to three or four.

Yards lost per take-a-knee play

In 1986, there were 291 take-a-knee plays in the NFL. They lost a total of 600 yards or about **two yards per play**. There are times when you might want to **reduce** that to one yard or zero—for example when you start on your own three-yard line. In the typical take-a-knee play, the quarterback receives the snap, which moves the ball back about one yard, then steps back another yard before he drops to one knee.

To reduce it to a **one-yard loss**, he could take a knee right where he receives the snap. To reduce it to **zero**, the quarterback will have to run a sneak, but he should make it a low-head-for-the-ground-at-the-original-spot-of-the-ball charge. *You do **not** risk a tackle and fumble when you have passed the take-a-knee point.*

You should, at least once per season, have each quarterback take a knee three times starting at his own two- or three-yard-line.

Greatest NFL game ever—no take a knee!

I was amazed when I analyzed the Miami-Raiders Divisional Playoff game of 12/21/74, a game which many believe was the greatest NFL game ever, that the winning team, the Raiders, **never took a knee**, even though they were ahead and in possession at the end of the game. The Raiders were ahead 28-26.

The Raiders' Phil Villapiano intercepted Griese's pass with :13 left in the game. Miami had at least two timeouts left. That would make the Raiders' take-a-knee point **:46** according to my worst-case take-a-knee table. So they were already in take-a-knee. Even if the Dolphins had **three** timeouts, the worst-case take-a-knee point would still be **:08**.

On the first play, Raiders' fullback Marv Hubbard ran over left guard for 6 yards. If Miami had three timeouts left, the Raiders needed to get **another first down**. In high school, I'd have the quarterback keep. In the NFL, the quarterbacks are too valuable for that. So no complaint about the first down handoff call—if Miami had three timeouts.

Miami stopped the clock at :07 with a timeout after the play. At this point, it seems to me that Oakland should take a knee for the rest of the game. Running with the ball risks a fumble and is unnecessary. But run they did. Hubbard went over left guard again for a gain of one. Miami called another timeout stopping the clock at :03. This situation, third down with :03 left, is **definitely** take-a-knee no matter how many timeouts Miami has. But again Oakland did a handoff and Hubbard ran around left end for a 9-yard gain, ending the game. The Raiders should not have risked **either** a handoff or a strip once they passed the take-a-knee point. It may have been the greatest game, but it wasn't the smartest last series.

Injury on the take-a-knee play

A friend of mine's freshman team took a knee at the end of a game. An enraged defensive lineman, apparently angry about losing, charged through the line and hit the quarterback, twisting his leg such that he was out for the rest of the season. The other members of the team must **block** on the take-a-knee play. Hard feelings are common in take-a-knee situations and injuries are likely if one team attacks while the other relaxes.

In addition, the quarterback can protect himself by not literally taking a knee. Instead, *drop to a fumble recovery position with your back to the line of scrimmage.*

In the NFL, which is the take-a-knee situation we see the most on TV, defenders usually behave in an injury-avoiding and gentlemanly way when the quarterback begins to take a knee. Also, I suspect the NFL would hit a defender who injured a quarterback during a take-a-knee play with a big fine. You can't count on that in high school or college.

The quarterback-keep-sweep-slide

An argument could be made that the take-a-knee play is **not** the **best** one to run in situations where the amount of time left makes the decision to take a knee a close call. Taking a knee, **slowly**, takes about three or four seconds per play off the clock.

Running a quarterback-keep sweep can increase both the play time (at all levels) as well as the referee's fetch-and-move-the-ball-back-to-the-hash-mark time (in high school and college). As with a take-a-knee play, you should avoid both a handoff and being tackled. You can do that by making the sweep a quarterback keeper and by telling the quarterback to slide NFL-style when he is about to be hit. He must also make sure to **stay in bounds**.

As described in the Overview chapter, a sweep takes about **seven** seconds, especially when run to the **wide** side of the field. Furthermore, when the play is over, the ref must move the ball back to the hash mark, which takes extra game-clock time in high school and college. On a take-a-knee play, the refs simply put the ball on the ground where it is and can blow the ready-to-play whistle faster in high school and college. In the NFL, this would be a 40-second-clock situation and there would be no game-clock benefit to making the ref bring the ball back into a hash.

An extra ten seconds

You can't be sure, but I figure the keep-sweep-slide play would run off about ten more seconds than a take-a-knee play in high school and college, seven seconds more in the NFL. If you got the ball on first down and your opponent had no timeouts left, ten seconds more per play would enable you to start your no-need-to-make-a-first-down offense 3 downs x 10 = **thirty seconds sooner**! Actually, by doing the same on the fourth-down play, you would run an extra 37 seconds off the clock!

Here's the table shown above, only redone using these formulas:

NFL	K = 46(D - 1 - T) + 7T + 7
High school and college	K = 41(D - 1 - T) + 10T + 7

Again, you must ignore opponent timeouts in excess of D - 1.

Sweep slide

H.S.&NCAA — **Opponent timeouts left**

Down	0	1	2	3
1	2:10	1:39	1:08	:37
2	1:29	:58	:27	:27
3	:48	:17	:17	:17
4	:07	:07	:07	:07

NFL — **Opponent timeouts left**

Down	0	1	2	3
1	2:25	1:46	1:07	:28
2	1:39	1:00	:21	:21
3	:53	:14	:14	:14
4	:07	:07	:07	:07

If my figures are correct, **Wisconsin Coach Barry Alvarez could have won** that Northwestern game after all, not by taking a knee, but by doing quarterback sweep-slides. Remember, Wisconsin had first down with 1:33 left in the game and Northwestern had one timeout left. That means they were past the sweep-slide point of 1:39.

Actually, you'll also recall they subsequently **added twelve seconds back** onto the clock because of a clock operator error. So the situation **really** turned out to be 1:45, first down, and one opponent timeout left. No sweat. Alvarez could pick up an extra second or two by **deliberately taking a delay-of-game penalty**. Then he could **deliberately take a safety** on fourth down, which would take even more time off the clock than a sweep-slide play. The first three downs would be used to gradually move back toward the goal line to facilitate the fourth-down safety.

Remember he started at his own 32-yard line and was ahead by three. Between the delay-of-game penalty and running about 30 yards backward and about 30 yards sideways for the safety, he ought to be able to find another six seconds. The final gun should sound during the safety play.

If you start out inside your own ten-yard line or so, you probably cannot run more than one or two sweep-slide plays without giving up a safety.

On the other hand, you could use the quarterback-keep-sweep slide to set up taking a safety if you were out at midfield, ahead by three or more points, and within the quarterback-keep-sweep-slide period. You would run it one way, then the other, then back the first way, arriving around your own ten-yard line for your fourth-down play, like this:

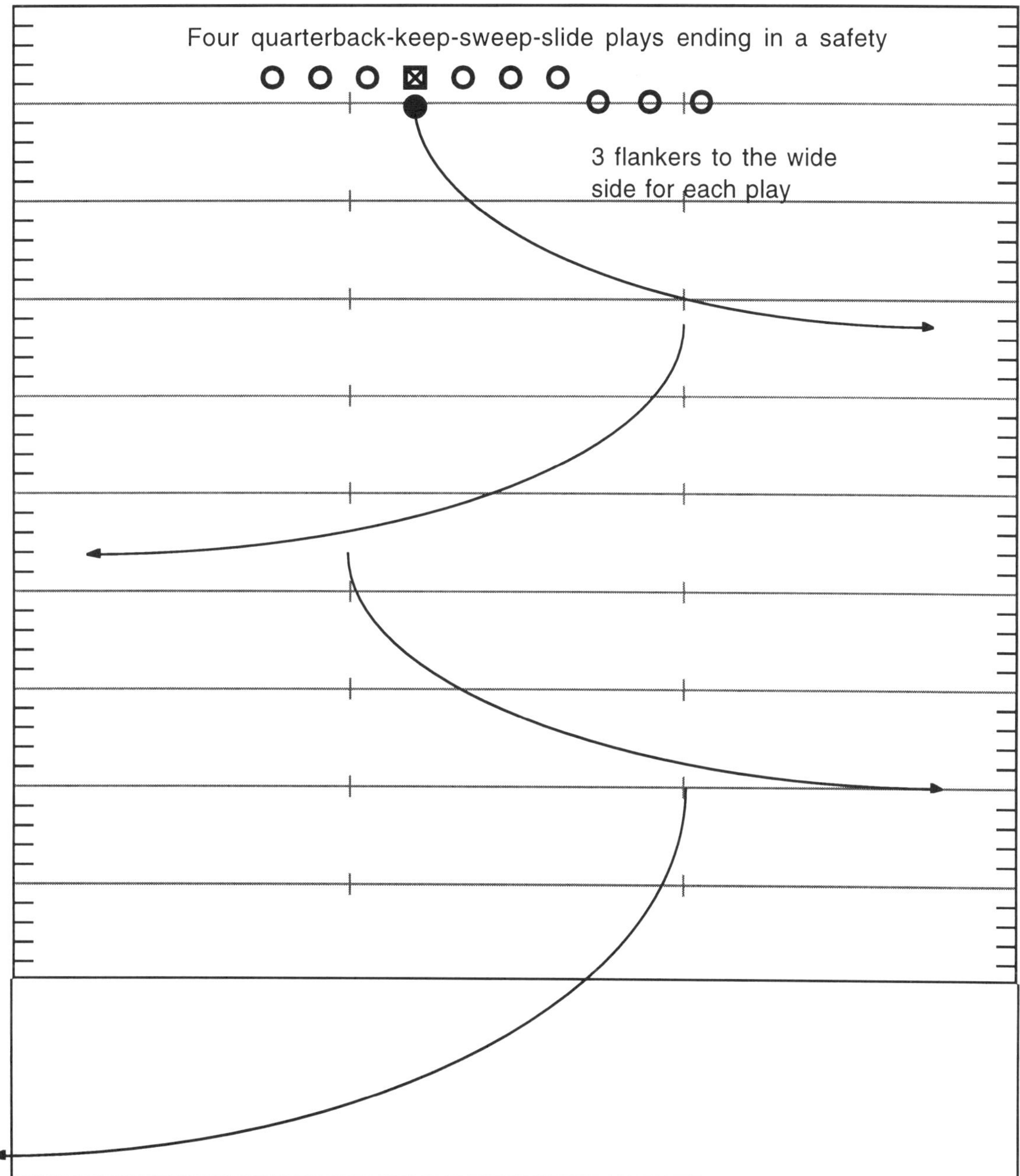

No play needed when game clock less than the play clock

When the **game** clock is running and has fewer seconds left in the period than the **play** clock, you do **not** need to run any more plays. And you **should not** run any more. In the **NFL**, this would happen when the previous play ended with less that **40 seconds** on the game clock, unless there was some extraordinary event like a timeout after the play. In high school and college, this would happen when the **ready-to-play whistle** came after there were less than **25 seconds** left on the game clock.

Actually, the play clock is not supposed to **start** in this situation, in college at least. NCAA Rule 3-2-2(f) says the play clock is not started when there is less than 25 seconds left in any of the four periods. I saw no rule against starting the play clock in the high school or the NFL rules, but since it is mathematically impossible to violate the delay-of-game rule in such a situation, there is no point in starting the play clock.

Fake take-a-knee play before halftime

Teams take a knee before the end of both halves. In the second half, there is no point in screwing around. You are ahead. Taking a knee wins the game.

But at the end of the **first** half, **either** team could be taking a knee: the **trailing** team or the **leading** team. And neither team can win the game by taking a knee at the end of the first half. Either team could use another score. Accordingly, the fake take-a-knee play **should** come to mind. Line up in your take-a-knee formation. Ostentatiously yell "Take a knee! Take a knee!" Then pop a pass.

In general, this would only work **deep in your own territory** because if you were farther out, your taking a knee would not be believable. Although at the lower levels, the defense may not be smart enough to recognize that you were playing possum.

I am not aware of any case histories. Bill Walsh did a fake take-a-knee play at the **end of a game** against the Cardinals in 1982. The pass was overthrown. *Sports Illustrated's* Paul Zimmerman said it "makes absolutely no sense at all" to do a fake take-a-knee at the end of a game. I agree. The Cardinals were ready to kill Walsh when the game ended.

Walsh apologized. "I don't know what I was thinking at the time."

Buddy Ryan also did this to Jimmy Johnson at the end of a game according to Zimmerman. Onetime 49er Russ Francis told Zimmerman that the fake take-a-knee play before halftime violates a "gentlemen's agreement" in the NFL. Maybe so, but as far as I'm concerned, it's a legitimate play. Like everything else, this play needs to be practiced.

Reaching take-a-knee on the fly

I have never heard anyone discuss this, but you often reach the take-a-knee point on the fly. That is, while your ball carrier is running with the ball, he passes the first-down marker, thereby turning a **pre**-take-a-knee situation into take-a-knee. So what?

Well, *one of the key principles of take-a-knee situations is that you never risk a tackle.* When you are in the series **before** the take-a-knee point, you must get one more first down. And you have to risk a tackle to gain yards and get the first down. But when you cross the first-down line, and thereby move into the take-a-knee period, you should no longer risk tackles. *So the ball carrier should slide as soon as he is about to be tackled after crossing the first down line, if that first down puts his team into the take-a-knee period.*

For example, you are ahead, the opponent has no timeouts, and you snap the ball with third and four. There's :58 left in the game. When your ball carrier crosses the four-yard point, the **new** situation is first and ten with about :54 left.

Third down with :58 left and no opponent timeouts left is **pre**-take-a-knee (in high school and college). But **first** down with :54 left **is** take-a-knee. As soon as the ball carrier gains the yards needed to get a first down, the game is over, if he's smart. But every step he takes in the vicinity of a defender risks snatching defeat from the jaws of victory.

You must teach your offense that *when they get the last first down you need, they must slide before being tackled.* You must practice this. You should have a word or phrase to describe this situation, like "First down and slide," and that word or phrase should be repeated in the huddle before each next-to-last-series play.

The same applies when you are ahead **on defense** near the end of a game. *If your defense recovers a fumble or makes an interception after your team has reached take-a-knee, they should not advance the ball. Rather they should take a knee.* Your clock-management assistant coach should be holding up his **checkered-pattern panel** starting the moment the time remaining and opponent timeouts left means your team has reached take-a-knee. Furthermore, he should call the attention of your defensive players to the checkered pattern and they should tell each other, "Take a knee if you get possession! Take a knee if you get possession!" If a defender does acquire possession during a play, his teammates should yell, "Take a knee! Take a knee!" to remind him not to run with the ball.

10

Turnover avoidance

Many late, come-from-nine-or-more-points-behind victories involve turnovers. So preserving victory when you have the lead necessarily means turnover avoidance. There are four kinds of turnovers:

- fumbles
- interceptions
- punts
- missed field goals

Most people don't think of punts and missed field goals as turnovers. Does possession change on a punt or missed field goal? I rest my case.

To put it in a way that most people agree with, in a close game, you need to keep the ball out of the other team's hands. That means not fumbling, throwing an interception, or failing to get a first down.

Fumbles

You have to **coach basics** like carrying the ball properly and protecting it in traffic. You need to give the ball to **experienced ball carriers** in pressure situations. And you need to **bench** or move to a non-ball-handling role any **player who chronically fumbles**. The NFL's Dexter Carter was an excellent kick returner, but he was a chronic fumbler and lost several NFL jobs as a result.

Second-stringers

Second-stringers are often a source of key fumbles. Many experts consider the 1935 Notre Dame-Ohio State game the **greatest college football game ever**.

With just over a minute left, Notre Dame missed a PAT leaving Ohio State ahead 13-12. Ohio State returned Notre Dame's ensuing onside kick to their own 47-yard line. Bill Shanklin's book *Against All Odds* did not say how many timeouts Notre Dame had left, if any. But he did say,

> *Now, all that stood between Ohio State and victory was for them to run out the clock, to freeze the ball.*

I would need to know the number of timeouts Notre Dame had to determine if Ohio State had reached the take-a-knee point. According to my table in the "Take a knee" chapter, Ohio State could start taking a knee if Notre Dame had fewer than two timeouts left. (You can start taking a knee on first down at 1:06 if your opponent has one timeout left. If they have two or three, you have to get one more first down.)

But Ohio State had a **substitute** halfback named Dick Beltz, carry the ball. He fumbled to Notre Dame, stopping the clock because the play also went out of bounds. Ohio State ran a fake-punt pass or a roll-out pass from a short-punt formation (an old-time offense where you were in a sort of punt formation for all four downs). The punter pulled the ball down and ran all the way to Notre Dame's 19.

Ohio State's Beltz, playing both ways which was normal at the time, dropped an interception of a Notre Dame pass. There were 40 seconds left. Notre Dame threw a pass for the game-winning touchdown. Final score: Notre Dame 18, Ohio State 13. Sports writer Damon Runyon wrote,

> *Notre Dame suddenly grabs victory not only from the jaws of defeat—but from defeat's esophagus.*

Lesson learned: *avoid having second-stingers carry the ball in a close game*. Possible lesson also illustrated, *when you reach the take-a-knee point, take a knee.*

Some fumbles inevitable

But once you have taught the fundamentals and put the right people in the ball-carrying roles, there is not much you can do to further reduce fumbles. In the NFL, there appears to be no correlation between success and fumbles lost.

The 12/15/95 *Wall Street Journal* had an article on the meaning of fumbles and interceptions in the NFL. They showed that the top four teams in 1994, the 49ers, Cowboys, Chargers, and Steelers lost 50 fumbles among them. But the bottom four teams, the Oilers, Bengals, Redskins, and Rams, only lost 32 fumbles.

Fumbles, they said, were a matter of luck and not a very good indicator of a good or bad team. A fumble, of course, is not necessarily lost to the other team. Only about half of fumbles result in a change of possession. (Interceptions, on the other hand, were a very good indicator of success.)

The Hidden Game of Football authors tracked 431 NFL turnover fumbles and found the following:

- 30 were fumbled center-quarterback exchanges
- 177 were on running plays (1.3% of rushes)
- 155 were on passing plays
  - 69 by the passer
  - 86 by the receiver
- 35 were on punt returns
- 25 were on kickoff returns
- 5 were on pass interception returns
- 4 were by punters

The clock-management aspect of turnovers is that late in a close game, the value of everything, including turnovers, is orders of magnitude greater. Coaches must not make the mistake of giving **normal** weight to turnover risk when the game situation has **magnified** the cost of a turnover greatly.

Avoid tricky ball handling?

Some people say that you should avoid tricky ball-handling plays, like the triple option, to avoid fumbles. I disagree. Option teams generally **must** use their option to be successful. They have spent too much time on it and not enough on other types of plays to get away from the option in a crucial game situation. Furthermore, fumble avoidance is part of **teaching** the option. What you emphasize, you achieve. What you demand, you get. And if you want to play option football, you'd better emphasize and demand turnover avoidance.

Air Force has run the triple option for many years. In 1994, they were tied for eighth in the nation in **turnover margin** with an average of plus one per game. They had 16 fumbles lost, which tied them for **most fumbles lost** among the top 21 turnover margin teams that year. But they only lost 4 interceptions, the fewest among the top 21 turnover margin teams. **Interception avoidance** is one of the most **overlooked** benefits of the triple option offense. Air Force's 1994 team was also 13th in the nation in total offense with 435 yards per game.

One of the top high school football teams in the world, De La Salle, is located near me in Concord, CA. They run the veer triple option. In 1996, they lost only nine turnovers, second in the region to two teams that lost eight.

In 1996, I had my high school freshman team run the option. (We called the dive play in advance rather than reading a dive key and deciding whether to give the ball to the fullback. But we did a true option on the pitch key.)

We did not run the option well because our quarterbacks were not very good running backs. But whenever I saw a ball hit the ground in practice on an option pitch, I made both players, the quarterback and the pitchback, drop and give me five pushups. **Before** I instituted that penalty, about a third of the pitches hit the ground in drills. **After** I instituted it, the number of fumbles instantly fell to about one per day in practice. We **never** fumbled an option pitch in a game all season, even though our first-string quarterback had never played tackle football before.

Skip the handoff

In general, you need to stick with your normal running game when there is still so much time left in the game that you will have to get multiple first downs to preserve your lead. But *when you get down to where you only need one more first down to get to take-a-knee time, you might eliminate the handoff. Consider running one or more quarterback keepers.*

That's what Tom Cruise's player character said to Craig T. Nelson's coach character in the football movie, *All the Right Moves*. "If youda had Rifleman [the quarterback] hold onto the ball, we woulda won the game."

Wisconsin coach Barry Alvarez did **not** do a dumb thing when he called for the fatal handoff to Ron Dayne in their 1996 game with Northwestern. But it is true that there is **no** chance of fumbling the exchange if you **eliminate** the exchange. Alvarez's decision to do a handoff instead of a quarterback keeper does not seem like a **bad** idea absent hindsight. But neither does it seem that a handoff was **necessary** with second and four.

There is no handoff in a take-a-knee situation. One reason is to avoid the turnover danger. Taking a knee avoids **two** things:

- the possibility of fumbling an exchange with a running back

• the tackle.

The situation that immediately precedes the take-a-knee situation is the need-one-more-first-down-situation. Running a quarterback-keeper play in the last series before you reach the take-a-knee point is a sensible transition from your normal running game to the other extreme: taking a knee on every snap.

OK. I acknowledge that quarterback keepers are not appropriate in the NFL. But the NFL is weird compared to the rest of the football when it comes to the importance of quarterbacks. Pro football teams are like those singing groups with names like "Diana Ross and the Supremes" or "Dion and the Belmonts." If Dallas is really "Troy Aikman and the Cowboys," which it is, you'd better not have Troy running quarterback keepers that end in his being tackled by Chuck Cecil or some such. And you should probably extend that principle to some college teams like Danny Wurfel and the Gators. But for the rest of football, the quarterback keeper during the last series before the take-a-knee point makes sense if it does not prevent you from getting that last first down.

Center-quarterback exchange

It is just good football for you to make sure your centers and quarterbacks get enough reps to eliminate fumbled center-quarterback exchanges. That applies to your entire season, not just clock-management situations.

One of the lessons I learned coaching at Miramonte High School was to look for any excuse to give the centers reps snapping to the quarterbacks. My centers snapped to our quarterbacks during the beginning-of-practice warm-up throws, during pass-pattern practice, during option practice, during sled drills, during pre-game warm-ups, during bird-dog drills (offensive linemen take the first step only and point at the man they will block), during sled drills, as well as during scrimmages and eleven-man drills. My 1996 freshman team never fumbled the snap all season.

The only clock-management admonition I would make for a team that is ahead is to *avoid putting an inexperienced center or quarterback into the game.*

One of the least talked about reasons for failure in football is inexperienced substitutes. Just about any coach who has a few years experience can relate key plays in important games where his team lost because an injury sub didn't know what he was doing. With the center-quarterback exchange, where a great deal of experience is required even for the regular starters, an inexperienced player can be fatal.

Also, avoid centers playing with quarterbacks when there is a **dislike** between the two players in question. The center-quarterback exchange requires intimate cooperation. When the center and the quarterback do not like each other, the ball will end up on the ground even if that particular center is fine with other quarterbacks and that particular quarterback is fine with other centers.

I decide who plays what position normally. But centers are one exception. I pick them, but the quarterbacks have **veto power** over whom I pick. *Do not have an incompatible center-quarterback team at all*, especially late in a close game.

Interceptions

An interception is about five times more likely to be returned for a touchdown than a fumble according to the aforementioned *Wall Street Journal* article. And even if it's not returned for a touchdown, they can score on a subsequent play. The main thing is as long as you possess the ball outside of your own end zone, the other team cannot score. So an obvious way to avoid turnovers is to refrain from passing.

Virtually everyone reading this book knew that before they started reading. But let's examine the issue a bit more closely especially in light of my admonition to begin the slow-down, and therefore avoid passes, as soon as you are about to take the lead, which is often in the first quarter.

Interceptions are very important

In 1994, the **top** four NFL teams actually had a **worse** lost-fumble total than the **worst** four teams. But in **interceptions**, the top four were way ahead of the bottom four—79 to 55. The top two teams, the Niners and Cowboys, each lost more fumbles than it got: 12-13 and 9-10 respectively. But those two teams made far more interceptions than they gave up: 23-11 and 22-14.

Incidence of interceptions

In 1995, all **NFL** teams combined attempted 16,699 passes. Five hundred twelve or 3% were intercepted. The quarterbacks with the lowest interception percentages in each league were Jim Harbaugh and Troy Aikman, both at 1.6%.

With those kinds of interception percentages, I would not have much fear of passing. But most of the people reading this book are not coaching Troy Aikman on how to throw to Michael Irvin.

The number one passing offense in NCAA division I-A in 1994 was Georgia. They attempted 462 passes, of which 14 or 3% were intercepted. The number one passing **defense** in NCAA I-A was Miami of Florida. They intercepted the ball 6.14% of the time.

The 1994 percentages at lower college divisions were

Level	Best passing offense	Interception %	Best interception defense	Interception %
I-AA	Alcorn State	4%	Robert Morris Col.	9.45%
II	West TX A&M	3%	Bentley	8%
III	Hanover	4%	Albion	10%

The 1996 year-end **high school** stats in my local newspaper indicate that the highest-rated passer (Kearns of league champion Alhambra, 216.8 rating) attempted 151 passes and was intercepted 4 times or 3% of the time. The lowest-rated passer (Martin of Las Lomas, 75.8 rating) attempted 117 passes and was intercepted 13 times or 11% of the time.

I analyzed some **junior varsity** high school video in 1996 and found the completion rate was about 33% and the interception rate was about 9%.

Bottom line, every 15 passes or so, below the NFL level, you are going to throw an interception.

The other passing turnovers

Interceptions are not the only turnovers that come from calling pass plays. Often, the ball gets **knocked out of the quarterback's hand**. In 1995, quarterback Brett Favre led the Packers in fumbles with eight. Backup Packer quarterbacks Ty Detmer and T. J. Rubley each had one.

You can also complete the pass, only to have the **receiver**, who is in a vulnerable position after the catch, get **stripped** of the ball. The second highest number of fumbles on the Packers in 1995 was Antonio Freeman's seven. He's a receiver. In contrast, their best running back, Edgar Bennett, only had two fumbles all season.

When it gets to crunch time in a game, and you need to avoid turnovers. Far and away *the best method of avoiding turnovers in football is to refrain from passing, which you should do, **IF** you can get the first downs you need without passing.*

Punts are turnovers

A punt that goes beyond the line of scrimmage is a turnover. (Little known fact: you can punt to a teammate as long as the punt does not cross the LOS. He can then advance the ball.) If it's fourth down, **any** play that does not result in a first down for the punting team is a turnover.

So you cannot get so turnover-avoidance conscious that you fail to get a first down because you limited your offense too much and are forced to punt. You ought to have a list of plays for each situation when you go to your game. That list probably has both run and pass plays for most situations. The success probability ought to be about the same or you wouldn't have listed both plays for that situation.

When you are more turnover conscious than normal, namely when you are in the lead, prefer the running play to the equivalent passing play.

Just as passing has more than one kind of turnover—interception, fumble by the quarterback, and strip of the receiver—so do punt plays have more than one way to turn the ball over:

- punt which is returned
- punt which is not returned but stays in bounds
- punt which is not returned because it went out of bounds (or into the end zone in high school)
- blocked punt, bad snap, fumble by punter.

There are turnovers and there are turnovers

All turnovers are not created equal. A good punt that is fair caught or an unreturned interception of a deep pass at least has a good field-position result for the team that loses the ball. When the punt team is leading and trying to waste time, punts and deep interceptions that stay in bounds also have the benefit of running off some game-clock time.

I like to kick **out of bounds** on punts because I think the punt return is one of the most dangerous plays in football. In 1995, there were 1,042 punt returns in the NFL. The average return was 9.4 yards, but ten were returned all the way for **touchdowns**. And eleven were blocked.

Blocked-punt touchdowns

The total number of **fumbles** returned for touchdowns in the NFL in 1995 was 33, more than three times the number of **punt returns** for touchdowns! (There were a total of 403 fumbles lost in the NFL in 1995, so the percentage returned for touchdowns was 33 ÷ 403 = 8%.) In 1986, 28 punts were blocked in the NFL—and 14 or **half** were returned for touchdowns! The only thing more dangerous than a punt return is a blocked punt.

If the two stats above are representative, a regular NFL **fumble** has an **8%** chance of being picked up and run in for a touchdown while a **blocked punt** has a **50%** chance of the same end result. I suspect a **bad punt snap** has about as high a touchdown probability as a blocked punt.

One year when I was head coach of a youth football team, my line was so weak that I always ran a fake punt on fourth down rather than punt. I explained to my players and coaches that if we tried to punt, it would likely be blocked and run in for a touchdown. I'd rather turn the ball over on downs and make the other team get the touchdown the hard way.

One of my relatively inexperienced assistant coaches thought I was crazy and got so frustrated that he went behind my back and told our fake punter to actually punt on one occasion. It was blocked and run in for a touchdown.

An NFL Films segment discusses Pittsburgh's Chuck Noll making a similar decision in Super Bowl X against Dallas. With fourth and nine to go and about a minute left, Noll called an off-tackle play instead of a punt. Noll took into account that Dallas had no timeouts left and that they had almost blocked two earlier punts in the game. Plus his punter had dropped one snap in the game. Noll simply did not have confidence in his punting game and knew the danger of a blocked punt.

Quarterback Terry Hanratty gave the ball to running back Rocky Bleier. The play failed to gain the first down and the ball went over on downs. Dallas quarterback Roger Staubach then went to work against the Steel Curtain defense. He completed one pass to a wide-open Preston Pearson, but Pearson turned toward the middle of the field instead of getting out of bounds to stop the clock. Dallas's final Hail Mary passes were incomplete and Pittsburgh won 21-17.

The hierarchy of punt turnovers

Here's the hierarchy of punt turnovers from the perspective of a punt team which is leading in the game:

Worst: blocked punt, bad snap, fumble by punter, or return for big yards
Second best: punt out of bounds (uses **less time** than inbounds punt)
Best: zero-return inbounds punt (fair catch, tackled immediately, or downed after it stops rolling in high school or college) (Don't touch a scrimmage kick in the NFL.)

If your long snapper or punt protection are questionable, and you are ahead at the end of a game, attempting a punt is ***not*** *advisable because of the instant touchdown return potential if the punt does not get off.*

Fake punt

If your long snapper is solid, but your line is the problem, you can run a fake punt. That will burn time off the clock and eliminate the possibility of a blocked punt. The fake punt is the most overlooked, underrated play in football. It was only attempted eight times in the NFL in 1995, all in the NFC. I have the 1995 third- and fourth-down efficiencies of each NFL team. The fourth-down efficiency (success rate at getting a first down when they go for it on fourth down) is higher than the third-down efficiency. Here are some examples:

Team	third-down efficiency	fourth-down efficiency
Bills	31.6%	53.8%
Broncos	43.0%	44.4%
Colts	39.0%	63.2%
Chiefs	35.5%	68.2%
Dolphins	45.9%	76.9%
Steelers	42.2%	55.0%
Cowboys	44.6%	61.5%
Packers	49.1%	62.5%
49ers	48.9%	61.1%

The only team in this list that did not make the first down **most of the time** when they went for it on fourth down was the 8-8 Broncos. And **every** team had a higher fourth-down conversion rate than their third-down conversion rate.

In 1986 in the NFL, twelve fake punts were called by their coaches and 8 resulted in first downs! Furthermore, the punters also ran or passed for **four more** first downs when they got bad snaps and had to **improvise**. Like I said, an underrated play.

Which is the 'gamble' when you are ahead late in the game?

When you "gamble" by going for it on fourth down, about the worst that can happen is that you fall short and turn the ball over on downs after a short gain. If you take the "conservative" approach and punt, you **may lose the game right on that play** if the receiving teams runs either the punt or a blocked punt or bad snap in for a touchdown. And what's the **best** thing that can happen if the punt gets off and there is no return?

The average punt in the NFL in 1995 was 41.8 yards and the average return was 9.4 yards. That gives an average **net punt** of 41.8 - 9.4 = 32.4 yards. If you figure the average failed fourth-down conversion attempt gained two yards, the net benefit of punting compared to going for it unsuccessfully is about 30 yards—in the NFL. But most coaches don't coach in the NFL.

Shorter net punts at lower levels

At the lower levels, the average punt **returns** are longer. In 1995 the best NFL punt return team was Minnesota at 11.8 yards. The best team punt return averages at the various **college** levels in 1995 were:

Division	Team	Average punt return
I-A	Ball State	19.9
I-AA	Towson State	19.5
II	Adams State	16.6
III	Frostburg State	15.23

I do not have stats on the **average** net punts in college, high school, or youth levels. The top twenty NCAA Division I and II teams had net punts ranging from the high 30s to the low 40s in 1995. The top twenty NCAA Division III schools had average net punts of about 33 to about 38 yards. Remember, those figures are for the **top twenty** teams. The **average** college team has shorter net punts.

High school and youth players are smaller and younger so their punts will clearly travel fewer yards. Net punts at the lowest youth levels (ten-year olds) are about ten to fifteen yards. You wonder why they bother. (I watched all four levels of the Pop Warner Super Bowl one year. Hardly any team punted all day—even in situations like fourth and 18.) You can probably draw a steadily rising continuum from that level to the lowest college levels. That would work out as follows:

Punter's age	average net punt
10	12 yards
11	14
12	16
13	18
14	20
15	22
16	24
17	26
18	28

Returning the punt is instinctive, but **covering** it is not. Young returners can juke their peers as well as college and pro players. But inexperienced high school and youth coverage men give up longer returns than college and pro players. So the younger you go, the fewer yards the kick travels and the more yards it comes back at the punt team.

More punts returned for touchdowns at lower levels

There appear to be a higher percentage of returns for touchdowns in college as well. The average NFL team returned .3 punts for touchdowns in the 1995 season. (Most teams had none, a dozen had one, and the Giants had two.) The top twenty NCAA Division I-A teams returned 1.15 punts for touchdowns that same season—four times as many as the NFL average! And college teams only play about **eleven games** a season compared with **sixteen plus** in the NFL.

Weaker long snappers

The younger you go, the poorer the quality of the long snappers. One year every high school game I watched had at least one bad long snap. Younger long snappers are also weaker. Except when the ball in inside the five-yard line, **NFL** punters stand about **15 to 18 yards** behind the long snapper to receive the snap. Augustana College coach Bob Reade and Dan DeMonbrun, a **high school** special teams coach, each wrote a book in which he recommends the punter stand **13 yards** behind the long snapper. The *Boys Club Guide to Youth Football* says the punter stands **12 yards** behind the long snapper. In the book *Youth League Football*, authors Tom Flores and Bob O'Connor say

> *The depth of the punter should be ten yards behind the line of scrimmage in a tight punt formation, 12 to 14 yards for a high school spread punt, and 15 yards for a college spread punt. Youth teams, of course, should shorten the distance relative to the age of their players.*

In his book, *A Parent's Guide to Coaching Football*, Jack McCarthy says,

> *At the youth level, [the punter lines up]* ***7 to 10 yards*** *[behind the line of scrimmage] and that's still quite a hike for a young center.*

In my own book, *Coaching Youth Football*, I said we lined up a mere **five yards** behind the center to punt—although we ran the single wing and always did what I called a "fourth-down quick kick" rather than a regular punt formation. That is, we lined up like we were going for it on fourth down in our regular offensive formation, then we punted quick-kick style. Because there was usually no one back to receive it, we would get rolling, unreturned punts that would go net 30 yards or more. I further said in my book that I recommend punters in regular punt formations be no more than **eight yards** behind the long snapper in youth football.

The bottom line is that the younger you go, the closer the punter is to the defensive guys who want to block the punt, thereby increasing the incidence of blocked punts.

Poorer blocking, too

The younger you go, the poorer the quality of the offensive line play. I know of no stats to prove this. But it's safe to say that anyone who has watched high school or youth football games can vouch that those games feature a lot more blocked punts than in the college and pro games they see on TV.

Field goals

Almost everything that I said about punts applies to field goals as well. They can be blocked. There can be bad long snaps. Field-goal attempts that come down short of the end zone can be returned. The field goal at least has the virtue of scoring three points if it succeeds. A successful field goal also gives the kicking team a chance to kick off from their 30-, 35-, or 40-yard line. A successful punt, on the other hand, scores no points and can be returned big.

Coaches who have a lead of less than nine points, and who have questionable long snappers, holders, or offensive lines, ought to think twice about risking the disaster a field goal attempt can lead to.

In the 9/8/90 Utah-Minnesota game, Minnesota tried a field goal to win on the last play of the game. It was blocked and Utah's Lavon Edwards ran it back 91 yards for the winning touchdown. Utah, 35; Minnesota, 29.

In the 1997 Rose Bowl, Arizona State's spectacular come-from-behind fourth-quarter touchdown drive **started** with a blocked field goal. Indeed, the blocked field goal was picked up and run in for a **touchdown**, but it was called back because there was a **forward lateral** during the runback.

In 1986 in the NFL, 32 field goal attempts were blocked. Two of those were run back for touchdowns.

Kansas City vs. Pittsburgh, 1986

With 26 seconds left in the first half, Pittsburgh was trailing the Chiefs 17-6, and at the Kansas City three-yard line. Needing both a field goal and a touchdown, they chose the "conservative" route, a field goal. Only it didn't turn out so conservative. Chiefs' nose tackle Bill Maas blocked the kick and his teammate Lloyd Burruss ran it all the way for a touchdown.

If the **field goal** had been **successful**, Pittsburgh's win probability would have been **.189**. If they tried for the **touchdown** and **failed**, their win probability would have been **.127**. But if they got the **touchdown** and **extra point**, their win probability would have risen to **.334**. As it turned out, their win probability after the blocked field goal and touchdown runback was a mere **.041**.

So Pittsburgh feared the .189 - .127 = .062 loss in win probability if they tried for a touchdown and failed. But they overlooked the field goal's risk of a block and touchdown runback, with its .189 - .041 = .148 price tag. In other words, the field goal has a high probability of success, but also a small probability of absolute **disaster**. Furthermore, field goals don't pay off very well (just three points) when they succeed, except in the case of last-second game winners.

Remember, this was an **end-of-the-first-half** play. The analysis for similar situations at the **end of the game**, like that faced by the Colts in Super Bowl III, is quite different.

On the other hand, a three-yard "go for it" has the great upside of seven or eight points and a relatively safe downside of turning the ball over on downs at the other team's one or two yard line.

True, the announcers (or alumni or parents depending on your level) are going to beat you up for getting all the way to the three and "coming away empty handed." But as the 1986 Kansas City-Pittsburgh game shows, there are **worse** things than "coming away empty handed." Kansas City went on to beat the favored-by-two-points Steelers 24-19.

I said that field goals and punts are normally fairly safe plays at football's higher levels. But I also said think twice about risking a blocked kick if your line or long snapper are questionable. The authors of *The Hidden Game of Football* characterized Pittsburgh's 1986 special teams as "an embarrassment all year." That being the case, the "safe" field goal looks even riskier in Pittsburgh's case.

Turnover-avoidance principles

When you are ahead, you must avoid turnovers. That means calling plays which reduce the likelihood of a fumble or interception. But you also have to get your first downs prior to the take-a-knee point. So you may have to take some calculated risks, like passing, to avoid the turnover known as a fourth down.

During the last series where you need to get a first down before the take-a-knee point, you should probably look for opportunities to run quarterback keeper plays. But *above all, you must avoid the blocked punt or bad punt snap.* And the lower the level you coach at, the more crucial this becomes.

- *Prefer running plays to passes if you can still get your first downs.*
- *Prefer quarterback keepers to handoff running plays when doing so will not prevent you from getting your first downs.*
- *Think twice before you risk a punt or field goal when you have the lead late in a game, especially when you are below the NCAA Division I level.*

11

Ahead on defense

You are ahead, but only by one score, there is less than a quarter left, and you're on defense. What do you do?

The opposing offense is running their hurry-up offense. You need to call the defenses that best stop those plays.

'Prevent' defense

TV announcers are fond of denouncing so-called "prevent" defenses. A common knock is that they "prevent you from winning."

As the clock runs down, the choices the trailing offensive coordinator must make become more constricted. That, in turn, means you have a petty good idea what play is coming.

For example, if the opposing offense has a long way to go for the winning score, you can expect that they will pass. Everybody's got that figured out.

Pass defense

But the key question is how do you defend a pass?

There are three ways:

- **pressure** or sack the passer
- **delay** the release of the receivers
- **cover** the receivers in the secondary.

Most teams do a mixture of all three. It's common to delay tight ends at the line of scrimmage. Most teams blitz at times in passing situations. Some teams bump wide receivers at the line of scrimmage.

You should keep detailed statistics on your defense, including how much success each defense and blitz has in various situations. Having done that, it seems obvious to me that you should *run your most successful defense for the situation in question.*

Best, not 'prevent'

Your best defense is whatever worked best thus far in the season. It is a function of your personnel. Good defensive backs are hard to come by. So if you are like most teams, and have fewer than you'd like, the so-called prevent defense, with its extra defensive backs, is probably **not** a good idea.

In the 1997 playoff game between New England and Jacksonville, The Patriots were leading 10-3 and had the ball with :15 left in the first half. It was second and eleven at the Jacksonville 41. There was also a 20 mph wind blowing in the Patriots' faces. Too far out to kick a field goal. Jacksonville put in seven, count 'em, **seven** defensive backs. Jacksonville only rushed three guys.

What happened next? Drew Bledsoe completed a bomb to the two-yard line. The receiver got out of bounds stopping the clock at :08. One of Jacksonville's double-teamed rushers got injured on the play and had to leave the game. After an incomplete pass that took the game clock down to :04, New England kicked a field goal. They went on to win and advanced to the Super Bowl.

NFL quarterback Brian Sipe said, "I'd rather pass against a prevent than a hard rush any time. Coaches just don't seem to realize that three medium passes come out to 60 yards, same a one long one."

If you've had your best success with a mixture of blitzing and bumping, you'd better blitz and bump when you know the other team is going to pass—even in an end-of-game situation. I suspect that many coaches agree with this, but use the prevent because they do not want to be criticized by powerful people who don't understand football, namely, fans, owners, and school administrators.

'Prevent' is not conservative

We've all seen games where a team that struggled all day suddenly gets into their two-minute drill and marches right down the field. "Why didn't they do that earlier?" people ask. "It's easier in this situation," color men explain, "because the defense is in a prevent. The quarterback has more time to throw. The defense is sideline conscious opening the middle. There are more receivers out."

The only time I can see a prevent making sense is on the last play of the game when the opposing offense is sure to throw a Hail Mary pass and the field position is such that the quarterback can release the pass on a three-step drop. With that drop, you probably cannot get pressure on the quarterback. So you might as well get more bodies around ground zero.

Don't be too afraid of defensive penalties

Defensive backs sometimes get too conservative about penalty avoidance in late-game situations. There is no doubt **penalties** are **more important** late in a close game. But neither is there any doubt that **completions** are **more important, too**. This is a tricky mental issue. Just make sure you do not contribute to overcaution with anything you say. What you want, when you are ahead and on defense at the end of a game is what you always want: **good defense**. You do **not** want conservative or cautious defense.

Timeouts

As a general rule, you do **not** use timeouts on defense to make adjustments, as in "Junior Seau doesn't like what he sees. He's calling timeout." But you may need to use one or more to avoid a play which you are not prepared for. Instruct your defensive players when to use timeouts and give them some practice calling them in clock-management situations. For example, they need to know how and when to call "green" (just before the offensive gets ready to snap) or "red" (as soon as the previous play ends) timeouts.

Controlling the offense's pace

In the slowdown chapter, I said the offense should adopt a pace appropriate to the distance they have to travel and the time remaining. There are graphs in that chapter to show you what pace that should be.

Obviously, the defense should do the opposite. There was a play discussed in the slowdown chapter from the 1997 Rose Bowl. In that play, an ASU receiver was trying to get out of bounds and an OSU defender was trying to prevent him from doing so. Actually, they both were trying to do the wrong thing.

Remember the offense wants to score and do so at a pace that leaves little time for the opponent to come back and score. The defense's goal is the opposite: to prevent the score and to preserve maximum clock time for themselves if they are not able to prevent it. That's a little tricky so stay with me here.

You will read a little later in the book where one of my freshman receivers was held up by our opponent in a tackle that lasted four seconds. If it had lasted five, we would have lost the game. We won the game by one point on a play that started with :01 left.

We were operating at a red or top-speed hurry-up pace. We had taken possession at our own 38 with 2:01 remaining and no timeouts. By keeping my receiver inbounds and standing up, the defense was trying to force us out of red and into green, the opposite of what we needed. Most people can understand the idea of a defense on a team which is ahead preventing the trailing offense from getting out of bounds or to the ground near the end of a game. The defense is trying to run the clock out before the offense can score.

But what about when the team which is on offense and behind is operating at a green or maximum slowdown pace? For example, the 1997 Rose Bowl after Arizona State completed the bomb to the Ohio State eight-yard line with about 2:54 left in the game. That pass took ASU out of the yellow or inbounds hurry-up pace and put them into green or maximum slowdown. Should it also take OSU out of their run-out-the-clock mode? Yes.

I said in the chapter on using timeouts that the best time to use a timeout was when the opposing offense was in their slowdown. Was Arizona State in their slowdown after they completed the pass to the eight? Yes, they were. Did Ohio State have any timeouts left? Yes, one. Should they have used it as soon as Arizona State completed that pass? Yes.

Doing so would have shocked the crowd and the announcers. But then they hadn't read this book. Think about it. Arizona State no longer needs time. They have all the time in the world when you realize they have eight yards to go and only can run four plays maximum. Time saved now can only benefit Ohio State.

Had Ohio State called their timeout immediately after the completion, how much time would they have saved? Arizona State snapped the ball at 2:32 for the next play. So Ohio State could have saved 2:54 - 2:32 = 22 seconds. If Arizona State had used as much time as they should have, Ohio State would have saved 23 + 15 = **38 seconds** by calling timeout.

Ohio State got the ball back with 1:40 and was able to comeback and score the winning touchdown. But wouldn't they have much preferred to have had 1:40 + :38 = 2:18?

The logic of Ohio State calling timeout immediately after the Arizona State completion at the eight would have been,

> *ASU is now likely to score, they have more time than they need to do so. If they* ***do*** *score, it is* ***we****, OSU, that will be needing time. So let's conserve time in case we fall behind.*

Stated more crudely,

> *If my opponent wants to waste time, I want to conserve it.*

I would add this assumes your opponent knows what he is doing. You want to do the opposite of what your opponent **should** be doing, which may not be what they **are** doing.

I would not worry about pushing Arizona State ball carriers out of bounds to conserve time inside my own ten yard line. I would have my players focus entirely on just stopping them from scoring. But I would call **timeouts** immediately to conserve time.

Some coaches might wonder if calling a timeout, indicating you were now worried about having enough time to make a comeback, shows lack of confidence in your defense and will demoralize them. They should be taught throughout their college careers that you will call timeout in this situation—that it is strictly a function of the distance and time remaining and has nothing to do with your confidence in the defense.

In other words, you should teach them the clock-management principles that are in this book. I think the players can understand that there sometimes comes a time when the opposing team is no longer worried about the clock even though they are behind. And they can also understand, if my opponent wants to waste time, I want to conserve it.

The alumni and sports writers may take a little longer to figure it out, but that's what post-game press conferences are for.

Play sheet

Your offensive coordinator should have a list of clock-management situations and plays to call in those situations. Your **defensive** coordinator should also have a list of what opposing offensive coordinators call in clock-management situations so he can tell his players what to look for.

Scouts should be looking not only for down-and-distance tendencies, but also for **clock-management tendencies**. Teams tend to get real simple, and predictable, in their two-minute drill. You can reap a tremendous intelligence bonus if your figure out your opponent's standard two-minute drill. And you probably can easily do so if you happen to get a video which has one of the opponent's two-minute drills.

Unpiling

There are three modes of unpiling:

- fast
- normal speed
- slow.

When you are ahead and on defense, you should have a code word to remind each other not to get up quickly in this situation. It should be a word which only **your** players understand. For example, you might call the nickname of the slowest player on the team, e.g., "Lurch! Lurch!" You should **not** unpile slower than normal because it's unethical and against the rules. The NFICA Ethics code prohibits:

> *2. Teaching illegal techniques that violate principals [sic] of sportsmanship and fair play.*

The NCAA Football Code says,

> *The football player who intentionally violates a rule is guilty of unfair play and unsportsmanlike conduct; and whether or not he escapes being penalized, he brings discredit to the good name of the game, which it is his duty as a player to uphold.*

The American Football Coaches Association Code of Ethics says in pertinent part:

> *The welfare of the game depends on how the coaches live up to the spirit and letter of ethical conduct...*
>
> ***Article One***
>
> ***Responsibilities to Players***
>
> *1. The coach should never place the value of a win above that of instilling the highest desirable ideals and character traits in his players.*
>
> *2. Any attempts to beat [the rules], to take unfair advantage of an opponent, or to teach deliberate unsportsmanlike conduct, have no place in the game of football, nor has any coach guilty of such teaching any right to call himself a coach.*

Article Three
Rules of the Game
3. Both the letter and spirit of the rules must be adhered to by the coaches.
4. To gain an advantage by circumvention or disregard for the rules brands a coach or player as unfit to be associated with football.

Take-a-knee-period interception

When you are ahead on defense, you frequently end your opponent's last possession with an interception. When you are ahead on defense, and the time remaining and number of opponent timeouts left is such that you would be in take-a-knee if you had the ball, and make an interception on the last play of the game, your interceptor should slide or get out of bounds to end the play. *Under no circumstances should he allow himself to be tackled once you have reached the take-a-knee point.*

The clock-management assistant should show the checkered panel as soon as the time remaining hits the take-a-knee point, even though the other team still has the ball. Because as soon as there is a turnover, you are in take-a-knee. *Whenever you are in take-a-knee, you must take a knee. That applies to a defensive player intercepting or recovering a fumble as well as to offensive players.*

In 1995, when I was an assistant coach with the Miramonte High School varsity, we intercepted a pass on the last play of a game in which we were ahead of San Ramon Valley by 20-14. The final horn sounded while the pass was in the air. The interceptor then commenced to try to run it back for a touchdown and was tackled.

I gave him a mild chewing out and explained that once the horn sounded, we had **won** the game. We couldn't win it any **more** by him scoring. And, if he had been stripped or fumbled, and the other team had picked it up and ran it for a touchdown, we probably would have **lost**. He would have been the biggest goat in Miramonte history.

In Michigan's 1996 upset of Ohio State, a Michigan defender (#89) **almost** showed the correct approach. He intercepted the last play Hail Mary pass. Time had run out right after the snap which took place with :01 left.

The defender ran the interception back zig-zagging across the field. But when he approached a member of the Ohio State team, he **slid**, ending the play and preventing any possibility of a turnover. His slide was the right idea to avoid a tackle, but he should have just taken a knee right after the interception. The run was gratuitous and had a slight danger. In that situation, you hold victory in your knee. Touch it down, and you win. Every second you delay touching it down risks catastrophe.

In the 1997 Peach Bowl, a similar incident happened on a deflected field goal. Clemson, trailing 10-7 tried a field goal on fourth and six from the LSU 35. Clemson had no timeouts left and there was 1:10 left with the clock stopped until the snap by an incomplete pass. An LSU defensive back caught the deflected field goal attempt in the air and returned it from the LSU 27. He was knocked out of bounds at the Clemson 45.

Again, the LSU defensive back was handling the ball **after** his team's take-a-knee point so he should have taken a knee or gone out of bounds rather than risked fumbling by running with the ball. Going out of bounds is generally a no-no when you are ahead. But on a **turnover**, it matters not because the **clock will stop on the change of possession** regardless of whether you stay in bounds or not. Going out of bounds usually avoids the injury possibility inherent in contact.

Coaches need to practice proper defensive behavior for these situations. It should only take a couple of reps in one practice session. Coaches must also have some sort of word or phrase, like "Take-a-knee defense!" which they yell to alert the players that they are past their own take-a-knee point even though their opponent still has the ball.

Defenders who get the ball should take a knee

Actually, it's not just the last play of the game. *A defender who obtains possession by any means after his team has passed the take-a-knee point should do just that: take a knee.* For example, suppose you are ahead by five and intercept a pass with 1:01 left and your opponent has no timeouts. The take-a-knee table says you can start to take a knee when the clock passes 1:35 if it's first down and the opponent has no timeouts. That is the situation on this hypothetical interception. The taking of a knee should start with the **interceptor**, **not** the first offensive snap after the interception.

Remember the idea behind taking a knee is to *avoid being tackled* because of the danger of a turnover. On an interception, you cannot form the protective take-a-knee formation. So the defender who gets the ball should just take a knee or slide in the open field.

I generally recommend that defenders pick up fumbles rather than fall on them. But teams that are ahead on defense in the last minute of a game would be an exception to that rule. Once you are past your team's take-a-knee point, there is no point to one of your defenders picking up a fumble and advancing it.

Keep them inbounds and upright

When your opponent is trailing and in their two-minute drill, keep them inbounds and upright. The game clock stops when they go out of bounds. Don't let them out of bounds if you can avoid it. Run defensive alignments that make it harder for them to complete the out or fade pass. Funnel their runs and passes to the time-wasting middle of the field.

Remember, every time they get out of bounds, they save about 12 seconds. (When they are in their **hurry-up**, the most they will take to snap if they **don't** get out of bounds is about 20 seconds. The play itself lasts about six seconds.) In a top-speed hurry-up, 12 seconds is about **enough to run two plays**. Don't let your opponent have two more plays by letting them get out of bounds.

Keep them upright, too. In our 1996 freshman game against Campolindo, the defense stopped my tight end after he caught a two-minute drill pass. But they did not tackle him to the ground. They sort of danced with him to run time off the clock.

We had first and ten with no timeouts left and :35 on the clock when we snapped the ball. We were trailing by two. We threw a quick out to our tight end but he was far from the sideline when he caught it.

From the time he was hit until the referees blew the play dead, **four seconds** elapsed. The defenders did not want him to go down. They walked him sideways. The refs finally blew the play dead when he began to go backwards. The clock continued to run.

We immediately lined up and spiked the ball leaving **:01** on the clock. Then we kicked a 26-yard field goal to win the game by one point. Had Campo held our tight end up **one second longer**, or held another ball carrier up one more second on a previous play, they **would have won the game**.

Colored panels for the defense

Your clock-management assistant should use his colored panels when you are on defense, too. But they have a different meaning:

- Green — Keep the offense inbounds and upright, don't hurry to unpile or get back to your side of the line of scrimmage. Avoid calling timeout, but if you must call timeout, wait until just before the opposing offense is ready to snap.
- Yellow — No meaning when you are ahead.
- Red — Players focus on stopping the offense from scoring, get up off the pile and lined up quickly. Coaches call immediate timeouts after plays which keep the clock running.
- Checkered — We are in our take-a-knee period. If you recover a fumble or intercept, immediately take a knee, slide, or get out of bounds.

12

Behind on offense

1997 Rose Bowl

In the 1997 Rose Bowl, undefeated Arizona State University was behind Ohio State by a score of 14-10. ASU, led by greatly heralded quarterback Jake Plummer got the ball at their own 42 with 5:36 left in the game. Plummer, who had led his team to five come-from-behind wins during the 1996 regular season and came in third in Heisman balloting, led a 10-play drive and scored in spectacular fashion on a desperate third-and-goal scramble from 11 yards out. Plummer's touchdown and the ensuing successful kick made the score ASU 17, OSU 14, but he left 1:40 on the clock. Too much, it turned out.

The kick return used 8 seconds of game-clock time. Ohio State's backup quarterback, Joe Germaine, looking more like Joe Montana, led his team 65 yards in 12 plays and 1:13 of game-clock time (helped by 30 yards worth of defensive pass interference calls) to score the winning touchdown with 0:19 left. The extra point was blocked leaving the score OSU 20, ASU 17.

Plummer then led his team to OSU's 35 where time ran out while his receiver was zigging and zagging in the middle of the field after catching a pass.

Nice to score, better to score slowly

Early in his pro career, New York Jets quarterback Joe Namath found himself **behind** at the end of a game and driving for a score. Back then, quarterbacks called their own plays. Namath felt confident his team was going to score the go ahead touchdown. But it also occurred to him that he ought to do it **slowly**, so there would be less time left of the clock after he scored. He characterized that realization as the moment when he felt he had become a pro. He then led his team—slowly—to the victory, as planned

Too bad for ASU that they were not able to do the same in the 1997 Rose Bowl.

Enough

Remember the watchword in football clock management is "**enough**." When you are behind at the end of a game, you need to score **enough points** to win. But you also need to score them with **enough speed** to get it done before the final gun. You do **not**, and should not, get it done with **more than enough speed**—because if you do, you're liable to give your opponent **enough** time to come back and beat you.

Too often, when it appears that the trailing team is on their last possession of the game, they wage a frantic two-minute drill to score as fast as possible. That's a mistake.

True, you have to score on **this** drive, but you don't have to score in **one** minute if you have **four** minutes left. Parkinson's Law says,

Work expands so as to fill the time available for its completion.

Would that it were also true of fourth-quarter, come-from-behind, go-ahead scoring drives. It **should** be.

When a field goal is enough

If you can win or tie with a field goal, you must keep in mind a particular problem with field-goal teams: they take a long time to get onto the field and lined up. Stanford offensive coordinator Dana Bible says he can get his field goal team onto the field and snap the ball in about seventeen seconds, but only after much practice. The authors of *The Hidden Game of Football* say it takes about 27 seconds.

Stop the clock

The best way to get your field-goal team onto the field in time is to **stop the clock**. You can do that with:

- timeout if you have one
- out-of-bounds play (if not fourth down)
- spiking the ball (if not fourth down)
- incomplete pass (if not fourth down)
- opponent timeout that you cause
- referee's timeout (for moving the chains, penalty, or some such).

Opponent timeouts can sometimes be obtained by lining up in an unexpected formation. Of course, the opponent may **not** call a timeout, in which case you need to be ready to run a **touchdown** play from the unexpected formation.

Leave enough time

If you cannot stop the clock, you must be careful to call for the field-goal team early enough that you have time to get them out there. They should be "in the blocks" on the sideline ready to run out as soon as the previous play is completed. In high school and lower levels, this is a problem because there are typically several players who are on both the offense and the field-goal teams.

Furthermore, any injuries that have occurred earlier in the game complicate making sure the right guys are on the field. High school and younger coaches probably need to call for the field-goal team 30 seconds before the end of the half to make sure they can end up with the right eleven guys on the field lined up correctly.

In college and higher levels, they can probably get their field goal team out there and snap in less than 20. Each team needs to practice it and thereby learn how much time they need. The responsible coach needs to know the **yard line** his kicker needs the ball on to be accurate enough and how much **time** his field goal team needs to get out, line up, and get the snap off.

Remind the ball carrier on the play just before the field goal to get out of bounds or take a knee or slide after a certain number of seconds. His normal instinct is to avoid tackle as long as possible. In the 1997 Rose Bowl, Arizona State's final ball carrier got his team within field goal range, but the clock ran out while he was zigging and zagging. Had he taken a knee or slid as soon as he made the first down, his team might have been able to kick the tying field goal. Arizona State lost 17-14.

Some interceptions are not permanent

When you are behind on offense at the end of a game, you are likely to be throwing passes. Interception usually ends your chances. But don't let your players give up too fast when a defender seems about to intercept.

Jets versus Browns, 1985

The Jets threw downfield where it was intercepted by a Brown. But he barely got hold of it before the intended receiver stripped it and took it into the end zone for a Jet touchdown.

Foothill Athletic League junior varsity league championship, 1994

The 1994 Miramonte junior varsity team, on which I was a coach, won the league championship in the final game of the season against Campolindo. We threw a pass to around Campo's two-yard line. Campo intercepted but our intended receiver immediately snatched the ball out of his hands and took it in for the touchdown. We won 7-6.

This is a good skill to practice once or twice. Have your receivers snatch an interception out of the hands of a defender. The defender should play patsy for this drill. It's mainly to plant the seed in your receivers' minds that the play is not over just because the defender has hold of the ball.

Some fumbles are not permanent

In 1992, San Francisco's Joe Montana completed a pass to tight end Brent Jones. But he fumbled when he was hit. A Cardinal lineman picked it up, but he was soon stripped by 49er Mike Sherrard, who ran the ball in for a touchdown.

Need to score more than once

If you need to score more than once, you must go at a top-speed hurry-up pace on all but the last drive. You may need to go top-speed on the last drive, too, but you can't tell until it starts. If you get a fourth down, and you need a field goal as one of your two scores, go for the field goal if the down and distance are such that you would normally (early in the game) kick.

If time is short, your victory plan is score, recover an onside kick, and score again. You must go on the **working assumption that you will succeed** at each of those things. You must exude confidence as a coach and you should practice this so that your team can feel confident, too. Practicing against air (no opposition) is advisable because you don't have time to do this very many times and every repetition that fails diminishes confidence.

Your players need successful reps so they feel, "Score, recover an onside kick, and score again? No problem. Been there, done that."

13

Tie or win

Ara Parseghian is one of the most successful coaches in Notre Dame history. His winning percentage there was .836. But he is not remembered for that. He will forever be remembered mainly as the guy who went for a **tie** against Michigan State in 1966.

He did not go for a tying **score**. Rather he just **sat on the ball** and ran out the clock when the game was already tied—at a time when there was no overtime in college football.

Parseghian's rationale was that if he went for the win and lost the game as a result (on a turnover), he would lose the national championship he expected to win. On the other hand, if they tied, they'd still probably get the national championship.

He was right. Notre Dame was voted the national champion in 14 polls. In three, they shared the title with Michigan State. Michigan State won one poll outright, as did Alabama. But not many people remember the poll results that year. Rather they remember the mocking headlines: "Old Notre Dame will tie over all" and "Tie one for the Gipper."

Utah versus Minnesota

The University of Minnesota had a similar choice in a less famous game on 9/8/90. They were tied at 29 and tried a field goal to win on the last play of the game. It was blocked and Utah's Lavon Edwards ran it back 91 yards for the winning touchdown.

In hindsight, it would appear a running play would have been a better choice. But given the accuracy of most Division I-A college kickers (.975 inside 20 in 1994) and the low incidence of blocked field goals (the career record is 8 field goals blocked 1978-81 by James Ferebee of New Mexico State), Minnesota made the right decision. It just didn't work out.

Tennessee Chattanooga versus Western Carolina

Going for the win in a tie game, and losing also happened to Division I-AA Tennessee Chattanooga in a 9/16/89 game against Western Carolina. With the score tied at 20, Chattanooga had the ball for the last play of the game. They chose to pass. It was intercepted by Terrell Wagner at his 32. He then returned it for the winning touchdown. Final score: Western Carolina 26, Tennessee Chattanooga 20.

I do not know what Chattanooga's field position was. But if the opponent intercepted at his own 32, it sounds like Chattanooga was too far out to win with a running play or field goal. The Chattanooga coach made the right choice. He lost his gamble, but he did so while trying to win the game.

> *His place shall never be with those cold and timid souls who know neither victory nor defeat.*

LSU–Tennessee, 1959

LSU scored a fourth-quarter touchdown against Tennessee in a 1959 game, bringing the score to Tennessee, 14; LSU, 13. LSU coach Paul Dietzel could have kicked the extra point to tie. But he elected to go for the win, and failed. Dietzel said, "...if I had it to do over a hundred times, I would do the same thing." I agree with Dietzel. *Against All Odds* author Bill Shanklin characterized LSU's decision this way,

> *But LSU went down like champions, with guns blazing, playing to win.*

But it must be noted that there was no tiebreaker then. That rule went in during the 1996 season. Nowadays, a tie in regulation is not a tie at all, it's just a ticket to overtime.

1996 Independence Bowl

On 12/31/96, Army played Auburn in the Independence Bowl. Army was losing 32-7 at the start of the fourth quarter. They then scored 22 unanswered points making the score Auburn, 32; Army, 29. Army did an unsuccessful onside kick after one of the scores. Then, after scoring to bring the score to 29, Army again kicked onside with 1:27 left in the game. This time, they were successful. They reached Auburn's 10-yard line with 33 seconds left. Although it was only third down, Army decided to attempt a 27-yard field goal, which would tie the game.

The announcers questioned the call, wondering why he wouldn't take at least one shot at a winning touchdown before kicking the field goal. Army's quarterback, Ronnie McAda had not thrown an interception all season.

True, Army's kicker had made 17 straight field goals from inside the 30.

In the event, the kick was wide right and Army lost the game.

Thirty-three seconds seems like more than enough time to use both of Army's remaining downs. I saw no accounts of the Army coach's explanation. But I agree with the announcers. The third down should have been used to try to **win**. Maybe, I repeat, maybe, try to put the game into overtime by kicking a field goal on fourth down.

1996 high school playoff game

A high school playoff game I attended ended similarly. Tied at the end of regulation, the two teams began the high school tie-breaking scheme: each team gets the ball on the other team's 10 and gets four downs to score. The first team scored on fourth down and kicked the extra point for a seven-point lead. Then the other team scored, on third down, and went for the tying kick, which, if successful, would have triggered a second pair of possessions. Had they gone for two and succeeded, the game would be over. But the kick was blocked. They lost.

10/16/94 Cardinals-Redskins game

Buddy Ryan's Arizona Cardinals had just scored to make it Skins, 16; Cards, 15 with 19 seconds left in the game. Had he gone for two, and made it, the Cards would have won the game He went for the tie—got it—and won in overtime on a 29-yard field goal—but not until 4:56 was left in the first overtime period. Remember, in the NFL, the extra point is from the **two**-yard line, not the **three** as in high school and college.

It's hard to argue with success. But the decision on whether to go for two and win it or go for one and tie was not clear-cut. It is possible the Cardinals might never have gotten the ball back after the extra-point try. The Redskins, indeed, won the toss. Although at the time he made his kick-the-PAT decision, Ryan only knew that there was a 50-50 chance that Washington would win the toss. Of course, he also knew his defense stopped them all day long (The Skins had scored on a 46-yard TD pass, an interception runback, and a safety deliberately given up by the Cardinals) and apparently was confident he would get possession if the Skins did win the toss.

Arizona's 1994 PAT run success rate from the two-yard line in 1995 was 0% (0 for 1) but their **passing** two-point conversion rate was 100% (5 for 5) for an overall two-point conversion rate of .833.

Not symmetrical

One thing that bothers me about going for a tying score when you have a comparable chance to go for the win is that the outcomes are **not symmetrical**. By comparable I mean that the probability of success is similar. On the other hand, the probability of kicking a **field goal** from the other team's 30-yard line is usually much higher than the probability of scoring a **touchdown** from the 30. If you're on the 30, and you can tie with a field goal, you should probably kick on fourth down.

If you go for the **tie**, and succeed, all you get is a tie. But if you go for the **win** and succeed, you win.

But in both cases, if you **fail**, you **lose**.

Burn the boats

An ancient European military leader supposedly gathered his soldiers on a cliff overlooking the boats they had used to get to England—so they could see him burn them. That's the way they motivated their "players" in the old days.

If you tell your players, "We're going for it," I guarantee the news will electrify them. You're telling them, "This is it. Put everything you have left into this one play. If you do your job, we win. If not, it's over. One way or the other, this is the last play of this game."

Not only does it send a shock through your team, it electrifies the crowd, the public address announcer, and the officials.

Army-Navy, 1971

Navy was trailing 24-21 with :13 left in the 1971 Army-Navy Game. They had fourth down at the Army seven-yard line. A field goal would tie the game. Navy went for the touchdown, but their pass fell incomplete. The ball went over on downs to Army and they ended the game be deliberately taking a safety.

After the game, which was played before the NCAA adopted its tiebreaker rule, Navy coach Rick Forzano said,

> *In no way were we going for a field goal at the end. We aren't a tying team.*

I agree with Forzano. The stirring line in Navy's fight song, *Anchors Aweigh*, is not "Tie the Army!" it's "Sink the Army!"

Notre Dame-Penn State, 1992

Notre Dame was trailing 16-15 with 20 seconds left in the game after scoring a touchdown. Lou Holtz, perhaps thinking of Ara Parseghian, decided to go for the win. According to Michael Steele in the *Fighting Irish Football Encyclopedia*,

> *...the stadium was literally shaking as the crowd went ballistic.*

Quarterback Rick Mirer completed a pass to Reggie Brooks who caught the ball in the end zone. Says Steele,

> *This incredible win has to be ranked in anyone's list of top ten Irish triumphs.*

Not if he goes for the tie. Compare that to going for the tie. If you go for the tie, the **other team's coach** can tell his guys, "This can be it. If you do your job on this play, we can win right now." By going for the tie, you create an asymmetrical motivation for each team. If **your** team succeeds in scoring, you only have a **tie**. But if the **other** team succeeds in stopping you, they **win**. If you go for the tie, you are involved in a play in which the stakes are quite different for the two teams, unfavorably so from your perspective. It's far better to lose while trying to **win** than to lose while trying to **tie**.

This play versus overtime

Go for the tie if you think your chances of winning are better in overtime than in the final regulation scoring play. The overtime rules at your level and how the game has gone thus far tell you how likely you are to win under the overtime rules.

- NFL—coin toss to determine first possessor and sudden death
- NCAA—each team gets two series from the 25-yard line
- NFICA—each team gets a series from the 10-yard line

In the **NFL**, you must consider the **50% chance** that you will **lose the toss**. If the opponent has been moving the ball against you in the game, you may want to take your shot at winning in regulation. But if your defense has been effective, as was the case with Buddy Ryan's 1994 Cardinals against the Redskins, you will likely go for the temporary tie expecting to make a winning drive in overtime.

In **college**, the question is **which team has the better red-zone offense today**. If it's you and tying is more certain than winning in regulation, go for the temporary tie. If the other team's red-zone offense has been better, you'd better try to win in regulation. In **high school**, the question is which team has the better goal-line offense today.

Miramonte versus Foothill, 1994

In the 1994 semi-final playoff game of the North Coast Section Championship (the highest championship you can win on the field), Miramonte was playing Foothill. The game was tied at 10. It was clear to everyone at the stadium that the overtime rules favored Miramonte on this day. That is, Miramonte had been moving the ball reasonably well. Foothill had scored on a couple of breaks.

It came down to Foothill having third and long at around their own 45. Everyone in the stadium knew Foothill did not want the game to go into overtime. Everyone expected some sort of trick play. And we got it, a fumblerooski, (not legal in college or NFL) which went for the game-winning touchdown. A week later, Foothill beat Alhambra to win NCS.

Clock management in overtime

There is a play clock but no game clock in high school or college overtime. Some clock-management principles still apply.

High school and college overtime

Special rules apply. In high school, any unused timeouts from the second half may be used in overtime. Plus each team gets one additional timeout. Overtime timeouts are for conferences and to get more than the play-clock time to make substitutions and such. You cannot use them to conserve time because no game clock is running. You might as well use your timeouts as fast as you can because they are of little use and every play could be the one you score on. You can place the ball anywhere between the hashes for the first play.

The winner of a coin toss gets to pick either:

- possession or
- which end of the field the overtime will be played in.

If you win, you should choose to go on defense first. That, in turn, means you get to choose which end of the field. Pick the one that favors your team's strengths and weaknesses on that day. Factors include:

- sun angle
- footing at each end of the field
- wind direction and speed.

Which end of the field rarely matters. But going on defense first **does** matter.

The team that goes on defense first, gets to see what score, if any, the opponent makes during the first series. The more-versus-enough principle applies. If the opponent fails to score at all, you can then kick a field goal on your **first** down, which you should if you have a normally effective field-goal unit. In general, there is little or no increase in field-goal accuracy achieved by moving closer than the ten-yard line, which is your starting point in high-school overtime.

I have seen teams penalized in high school overtime. If you are penalized back to the 15, 20 or 25, you probably will want to use one or more of your downs to get closer before you kick.

If your opponent scores only a field goal, you should then go for a touchdown, settling for a field goal to go into another overtime only if the touchdown seems unlikely on fourth down. *If you have to go first, score a touchdown if you can, and kick the extra point, unless you are fairly certain the opponent can score eight points.* Settle for a field goal only in extreme circumstances, like you have been penalized back to the 20 or some such.

Not PAT rules

Overtime seems PAT-like. But it is not. Unlike high-school PATs, the defense can score. Unlike college PATs, the defensive touchdowns are worth six points, not two. If the defense scores in the first series, the game is over and the defense wins. If you are a high-school coach and have a series of risky plays you use for two-point conversions, because you have no fear of a defensive score, do **not** use those plays. *Use regular goal-line plays.*

Furthermore, your offense must be defense-minded as they execute their overtime offensive plays. That is, *if there is a turnover during the first series, they must stop the defense from scoring or they lose.*

If the first team to get the ball scores, and there is a turnover during the second series, the game is over because the second team can no longer match the score of the team that went first. That is essentially a sort of take-a-knee situation. *Your defender should immediately take a knee or go out of bounds if he gets possession during an overtime series in which your team is ahead in the score.* Running the ball back for a touchdown cannot win the game any more and it risks a second turnover back to the original offense which could enable them to win. If you are on defense and ahead during the second series, and you get possession, kneel or run out of bounds. You've won.

Green pace or surprise red pace

You can operate at a "green" pace, that is maximum slowdown. A top-speed no-huddle might be effective as a **surprise** tactic. Or maybe a combination: say, two downs at maximum slowdown then suddenly shift into top speed for the last two downs.

14

Hail Mary pass

If a team is on offense, behind by more than three, 30 to 50 yards from the goal line, and has time for only one more play, their last play frequently is the Hail Mary pass.

Doug Flutie

The most famous Hail Mary I know of happened 11/23/84. Boston College quarterback Doug Flutie threw a dramatic, last second, 48-yard Hail Mary to Gerard Phelan in the end zone to give BC a 47-45 victory over Miami (Florida). The play also arguably won the diminutive Flutie the Heisman Trophy.

1997 Cotton Bowl

On New Year's Day, 1997, Kansas State's quarterback Brian Kavanagh threw a last-second-of-the-half Hail Mary to the end zone against BYU. It was tipped and caught inches from the ground by Andre Anderson, who was on his back. Touchdown!

What's the big deal?

I do not understand the amazement people express when the Hail Mary succeeds.

What's the big deal?

Is it a big deal that your quarterback can throw the ball to the end zone? Most quarterbacks can throw the ball 50 yards. (Kordell Stewart can throw even farther, as he did when he won the 9/24/94 Colorado-Michigan game 27-26 on the final play of the game with a 64-yard Hail Mary pass to Michael Westbrook.)

Is it a big deal that a receiver can catch a "jump ball" when there are a couple of guys from each team going up for it? Basketball players grab rebounds in similar situations dozens of times in every game.

I suspect that the completion percentage on Hail Mary passes is much higher than people would think. The 1996 *Pro Football Revealed* says in 1995, the average NFL team threw 71 "bombs" (passes of 20 yards or more) and completed 20 or 28%. An average of 6 or 8.4% went for TDs.

Rep it

You should practice the Hail Mary pass. You may need it. If and when you do need it, you don't want your players to regard it as a hopeless long shot—which is the general public's perception of the play.

Rep it to show your players that the pass can often be caught, if not directly, then on a tip. Rep it to teach your receivers what position to get into and how to time their jump. Rep it to give you players experience judging the ball. Catching the Hail Mary is like playing outfield—a position that benefits greatly from experience judging fly balls.

Alley Oop

San Francisco 49er R.C. Owens was the receiver for a play called the Alley Oop. He was very tall and told the quarterback to make the ball **wobble** a bit because it made it easier to judge. The Alley Oop was a sort of one-receiver Hail Mary, and it was used in all sorts of situations, not just the last play of a game.

In 1957, the 49ers used the Alley Oop to beat the Lions 35-31. Later that season, the 49ers again met the Lions in the playoffs. The Niners first play of that second game was the Alley Oop, and it worked again.

My son and I played football catch a lot prior to his freshman football season. One drill we did was to throw the ball end over end. We were trying to make it more difficult to catch, simulating a bad or deflected pass. To our surprise, it was **easier** to catch than a spiral pass. Apparently we saw the same phenomenon R.C. Owens did.

The original Hail Mary, Staubach to Pearson, 12/28/75

The original Hail Mary, the play that inspired a sports writer to use that label, is not like the current version. Nowadays, there are several players from each team at ground zero, which is typically in the end zone. In the 1975 Dallas-Minnesota Divisional playoff game, Dallas had second and ten at the 50-yard line with :32 remaining. Minnesota was up 14-10. Drew Pearson ran what Staubach called an in-and-take-it-deep route. I'd call it a post-corner.

Staubach pump-faked to the left, then, because the pump-fake took so much time, underthrew Pearson on the right side of the field. Pearson came back to catch the ball at the five-yard line. The defender fell down when he tried to stop and come back with Pearson.

Pearson was unable to hold onto the ball and thought he had dropped it. Then he discovered it between his right elbow and hip pad and trotted into the end zone for the winning score. NFL Films called it the fifth greatest touchdown in NFL history. Staubach said it was the most memorable play he was ever involved with.

Differences between the original Hail Mary and today's

The differences between the original Hail Mary, which was successful, and the recent Hail Marys, which often fail, are interesting.

For one thing, it was **not Dallas's last play**. Today, Hail Marys are thrown on **fourth down** or when there is **time for only one more play**. *Maybe the Hail Mary has a better chance of succeeding when the defense thinks you are still just going for a first down, that is, a little earlier than the last play.* In this game, Dallas had **second** down, not fourth, and :32 left, not :05. At a top-speed hurry-up pace, that's enough time to run about five plays. Dallas was in **their** Hail Mary mode, but Minnesota was **not** in their Hail Mary defense mode. The element of surprise.

For another thing, this was **a real play**. It was not just a Bill Cosbyesque "Go long" like the modern Hail Mary. Dallas did a pump fake and a route with a planned cut as well as an unplanned one—the comeback.

There was **only one intended receiver**. The Dallas receivers did not all assemble in the end zone as we now expect in Hail Marys. Pearson had only one guy to beat, and he beat him. Actually, he didn't beat him until he had to make the unplanned comeback cut.

When you analyze it, the original Hail Mary was actually a somewhat screwed-up play. Staubach and Pearson say so themselves.

Staubach sort of designed it on the spot, and its design was flawed. Staubach simply did not have the arm to pump-fake to the left then hit Pearson in stride on a post-corner to the other side. Maybe no quarterback did. That is, the **timing was incorrect**.

Where Pearson could get to in the time it took Staubach to pump-fake then throw deep, was farther than Staubach could throw. Had they worked on this more in practice, they no doubt would have corrected the timing either by eliminating the pump fake or by giving Pearson a little more to do before his final break. Or maybe they would have designed in the comeback at the end.

Pearson was well covered. Staubach did **not** throw to an open receiver. Had the defender not fallen down, he was actually in a slightly better position to make the catch than Pearson. The defender had **inside** position and was running stride-for-stride with Pearson. The underthrow meant the ball was not only short, it was also coming to Pearson's **inside**, where the defender was. The defender seemed to fall, and Pearson did not, because Pearson saw the ball sooner than the defender. The defender had to slam on the brakes. Pearson was able to apply the brakes more gradually. The defense complained that Pearson interfered, knocking the defender down. I watched the video a bunch of times. I would say it's possible that Pearson pushed the defender but it was awfully subtle if he did.

Consider throwing your Hail Mary sooner than the defense expects, running a real pattern rather than the "everybody go long" that the defense expects, and try a comeback ending to increase the probability of separation.

Basketball center at ground zero

Grand Valley State's coach Tom Beck puts a tall player at ground zero and has two other receivers trail him about three or four yards for a tip from him, like a basketball jump ball. Beck wants the "center" to get near the back of the end zone then come back toward the pass to catch it.

A logical play

I have no experience with the Hail Mary pass. But the following makes sense to me from a logic standpoint. Line up in a quads formation. On the snap, have the five receivers run downfield and line up in the end zone like a basketball jumpoff. The top jumper is in the middle and is the intended receiver. He goes to a spot smack in the middle of the end zone. The other four go to the four points of the football-field compass around him:

- one on the end line directly behind him
- one on the goal line directly in front of him
- one about five yards to the right of the center
- one about five yards to the left of the center.

Here's a diagram:

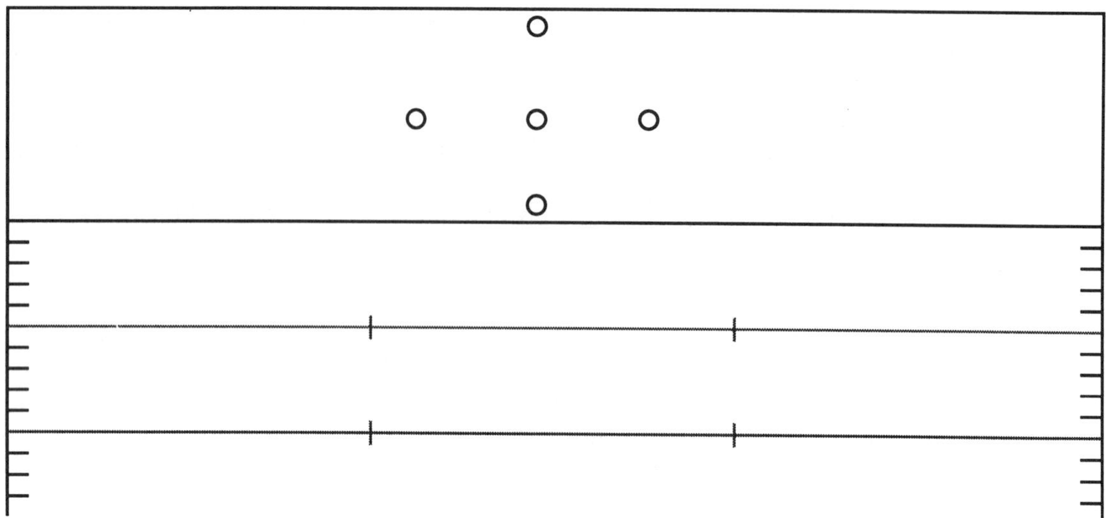

The intended receiver tries to out jump the defenders. If he cannot catch the ball, he tips it to a teammate. The four teammates are in a "good football position" ready to dive or jump in whatever direction to catch the ball. You should get a bunch of static reps with the players already in this position. You should also practice the entire actual play from scrimmage.

Fake Hail Mary screen pass

Beck likes to fake a Hail Mary and throw a screen pass when there is about 25 to 30 seconds left in the game. He says it is easy to get 20 to 30 yards on the screen in such situations. Then you get out of bounds.

That's probably a good last play if you are outside your quarterback's throwing range to the end zone.

Eagles versus Vikings, 1962

From his own 20, Hall of Fame quarterback Sonny Jurgensen threw a screen pass to Timmy Brown. It went 80 yards for a touchdown.

In recent years, statisticians have looked at two new stats:

- yards at catch (Y@C)
- yards after catch (YAC).

The Hail Mary has a zero YAC in most cases. But where does it say you have to score with strictly Y@C? Why not get the yards needed to score with YAC?

The NFL Films video *100 Greatest Touchdowns* gives you one great touchdown after another with little discussion. Most are long plays. As I watched, I was struck by all the downfield blocking I saw, most notably the seven perfect blocks on Dolphin Dick Anderson's interception runback of Johnny Unitas's pass in the 1971 AFC Championship game.

Few long touchdowns are solo acts. What better way to get downfield blocking than a screen?

Whatever your best long gainer is

Actually, the debate in your coaching staff should not necessarily be between the Hail Mary and the screen. Go over your stats for the last several years and figure out *what has been your best long-gaining play*. Then use that as your last play of the game when you are behind and far away from the goal line. It may be an inside trap. Go with what has worked for you, not the conventional wisdom's Hail Mary.

'...and two of them are good'

Woody Hayes is widely believed to have said,

When you pass, three things can happen and two of them are bad.

Actually it was coach Bob Neyland of Tennessee who said that. He is a fellow member of the Long Gray Line, so I rise to his defense.

But when it comes to last-play-of-the-game Hail Mary passes, remember that many things can happen and **two of them are good**:

- **complete** to one of your players
- defensive pass **interference**.

In the event of a catch, you score six points. In the event of defensive pass interference, you get to try again, even if the final gun went off during the play. The game cannot end on a defensive penalty without the offense's permission. You would accept the penalty if you did not score on the play. Then you would get to run one more untimed play.

In **high school**, the penalty is 15 yards from the previous spot (where the ball was snapped at the start of the play) and an automatic first down. If the interference was deemed **intentional**, the penalty is **30 yards** from the previous spot. (NFICA 7-5-10). So you not only get to try again, you get to try from closer to the goal. And if there is time left on the clock, you also get a first down. All of that is almost as good as a score and may well result in one.

In **college**, the rule is similar, only the offense gets the ball at the spot of the interference and an automatic first down if the spot of the interference was within 15 yards of the previous spot. If the interference occurred more than 15 yards beyond the previous spot, the 15-yard penalty in marked off from the pervious spot. But if the previous spot was between the defense's 17- and 2-yard line, the offense gets first down at the defense's two-yard line! If the previous spot was inside the defense's two yard line, the offense gets first down half way between the previous spot and the goal line. (NCAA 7-3-8)

In the **NFL**, defensive pass interference is generally first down at the spot of the foul. But if the defensive pass interference is **in the defense's end zone**, the offense gets first down on the defense's **one-yard line**. As in college, if the previous spot was inside the defense's two yard line, the offense get first down halfway between the previous spot and the goal line. (NFL 8-2)

Do you have a **case history**? If you've seen a play or game that well illustrates a principle of clock management (not just about Hail Mary passes), please contact me and tell me about it. I'll put the best ones in the second edition of this book.

15

Top-speed hurry-up offense

There are three main types of no-huddle offense: the **top-speed** hurry-up used by teams which need to use the minimum time (about six seconds) for each play to score before the half runs out, the **inbounds** no-huddle (about 20 seconds per play) where the offense does not huddle but neither do they try to stop the clock after every play, and the **whole-game** no-huddle whose purpose is to confuse and tire out the opponent regardless of the score. I'll cover the top-speed in this chapter and the whole-game no-huddle in the next chapter. The inbounds no-huddle is covered in the slowdown chapter.

Go to the hurry-up as soon as you fall behind

Most people think you don't start that until late in the first half or late in the game. By "late," I mean like the time when the rules change in the pros: the last two minutes of the first half and the last five minutes of the game.

Seems to me that if the team that scores first wins 70% to 84% of the time, which they do, you are in big trouble **whenever** you are behind and you had better take drastic action, **now**. If you are currently behind, there is around a 70% to 84% chance that you will still be behind in the last minutes of the game.

When those last minutes arrive and you are still behind, you will wish you had conserved time earlier in the game. So my conclusion is that you should *start your hurry-up as soon as you fall behind*. There is an exception which I discussed in the Slowdown offense chapter. (When you are on your last possession of the **first half**, you operate at whatever pace is required to leave about 20 seconds on the clock after you score. When you are on your last possession of the **game**, and you are behind by eight points or fewer, you operate at whatever pace is required to leave about 20 seconds on the clock after you score.)

'Plenty of time'

Most coaches believe they should not go to a hurry-up in the first quarter, or even the second or third quarter—except possibly for a just-before-half-time possession. They regard going to a hurry-up that early as **panicking**. "There's still plenty of time," they would tell you."

They're wrong. Slowing up whenever you are ahead and speeding up whenever you are behind is the most controversial advice in this book. So I'll devote extra space to making the case.

Between plays time span

Video of the 1996 Liberty Bowl made it clear that the refs were taking about 15-17 seconds per play because the game-clock time run off between the end of one play and the next snap was about 40 seconds.

When I analyzed youth football video, the time from end-of-play whistle to ready-to-play whistle was about 19 seconds on average. Youth football uses high school rules which are generally the same as college and pro rules, and high school referees.

I ran a hurry-up offense for almost an entire season one year. I found that the officials **shortened** their end-of-play to ready-to-play interval to about **eleven seconds** when they saw that they were holding us up. (My players would line up with their hands on their knees waiting for the ready-to-play whistle. They would get **set** on the ready-to-play whistle and snap the ball within two or three seconds of that whistle.)

Play clock

In the NFL, there is no ready-to-play whistle on many plays. Rather the play clock starts when the previous play is blown dead. The offense then gets 40 seconds from the end of the last play to snap the ball. In the NFL, there is only a ready-to-play whistle, which starts a 25-second play clock, when something unusual happens, like a first down, injury timeout, change of possession, and so forth.

One of the conclusions I have come to while researching this book is that the college and high school rule committees really need to adopt the pro 40-second clock rule. As it is now, the time the refs take between blowing the last play dead and blowing the ready-to-play whistle is an unknown and uncontrollable variable, and it can decide the outcome of a game. That should not be.

I found the following typical times in games following high school rules:

period	average elapsed time
• snap to end-of-play whistle	5 seconds
• end-of-play whistle to ready-to-play whistle	19 seconds
• ready-to-play whistle to snap	16 seconds
total	40 seconds

Here are the rules regarding the maximum play clock at each level:

• high school	25 seconds
• college	25 seconds
• NFL	40 seconds usually 25 seconds after certain events

Conserving time

You conserve game-clock time by stopping the game clock whenever possible and by shortening the amount of time you spend on each of the three phases of a play.

Here's a discussion of some hurry-up no-huddle techniques and considerations by Raider managing partner Al Davis from Paul Zimmerman's book, *The New Thinking Man's Guide to Pro Football*:

A quarterback can complete a 10- to 15-yard pass, turn to an official and call timeout, and only six seconds will have run off. A 30-yard completion downfield takes 10 seconds, and if you've called two plays in the huddle, it'll take another seven to 10 seconds to put the ball in play again. If you complete that pass and call a timeout, it's another 10 seconds, but you can run up and throw the ball away and the whole thing has only taken 12 seconds and you've saved a timeout. Those are things a quarterback and a coach have to know, but you'd be surprised how many of them don't.

Snap to end-of-play whistle

Some plays take longer than others. The play that takes the **least** time is the game-clock-stopping **spike** of the ball. Other usually quick plays include quarterback sneaks and quick slant passes. But with the exception of the spiking play, most plays are chosen for the yards they are likely to gain, the points they are likely to score, or their ability to stop the clock if they fail to score—like incomplete passes and running out of bounds.

End-of-play whistle to ready-to-play whistle

What has to happen during this period? At the very least, the referees have to get hold of the ball and place it for the next play. That consists of two things:

- fetching the ball
- moving it to the hash if the play went outside of the hashes.

They also have to get to the spot of the tackle or leaving fair territory to perform the chores of stopping the players from piling on and of spotting the ball for the next play. Then they like to get to the spots where each stands at the beginning of a play: the head linesman, side judge, back judge, and line judge outside the widest receivers; the field judge and umpire behind the defense, and the referee behind the offense.

In the NFL, this period means zilch because the 40-second clock is already running.

Hand the ball to the ref

Your players can reduce the fetching time by simply *handing the ball to the referee.* They should be trained to do so. Recently, many have gotten into the habit of disdainfully tossing the ball aside. The implication of the discard-the-ball body language is, "I am king. The official is my servant who must clean up after me."

This is unseemly at best. It probably annoys the refs who, after all, have to fetch the ball about 80 to 130 times a game. As far as game-clock management is concerned, referees fetching a ball off the ground wastes precious time. Train your players to hand the ball to the nearest official after each play whenever you are in a hurry-up or normal mode. (When you are trying to waste time, your ball carriers should leave the ball on the ground. Deliberately tossing the ball so it rolls away from the official is unsportsmanlike in the general sense of that word. And it may be a violation of the rules.)

Defenses that unpile slowly

When they are ahead and approaching the end of a half, teams often unpile slowly. That increases the referee's fetch time in high school and college football. Navy defeated Army in 1963 with that trick.

Unpiling slowly is **unethical** and **illegal**. But you cannot rely on either the ethics of your opponent or the strictness of the referees. Your players need to find a way to get up fast. Your players can and should help their teammates up, but they cannot pull opposing players off the pile because of the danger of a penalty.

Generally, teams trying to conserve time can avoid this problem if they run **outside the tight ends**. But that usually creates another problem: forcing the refs to take extra time to move the ball back inside the hashes. Although the refs moving the ball back inside almost always takes less time than trying to get out from under a pile.

On offense when you are in a hurry, you may also reduce the slow-unpiling problem if your blockers are conscious of it and refuse to allow defenders to pile on to begin with. That is, they sustain their blocks after the dead-ball whistle if they are near the ball carrier.

Stay between the hashes

You can save a little moving-the-ball time if you keep your plays **inside the hash marks**. But generally, your play selection will be based on the play's probability of success rather than whether it will stay between the hashes. However, if you have a choice between two plays with **equal** probability of success, choose the one most likely to stay between the hashes.

Handing the ball to the official will save up to **five seconds per play**. Avoiding the need to move the ball back inside to the hash mark will save maybe another five seconds per play.

Ready-to-play whistle to snap

Often, the game clock does not run during all or part of the ready-to-play-whistle-to-snap phase. That happens after timeouts, incomplete passes, out-of-bounds plays, penalty decisions and enforcements, and so forth. See the chapter on the rules for details. But when the game clock **is** running, this is the most prominent phase of the so-called "two-minute drill."

Look at what normally happens during this phase:

- move from end-of-previous-play positions to huddle
- wait for play messenger or play signal from sideline
- quarterback gets play
- quarterback repeats play to huddle
- break huddle and move to play-formation positions
- get set for one second
- shift, if used, then get set for one second again
- motion (after everyone is set for one second), if used
- call cadence
- snap.

No huddle

The obvious thing to eliminate when you want to save time is the huddle. Indeed, the two-minute drill is invariably a no-huddle sequence of plays.

Only one item in the above list can**not** be eliminated: **getting set for one second**. The rules require it. But the rest **can** be eliminated, and **should** be.

Play signals

The rules do not require play signals, but you cannot run a play without communicating to the players which play you want. This is sometimes done by the quarterback verbally calling a coded **audible** at the line of scrimmage. In the most famous Super Bowl, Super Bowl III, winning quarterback Joe Namath generally just said "Check with me" in the huddle. That is, he would give the team the play after he got to the line of scrimmage—after he saw the defense.

Some teams use quarterback **hand signals**.

Two-minute drills often involve **memorized play sequences**. In that case, only the identity of the **sequence** must be communicated. The players can then execute several plays without waiting for a play to be communicated to them. Or at least that's the plan.

I prefer **coded play numbers** sent in to **all the players simultaneously** from a **sign board** on the sideline.

In the 1996 season, I used a down-related system for one two-minute drill sequence on my freshman team. I would signal that we were using this sequence by waving my arm in a circle like a referee's start-the-clock signal. My players would then execute plays according to the **down**.

- If it was **1**st down, they would run I left quasar **91** (quick out pass).
- If it was **2**nd down, they would execute I left quasar **92** (quick slant pass).
- If it was **3**rd down, they would execute I left dark **393** (5-step out & streak pass routes)
- If it was **4**th down, they would execute I left dark **444** (all curl-in pass).

This worked well enough for freshman football. We won one game against Campolindo with a last-second, literally, field goal, 15-14. Our down-sequence two-minute drill played an important part of our final, no-timeouts-left scoring drive.

But in retrospect, I do **not** like this down-based approach. The reason is, when it works, you keep having **first** down and therefore run the same quasar 91 pattern over and over. Better we should have used all four plays of the sequence in order **regardless** of down. In that case, the quarterback could simply hold up one, two, three, or four fingers to the other players to signify the play. Or he could simply assume that they knew where they were in the sequence.

The disadvantage of this is that you cannot do this more than one or two times in a particular game because the opponents will figure out the code. A sharp-eyed **scout** may even figure it out and teach it to his players **before** the game.

The warp-speed no-huddle

The no-huddle approach I recommend is what I call the warp-speed no-huddle. The players got set on the ready-to-play whistle or when we sent in the play, whichever came **last**. In the warp-speed, you number ten plays from 0 to 9. (You could have more plays if you use a slightly more complicated code.) You may want to match the numbers to hole or back or pass route numbers wherever possible. That's what I did with the down sequence described above. Here's an example play list:

Play #	No-huddle play	Type
0	I right 9**0** quick	quick pass
1	Quads right **11** inside trap	run
2	Offset I left **22** inside trap	run
3	Weak right double-tight unbalanced 2**3** base	run
4	Strong right **44** base	run
5	I left dark **555**	5-step drop-back pass
6	I right 5**6** lead base	run
7	I left dark **717** seam	5-step drop-back pass
8	I right 5**8** sweep crack	run
9	I left **99** quick	quick pass

Code numbers

In 1993, I used a 24" x 18" white board and a Jumbo Expo II dry erase marker to send in the plays. We wrote a three-digit number on it. All eleven players were to look at the white board to get the play.

The first digit meant nothing. The last two digits were added together and the play number was the last digit of the answer. For example, 984 would mean 8 + 4 = 12 or play #2. 723 would decode as 2 + 3 = 5 or play #5. This may sound too complicated. It's not. My 1993 team **never** ran the wrong play a single time all season—and they were nine- and ten-year olds!

Magna Doodle®

I was concerned in 1993 that our white board and dry erase marker would not work in the **rain**. We had a little rain one game, but it was not a problem.

In 1996, my assistant coach, Cy Doerner, got the idea to use a Magna Doodle® instead of a white board. A Magna Doodle® is a magnetic drawing toy. It consists of a blue plastic rectangle with about an 8 1/2" x 11" white screen. You write on the screen with a magnet that is about the size of a quarter. It makes a roughly one-inch wide black mark.

You can fit up to four large numbers on the Magna Doodle®. These numbers are readable from 50 yards away, which is the farthest distance your players will ever be from the Magna Doodle® (they at the far hash on the one-yard line and you on your sideline at the 30-yard line). But they are small enough to be diabolically difficult to read from the opposing sideline, which is 53 1/3 yards away.

There is a slide along one side of the Magna Doodle® which erases the screen. It should work rain or shine.

For a time during the 1996 season, we sent our formations and plays in using the Magna Doodle®. The code was that the **lower left digit** indicated the **formation** and the last digit of the sum of the upper left and lower right numbers was the play. The upper right number was meaningless. Here's an example:

5	4
3	9

The formation number, 3, is odd. That means the formation strong side is right. The word "right" has five letters. Five is an odd number. "Left" is a four-letter word and four is an even number. An odd number in the lower left indicates right formation; an even, left.

The play number is 5 + 9 = 14 or play #4. So the translation of the above four-digit sign is,

Right formation, Play 4.

Obviously, you can use the four digits in many other ways. You could make the bottom two the play. You could make the left two the back number and the right two the hole number. And so forth.

You could have more than one Magna Doodle® to signal more complicated plays. If your team colors were green and gold, you might have a person in a **green** shirt whose Magna Doodle® indicates the **formation** and a person in a **gold** shirt whose Magna Doodle® indicates the **play**.

My main point here is that when you are trying to conserve time, and you are not using memorized play sequences, you need the fastest way possible to send in plays. Memorized play sequences are faster than even Magna Doodle® signals. But they are less flexible and more likely to result in error.

Our Magna Doodle® never malfunctioned. But you may want to have a spare in case it does. One brand new one I saw in a toy store had a broken eraser slide. Also, I never used the Magna Doodle® in bad weather. Cold or rain may foul it up. Test it in practice.

The best solution is probably a set of flip numbers like the old-style down markers. You could get three or four sets of ten (0 to 9) and hinge them on top of a board. You select the play by flipping the numbers before the ones you want over to the back of the board then show the desired numbers. This should be both rain- and malfunction-proof.

Can opponents crack the code?

Coaches may worry that the opponents can crack the above play code. Actually, most traditional play signals are even easier to break. For example, I saw a coach signal a quarterback sneak by steepling his hands together and making a diving motion. That's rather obvious. A scout could train his video camera on the signaling coach between plays. I've done it in high school football. (Video scouting was illegal in our youth leagues.)

With the warp-speed no-huddle, the **defensive players on the field** have to crack the offensive code—because there is not enough time for the opposing **coaches** to decode, then signal their defense.

Most importantly, the code is **too hard to crack**. Unless you've read this book or one of my other books, the notion of adding numbers together is unlikely to even **occur** to you. And if you **have** read this book, you still have to figure out **which** numbers to add.

One live, one decoy

There are numerous things the offense could do to make it harder. For example, you could have **two** guys holding up Magna Doodles®—one live, one meaningless. You could add a Magna Doodle® digit to the last number of your team's **score**. You could make the **hand position** of the guy holding the Magna Doodle® part of the code. You could have a "wild card" number that means the "Play of the Week" or that means use an audible or use the play of the last digit of your team's score. That'll drive would-be code-breakers nuts.

Basically, there are just too many ways to code the play for the defense to ever feel confident they have it. And if the offense ever suspected their code had been broken, they could run a **wrong-way play**. That is, tell the players to run one play when they are on the sideline, then signal an opposite play on the Magna Doodle® and watch the opponent's linebackers. The ideal wrong-way play would be to signal a play, then actually run the misdirection play that starts out looking like the signaled play. Or you could signal a running play then run the play action pass off that running play.

Single-wing coaches use occasional wrong-way plays to discourage opposing linebackers from keying on their blocking back. If the defense reacts to the Magna Doodle® play, as opposed to the play the offense runs, immediately change the code so that the defense is going the opposite way from the play. After two or three such plays, they'll stop looking at the board.

Before a game, an opposing coach in 1994 told me he had broken our code in our game the previous year. "Oh, really?" we said. Then we went out and used the exact same code in the 1994 game. At half-time, we were winning 14-0. In fact, the opposing coach was crazy. He may have **thought** he broke our code. But we were always on the lookout for opposing players looking at our white board. They invariably tried to figure it out on the first series, then gave up. And that's exactly what had happened in the 1993 game in question. If no one on the other side is looking at your play board, they have not broken the code. No one ever looked at our board after the first five or six plays.

Appallingly transparent codes

I have long been interested in codes. As a kid, I was a member of the American Cryptogram Association. When I was in school as an Army officer, a bunch of us started solving newspaper cryptograms for fun. We got so good at it, we could often break them at a glance without pencil and paper.

My training and work in the army was in communications and that included codes. I spent a tour in Vietnam where preventing the other "team" from breaking our codes was literally a matter of life or death.

I was appalled at the lax codes in Vietnam. For example, in radio transmissions, "Six" was always the **commander** and "twenty" was always **location**. As in, "Six is on his way to your twenty." That's a good way for "six " to get his butt shot down.

Or a particular officer would use some macho handle like "Ball breaker" for his entire one-year tour. Another common trick was to assign car names to grid coordinates, as in, "We're going to set six down two clicks northeast of Camaro." Later, documents were discovered which revealed that North Vietnamese soldiers monitoring our radio transmissions would mark the secret "two clicks northeast of Camaro" location on a map instantly upon hearing the words. Typically, they had been assigned to that duty for years and had been listening to Americans say Camaro in that area for years. They had no idea what a Camaro was, but they had long ago figured out that it was a spot one kilometer south southeast of the village of Phu Loi.

I spent much of my tour in Vietnam fruitlessly trying to get my colleagues to switch to better codes, which were readily available in our military code books, and to change them frequently, which is also good code practice.

Football's equivalents

After Vietnam, I was only mildly surprised to learn that football teams use incredibly transparent codes within sight or earshot of the opposing team. A coach might signal a long bomb pass play by making an exploding motion with his hands. A defensive coordinator might touch his nose then hold up his right arm at a 45-degree angle signaling for the nose tackle to slant to his right.

A quarterback might call an off-tackle play in the huddle, add "Check with me," then walk up to the line of scrimmage, observe that the opposing defense had their strong safety on the right and yell "Odd!" meaning run the **left** version of the off-tackle play. How many times can they do that before the defense figures out that odd means to the offense's left and even means to the right?

Actually, forever according to Roger Theder, an NFL and college coach of many years experience. He said when he first got to the NFL, he was astounded at how easy the audibles were to decode. Twelve was a quarterback sneak through the right A gap. 85 was a five-step drop medium depth pass route.

But the players assured him it was not a problem. And Theder found that they were correct. That notwithstanding, I still recommend better codes. The Germans and Japanese lost World War II in large part because we broke their codes. According to *Sports Illustrated* football writer Paul Zimmerman, the Oilers beat the Chargers in the 1979 AFC divisional playoff 17-14 by a combination of stealing Charger signals and tipoffs in the alignment of Dan Fouts' pre-snap feet alignment. Houston intercepted four Fouts passes in that game. Theder coached at the Chargers in the late eighties.

Audibles

Audibles are typically sequences like a color followed by a two-digit number. When the "hot" color is said, the numbers that follow are the new play. For example, a team whose colors are blue and gold might make blue its "hot" color. "Green 34" would mean run the play called in the huddle, the phrase "Green 34" being a decoy audible. But "Blue 26" would be a **change** in play from the one called in the huddle to a 26 play—two back through the six hole.

If I'm a linebacker, I make a mental note of the color and see if they run that play. Before long, I'll have the "hot" color. Then the opponent's numbering system is probably similar to the defense's. It may even be the same.

For example, two is usually the tailback, three the fullback, and so forth. Holes are generally numbered from the inside out with even on the right—2, 4, 6, 8 and odd, on the left—1, 3, 5, 7. When I crack the code, I tell my teammates in the defensive huddle and the offense's audibles suddenly start averaging minus yardage.

I have heard that college and pro football coaches hiring all sorts of outside experts on everything from ballet dancing to psychology. They need to hire some **code experts** for both designing their own codes and breaking their opponents'. The security level of the vast majority of football play codes is ridiculous.

I'm no code expert, but here are a few principles:

- include **meaningless information** in every signal
- make the code **simple** enough that your guys decode it correctly every time
- do **not** use charade-like hand signals whose meaning could be recognized by an opponent
- do **not** use two hand signals which closely resemble each other

Meaningless information

Baseball base coaches are good at sending meaningless information with every signal. They typically give a flurry of hand signals, only one of which is "live." I assume football coaches do **not** do that because:

1. they are in a hurry because of the play clock
2. they have to communicate multiple bits of information, e.g., formation, ball carrier, hole, etc.

Football coaches must find a way to send meaningless information to throw the opponent off. In the NFL, they often have two or three coaches or players signaling in plays. Only one is live. My numbers on a sign system simply had one meaningless digit. That's fast and simple and unlikely to confuse your own players. But it adds immense complexity to the opponent's task of breaking your code.

In the Buffalo Bills no-huddle, which uses quarterback audibles to call the plays, the quarterback calls many dummy signals.

Belvidere (IL) High School Pottinger, whose team holds the record for most plays and most rushing attempts in a season, has two signalers. One is live the other is a dummy. They change which one is live during each game. Pottinger, like most coaches, uses backup quarterbacks to signal in the plays.

Reliability

I have long been amazed at the level of miscommunication football coaches are willing to tolerate. Many's the time I have been on the sideline when an offensive coordinator would watch a play and exclaim, "What the heck play is he running!?" Typically, the messenger forgot on the way to the quarterback. Or the messenger did not hear the coach clearly. Or the quarterback mistook one hand signal for a similar one.

Seems to me that no system that is not 100% reliable should be used. My numbers-on-a-white-board system **never** produced a single wrong play all season. Good coaches spend hours analyzing their plays to figure out what works when. A mistaken play is not only less likely to work, it may well be a **terrible** play for the situation in question, since it is chosen more or less randomly.

In a two-minute drill situation, there is no time for messengers. What's worse, messengers require huddles to relay the play from the quarterback to the players. Finally, the messenger method replicates a party game where a message is whispered to one person who repeats it to another and so on down the line. The final version is invariably comically garbled. That's funny at a party, but not in the final minutes of a football game.

Opaque, unmistakable hand signals

If you are going to use hand signals, you should use signals that give no charades-like clues to the opponent. For example, do not use a signal that involves the signaler's nose when you want to say, in code, nose guard or nose tackle. Rather use hand signals that have meaning **only** to **your** players and coaches.

Semaphore is a good model. That is a system of signals sent by a man holding a small flag in each hand. The military used to use it. You see it sometimes in World War II movies. It was in Boy Scout manuals last time I saw one. There is a position for each letter of the alphabet and for the numbers 0 through 9. Each signal is explicitly designed to be as different as possible from all others to minimize the danger of confusion.

In football, you would not need to learn all 36 signals. You could probably communicate all your plays with a shorter list of signals. If you did use semaphore, you should deliberately **not** use the standard signals to mean the same letters and numbers as they do in the *Boy Scout Manual*. No need to help an opponent. You could signal a play like "I right 26 power" with the semaphore signals

I R 2 6 P 4

where the final 4 is meaningless.

I still prefer the sign board method. It's faster. Semaphore requires **sequential** signals, as does the standard football method of touching the eye for I formation and all that. The sign board communicates the whole schmear at once. Tennessee head coach Phillip Fulmer says he uses just one or two quick hand signals for two-minute drill plays.

Hand signals also get missed if everyone is not watching at precisely the moment you send each one. Baseball players often signal a base coach to "retransmit" by circling their index finger—so do quarterbacks. But baseball players don't have a 25-second clock—or worse—a two-minute drill. And there's usually only one or two baseball players, not eleven, with whom you have to communicate. With the sign board, everyone can blink, tie their shoe, or whatever, and still get the play.

Longer play names

In 1996, I was a high school freshman offensive coordinator. The varsity head coach would **not** let me reduce any play names to one digit. So I tried various ways to run the warp-speed with his system, which required as many as 8 instructions for a running play and 9 for a pass play. The best way I found was to have pads printed up at Kinkos. The pads had four blank boxes where I wrote the formation, motion, pass drop, back, and hole numbers. It also had about a dozen words like "power" and "inside trap" to indicate blocking schemes, special plays, and pass routes for backs. I would scribble things like

S L
DTU
D
717

then circle the word

seam.

That meant "strong left, double tight unbalanced, dark, 717 seam." That, in turn, meant that the fullback was behind the quarterback and the tailback was behind the right tackle. Unbalanced meant that the left tackle went over to the right side between the tight end and tackle. The left wide receiver became the left tight end and the right wide receiver became the right wing. D means dark or 5-step drop. 717 meant that the three receivers ran 7 (flag), 1 (out), and 7 routes respectively from left to right. Seam was the pass route for the tailback.

The messenger player would hold the play note on his chest at the ball with his back to the opponent. The players would form a tight huddle for the sole purpose of seeing the play note. Once each player had seen it, he would hurry to his position and get ready to run the play. The messenger would stuff the play into his pants and get set himself.

This worked well enough to discombobulate the opponents to an extent, but I did **not** like this system. It took too long to write the plays down, even with the pre-printed forms. And they still had to be run in. Long play names are not feasible in two-minute drills. Some sort of shorthand **must** be worked out.

Memorized play sequences

Many coaches use memorized play sequences for their two-minute drill. I sort of did that with my if-it's-first-down-run-91 approach. A common format is to memorize two plays at a time. That's the way Tom Beck did it at Grand Valley State, which led the nation in total offense and scoring offense the year his clinic on the two-minute drill appeared in the *Coach of the Year Clinic Manual*, 1990.

Those coaches figure that the clock will stop after one of those two plays on account of going out of bounds or falling incomplete or calling a timeout. If none of those happen, there must be a hand signal or audible for the third play. Remember you should not have any timeouts because they are best used when you are on defense and your opponent is running their slowdown.

Silent 'cadence'

We used a silent "cadence" in my youth teams. And we used it for a while in my freshman team. Silent "cadence" meant no "Ready! Hut!" or any of that. When we ran the single wing, the center was looking through his legs at the tailback. The tailback would call for the ball by flicking his thumb as if he were flipping an invisible coin sideways. When we ran an offense with the quarterback under center, we had the quarterback use hand pressure to tell the center when to snap.

The silent "cadence" has three advantages:

- At the beginning of the game, the defense is often unaware that the ball is being snapped until it's too late
- Silent "cadence" saves one to three seconds per play
- Rarely a false start.

We often snapped the ball when the defense was still in its huddle or when some of the defensive players had their backs turned to the line of scrimmage. Regular verbal cadence acts as a **wake-up call** for the defense.

The silent cadence had the unexpected benefit of all but eliminating illegal procedure penalties. We only had two all season in 1993, both caused by defensive players making a sudden movement to trick our players into moving.

Line coaches are typically horrified at my silent cadence recommendation. But when you think about it, there is already a lot of silent cadence in football. Silent cadence is normal in:

- wide receiver get-off
- field goal attempts
- PAT kick attempts
- punts
- shotgun offense

South Carolina's Brad Scott uses a silent cadence in his shotgun no-huddle. But he has a twist. He has the center yell, "Hike!" when he snaps the ball so the linemen don't have to turn their heads toward the center to see the ball move. I like that idea, but I would instruct the center to keep quiet if he saw that we were going to snap with one or more defenders not paying attention. In other words, no wake-up calls for our line, which also wake up the defense, unless everyone on the defense is already awake. You would typically catch some defenders napping at the beginning of the game.

First sound

Regular cadence also takes about one second per word. In a tight game, those extra seconds add up. And if the number of seconds left is below three, and the clock is not stopped, your need to call cadence to get the play started could doom you to defeat before the snap. If you must use a verbal cadence, go on **first or second sound** during your two-minute drill. First sound is **fastest**. Second sound is slower but gives your line a chance to tee off on the defense if your quarterback uses a **rhythmic** cadence (always the same time interval between the first and second sound).

Snap count matched to play

Many teams vary the snap count during their two-minute drill by making it part of the play. For example, "Whenever we call 32 or 33 dive, it will be on one. Whenever we call 25 or 26 power, it will be on first sound. And so forth." The complexity of that scares me. I can easily envision players jumping offside.

Practicing the warp-speed

The warp-speed takes a little practice. I found the best way was to play the role of referee/coach. I would blow the ready-to-play whistle then count out loud, "One thousand one! One thousand two! One thousand three!" If I got to three and the ball had not yet been snapped, I would admonish the players. For repeatedly being too slow, I would have them do five push-ups or five up-downs or some such.

Basically, the warp-speed is a **habit**, a rhythm your players get into. They need prodding at first, then an occasional reminder.

Hustle to the ball

All offensive players must get into the habit of following the play. Normally, they do their block then stand and watch. That's never a good idea. But it is absolutely verboten when you are running a hurry-up pace.

Defensive coaches run double-whistle drills (The first whistle ends the play, but all defenders run to the ball. Second whistle authorizes them to return and line up for the next play.) and others to inculcate the fly-to-the-ball habit. Two-minute drill **offensive** coaches should take a page from their **defensive** counterparts practice book on this one.

Shifts and motion

You probably need to **forget** shifts and motion in your hurry-up mode. They take time. All eleven players have to be set for one second before any one can go in motion and before the ball can be snapped. Using shifts and motion **increase penalties** in general. They especially are likely to result in a penalty when you are in a hurry.

Here are some actual two-minute drill successes and failures in games you may remember and some more obscure games.

Navy blows it

In the more-versus-enough discussion in the overview chapter, I told how Navy stupidly went for a touchdown when they could have locked the game up with an easy field goal in the 1995 Army-Navy Game.

As bad as Navy's decision to go for six was, Navy's clock management during the final 63 seconds was **worse**. After Army's late score to go ahead 14-13, Navy received the kickoff. Navy had no timeouts left when they began their final drive. They returned Army's kickoff to their own 30.

Get out of bounds

They should have run out of bounds to stop the clock on their first play from scrimmage. Instead, they had to line up and **spike** the ball to stop the clock. That took **31** seconds and left them with **third** and ten.

The **third**-down pass was incomplete, stopping the clock. The **fourth**-down pass was complete and the receiver got out of bounds at the Army 42—first down. There were now 26 seconds left.

The **first**-down pass—over the middle—was incomplete. Had a pass in that area been **complete**, the receiver would **not** have been able to get out of bounds and the clock would keep running after the tackle. Not smart with only 26 seconds left. Had the pass been complete, the receiver would have had to run to the first-down yard line then slide to stop the clock if it was apparent that he could not score on the play.

Navy's quarterback then rolled right looking for a receiver. Finding none, he ran and gained five yards, to the Army 37, but as on the first play of the drive, he did **not get out of bounds**! Navy had to scramble to line up and **spike** the ball to stop the clock. All of that took 24 seconds!

With just two seconds left, and needing to kick a 54-yard field goal or score a touchdown, Navy threw to the end zone and got intercepted. Army won: 14-13.

Army runs out of time

At the 1963 Army-Navy Game, clock management went the other way. Navy, led by Heisman Trophy-winning junior, Roger Staubach, was ahead 21-15 with 6:19 left in the game. Army's onside kick was successful at their 49-yard line.

With no time outs left Army drove to Navy's seven-yard line. The clock read 1:38.

Don Parcells, brother of NFL coach Bill Parcells, gained two yards on a dive. Ken Waldrop gained a yard to the four. Army was huddling between plays. That's OK. They were in an inbounds hurry-up situation.

The pertinent reference here is the **first-and-goal table** in the slowdown chapter. It shows that Army should have been in an **inbounds hurry-up** pace for the first two downs, then switched to a top-speed hurry-up pace during the third down. In other words, if Army had had a clock-management assistant coach, he would have flipped his colored panels from yellow to red during the interval between the end of the second-down play and the snap for the third-down play. At 45 seconds, Army quarterback Rollie Stichweh signaled for the crowd of 100,000 to quiet. The clock stopped briefly to wait for quiet.

It was third down and there were 29 seconds left when Army ran their last play, another inside run. It got to the two-yard line. But Navy's players would not let the Army players up, the referees refused to stop the clock, and the whole 29 seconds got used up trying to pull the Navy players off the ball carrier. Navy won: 21-15.

Given that they played in front of 100,000 rabid fans at the time, they should have been prepared to snap the ball without needing to **hear** a cadence. As I said above, I had my offense go on **ball movement** for an entire season in youth football and for much of a season in freshman ball. I could never tell the difference between a normal snap count and going on ball movement as far as the linemen's jump was concerned. I understand the logic of getting a jump. I just couldn't see the theoretical benefit with my own eyes when I watched films of us going on movement and our opponents going on a count.

Navy's behavior was unethical. The last play probably took **four** of the 29 seconds that remained. Twenty-five more seconds to unpile is obvious delay. Navy's linebacker, Fred Marlin, admitted as much, "The more they pulled, the more we tried to stay down. You're going to take as much time as you can. That's football." The leading team should try to waste time. That's what much of this book is about. But unpiling that slowly is **not** a part of this book and should not be a part of your coaching.

Of course, the referees should have at least stopped the clock during the unpiling and probably should have penalized Navy for the delay. But this is a book for coaches, not referees. We coaches have to find a way to win in spite of poor officiating.

It appears this game could have been won, in spite of Navy's refusal to unpile, had Army been more efficient **throughout** the final possession. Army only ran three plays in the last 1:38. That's over 32 seconds per play. 32 seconds per play is a good rate for a **maximum slowdown** offense, **not** for the inbounds hurry-up they should have been in.

Army correctly did an inbounds hurry-up, albeit a slow one, on the first two plays after they got to the Navy seven. But when the crowd prevented snapping on time after second down, the inbounds hurry-up situation evaporated. When you get to 40 seconds left in the game, and you have two downs and four yards to go, you need to get **out** of your **30-seconds-per-play pace**. To score leaving :20 on the clock, you now have to operate at a **10-seconds-per-play pace**, which is a top-speed hurry-up mode.

Colorado's no-huddle

Coach Rick Neuheisel described his no-huddle in the 1996 *Coach of the Year Clinic Manual*. His discussion of passing is interesting. He says you need both a "control" pass and a "chuck" pass in your two-minute drill.

He defines a "control" pass as one which is completed at least 80% of the time for ten yards. That sounds like what Ohio State used in their final scoring drive in the '97 Rose Bowl. You should have two control passes for every formation in your two-minute drill.

Neuheisel defines a "chuck" pass as one that gains 20 yards or more.

Colorado's experience is that college defensive coaches have one or two base defenses that they use against no-huddle offenses. The defenses start out trying to keep everything in front of them, not giving up the big play—a prevent **mentality** if not prevent personnel and alignment. But after seeing a number of control passes completed underneath, the defensive coordinator "...goes for his guns and comes with a blitz."

Accordingly, your two-minute drill must be able to handle both the bend-don't-break zone defense and the blitz. Your players have to be able to pick up the blitzers and block them or throw hot passes behind them. Your receivers need to recognize zone and man coverage and know how to get open in each case.

Neuheisel says you also need several specialty plays:

- red zone plays
- clock stoppers (spike the ball, get out of bounds)
- Hail Mary
- last play (Colorado has three: inside the 20, 20 to 35, outside the 35)
- maneuver play (to position the ball in the middle for a field goal)

Colorado's get-out-of-bounds pass has receivers at all depths. That sounds like a play we ran at both Miramonte and Granada High Schools. It looked roughly like this:

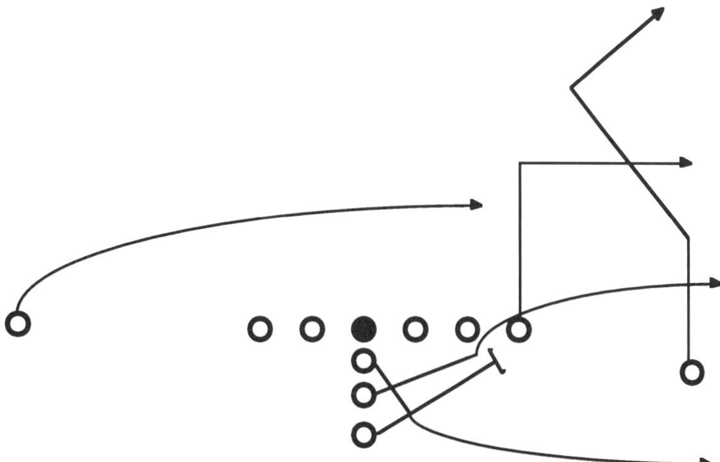

As you can see, the quarterback fakes to the tailback who replaces he tight end as a blocker. The fullback pretends to do a lead kick-out block against the defensive end or outside linebacker then slips through to become a shallow receiver. The tight end runs a medium-deep out and the flanker runs a deep post corner.

This puts four of your players heading toward the sideline and different depths. The quarterback can run out of bounds himself if necessary.

This is a relatively easy pass to complete to the shallow receiver, even at the lowest youth levels. The Miramonte freshman team, on which my son played in 1995, ran this against my Granada freshman team in 1996. Even though I warned the Granada defense and ran Miramonte's play on scout team in practice, Miramonte threw one to the fullback for a touchdown. It had a yards **at** catch of about one and a yards **after** catch of about 60.

Of course, this is a **play-action** pass so it would only be appropriate in a situation when the defense would **believe** you were really running an off-tackle play. The obvious-passing-situation version of this play would be a sprint out without the run fake.

Belvidere (IL) High School's no-huddle

In the ten years after they added the no-huddle to their wishbone offense in 1985, Belvidere (IL) High School won 80% of its games including seven conference titles, 10 play-off berths, and two state championships. (See the 8/95 *Scholastic Coach*)

Belvidere coach Kevin Reilly runs three speeds: "Amtrak" which is full-speed, "Locomotive" which is moderate speed, and "Mule train," which is his slowdown offense. Reilly's 1988 team set a national high school record for most plays per game, 66.1.

Reilly's main plays are the Inside Veer, Outside Veer, Belly, Double Option, and Counter Option. He says he only has seven running plays in his base offense, and only uses five a game. In one state championship game, he ran 65 running plays and six passes and held the ball for 33:17 of the 48-minute game and won 28-0. He admits to some complexity in his blocking adjustments.

Colonia (NJ) High School's no-huddle

Richard Strack, the freshman coach at Colonia (NJ) High School, said in his 4/97 *Scholastic Coach and Athletic Director* article that his team has gone 95-43-7 with three undefeated seasons. Their 1996 team went 9-0 and set a freshman scoring record with 334 points. They did **not** use a no-huddle the **whole game**, but they did use it randomly **throughout** the game. They also rarely ran two no-huddle plays in a row.

Strack uses just seven plays in his no-huddle sequence:

- five high-percentage passes (play-action bench, flare, hitch, slant, TE hot pass)
- a big-play run (pitch sweep)
- a short-yardage power run (inside veer dive).

He sends his plays in with hand signals to all eleven players. And he always goes on "One" when in the no-huddle mode.

The Quads two-minute offense

The Quads two-minute offense was invented in the early '80s by Archie Cooley. He was at that time, head coach of Mississippi Valley State. The main receiver he was trying to get open with this offense was a player named Jerry Rice.

St. John Fisher College in Rochester, NY used a variation of this offense to win 20 of 24 games in 1985 and 1986. They were NCFA national champions both years. Here's the basic formation.

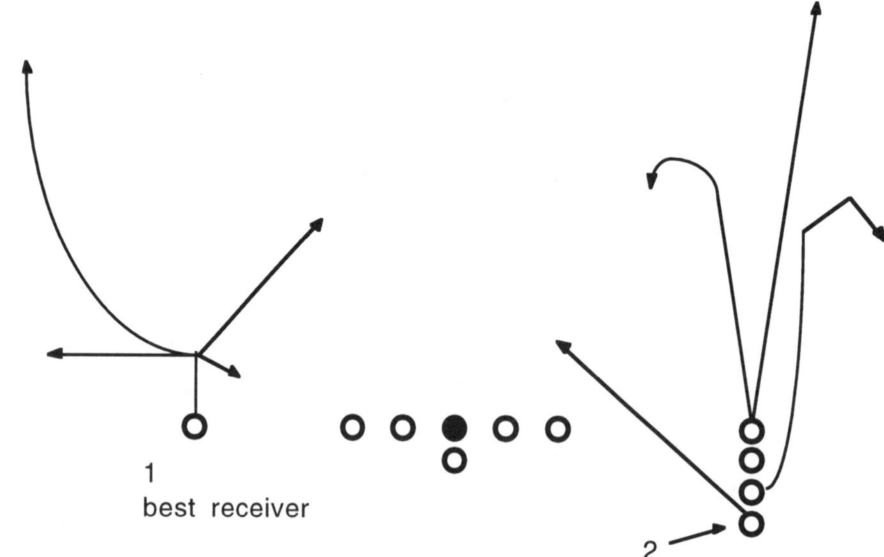

Your best receiver is 12 to 15 yards wide to the weak side and he is your quarterback's first read. Mississippi State would throw to Jerry Rice if he had single coverage. If double coverage on the weak-side wideout, he would throw to the open receiver on the strong side. The second read is the deepest receiver in the quad stack. I suspect this formation might inspire your opponents to call a timeout. As such, it would be a good one to call when you need a timeout, but no longer have any.

Obviously, you can only run one-, three-, or maybe five-step drops from this formation because of the lack of pass-protection blockers. St. John Fisher also **ran** out of this formation. They pitched to the deepest wide receiver. The quarterback ran a keep inside trap. They could shift into a more normal formation. They could put the deepest quads receiver in motion and run the **speed option** to the weak side.

The St. John Fisher player, Bill Teeter, who wrote about this offense in the 2/95 issue of *Scholastic Coach and Athletic Director* said this offense could be used to run the defense into the ground, when you substitute frequently for the wide receivers. As others have said, he says this can be used in practice in lieu of gassers and that it's fun for the players.

Trips no-huddle offense

Here's another similar-sounding approach, also from a *Scholastic Coach and Athletic Director* article (9/92). Tom Muhs of Westhampton Beach (NY) High School evolved into a 15-play no-huddle offense. The formation flips right or left and the quarterback audibles the play based on the defensive alignment. Here's the right formation.

This is a one-back version of Teeter's quad stack. As with Teeter's, there is a pitch to the deepest wide receiver, who can then pass or run. Muhs also has

- Look-in to tight end
- Out to the deepest wide receiver
- Out and up to the deepest wide receiver
- Fullback screen to either side
- Shovel pass to the fullback
- Slot back counter
- Fullback trap
- Speed option
- Fly pattern
- Post pattern
- Flag pattern
- Fullback dive
- Pitch to the fullback who throws back to the quarterback

Muhs scored five touchdowns in one game with this offense. As with everybody else who has experience with the whole-game no-huddle, Muhs says the offense is fun.

Washburn's no-huddle

Peter Moe, head coach of Washburn (ND) High School, says he originally put in the no-huddle just for game-ending come-from-behind drives. But it evolved into a normal part of the offense.

Like other no-huddle coaches, Moe found he had to simplify his offense. He uses just one formation. It looks like the next evolutionary step from Muhs' trips no-huddle.

He always puts the two-wide receiver side to the wide side of the field, the right if the ball is in the middle. As I did with my youth team, Moe numbered his no-huddle plays from zero to nine. He says he puts wrist bands with the numbers on his players early in the season, but gets rid of them after the first few weeks. I never did that, but I found I could only put in one play a day over the first three weeks.

Moe made numbers one through five, passes. I used **even** numbers for passes. Either is probably equally acceptable. His plays are:

1-3 Sprint-out pass
4 Screen
5 Three-step drop to weak end
6 Draw
7 Option
8 Counter trey
9 Reverse

Moe signals the play to the quarterback who, in turn, uses an **audible** system in which the quarterback yells a color and two-digit number. One digit is live; the rest is meaningless. Moe uses a standard snap count with the no-huddle.

Moe huddles when the game clock stops. In the huddle, he changes the snap count. They also sometimes call plays other than the nine no-huddle plays when they huddle.

Hill Park (Ontario, Canada) High School's no-huddle

Hill Park (*Scholastic Coach & Athletic Director* May/June 1997) restricts its no-huddle offense to just four formations:

- wishbone
- power I
- I
- shotgun.

To keep things simple, they stay in the same formation for an entire possession. But they use slightly different personnel for each formation, for example, the power I has extra fullback types.

They mainly run four similar running plays out of each formation:

- freeze option to fullback
- freeze option right to tailback
- off tackle right
- counter left.

Passes are read routes, that is, they are determined by the alignment and behavior of the defensive backs. Hill Park never huddles. They call their plays by audible. The code uses the "police phonetic alphabet" (Alpha, Bravo, Charlie, etc.) and numbers 0 to 9. Quarterbacks are required to take the snap within 8 seconds of the ready-to-play whistle.

Hill Park coach Gino Arcaro says high school defenses react to the whole-game no-huddle in a predictable manner:

- base defense for whole possession
- cautious play
- delayed reaction to plays
- less aggressive pass rush.

Arcaro says his team averages 19 more plays per game than teams not using a whole-game no-huddle. South Carolina's Scott says his high school team always got into a base defense when the opposing team went into a no-huddle pace.

One-play two-minute drill

Colorado head coach Rick Neuheisel says he once scouted a high school team whose two-minute drill was one play out of one formation. They kept running the same play over and over again. He thought that was "a little simplistic, but there is a lesson to learn."

I once ran the same play seven times in a row in 1994. I was special teams coordinator on a San Ramon Bears youth team. The previous year I had been head coach there and had great success with a no-huddle single-wing offense. Many of my players from the previous year were on the team where I was coaching in 1994.

In the first two games of the season, we had won easily against weak opposition. We were using a wing-T because that's what the local high school ran.

But in the next two games, we were unable to make a single first down (although we did win one 6-2 on an interception runback and deliberately taking a safety). In the fourth quarter of the second game, against Napa, I asked the head coach if I could try a single-wing play. He said OK.

We called timeout. I ran out and told the guys to line up in the single-wing like the previous year and run our "student body forward" play, a wedge, from right formation at a no-huddle pace again and again until further notice. The center had been a backup long snapper the previous year. But about half the team on the field had **not** been on my team the previous year and had no idea what I was talking about.

They gained 31 yards and three first downs in seven plays that took about two minutes. Remember this is a team that had not gained a first down in the last two games. Yet with no practice or warning, they were instantly transformed into an unstoppable force. The unbalanced-line single wing was part of the reason for the success. But the warp-speed no-huddle pace was also a big factor. And they ran the exact same play, one play, to the exact same side, over and over during this seven play drive. Then the head coach decided to go back to the wing-T. He has since become strictly a single-wing coach.

You can do a lot with just one play especially if it's combined with a no-huddle pace.

Audible no-huddle system lets quarterback call own plays

Buffalo's Jim Kelly liked the fact that the Bills' no-huddle let him call his own plays. My warp-speed, which runs more plays per minute than the Bills' audible approach, does **not** require the quarterback to call the plays. The quarterback **does** have the advantage of being closer to the action than the coach, although that can work both ways. The coach is in a better position to think things through.

Whether the quarterback calling his own plays makes the team more competitive depends on the quarterback and his coach. That could be either an advantage or a disadvantage of the no-huddle, if you feel you have to use an audible-based play-calling system. Colorado's Rick Neuheisel says,

> *There is less pressure on the quarterback to call the plays in the two-minute offense than there is on all the crazy people on the sideline. If you have an experienced quarterback who can call the plays, that is the way to go.*

I have never had such a quarterback so I had to develop ways to do it from the "crazy" sideline. Youth and high school coaches probably all have horror stories of the time their quarterback called an audible.

At the end of the 1996 season, I watched nationally-ranked DeLaSalle High School, a team with the current longest winning streak in the U.S. (64), a team which slaughters nearly every opponent, struggle in the first half of the North Coast Section championship game at the Oakland Coliseum. Their quarterback called a number of audibles and they went into the locker room leading, but only by 14-7. In the second half, there were no audibles and they won going away 35-7.

Our warp-speed no-huddle worked like a charm and actually got the plays in faster from the sideline than the quarterback on the field could get them in. We had no problem with it. Of course, we never had headsets or guys in the press box. Maybe that's why our sideline was less "crazy."

Take no sacks when you are trying to save time

When you are in the time-conserving, no-huddle mode, your *quarterback must avoid taking a sack.* The clock keeps running after a sack. Rather he must find a receiver to throw toward so it will be an incomplete pass and stop the clock.

You need to practice this. Run a pass play and tell the quarterback that his receivers are covered even if they do not **look** covered, but he must not take a sack. One or two reps of this a week is probably enough. But I think it's a bad idea to simply **tell** your quarterbacks this point and never give them any practice. Remember, **one** rep is infinitely better than **no** reps and one rep takes very little time. It takes much longer to get ready for the next play when you take a sack than in a regular play because everyone was going the other direction and expected the ball to do likewise.

Injuries

Injuries create referee's timeouts. But it is unethical (Provision h of the NCAA Football Code, Provision 2 of the NFICA Safety and Ethics Code), dishonest, unsportsmanlike, contrary to the spirit of the rules, and illegal to feign injury to trigger a referee's timeout. When the Bengals started their whole-game no-huddle in the late '80s, some Bengal opponent coaches apparently told their players to fake injuries to enable them to get their substitutes into the game before the snap. The pertinent rules are NFL 4-3-4,5,6 and 4-3-10); NCAA Rule 3-3-5; and NFICA 3-5-10.

Penalties vary including such things as taking time off the clock, forcing removal of the injured player from the game, five yards, loss of a timeout.

After a legitimate injury, the clock generally starts on the referee's ready-to-play signal. You need to *practice getting lined up ready to snap the ball as soon as the referee gives the ready-to-play signal* so as to conserve time.

Crowd noise

If your games are played in front of crowds loud enough to prevent your players from hearing the cadence or quarterback audibles, you need to learn the appropriate rules (NCAA 3-3-3f.4 NFL 4-3-7-[13]), teach them to your players, and practice dealing with excessive crowd noise. You should also have a signaling system, like the sign board, which functions without regard to crowd noise.

Getting out of bounds

You should have no timeouts available when you are running the top-speed hurry-up. (They should be used when the **opposing offense** is running their **slowdown** offense.) So your ball carrier needs to get out of bounds whenever possible.

Getting out of bounds is not rocket science. But you will need to give your backs and receivers each a few reps at doing it, mainly so they become mentally conscious of the need the do it when you are behind and on a top-speed schedule.

But one aspect of it reportedly **is** rocket science to many players: the need to remember that you *don't go out of bounds until you are about to be tackled.* Many players, once they have been trained to get out of bounds in top-speed hurry-up situations, go out of bounds long before they are about to be tackled, thereby giving up yards they could have had for the taking.

You always gain as many yards as you can when you are trailing **before** you go out of bounds—with **one exception**. *In the last ten seconds of the game, when you are carrying the ball and it becomes apparent that you cannot score, you must stop the clock before* ***all*** *the remaining game time expires.*

In the 1997 Rose Bowl, Arizona State made a spectacular come-back to take the lead in the final minutes. Then, Ohio State made an even more spectacular come-back to take the lead back by three points. Then, ASU drove down the field one last time. But on the final play of the game, a receiver caught a pass over the middle. He should have immediately slid or taken a knee which would have been around the 33. He had gained a first down which would have stopped the clock until the chains were moved. But he zigged and zagged even though he was hemmed in and time ran out while he was zigging.

Ohio State's comeback in the 1997 Rose Bowl

The dramatic comeback by Ohio State in the 1997 Rose Bowl is one of the great two-minute drills of all time. Let's look at it in detail.

Ohio State had been leading 14-10 when their field-goal attempt was blocked and run in for a touchdown by Arizona State. The touchdown was called back on a forward lateral penalty, but ASU proceeded to march down the field and score to make it 17-14 with 1:40 left. After the kick return, which took seven seconds, Ohio State had 1:33 to go 65 yards. They had one timeout left.

Play #1: Seam pass to tight end down the middle, could not hang on, incomplete. Second and ten at the Ohio State 35 with 1:29 left.

#2: Lot of time. Hit wide-open receiver in the hand. Dropped. Third and ten. 1:22.

#3: Lot of time. Complete curl just beyond first down marker. First and ten. 1:16. Clock stops to move chains but will restart on referee's ready-to-play signal.

#4: Snaps at 1:14, within two seconds of ready-to-play signal. Out pass. Incomplete. Penalty. Ineligible receiver downfield. Declined because possession is now more important than field position and loss of a down increases the chances that Ohio State will lose possession. Second and ten at the Ohio State 45. 1:09.

#5: Pass over the middle overthrown. Incomplete. Third and ten. 1:04.

#6: Pass over the middle complete at the Arizona State 41. First and ten. Clock stops at :54 until the chains are moved. Ohio State is not blitzing. Four-man rush throughout this series. Sideline shots of Arizona State's Plummer indicate that he has stopped smiling and exchanging high fives.

#7: Ohio State lines up before the ready-to-play whistle and snaps within four seconds of the whistle restarting the clock. Out pass complete for another first down at the 29. Receiver gets out of bounds to stop the clock until the next snap. :46.

#8: Arizona State shows blitz. Ohio State quarterback Germaine gets rattled and jumps out from behind center without ball. False start dead-ball penalty. Opponent has no choice in whether to accept a dead-ball penalty. First and fifteen at the 34. The ref instructs the clock operator to put three seconds back on the clock. Clock operator had run three seconds off during the aborted play. :46. Much field-goal talk by TV announcers.

#9: Deep fade pass down right sideline. Incomplete. Contact. Penalty flag. Defensive pass interference. 15-yard penalty and automatic first down. First and ten at the Arizona State 20. :41

#10: Pass. No one open. Scrambles right. Alley open to run probably all the way to the end zone but threw ball away over receiver's head out of bounds. Incomplete. Second and ten. :33.

#11: Pass. Batted away. Announcer Dick Vermiel calls for pass interference. Replay shows defender grabbed receiver's shirt and pulled his shoulder down about eight inches. No flag. Incomplete. Third and ten. :28.

#12: Post incomplete. More obvious pass interference. Replay confirms the interference. Flag. Pass interference on the defense. First and ten at the five. :24.

#13: Right split end runs slant in then twirls (turns counterclockwise 380 degrees) and drifts out. Wide open. Touchdown. :19. Ohio State 20 Arizona State 17.

PAT: Disarray on PAT. Ohio State sends the fastest man on the team into the game to call a timeout. The kick is blocked, thereby leaving Arizona State within a field goal.

There is no great mystery in this drive. Backup quarterback Joe Germaine had to complete at least one pass for more than ten yards per set of four downs, and he did. He ran twelve plays in 1:21—a rate of one play every 6.75 seconds. Of course, you can get it down to about five seconds if you throw incomplete passes. Ohio State had a timeout throughout the drive, but never used it until the PAT.

About the only clock-management tricks they had to perform were to get out of bounds and to line up during the moving of the chains after first downs. They did both smoothly and efficiently. Basically, the ASU defense, which had been number one in the Pac-10 against both the pass and the run, was unable to stop Ohio State's Germaine except with interference, and they only got away with that once.

Ohio State permitted ASU to block their PAT, even after a timeout, and even by the same guy who blocked a field goal to start the ASU scoring drive. That's terrible special teams play and it left ASU within a field goal of a tie. That's means ASU has to go about 40 fewer yards than if Ohio State had gotten a four-point margin.

Arizona State's 19-second comeback attempt

Now it's 19 seconds left and Arizona State needs a great kick return and/or two-minute drill. ASU has one timeout left.

Kickoff: Ohio State kicks deep to the 15. He returns it to the 34. First and ten with :14 left in the game. ASU needs a touchdown or a field goal. Clock stopped until the snap.

Play #1: Out pass complete for a first down to the Arizona State 47. :07. Clock stops until the next snap because the play went out of bounds. Arizona State now needs to get to field-goal range, and get to the ground or out of bounds to stop the clock. If they stay in bounds, they need to use their final timeout to get their field goal team onto the field. They must be careful not to use all seven seconds on the play. Dick Vermiel points that out.

#2: ASU's Jake Plummer completes the pass over the middle for a first down to the 35. But the receiver spins and dances the remaining time away. The game ends as he is being tackled. He *should have taken a knee or lateraled.* Had he taken a knee, ASU could have called timeout during the moving of the chains and run one more play. The 52-yard field goal may not be as likely to succeed as a Hail Mary or other play. ASU's place kicker was sixth in the Pac-10 with a .688 success rate. ASU's goose was cooked pretty much when they let Ohio State score with only :19 left. But Jake Plummer might have pulled off another miracle on that last play, had their receiver been smarter about his "run after catch."

Navy's come-from-behind 1996 Aloha Bowl 2-minute drill

Cal was leading 38-35 in the fourth quarter of the 1996 Aloha Bowl against Navy. Cal quarterback Pat Barnes, with 3rd and 9 at Navy's 32, scrambled. He appeared to have the first down but he reached out for an extra yard or two as he was being tackled at the 21 and fumbled the ball to Navy at Navy's 16 with 3:00 to go in the game.

Play #1: Clock stopped on change of possession. Option pitch to the boundary (closest sideline). Runner gets out of bounds at the 18 at 2:55. Second and 8. Clock stops.

Play #2: Play-action bomb down the middle, way overthrown. Clock stopped at 2:49. Third and 8.

Play #3: Quick pass to right tight end, tipped but caught. First down at the Navy 32 with 2:44 left. Navy has used motion on each of their plays. Normally, you would not do that in a two-minute drill because it wastes time. But in Navy's case, the clock was stopped on each down by the previous play. So they could use motion without wasting game-clock time and did.

Play #4: Motion. Crossing route by motion man. Completed over the middle with the run after catch taking the ball down to the Cal 16-yard line with 2:27 left. The ball carrier runs out of bounds stopping the clock until the next snap. The first down alone would have stopped the clock to move the chains, but would have restarted on the referee's signal. Navy has managed to stop the clock until the next snap on every single play of this drive so far—without using a timeout.

Play #5: Motion. Inside handoff, runner breaks outside. Tackled at the ten with 2:24 left. He did not get out of bounds. The clock is running. Second and four.

At this point, Navy needs to go ten yards and they need to take about two full minutes to do it. The slowest they can go is about 36 seconds per play if the play takes, say, four seconds, the refs take ten seconds to give the ready-to-play whistle, and Navy takes 23 seconds of play-clock time. The most plays they can run is seven: three to get the first down and four more to score.

Their first three plays must average 4 ÷ 3 = 1.33 yards per carry to get the first down. Then they can take as many as four more to score. Throughout, they should stay in bounds and avoid passes. In fact, the receiver who caught the 52-yard pass should have stayed in bounds. By gaining that many yards in one play, he got Navy **ahead of schedule** and took them out of a hurry-up and into a maximum slowdown situation.

Play #6: Clock running. Snap at 1:46. Fake dive to fullback, quarterback keep (sort of a draw) off tackle. Touchdown. Much celebration. But they leave 1:42 left on the clock for Cal to come back. That's two seconds more than Arizona State left in the 1997 Rose Bowl. 1:40 was enough time for Ohio State to come back and win in the Rose Bowl. But fortunately for Navy, it turned out **not** to be enough for Cal in the Aloha Bowl. Navy's PAT was good making the score Navy 42, Cal 38.

At the start of their final possession, Navy needed to go 84 yards in three minutes. In a hurry-up mode, they could have run a play every ten to twenty seconds or eight to 16 plays, assuming a twenty-second margin at the end. An eight-play pace requires them to gain over ten yards per play; 16-play pace, five yards per carry. Except for the long-pass receiver running out of bounds, Navy managed the clock about as well as they could.

Cal's comeback attempt

Navy kicks a line drive to the Cal six. The returner runs to the middle and is tackled at his own 15. The clock stops at 1:35 until the snap. Cal needs a touchdown and therefore needs to go 87 yards in 1:35. That means they can run about six to twelve plays and need to average at least 7.25 yards per play. That is, they need an archetype **full-speed, stop-the-clock, two-minute drill** unless they get a big gainer.

Play #1: Quick out to tight end who gets out of bounds at the Cal 21 stopping the clock at 1:30. Second and two.

Play #2: Drop-back. Blitz. Sack. Desperation pass while falling batted and almost intercepted. It's smart to avoid a sack in this situation, but better a sack than a turnover. Refs rule the quarterback down at the 14 **before** the pass. So the clock keeps running. Third and eleven.

Play #3: Drop-back pass. Tipped. Incomplete at 1:05. Fourth and eleven. Now Cal has a reasonable amount of time. But they gotta get eleven yards on the next play or the game's over. Cal coach Steve Marriucci calls his last time out. Navy still has two. Calling your last timeout when the clock is already stopped does not strike me as a brilliant move. He will almost certainly need that timeout during the rest of the drive.

Play #4: Drop back. Scramble. Sacked. Ball goes over on downs to Navy.

Except for the use of the timeout after an incomplete pass, which did not matter as it turned out, Cal does not seem to have fouled up their clock management. They just were unable to get their first downs.

Army's 1996 Independence Bowl end game

Army got the ball on downs at their own 30, first and ten with 3:37 to go in the game. They were losing 32-21. They had used their last timeout on defense to stop Auburn's slowdown. In view of the fact that they need to score **twice** to win or tie, they should have been in a **top-speed hurry-up**.

But Army proceeded to run an **inbounds hurry-up**—and it almost worked!

Play #1: Pass complete to the 35 but receiver stayed inbounds. Clock kept running and was at 3:14 for the next snap—a twenty-seconds per play pace, which is what you get with the inbounds hurry-up.
Play #2: Draw to the 37, clock still running.
Play #3: 2:40 Inbounds pass complete, but short of first down. Fourth and one at the Army 39.
Play #4: 2:12. Last play took 28 seconds! Fourth-down pass is complete over the middle for a first down—temporarily stopping the clock while the chains are moved.
Play #5: 2:02 Option play sacked
Play #6: 1:35 Pass over the middle complete for a touchdown. Army 27, Auburn 32
Play #7: 1:27 two point conversion counter play is good. Army 29, Auburn 32.

Army then kicked onside and recovered!

There is now 1:22 left in the game. Army is down by a field goal and has the ball at the Auburn 45-yard line. According to the table you saw in the slowdown chapter, Army has to go 45 yards in 1:22 to win so they should do a **top-speed hurry-up**. That is, stop the clock after each play, with no timeouts! Here's what they actually did.

Play #8: Incomplete pass over the middle. Clock stops.
Play #9: 1:15 Second and ten. Pass complete. Receiver does not try to get out of bounds. First down. Clock stops to move the chains.
Play #10: 1:08 Long pass complete to the 13 where the receiver is cold cocked out of bounds and has to leave the game. Clock stops. First and ten. Also referee's timeout for injured Army receiver.
Play #11: :55 Option dive to the ten-yard line. Second and seven. Clock running
Play #12: :40 Army spikes the ball stopping the clock.
Play #13: :33 Third down 27-yard field goal attempt misses. Auburn wins 32-29.

Did Army do a good job of clock management on these two drives? Well, they darned near tied a game in which they were trailing by 25 points when the fourth quarter started! But they sure had a strange way of doing it. One might say that Army decided to pass over the middle to use the element of **surprise**. In their situation, a team will generally try to get out of bounds on each play to stop the clock.

Army put themselves in a position where they **had** to complete long passes. That's not a good thing to do—unless you **can** complete the passes—which they did!

When Army got the ball with 3:37 left they had to figure

We need to drive 70 yards to score, recover an onside kick, and drive another 50 yards to score again. If we get a two-point conversion after our touchdown, we only have to drive about 30 yards to get into field goal position and tie after the onside kick recovery.

That's a total of 100 yards worth of drives just for a tie, 120 to win. Plus they have to throw in the time necessary for an onside kick, and they have no timeouts. If that's not a top-speed hurry-up situation, I don't know what is.

But Army used a relatively leisurely **inbounds hurry-up** pace—about twenty seconds per play. Army seemingly made it hard on themselves but, except for the inaccuracy of the field goal, they pulled it off.

I have heard Bill Walsh say that it is often a good idea to throw over the middle in a hurry-up situation when the opponent expects sideline passes. Army's last two drives in the Independence Bowl would appear to back that up. But don't try this at home.

In general, I believe percentages favor running a top-speed hurry-up in the situation in which Army found itself. Running a top-speed would have allowed them to run about two or three times as many plays. That, in turn, would enable them to gain one half to one third as many yards per play. As it was, they had to gain 100 yards and do it in only 12 plays, an average of eight and a third yards per play. Had they run the top-speed hurry-up, they could have increased the number of plays to 24 to 30 or so, thereby reducing the average yards per carry to 3.3 to 4.

It is especially surprising to see **Army** try to pass their way to two scores in three and half minutes when you consider that, in 1996, Army ranked 108 out of the 111 NCAA Division I-A football teams in **passing**. Where did they rank in **rushing** offense? Would you believe **first**?

Lesson learned? If it works, you can do anything you want. But if it doesn't work, you'd better do something intelligent if you want to keep your job.

1996 freshman Granada-Campolindo two-minute drill

My 1996 Granada High School freshman team ran a two-minute drill in the Campolindo game which the world will little note nor long remember. But I was darned proud of it and still get a thrill every time I watch the video. I'll describe it here mainly to disprove the notion that freshman are too young to execute a two-minute drill competently. You should be aware that my quarterback and most of his teammates had never played football before the 1996 season.

We were trailing 14-12 in the fourth quarter. After using all our timeouts on defense, we took over on downs at our own 38-yard line with 2:01 remaining. Rookie quarterback Chris Peart handed off to MVP fullback Mike Kukahiko on 32 dive. It gained four yards. Sounds like a dumb choice, but the flip-side version of that play had gone 60 yards for a touchdown with the same ball carrier earlier in the game.

Second and six. Clock running. Peart throws a three-step drop streak pass to left tight end Mike Wooten for ten yards to the Campolindo 48 and a first down. Clock stops for the chains to move. Referees move the chains at record speed—so fast that our play messenger is ordered off the field by the quarterback, who apparently yelled to his team to run our standard first-down hurry-up play. 1:27 left. Pretty impressive thinking on your feet for a rookie 15-year old. Out pass batted away at last instant. Incomplete. Clock stops.

1:14. 27 pitch sweep crack to tailback Jeff Aires who goes around left end for ten yards and gets out of bounds to stop the clock. First down. We are doing our warp-speed no-huddle with the tailbacks taking a written play in on a Kinko's play pad sheet. They hold it on their chest right at the ball. As each player sees it, he immediately goes to the line of scrimmage and gets set. Derisive Campo parent comments about the play "diagrams" our tailbacks are showing their teammates can be heard on the audio from the press box.

1:07 Streak pass to tight end, overthrown. Incomplete. Clock stops. Second and ten.

1:02 Quads right formation. Flood sprint-out pass. Incomplete because of apparent defensive pass interference. Not called. Clock stops.

:58 31 inside trap to Mike Kukahiko behind the trap block of Jeff Cooley, a running back whom I asked to convert to guard. Cooley was our Lineman of the Year. Normally, not a top-speed two-minute drill play. But it was one of our best plays all season and worked especially well against Campolindo. Kukahiko gains 15 yards to the 23 and gets out of bounds stopping the clock. First and ten.

:52 28 pitch sweep crack to tailback Jeff Aires who gains eight yards to the 15 and runs out of bounds stopping the clock. Second and two.

:43 31 dive. Mike Kukahiko gets to the Campolindo nine-yard line. First and goal. Clock stops, but only as long as it takes to move the chains.

:35 I am now giving my wind-the-clock signal which means run the play that corresponds to the down. First down means quasar 91, an out pass. Tight end Dahlin Wilson catches the pass, then is hit by several Campolindo players who hold him up and keep him from getting out of bounds as well. Their tackle lasts **four seconds** from the time they first hit him until the refs blew the whistle. The ball is now on the left hash mark.

:05 and running Quarterback Peart orders his teammates to line up for a spike. They respond instantly and he spikes the ball leaving **:01** on the clock.

:01 Campolindo helpfully calls timeout, thereby enabling our head coach to go out and make sure we have the right eleven guys and that they are lined up correctly. Attempting our first field goal of the year, long snapper Justin Nordgren snaps to holder Justin Gonzales. Kicker Jeff Aires splits the uprights, a 26-yard field goal that would have been good from another ten or fifteen yards out. Pandemonium. We win 15-14.

The quick out pass

The quintessential two-minute drill play is the quick out. That play works best to the **short side of the field** according to Tennessee head coach Phillip Fulmer.

Your quarterbacks and receivers need many reps to perfect this. They need to run it against a defense, too because it is imperative that you avoid an interception, which is generally fatal late in a game in which you trail. *The quarterback must practice:*

- *completing the out pass*
- *throwing the ball away safely and legally when the receiver is covered*

Favorite two-minute drill plays

Fulmer also like the screen, draw, and fullback trap in two-minute drill situations. Tom Beck, of Grand Valley State likes the trap, draw, and lead option.

Boise State head coach Tom Knap says to use basic plays. You need at least one each short, medium, and deep pass so you can take what the defense gives you.

Stance

I always used my normal stances. Most coaches do. But Grand Valley State's Tom Beck has his whole team in a **two-point stance** when they run the two-minute drill.

Substitutions

You should stick with your main players in two-minute drills. Often a coach will decide the last minutes of a game in which he is trailing are a special situation requiring a special group of personnel. That's a bad idea. Many's the time I have seen a team get penalized because they tried to get cute when they were running out of time. They tried to run some unusual play they had rarely practiced and had the wrong number of men on the field.

When in your two-minute drill, avoid plays that require unusual personnel or unusual substitutions.

16

Whole-game no-huddle

The no-huddle as a non-clock-conscious tactic

The vast majority of people think the no-huddle is desperation measure to be used only for trailing teams late in a game. Not I.

To me, the no-huddle in an awesome, multi-purpose, offensive weapon. Does it save time? You bet. Nothing does it better. But that's not all it does.

In 1993, I decided to try running what I called the warp-speed no-huddle the entire season with my youth team. That's **all game, every game**.

How'd it work? My team was second only to the league champions in points scored against our opponents. They don't keep stats. But as far as I can tell, that team was, and still remains, the best offensive team (most points, most yards, most plays, fewest turnovers, etc.) in the history of the San Ramon Bears. The San Ramon Bears started play in 1988 and they field four teams each year. As of 1997, that's 9 x 4 = 36 teams.

The warp-speed no-huddle was not the only reason for that team's success. Our star tailback, Will Sykes, gained 1,583 all-purpose yards even though he only played in 7 1/4 games—forty-minute games at that. In one of those game, he gained 354 yards. The NFL single-game (60 minutes) record is 276 yards by Walter Payton.

Like any successful team, we had good linemen: Artie Cervantes, Kyle DeYoung, Josh Brown, Dan Pinney, Aaron Ricks, and Tim Holt. Our center, Richard Chinn, made 402 straight long snaps without a mistake (we ran the single wing) and was the subject of a story in *Sports Illustrated for Kids* as a result. Blocking back Paul Doerner and wing/tailback Ryan Chiarelli were also crucial. But the no-huddle was a big factor. Unfortunately, Sykes never had another season remotely resembling his warp-speed no-huddle adventure, before or after that year.

Run your opponents into the ground

After one game, in 90 plus-degree heat, the Benicia head coach expressed amazement at our no-huddle. "My first-string defense guys were begging to be taken out of the game!" he told me—because of the pace we set. We ran an even 75 plays on offense that day. In youth football, the quarters are only **ten minutes** long and the clock rarely stops because **hardly any passes** are thrown. The national high school record for most plays per game average for a season is 68.9 (Hemingford, NE 1989). And they have **twelve**-minute quarters.

I attended a clinic on the no-huddle in Burlingame, CA on 2/2/96 where Tom Craft, offensive coordinator of the San Diego State team, told about his no-huddle. He said coach friends on one of his opponents' teams admitted to him after their game that their defense was vomiting on the sidelines during the game because they could not handle the no-huddle pace.

In a Bills all-no-huddle game, the Colts coaches had to call what Jim Kelly called "a timeout like a basketball team on the wrong end of a big point run." In their 1990 regular-season victory over the Giants, Bills book author Vic Carucci said, "Many of the New York defenders were doubled over in exhaustion, their huffing and puffing visible in the cold air, as Kelly drove the Bills to a pair of lightning-quick touchdowns on their first two possessions." "Fatigue does set in," Giant defensive end Leonard Marshall admitted.

In a 1990 game with the Philadelphia Eagles, Eagle defender Jerome Brown said to Bill quarterback Jim Kelly, "Come on, slow it down, bro! What are you trying to do, kill us?"

South Carolina's shotgun no-huddle

South Carolina head coach Brad Scott's shotgun no-huddle is described in the 1996 *Coach of the Year Clinic Manual.* He says,

> *The shotgun fatigues the defense, especially the defensive line. I'm talking about the shotgun and the no-huddle attack.*

Scott had an extra twist,

> *We used different cadences to keep the defensive linemen in their stances for long periods of time. If you do that 60-70 times a game that defensive lineman is looking for relief.*

Scott found some disadvantages from his shotgun. He felt his line got a little too pass-blocking oriented and was unable to run block as well as he wanted. He also said the shotgun requires depth at wide receiver. It also requires a passing quarterback. And the shotgun snap requires extra practice. Scott says to move in and out of the shotgun, don't use it every play.

Fatigue management

The team using the no-huddle has to learn to manage fatigue, too. Buffalo's Kent Hull would sometimes tell Kelly, "Slow it down just one beat, Jim, so we can catch our breath." After a long run, my youth tailback would sometimes signal me that he was tired. I would either have him and the wing switch positions or I would call a wing reverse in which the tailback handed off to the wing, to give the tailback a breather.

We also noticed that some players took longer to get in shape than others. In 1996, my star freshman fullback skipped summer football conditioning and frequently asked for a break from our no-huddle during games. But about half way through the season, he stopped asking. I questioned him about it and he said he no longer was getting tired.

Most teams have learned to manage fatigue when it comes to **wide receivers**. They routinely substitute after a long route. But all other players are used continuously. When you run the warp-speed no-huddle, you learn the fatigue breaking points of more of your positions.

That's not a put down. I told my players,

> *The warp-speed will make you hot, sweaty, and tired. That's the* ***bad*** *news. But the* ***good*** *news is that it will do the same to the other team. The* ***even better*** *news is that we will be used to it both physically and mentally and the opposing players and their coaches will not. You should regard the onset of fatigue in a game as the return of an old friend and ally.*

They did. The fatigue of our warp-speed was sort of an inside joke. Our players would slyly watch the opposing players wheezing and gasping.

The first reaction of an opposing defensive coach when one of his players asks to for a break is **anger**. On my team, in contrast, we **knew** our kids would get tired and expected them to tell us when they did and we had a routine way of dealing with that fatigue. Our superior knowledge of the fatigue points in a warp-speed no-huddle and the correct ways to deal with them were powerful competitive weapons which we wielded against our opponents.

'Supermen syndrome'

I surmised that a sort of "Supermen syndrome" set in among our opponents when we ran the warp-speed. In youth football, there are representatives from each team on each sideline. In one of our warp-speed games, our representative told me after the game that the opposing coaches kept telling their kids, "Don't worry. They can't keep that up the whole game."

The hell we couldn't. Keep it up the whole game was exactly what we did every week. But imagine your morale when you are on the opposing team, tripping over your tongue in the first quarter from exhaustion, and your coach's prediction that "They can't keep it up" keeps not coming true.

Two quick scores

Like Jim Kelly's Bills, we generally found that we could rip off a couple of quick scoring drives at the beginning of a game. In high school, where I had to run a much-slower no-huddle because of the varsity head coach's restrictions, we still often drove right down the field to score on our first two possessions.

In the last game of our 1996 freshman season, we played the undefeated league champion Foothill team, which was coached by Fox-TV football analyst John Madden's two sons. We were no longer running even the modified no-huddle. But our kids were in the no-huddle habit and still ran at a significantly faster pace than normal teams. On our first possession, we drove right down the field to miss a field goal from the four. On the next, we drove down and scored a touchdown. We ended up losing 8-6. But you could still see the knock-the-opponent-off-balance effect of a rapid-pace offense.

In my youth season running the warp-speed no-huddle, opposing players and coaches would panic, as evidenced by their frantic signals and yelling and those basketball-style timeouts. They seemed to be asking the question that Butch Cassidy and the Sundance Kid asked each other in their movie, "Who **are** those guys?"

'You win the first race, but how 'bout the 40th?'

The superior conditioning of whole-game, no-huddle teams is not only an **equalizer** versus superior talent teams, it **erases** that talent advantage. South Carolina's Brad Scott:

> *My first year at South Carolina we beat some teams we were not as good as. It was a difference maker in several games because we kept the pressure on the defense.*

Your 4.5 guy can beat my 4.8 guy in a race in which both men are **rested**, and come track season, he will. But football ain't track, and I will not let it **become** a track meet by letting your 4.5 guy get his normal rest between plays. I have conditioned my 4.8 guy so he can run forties all day long almost at that pace. And when I am on offense, and therefore in control of the tempo of the game, I will set a pace that has your 4.5 guy so tired that he can no longer keep up with my 4.8 guy.

> *The race is not always to the swift, but to the one who keeps on running.*
> Anonymous.

You can coach stamina, but you cannot coach speed. So coaches whose teams lack speed had better turn the game into a stamina contest.

Cincinnati Bengals no-huddle

The all-game no-huddle was popularized by the 1988 and 1989 Cincinnati Bengals. Stanford offensive coordinator Dana Bible, who was kind enough to read this book before publication, was a part of the Bengal coaching staff in those years. The whole-game no-huddle gave their opponents fits and was a big part of the reason the Bengals outscored all other teams in the AFC in 1988 and went to the Super Bowl. They also led the AFC in yards gained both years. In 1987, their last year **before** the all-game no-huddle, they had finished **last** in their division.

Buffalo Bills no-huddle

Probably the most-famous all-game, every-game, no-huddle team is the Buffalo Bills. The Bills were impressed when the 1988 Bengals beat them in the AFC championship game, 21-10. They also noticed that their own no-huddle was maybe worth using in other than just last-minute situations. Buffalo used the no-huddle as a sort of standard offense in a 1989 overtime 47-41 victory over the Oilers.

After seeing the no-huddle also do well in another 1989 playoff game against Cleveland, the Bills coaches decided to try their "K-Gun" (named after tight end Keith "Killer" McKeller according to Jim Kelly) at the opening game of the 1990 season against the Colts. They evolved into using it throughout each of their games, averaging only 18 to 20 seconds between snaps. The Bills then led the AFC in scoring for the next three years and in yards gained in 1991 and 1992. Of course, they also went to the Super Bowl for the next four years, too.

Interesting note on the Bills no-huddle. In his 1984 book, *The New Thinking Man's Guide to Pro Football*, Paul Zimmerman wondered,

> *...why not run a hurry-up, no-huddle offense early in the game and keep coming back to it from time to time?*

That was before anyone ever did a whole-game no-huddle. Steelers backfield coach Tom Moore told Zimmerman he ran a whole-game no-huddle against Iowa when he was offensive coordinator of the University of Minnesota. Tony Dungy was his quarterback. The result:

> *...we killed 'em. They couldn't get their defensive calls right."*

Zimmerman asked then former Chiefs coach Marv Levy why you couldn't do that in the NFL. Remember this is in 1984, four years **before** Levy's Bills ran a whole-game no-huddle with great success. Marv said,

> *An offense can run itself out of steam in a hurry that way. You can't really duplicate a two-minute situation in the middle of a game.*

Keep that Levy quote in mind next time an experienced coach tells you why some new football idea can't be done.

The main idea behind the whole-game no-huddle

The main idea of the whole-game no-huddle is two-fold:

1. By running a warp-speed, no-huddle pace in **practice** you get two or three times as many reps and it conditions the players without their realizing they're being conditioned.
2. By being highly conditioned as a result of warp-speed practices and being used to the warp-speed, no-huddle pace, both physically and mentally, you create the capability to run the opposing defense into the ground in **games**.

Don't huddle even when the game clock is stopped

Coach Howard Schnellenberger says a team running the two-minute drill in a game should huddle when the game clock is stopped. That's typical of most no-huddles.

When you're in a **whole-game**, no-huddle, you **never** huddle—even when the game clock is stopped. That's because your **purpose** is to **drive the other team into the ground**. Why give them a breather?

You need not snap the ball before the end of the 25-second play clock to save game-clock time when the game-clock is stopped. But saving game-clock time is **not** the purpose of a **whole-game** no-huddle. Accordingly, you snap the ball as fast as the officials will let you on **every** play, regardless of whether the game clock will be stopped until the snap.

If, on the other hand, you are **not** in a whole-game, drive-them-into-the-ground no-huddle, it **is** a good idea to huddle when the clock is stopped because of such benefits as catching your breath, time to think about your next play, and making substitutions. But as with timeouts, **both** teams benefit.

Other advantages

The no-huddle is not just a clock-management strategy. It has several other advantages:

- Tires out teams that are not used to it
- Hinders defensive substitutions
- Hinders defensive adjustments to offensive formations
- Eliminates defensive huddle
- Forces defense to simplify
- Encourages intensity and hustle
- Discourages stunts because no defensive huddle in which to communicate them.

Hinders defensive substitutions

The no-huddle makes it **hard for opposing defenses to substitute**. Former Bills offensive coordinator Ted Marchibroda says it's hard for the opponent to even call a defense, let alone substitute. So when you run the no-huddle all the time you tend to see far fewer defenses.

Buffalo's no-huddle caused defenses to stop all the situational substituting they prefer to do. In a 1990 game with the Bills, the Jets defense was penalized twice for too many men on the field. That's 10 yards for the offense just for selecting the no-huddle pace. In a high school game, you would typically benefit from **30 yards** in penalties for the opponent having too many men on the field twice (illegal participation NFICA 9-6-4a).

Better conditioning

Marchibroda also noted the **superior conditioning** of teams that run the no-huddle almost all the time in practice. Almost every coach in America claims his team is the best conditioned in the league. But talk is cheap. In that 1993 game where my opponent said his first-string defenders were begging to be taken out of the game, **none**, I repeat, **none**, of my players gave the slightest indication that they were bothered by the temperature or fatigue. It's hard to condition players with pure conditioning drills like running the stadium steps or gassers. Players inevitably pace themselves. They fake injury. They look for excuses to get out of practice.

But when you condition them by running plays at a three-a-minute pace, they are having **fun**. You can see them sweating profusely and hear them gasping for air in a warp-speed practice, but you do **not** see the **loafing** that you see with the exact same kids when you make them run gassers at the end of practice. The conditioning benefits alone are so great that it would make sense to run the warp-speed no-huddle in **practice** even if you **never** used it during **games**.

Hill Park High School's Gino Arcaro says his no-huddle produces better conditioned teams and wears down opponents. Colorado's Rick Neuheisel recommends using your two-minute drill as a conditioning drill during two-a-days practice in the preseason. He also recommends that you put the pass coverage portion of the defense out so the offense can get used to recognizing coverages—an 11-on-7 drill.

Aberdeen's 'Bingo!' 'transition' offense

Aberdeen (MD) High School coach Kevin Reilly sees the no-huddle as an opportunity to inject the basketball "transition" concept into football. The basketball transition game is basically a fast switch from defense to offense intended to catch the team that was just on offense off balance.

When there is an unexpected turnover to his team, Reilly yells "Bingo!" on the sideline and his offense runs onto the field and runs their first play with a predetermined snap count and without a huddle, even though the clock is stopped as a result of the change of possession. Virtually all other no-huddle offenses call for a huddle whenever the game clock is stopped.

I did a version of this with an **expected** turnover, the **kick return**. We practiced our kick return as a **two-play sequence**: the return itself followed by an instant, no-huddle offensive play, usually a sweep toward our bench. Our theory was that we might catch the opposing defense still making substitutions or otherwise not ready. Reilly, who explained his "Bingo!" concept in a brief *Coach and Athletic Director* article (12/95) said,

> *In the let down and confusion that follows a turnover, we have had wide receivers left completely uncovered, the opponents forced to use timeouts, or penalized for having too many men on the field.*

One of his "Bingo!" packages included a deep pass to either wideout, a perimeter play, and a quick-hitter up the middle. The players get the play by audible. The quarterback, who was going both ways for Coach Reilly, got the play from a messenger. If either wideout is uncovered, he immediately switches the play to a fade pass.

Players love it

San Diego State's Craft said his players **loved** the no-huddle. Kevin Reilly, coach at Aberdeen (MD) High School says his "Bingo!" is fun for his players. So do Peter Moe of Washburn (ND) High School and Gino Arcaro of Hill Park (Ontario, Canada) High School. My youth players loved the no-huddle.

Jim Kelly says that about the Bills. Here's his account of the scene at their first all-no-huddle game against Buddy Ryan's Eagles:

> *Looking around the locker room at halftime, with us holding a 24-16 lead, you saw everyone trying hard not to smile too much. It wasn't easy. We all knew something incredible had happened to us in those first thirty minutes and we were all feeling pretty giddy about it. Besides the quick points, we kept our mistakes to a minimum.*
>
> *We stuck with the "K-Gun" throughout our next game, at Indianapolis, and it worked every bit as well as the previous week.*

Better organized practices

Another benefit of running the no-huddle in practice is more reps. We tried to hit three plays per minute in my practices. Craft said his practices were better organized as a result of the no-huddle. So did Strack.

A chance to master a difficult skill

One of the most common mistakes football coaches make is to adopt a play or system that requires a certain amount of practice, then not devote that much practice to mastering it. The triple option is a typical example. The pass is another. The result is that the team cannot execute come game time. Colorado's Rick Neuheisel says,

> *When you talk about the two-minute offense, you are talking about something that somebody screws up every week. It doesn't matter whether you are talking high school, college, or pro.*

If what he says is true, and I believe it is, coaches need to spend **more** time on the two-minute drill. If you turn the two-minute drill into your regular offense, you will master it. As long as you treat it as a sort of special team, you will have the screw-ups of which Neuheisel speaks. Remember that although two-minute drills may be relatively rare, clock-management plays are more important than regular plays.

What you emphasize, you achieve. If you want to achieve competence in the two-minute drill, you must emphasize it more than the vast majority of coaches have been doing. Neuheisel goes on,

> *...when it gets to that time in a game and the game is on the line, that side line is not as calm as it might have been. The press box communication gets kind of garbled because people are losing their cool.*

I don't think that's necessary. The sideline **is** a hectic place during a football game. But I've seen worse. Taxi dispatchers. Live TV show producers, including those who televise football games. The stakes are high in football games. But I've seen higher. Aircraft carrier flight deck personnel. Air traffic controllers. In other words, it can be done. If coaches and players are **not** getting it done, it's because they are not getting enough practice.

Rhythm

The whole-game no-huddle facilitates the offense getting into a rhythm. In other sports where a no-huddle sort of pace is normal, like basketball and volleyball, coaches frequently use timeouts to snap an opponent's hot streak, to break their rhythm.

Indeed, in 1993, I found that my opponents typically called such a panic-stricken timeout around the third or fourth play of the game when I ran my warp-speed no-huddle. Their players were in disarray, knocked off balance, and reeling and their coaches had to go out and calm them down and get them reorganized and reprogrammed to handle our rapid pace. Not only were we **in** rhythm, they were **out** of it.

In 1990, when they started using the no-huddle the whole game, the Bills saw their quarterback Jim Kelly going on hot streaks like 8 for 8 against the Eagles and 7 for 9 against the Colts. Here's a passage from Vic Carucci's book, *The Buffalo Bills and the Almost-Dream Season.*

> *Kelly then threw 14 yards to Thomas and 15 to Reed to move the ball to the Raiders' 34. After a 5-yard Thomas run and a Kelly-to-Thomas pass for 9 more, the Raiders, like previous Buffalo opponents, called a basketball-style timeout to regroup. Although theirs figured to be one of the more formidable defense the Bills would face all season, they looked far more confused and disoriented than any Buffalo had faced to that point. It seemed as if the no-huddle, which everyone in the world expected from the Bills, had caught them by surprise.*

After the timeout, the Bills went on to score anyway, their tenth score and ninth touchdown in their last twelve opening drives.

17

Spiking the ball

Spiking the ball to stop the clock

Since 1995, **high school** quarterbacks can stop the clock by deliberately spiking the ball into the ground. Note carefully the wording of Rule 7-5-2d:

> *It is legal to conserve time by intentionally throwing the ball forward to the ground immediately after receiving a direct hand-to-hand snap.*

Note that the ball must be thrown **forward**. A referee told me of a quarterback who turned around and spiked the ball into the ground **backward**—which is a live ball. Note that the ball must be **thrown, not** just **dropped**. And finally note that it must be a hand-to-hand snap. That leaves out **shotgun** and **direct single-wing style snaps**.

College quarterbacks can also stop the clock legally with a forward spike. (Rule 7-3-2) They must do so **immediately** after the ball is first controlled after the snap. They can**not** legally spike the ball to stop the clock without penalty if the ball **hits the ground** before they spike it, for example, after a muffed snap. Shotgun and punt- or field-goal-style snaps can be legally spiked in college. Although I don't know why you would want to do that. A hand-to-hand snap is quicker and you're trying to stop the clock as soon as possible. Also, you lose more yards with a shotgun spike.

In the **NFL**, it's called an intentional forward fumble and it is considered a forward pass. (Rule 8-4-2 exception 1)

Hard part is getting lined up

The **tricky part** of spiking the ball to stop the clock is **not** the **spike**. It's getting everyone **lined up** in a legal formation fast so you can snap the ball.

In practicing spiking the ball to stop the clock, make sure your players comply with the usual pre-snap rules. That is,

- everyone must be **set for at least one second** after the ready-to-play whistle
- everyone must be **within 15 yards of the ball** at least momentarily after the ready-to-play whistle
- at least **seven** properly-numbered **men on the line**
- **no overlapping of legs** except between guards and center in high school (NFICA 7-2-2) and college (NCAA 7-1-3-5-2). In the NFL, all linemen may lock legs (NFL 7-2-1)

It is crucial that your team learn to be both fast and legal before the snap for a spike play. Remember that if you draw a **penalty** on your spike play, the clock will stop **during** enforcement of the penalty, but will restart on the official's ready-to-play signal as soon as the chains are moved.

Since the penalty in question will be a **dead-ball penalty**, the defense has no chance to decline or accept it. And the fact that you spiked the ball is irrelevant because a dead-ball penalty means your spike did not happen in the eyes of the rules. The whole play did not happen. There was no spike so there was no clock-stopping event.

After such a penalty, your team must immediately get lined up to run another play so they can snap the ball again.

At Colorado, when he signals "spike the ball," head coach Rick Neuheisel has his team line up in the same formation as the last play to speed things up.

When to spike to stop the clock

Obviously, there is one circumstance when you do **not** spike the ball to stop the clock: **fourth down**.

If you spike the ball on fourth down, it will go over to the other team on downs. Remember that the scoreboard and sideline down indicators may not be accurate. That is, they may **say** third down, when it's **really** fourth.

If you don't think they ever make mistakes about the down on the scoreboard or chain gang, check out two of the most famous college football games ever: Cornell vs. Dartmouth 1940 and Colorado vs. Missouri 1990. In both games, the officials mistakenly gave one team a fifth down, which used they used to achieve a last-play-of-the-game come-from-behind victory! In 1940, even though Dartmouth refused to say a word of complaint about it, Cornell graciously gave up the victory when the error was proven by film, thereby costing themselves a chance for a national championship.

In 1990, Missouri demanded the loss be reversed but Colorado disgraced themselves by refusing to concede victory, even after it was proven that they scored the winning touchdown a fifth down—and the poll voters disgraced themselves by awarding Colorado the national championship. What a difference 50 years makes!

What if timeouts left?

At first, I thought you should not spike the ball **if you have any timeouts left**. But there are a couple of things to be noted on that score. Spiking the ball allows you to stop the game clock until the snap—although at the cost of a down. But it does **not** allow the coach or water boy to go on the field. Timeouts are longer than the play-clock interval you get from a spike and they do not cost you a down.

Generally, if you have a timeout left, take it before you start spiking. Spiking the ball can be dangerous. You could fumble the snap or bobble the spike or draw a penalty flag. The timeout is a sure, no-risk, thing. Save your timeout if you anticipate a future need for the unique advantages of a timeout.

Stop the clock if you need extra time to:

- **substitute** (common when you need to get the field-goal team on the field)
- take time to **decide** what play to call
- take time to **explain** the play you want (reconsider—plays that haven't been practiced by the players who have to execute them generally fail).

The fake-spike play

Miami's Dan Marino did the most famous fake-spike play on 11/27/94. Dolphins at Jets. With 22 seconds left in the game, the Dolphins are down 24-21 at the Jets 8. Marino motions that he plans to spike the ball to stop the clock. The Jets relax. Suddenly, Marino throws to Mark Ingram. Touchdown! Dolphins win 28-24.

A fake-spike play should be an uninterceptible pass—a look-in or a fade. It should be set up by signaling that you are going to spike. The quarterback should make a throwing motion toward the ground. The coaches on the sideline can do the same, as well as other players making the signal to each other. The fake aspect of the play could be set up in advance. For example, before the game, the coach says, "If we get into a no-timeouts-left clock-management situation where the game clock is running after a play before fourth down, we will run the fake-spike pass play."

Or the quarterback could signal spike with his throwing arm while making another secret signal with his other hand. For example, the non-throwing hand on the belt buckle might signify the fake-spike play.

In theory, you could run a fake-spike running play. But the defense normally congregates near the ball when they anticipate a spike. Throwing takes advantage of that. Running does not. Plus, running results in the clock not stopping after the next play unless the runner gets out of bounds.

18

Downfield laterals

Downfield laterals

Downfield laterals are generally **not** a good idea for ball carriers other than option quarterbacks lateraling to their normal pitch backs. It is common for option teams to **always** have their quarterback lateral downfield in practice when they on keep the ball so the lateral possibility stays in both players' minds.

Laterals other than options are not a good idea in general. However, if the play in question is the *last play of the game, and you are behind by 8 points or less, and you are about to be tackled, you **must** lateral.* The normal danger of the lateral, that the other team will get the ball and subsequently score, is no longer an issue. The immediate problem is that once you are tackled, your team loses the game. So you **must** lateral.

Must have the lateral play

I once had an argument with a high school varsity coach about this. I said everyone needed to have the Cal-Stanford Band play in their repertoire. He disagreed. He said you should just have a good kick-return play and score on that.

I still disagree. Kick-return touchdowns are pretty rare. In 1995, there were 2,043 kickoff returns in the **NFL**. Just 9 or .4% were returned for touchdowns. If your plan for winning a game is to run a play that succeeds .4% of the time, you have a 99.6% probability of losing. Some sort of trick kick return would have a better chance of success. Heck, almost **anything** would have a better chance of success than .4%.

The lower the level, the more kick-returns for touchdowns. For example, the **Pac-10** had eight touchdown kick-returns out of 385 total kick-returns or **2%**.

My local **high school** football league, the East Bay Athletic League (EBAL), had 12 touchdown returns in 1996. Their stats do not give the total number of returns. But we can make an educated guess. Their games last 48 minutes which is 80% of the college's 60 minutes. Eighty percent of the Pac -10 total returns is 80% x 385 = 308. All but one of the Pac-10 teams played 11 games. High school teams play ten games except for the top two who go the playoffs. Figure the high school total will be 10/11 of the Pac-10 total or 10/11 x 308 = 280 total kick-returns in the EBAL of which the 12 touchdown returns represent **4%**.

Is the multiple-lateral kickoff return a better play than a regular kickoff return? We don't really know. There's not enough data. Coaches generally do not use it for kickoff returns because of its potential for disaster. But when you are executing the **last play of the game** and you are trailing, there is **little downside** to what would **normally** be a big gamble.

When the ball carrier on the trailing team is about to be tackled and there's no time for another play, there is no question that he should lateral rather than be tackled. So you do not need to plan on the lateral play **as** your kick return when the kick return is the final play of the game. But *you must teach your players the lateral-rather-than-be-tackled play* and give them some reps so that they have it in mind when necessary. This principle applies to **all** plays, not just kick returns.

1997 Rose Bowl lateral

In the 1997 Rose Bowl, Arizona State's Brent Burnstein blocked an Ohio State 37-yard field goal attempt—the fourth time he had done that in the 1996-1997 season. Teammate Derek Smith picked the ball up and began running. There were less than six minutes left in the game and his team was trailing 14-10. As he was about to get tackled, Smith lateraled to teammate Derrick Rodgers who made it to the end zone. However, the lateral was ruled an illegal forward pass, bringing the ball back to the Arizona State 42 with 5:36 left. That was the start of ASU's spectacular come-from-behind drive. Unfortunately, Ohio State came back with their own spectacular drive after ASU's.

You must practice the downfield lateral

I do not know how much time, if any, ASU spent practicing the downfield lateral. But the result of this play makes it sound as though whatever time they spent was not quite enough. You need to practice this at least a little, in part to make sure the trailing teammates know the rules and are conscious of them during the play.

Obviously, *the lateral must be sideways or backwards, not forward, once you are past the line of scrimmage.* It is less widely known that *any member of the team can receive the lateral.* **Linemen** who are normally **ineligible** to receive **forward** passes, **are** allowed to receive laterals. They need to know that, although you need to be careful not to make that a license for blockers to forget blocking and just look for laterals.

Everyone also needs to know that *the lateral can be caught on the bounce or picked up off the ground.* And you should deliberately practice that once or twice to make sure it's in your players' minds.

The whole team needs to know that *when you are behind, on the last play of the game, have the ball, and you are about to be tackled, you must lateral.* To do otherwise is to give up without the one last bit of fight which the rules permit.

The ball carrier needs to know the lateral rules and be conscious of the game situation and the need to lateral when he no longer has any hope of scoring. But it takes two to lateral. The recipient of the lateral needs to get into position to receive the lateral and receive it legally. ASU's Derrick Rodgers maneuvered to receive and did catch the lateral, but he did not get where he needed to be to make it legal.

Probably not a good idea with six minutes left

I must add that Derek Smith's decision to lateral to his teammate in the 1997 Rose Bowl was **not** on the last play of the game. Indeed, there were almost six minutes left.

At that point, it was crucial that his team gain **possession** of the ball. But the fact that Ohio State attempted a field goal took care of that. ASU didn't even need to recover it. They could have let the Ohio State holder or place kicker fall on the ball and ASU **still** would have had possession because it was fourth down.

I **agree** with Smith's decision to pick up the ball and run rather than just fall on it. Falling on a fourth-down fumble or blocked kick is terminally stupid 99% of the time. It's your ball already.

But his decision to lateral could have resulted in Ohio State regaining possession. Once Smith picked up the ball, the fact that it had been fourth down became irrelevant. Had Ohio State recovered or picked up Smith's lateral, it would have been Ohio State ball **first** and ten.

Whether Smith was wise to lateral is a judgment call. In general, I suspect it was a **bad** decision with that much time left on the clock. But it could be a good idea if the lateral could be made cleanly with little risk of a turnover. Certainly the fact that it was ruled a **forward** lateral indicates that it should **not** have been made. The penalty for an illegal forward pass is five yards and loss of down. (NCAA Rule 7-3-2) There was no loss of down on ASU's forward lateral, I presume because it was on a kicking play rather than a scrimmage down. They started first and ten after the five-yard penalty was marked off.

Laterals gone bad

In 1987, Saints quarterback John Fourcade threw an interception against the Rams. The interceptor, apparently trying to lateral, fumbled the ball forward (no longer allowed). But one of his linemen teammates picked it up. Being slow, he thought it wise to lateral to someone faster, but as he was holding the ball in both hands searching, it was slapped out by a Saint. Fourcade picked it up and ran 60 yards for a touchdown—Touchdown #100 in the NFL Films video *100 Greatest Touchdowns.*

Number 70 involved another lateral gone bad. In a 1986 game between the Bears and Tampa Bay, Chicago's Todd Bell intercepted a pass. During the runback, Bell lateraled to another Bear who also lateraled. But the second lateral was intercepted by the Bucs and run back for a 45-yard touchdown.

1997 Sugar Bowl lateral

An FSU linebacker lateraled as time ran out and he was about to be tackled just before halftime in the 1997 Sugar Bowl Game against Florida. The lateral receiver got tackled after time ran out, but the lateral was a good idea. As a matter of fact, the guy who received the lateral should have lateraled himself when he was about to be tackled.

Coaches generally do not like laterals—although quarterbacks lateral all the time when they pitch the ball. Downfield laterals used to be very popular. But then NFL coaches started fining players every time they lateraled and the practice generally ended. The coaches were probably right as far as normal game situations are concerned. But when it comes to the last play of the game, they overdid it. The lateral should be brought back, at least for the last play.

The Cal-Stanford Band five-lateral play

The most famous lateral play in football history was California's final play of the 11/30/82 "Big Game" with Stanford. Stanford had just scored a come-from-behind score to take the lead 20-19. But in doing so they had left enough time on the clock that they still had to kick off to Cal.

Stanford kicked short to Kevin Moen who caught the ball at his own 43. As he was about to be tackled, he lateraled to Richard Rodgers. When Rodgers was about to be tackled, he lateraled to Dwight Garner, who subsequently lateraled back to Rodgers. Rodgers lateraled to Mariet Ford, who crashed through the Stanford Band, which had begun marching onto the field when the final gun sounded during the return. It couldn't have happened to a nicer band.

Holy Cross imitates Cal

Four years after Stanford failed to stop Cal's Mariet Ford, Holy Cross followed Cal's example to win a I-AA game against Princeton. Darin Cromwell caught the kickoff on his own 30-yard line. Holy Cross was trailing 26-24. There was not enough time left for another play. After running 15 yards, he lateraled to Tim Donovan, who took the ball the remaining 55 yards for the winning touchdown: Holy Cross 30, Princeton 26.

Colts versus Browns, 1981

The Colts attempted a field goal from the Browns' 18. It was blocked. One Colt picked it up and tried to run. He got caught and lateraled to a lineman teammate. He, in turn, got caught, and lateraled to no one in particular. The holder then picked the ball up off the ground and ran it in for a touchdown.

Ollie Matson, 1952

In 1952, Chicago Cardinal Hall of Famer Ollie Matson started a series of fumbles and laterals that led to one of the NFL's greatest touchdowns. Matson fumbled as he was hit. Teammates tried to get the ball but just ended up kicking it around. Finally, 250-pound Cardinal lineman (big in those days) Bill Fisher got it and took off. As he ran down the sideline, he was grabbed repeatedly by a pursuer. But he kept swatting the guy away while holding the ball in his other hand looking for a lateral opportunity. As he was finally tackled, he flipped a pretty-as-you-please lateral to a trailing teammates who took it in for the touchdown. Total yards covered: 85 yards.

Design of the lateral play

By rule, every player is eligible to receive and advance a lateral. And if you take no action to prevent it, that's exactly what you'll have, your whole team trailing the runner and nobody blocking. You need to designate some of your players as blockers and the rest as ball carriers, that is, potential lateral recipients. Once you have done this, you must absolutely **prohibit** the blockers from receiving laterals. Truth be told, it's better to lateral to a blocker than no one. But if you tell your players that they'll **all** be looking for the lateral and no one will be blocking.

You should practice this but make sure your players understand that this is **not your standard procedure**. It is *only for the last play of a game*. There is a good chance you will never have occasion to use this play all season. But if you need it, you'd better have it. And you will **not** have it if you do not rep it.

You could choose up sides and run a competitive game where there are no plays but kick returns or scrimmage plays and there is only one down. If you fail to score on your only down, the ball goes "over on downs."

Not just short laterals

Most people figure any lateral should be short and underhand. Why? I suspect the longer the better. **Pass** the darned thing if the distance warrants.

In 1992, my youth team was facing a tough opponent, the Farifield Falcons, in the semi-finals of the league championship. For three weeks prior to the game, we worked on a cross-field lateral kickoff return—a backward pass would be a more accurate description. This was to be a **called** play, not a desperation last-play-of-the-game-only play.

We put our first- and second-string quarterbacks in the next-to-last rank of the kick return formation. We put our best two return men behind them. The play was that whichever quarterback received the ball, he was to run forward briefly then stop and pass back across to the other side of the field. The receiver opposite the quarterback who caught the kickoff was to **keep at least one yard line between him and the quarterback** to make sure it was a backward pass.

If the kick went to another player, we just ran our regular kick return. That's what happened after the Falcons scored in the first half.

In the event, they kicked the opening kickoff of the second half to our second-string quarterback, Shane Evans. He ran forward as if he were returning the kick, then stopped at just the right moment and passed back across the field to Chris Noon, who was exactly where he was supposed to be, one yard line behind the ball carrier. He caught the pass, although he did not need to under the rules. Unfortunately, the blocker assigned to the contain man was unable to sustain his block and we only got a 15-yard return.

My mistake was assigning only one man to block the contain man. We had seen in scouting that he was disciplined to maintain his sideline lane. We doubted the fake return on the far side would suck him in and it did not.

Or we could have stuck with the one-man block but **delayed** it until the strategic moment, so it would not have to be sustained. We were unable to debug the block in practice because we could not create the element of **surprise** in our scout team after the first rep. Probably, we should have run various normal kick returns that looked like the fake return we were planning to run with**out** the pass. We should have kept trying to make the block we needed for the backward-pass return until we got it right.

The main point, however, is that with just three weeks of practice (only about 10 minutes on this play per week) we got ten- and eleven-year olds to execute the ball-handling portion of it perfectly. (On the game video, you can hear the fathers of our players, who did not expect the play, raving about how great it was. If you've ever coached youth football you know what a tough audience they are.)

From scrimmage, too

That same year, we also had a scrimmage play which was a backward pass. The quarterback would reverse pivot counterclockwise faking a sweep-right pitch. Then he'd pass back to a flanker who dropped off the line during the fake pitch.

I told the offensive coordinator (I was defense and special teams) to deliberately one-hop the pass. He declined on the grounds that the shape of the football made bouncing it too unpredictable. But we practiced it enough that we got some inadvertent one-hoppers in practice, and our receiver thereby learned that such grounders are live balls.

In two **games**, we got inadvertent one-hoppers. One, which was the first play of the Richmond game, turned into a 60-yard touchdown. The opposing team assumed it was an incomplete pass. They did not know what we coaches meant as we yelled "No whistle! No whistle!" from the sidelines. Of course, it meant that the referees saw the play as a backward pass or lateral, not an incomplete pass.

In another game, we got a long gain out of a one-hopper backward pass which our receiver calmly picked up and advanced while the opposing defense was doing double takes. Most trick-play football books include that deliberate backward pass grounder. For example, it's Play #25 in Tom Simonton's *Directory of Surprise Plays for Winning Football* and it's on pages 25 and 36 of Patrick Wyatt's *The First Book of Trick and Special Plays.*

Long-distance downfield laterals

How about a long lateral or backward pass by a ball carrier who has gone downfield? He takes a sweep pitch, runs around the right end, then, as he's about to be tackled, he slings the ball 40 yards back across to the other side of the field. Remember this is the last play of the game and you are behind. He could probably even do it as a **blind pass**, NBA style. What the heck, you lose if you don't. You might as well go down with guns blazing.

The play design of this last-play-of-the-game would be a regular play with one exception. A player with good hands, maybe even an ineligible-for-a-forward-pass lineman, would loaf and drift out on the backside of a wide play like a sweep or option. A well-trained defense will "fly to the ball!" Especially when this is the last play of the game and the tackle seals the victory!

The ball carrier does his best to score. The lateral receiver stays one yard line behind the ball carrier in the vicinity of the backside field numbers. In high school, where there rarely are field numbers, the lateral receiver would be outside the backside hash marks.

When the ball carrier is cornered, he jump passes or hook shots Wilt Chamberlain-style or faces out toward the near sideline and hurls the ball over his head with two hands back across the field.

Whatever it takes. Forget style points. He need not even look as long as he puts it in the right general area **with some air under it** and **makes sure it is a backward pass**. Ideally, the receiver will catch it in the air, but he does not need to under the rules.

You could apply this principle to any kind of last play of the game—kickoff return, punt return, scrimmage play. You designate the player to make himself available to receive the lateral then tell your ball carriers,

> *On the last play of the game in which we are trailing by eight points or less, there will always be a good-hands teammate lagging behind you on the far side of the field. When you can go no farther with the ball, haul off and sling it back to the other side of the field. You don't even need to look. We will not get mad no matter what happens to the lateral. Just don't get tackled with the ball, thereby killing our last hope.*

This should be fun to practice and only a few reps should dramatically increase your chances of success over what they would be with no practice at all. You could designate this the "Last play of the game!" and yell those words both in practice and at the actual game to remind your players to what they need to do.

Backward over-the-head lateral to Tom Landry

Does the backward, over-the-head lateral seem a bit much? Obviously, you have not seen Touchdown Number 28 in the *100 Greatest Touchdowns* video. In that 1950 play, the New York Giants intercepted a Steelers' pass. The interceptor fumbled the ball back to the Steelers when he was tackled. Then another Giant simply took the ball out of the hands of the Steeler who had picked it up and begun running the other way. As he was being tackled, he lateraled backward over his head to teammate Tom Landry who took it in for the touchdown—70 yards from the point of the original interception. Yes, the same Tom Landy who later became head coach of the Cowboys.

Fake laterals work, too

If your opponent knows you tend to lateral on the last play of the game when you are behind, a fake lateral may work. It may work even without that scouting by the opponent.

Touchdown #96 in the NFL Films video *100 Greatest Touchdowns* shows the Brown Bo Scott fake a lateral just as the Raiders' #43 is about to tackle him in a 1970 game. The Raider goes for the fake and Scott goes 66 yards for the touchdown.

Hook-and-ladder play

Sports Illustrated football writer Paul Zimmerman says,

> *Every time I've seen the old Buck and Wing play, it's worked. That's the one where you pass to a wide receiver and he laterals to a trailer. Why not work something off that, such as a double lateral, or a fake lateral outside then one inside? Why not use it at the end of a game when there's nothing to lose anyway,*

> *instead of that tired old stuff like the three-wide-receiver, Big Ben play?* [I guess he means Hail Mary.]
>
> *"Because people want to play it safe, [Bill] Walsh says. "The conservative approach won't cost anyone his job."*

I coached freshman football at Granada High School in Livermore, CA in 1996. Our JV team, which used to scrimmage us in practice and which played my son's Miramonte JV team that year, loved the hook and lateral, more commonly called the "hook and ladder," (a short pass to the flat where the receiver immediately laterals to a back running outside), and they were good at it. They generally made it work against our freshman, and they used it twice, along with a blocked punt, to beat my son's team in a game where I thought Miramonte outplayed Granada otherwise.

In 1963, when I was on the Collingswood (NJ) High School varsity, our game with Audubon was postponed because it was supposed to have taken place the day after President Kennedy was assassinated. When we finally played the game, it was a stalemate until late in the fourth quarter. Then Audubon ran a hook and ladder that went about 60 yards for the winning touchdown.

Browns versus Vikings, 12/14/80

NFL Films archivist Ace Cacchiotti told me of a sequence involving two plays, each of which is the subject of chapters in this book. The Browns were ahead 23-22. Minnesota was at their own 20 when they ran a hook and ladder. Tight end Joe Senser caught the pass at his 25 then immediately lateraled to running back Ted Brown who ran all the way to the Browns' 46. That gave Minnesota first down but there were only about five seconds left in the game.

On the next play, Vikings quarterback Tommy Kramer threw a 46-yard Hail Mary. A defender deflected it, but Ahmad Rashad made a one-handed catch around the three and trotted into the end zone to score the winning touchdown. The delirious home crowd poured onto the field preventing the Vikings from running a PAT play. That's why the final score was only 28-23 Vikings.

Dolphins versus Chargers, Divisional Playoff 1/16/82

In the 1982 AFC divisional playoff game between Miami and San Diego, Miami used a hood and ladder just before half to great advantage. The Dolphins were down 24-0 when their quarterback Don Strock led them back to 24-10. Then, seconds before the half, with first and ten at the Charger 40, Strock threw a pass to wide receiver Duriel Harris who immediately lateraled to running back Tony Nathan. Touchdown Dolphins.

Tarkenton's best game

Zimmerman once told NFL Hall of Fame quarterback Fran Tarkenton that he thought Tarkenton's best game was a 1971 *Monday Night Football* 20-13 loss to Dallas. "It's my favorite, too," Tarkenton said.

Zimmerman described Tarkenton's final minutes in that game as a "quarterback in a competitive frenzy." The game ended with Tarkenton trying, in desperation, to lateral to a lineman.

All games in which the trailing team has possession should end that way.

19

Behind on defense

If you are behind on defense, you have a problem. About 70% to 90% of the teams in that situation lose. Some coaches say they never lost, they just ran out of time. This book is, in large part, about **not** running out of time when you are behind.

Defensive score

Is it possible to score without possession? Yes. There's one way: the **safety**. It gets you two points, which is enough to win if you are tied or one point behind and enough to tie if you are two points behind. If you are three to five points behind, scoring a safety enables you to tie or win with a subsequent field goal.

Can you do anything to increase the probability of a safety? Sure. Send lots of people, that is, blitz or run a gap-8 defense or some such to put maximum pressure on the quarterback or to increase the possibility of tackling another ball carrier in the backfield.

Safety just before half

We lost the 1996 Granada-Acalanes freshman game 10-0. We would have lost it 8-0 had it not been for the safety we gave up just before halftime. But the safety could have been the game winner had we ever scored eight points in the game.

We took over on downs on our own four or so with about ten seconds left in the half. The head coach said to just run out the clock, a decision I agreed with. Instead of having my regular quarterback run a quarterback sneak, I decided to send in my **two-point conversion quarterback**.

He was a big strong running back with years of tackle football experience. He had taken many snaps so I was fairly confident that he would not fumble the center-quarterback exchange.

The regular quarterback was a rookie who had never played football before. Great kid with a great arm, but we all held our breath whenever he ran with the ball. I figured he was more likely to have the ball stripped from him than the experienced running back. I did not want to risk a handoff.

Just before I sent the players on the field, I told the two-point conversion quarterback to run "I left, quarterback sneak, 11 base." 11 means the one back (quarterback) through the one hole (left center-guard gap). Base means base block, which more or less means every lineman puts his helmet between his man and the hole.

As I watched the play, the team lined up in **quads left**. "Uh oh," I thought. "What the heck is he doing?"

He then ran 17 sweep crack, and was tackled in our end zone for a safety.

I don't know how often one of your opponents will pull a stunt like that. But bringing a lot of guys enables you to take advantage when they do. If our opponent had been in a **prevent** defense for that play, it probably would have gained yards.

Taking risks on defense

Football coaches and fans alike have a good understanding of the logic of taking risks when you are behind on **offense**. Seems to me that the same principle applies when you are behind on **defense**. But coaches and fans seem far less comfortable with taking risks on defense.

Aside from the scoring-with-a-safety possibility above, the defense has one mission when you are behind:

Get the ball!

First, second, and third downs

How do you get the ball on first-second, or third down? **Strip or interception**.

To a large extent, clock-management **defense** is a mirror image of clock-management **offense**. The offensive portion of this book tells you what the offensive will **try** to do, or what they **should** try to do. I do not expect that every coach will read this or that all who do read it will adopt every principle in it.

Conversely, that tells you, the **defensive** coordinator, what your defense will have to **stop**.

The game ends sooner than you think

Here's one example of clock-management defense being the mirror image of clock-management offense. The game does not end when the final gun sounds. It ends when the leading team reaches the take-a-knee point and has possession. In this chapter, I assume you are on defense. If the other team can reach the take-a-knee point, the game is over.

Accordingly, your defenders must be trained to *savagely attack the ball carrier on a play where he appears to have made the last first down his team needs*. At all costs, they *must not let him get to the ground, stop his forward progress, or get out of bounds*. Rather they *must hold him up, keep him moving forward and inbounds, and* ***strip the ball***. If they allow the referee to blow the whistle before they strip the ball, the game is essentially over.

I suggest you come up with a code word that means, "if they get one more first down, they are in take-a-knee. Therefore we must strip the ball on any play that appears to have gained first down yardage."

The code word should **not** be understandable to the opponent. For example, "Strip time! would be a bad choice because it alerts the opponent to your plan. Rather use something like "Do-or-die time!" or "Crunch time!"

This is the trailing defense equivalent of the trailing offense's desperate last play, the lateral.

You must practice the hold-'em-up-and-strip play.

Turnover after take-a-knee?

I had never heard of a team turning a ball over in their take-a-knee period—until I mentioned that to my brother Bill.

We are from the Philadelphia area and he said it happened in an Eagles-Giants game in the seventies. So I called the Eagles and asked their public relations guy Todd Starowitz if he remembered such a play. "We get calls about it all the time," he said. I also got help from Giants public relations vice president Pat Hanlon on the details of this play.

'The Miracle of the Meadowlands'

On November 19, 1978, the Giants were ahead of the Eagles 17-12. Giant Odis McKinney intercepted Ron Jaworski's pass with 1:23 left. Giants quarterback Joe Pisarcik took a knee ending at 1:11 losing three yards and the Eagles used their last timeout. The Giants only needed to kneel two more times to win.

But with second and thirteen at the 18, the Giants called a **handoff** play! Csonka carried the ball over left guard for eleven yards.

Then, with :31 left at their own 29-yard line, on third and two, they called a handoff play again. The snap was bobbled. By the time Pisarcik got control and tried to handoff, Csonka was by him and the ball hit Csonka in the hip. As CBS rolled the credits on the TV screen, Eagles cornerback Herman Edwards caught the fumble on a short hop and ran it back 26 yards for the winning touchdown, scoring at :20 left. The Eagles won the game 19-17.

Giants offensive coordinator Bob Gibson was fired the next day and never worked in the NFL again. He was still refusing to comment on the play ten years later when contacted at his Florida real estate job. The Giants head coach John McVay and the director of operations Hall of Famer Andy Robustelli also were fired the day after the end of the season. The Giants won only won one of their four remaining games after the Eagles loss and began a multi-year bad spell (6-10, 4-12, 9-7, 4-5, 3-12). The Eagles, under Dick Vermiel, began a four-year string of playoff appearances culminating in their going to the 1981 Super Bowl. What a difference a play makes!

Giants owner Wellington Mara said the one play alone was **not** the **only** factor in the decision to fire McVay and Robustelli, but it was a **big** factor. Giants fans burned their tickets and one hired a plane to fly a banner over Giants Stadium saying, "15 yrs. of lousy football; we've had enough."

'Payback' time?

Why did the Giants run handoff plays during take-a-knee time? Eagles linebacker Bill Bergey said he thought another Eagles linebacker, Frank LeMaster instigated the sequence of events. On the take-a-knee play, LeMaster had crashed through the line and blasted Pisarcik. A brief scuffle ensued.

New York's owner, Wellington Mara, said after the game that he could hear Gibson arguing with wide receivers coach Lindy Infante about the next play. Giants tight end Al Dixon brought it in: "Pro up 65," a handoff to fullback Larry Csonka behind left guard.

As they lined up for the next play, Eagles players could hear the Giants arguing among themselves about the play call. Eagles nose Charlie Johnson asked the Giants center Jim Clack if they were going to take a knee. Clack said, "You won't believe this. We're going to run a play."

Giants were heard saying, "Joe, just fall on the damn ball!" But Pisarcik had been previously criticized for changing plays sent in from the sideline. He did not change this one.

Bergey believed the handoff to Csonka was an attempt to run a hard-hitting play at LeMaster to pay him back for hitting Pisarcik.

Clack later said, "...as we were coming up to the line, guys were asking about the snap count and still complaining about the call. It was chaos from the time the play was brought into the huddle." Csonka tried to persuade Pisarcik not to run the play.

NFL Films did a video titled *The 100 Greatest Touchdowns.* Herman Edwards' "Miracle of the Meadowlands" was number 10. (There have been over 41,000 touchdowns in the history of the NFL.) The current take-a-knee formation, with one guy playing safety, came into use after the '78 Eagles victory over the Giants. The phrase "Miracle of the Meadowlands" is used in Philadelphia and other non-New York places. In New York, the play has a different name. They just call it "The Fumble."

The legend of Barry Fry

I attended Harrington Public School when I lived in Harrington, Delaware in the early sixties. I played football there on the freshman team. One of my teammates and classmates was Barry Fry. I moved away at the beginning of our sophomore year. Barry went on to become team quarterback.

I later heard that when he was a senior in the 1963 season, Harrington was ahead of Millsboro by less than a touchdown at the end of the game. In that situation, Harrington's coach should have told the quarterback to take-a-knee, or at least trained him to call that play in that situation. Back then, quarterbacks generally called the plays, not coaches.

He did **not** take a knee. Rather he dropped back as if to pass, holding the ball in two hands up high. No damage was done. He held onto the ball when he was tackled. But he got his butt chewed by his teammates after the play for the damage it could have done. They still talk about it in Harrington.

Maybe a fumbled snap

You can't **count on** many Bob Gibsons or Barry Frys. But you should be ready to take advantage if your team encounters one.

It is possible that there could be a fumbled snap during a take-a-knee play. *Your defensive linemen should **assume** that the snap will be fumbled.* One defender should dive between the center's legs. Others should dive through the A and B gaps on each side. They are **not** looking to make the **tackle**, although they should get to the ball carrier as fast as possible if there is no fumble, to prevent him from running extra seconds off the clock during the play. In the take-a-knee chapter, I gave you the take-a-knee **offensive** formation. Here's the **defensive** counterpart.

Defensive alignment against take-a-knee formation

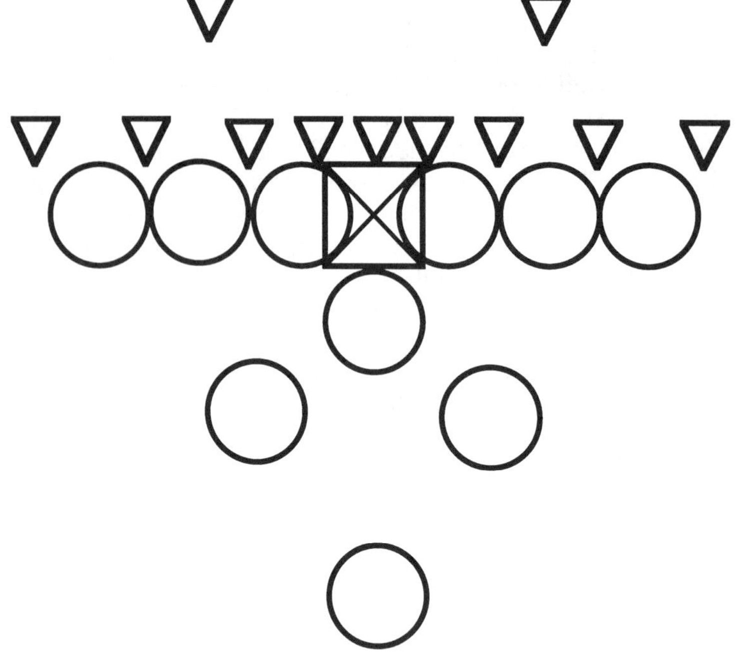

Before take-a-knee

This chapter is mainly concerned with what happens **before** the game reaches the take-a-knee point. *The trailing defense must not let the game reach the take-a-knee point.* Coaches who are willing to do all sorts of gambles on **offense** when they are behind at the end of a game are strangely content to wait for a punt on **defense**.

Forcing the other team to punt can work. It has worked. But forcing the other team to punt often does **not** work. In a game where the other team has been converting third downs at a high rate, it is a plan that is likely to **fail**.

No interceptions

When you are behind at the end of a game, you are not likely to get an interception. The offense will want to keep the ball **on the ground** to avoid a turnover and to avoid stopping the clock in the event of an incompletion. Although if you can force them into third and long in their own territory, they may risk the interception in an effort to get a first down.

Your best chance of a turnover is a **strip**.

The value of a takeaway

Everybody knows takeaways are good. But do you know how good?

A 12/15/95 *Wall Street Journal* article said that an interception was worth about 50 yards and a fumble was worth about 26 yards, although they did not explain how they arrived at those figures.

In the book *The Hidden Game of Football*, authors Carroll, Palmer, and Thorn say a fumble is worth about 50 yards and an interception is worth about 45 yards. Fifty yards is the distance the average team would have gained, or gained and punted, after the fumble, had they not fumbled.

Interceptions are worth five yards less because the average interception is returned 14 yards after traveling an average 19 yards downfield before it was intercepted. In high school and youth football, a turnover would be worth less because the average net punt at those levels is shorter than in the NFL games the *Hidden Game* authors analyzed.

The Hidden Game of Football also translates turnovers and other football events into the **points** they lead to. By analyzing hundreds of games, they found you score one point for every twelve yards you gain. If a turnover is worth 50 yards and there are twelve yards per point, a turnover is worth 50 ÷ 12 = 4 points.

The value of a takeaway as time is running out

As I have said elsewhere in the book, everything becomes more important as the end of the game draws nigh. Yards and points are useful as far as they go, but the final objective is not to gain yards or score points, it is to **win**.

Accordingly, the best measure of the value of a football play is how it affects **win probability**. A Miami-New England game is analyzed in *The Hidden Game of Football.* In that game, Miami fumbles on its first possession. Their win probability at the beginning of that drive was .507. After the fumble, it dropped to .498, a change of -.009. The time remaining in the game at the time was 56:37.

But later, in the second quarter, with 41:58 left in the game, New England's fumble resulted in a change in win probability change of -.091, **ten times as much**.

In another game, between the Chiefs and Steelers, Pittsburgh was trailing 24-19 when they threw an interception with 2:22 left in the game. Their win probability dropped from .178 to .055, a change of -.123, **fourteen times as much** as the first-quarter turnover.

Takeaways involved in most big comebacks

In the course of researching this book, I have watched many videos and read many books and other accounts of great comebacks. Virtually all great comebacks requiring more than one score involve a turnover by the leading team.

Stripping the ball

The strip has become a big part of the **pro** game in recent years. To an extent, college players have also increased the number of times they strip the ball. High school teams sometimes have the defensive back slap the ball when tackling from behind. Youth teams rarely try to strip except maybe in a game situation where the coaches send that specific instruction out to the players at the end of a game.

I suspect there is untapped potential in improving stripping technique. And if ever there was a time for it, it is when you are behind on defense at the end of a game.

Simple drill

I did a simple drill in youth football that paid big dividends. I had one player act as ball carrier, one act as tackler, and a third act as stripper. One big point we taught was that the **first** man in **never** strips, only the **second** man. But in a late-in-the-game, come-from-behind situation, the first man can become the stripper as well, because of your desperate straits.

We did **one rep** per player. The ball carrier was told to hold the ball loosely and let the stripper take it. Some would hand the stripper the ball, which we corrected. Others would hang on for dear life, which also disrupted the drill. We wanted some realism, but not competition between the stripper and the ball carrier. The ball carrier was to be a patsy for the stripper.

The objective of this drill was **not** to teach **technique**. Rather I just wanted to plant the seed in the players' minds that when they see a ball carrier being tackled, they should consider taking the ball out of his hands and running with it. Note that we did **not** want him to slap it **to the ground**. Once it's on the ground, **either** team can gain possession. In fact, the offense recovers about **half** of all fumbles. Just take the ball and run.

Later in the season, we played Napa. On three occasions in that one game, a Napa ball carrier would hit into the line on a dive or off tackle play, and after some unseen commotion, one of my defenders would come running out the other direction with the ball. All got tackled before they scored, but we obtained possession all three times.

One rep drills

I have found one-rep-per-season drills to be extremely productive. I said that elsewhere in this book, but it bears repeating. I have never seen or read about other coaches who use one-rep drills.

Coaches generally regard drills as repetitive practice of the same technique. That's fine as far as it goes, but there are many, many techniques that players must learn—far more than you have time to teach in multi-repetition practices. In fact there are **so many things** players must learn, that you can only teach the **majority** of them in one-rep-per-season drills.

Can you reduce **everything** to one-rep drills? Absolutely not. Skills like passing, option pitch, center-quarterback exchange, long-snapping, and so forth, all require **hundreds** of reps.

Can you truly **master** a technique in just one rep per season? Some simple techniques, like signaling for a fair catch, yes. But one rep will not give you mastery of very many techniques.

So why bother? Because *one rep is infinitely better than no reps*. There are all sorts of things which your players may be called on to do during a season, like take a safety or take a knee after making an interception on the last play of the game, or cover a kickoff that accidentally only goes one yard. Roughly speaking, the chances that your players will do it right if they get NO reps are close to **zero**. But the chances that they will do it right if they get just one rep all season rise to about 60 or 70%.

That improvement is worth the trouble. Here's a diagram of my understanding of the typical learning curve. One rep is much better than none. Two is better than one, but the second rep is significantly less valuable than the first. Eventually, the value of each additional rep approaches insignificance. That's called the point of diminishing returns.

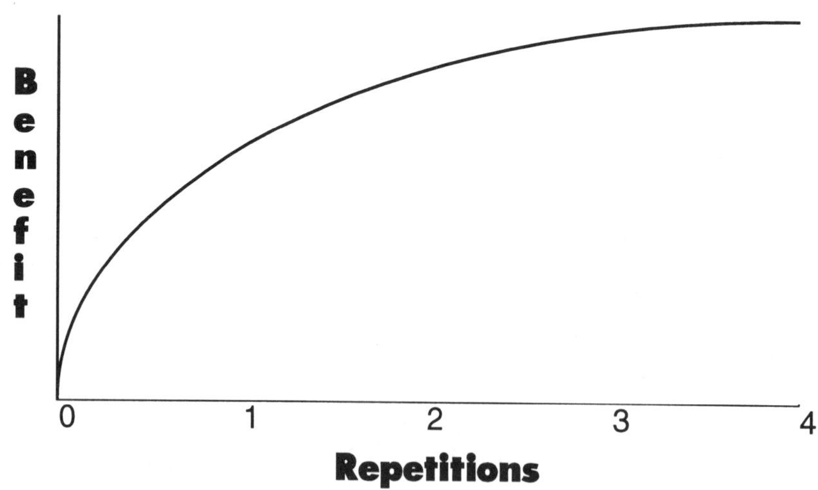

The learning curve varies from skill to skill. But a great many clock-management skills, like getting out of bounds at the end of a run or calling timeout at the end of the 25-second play clock, match this curve. That is, one or two reps are of great benefit. Not getting any reps almost guarantees that the player will forget to do the required thing. And numerous reps, like those needed for more traditional skills, are of little additional value.

Other drills

I have done other similar drills involving tackling from behind, receivers who had just caught the ball, loaf-of-bread running backs, and stripping quarterbacks who are trying to pass. Those drills all make sense to me, but I cannot point to an actual game situation where the drill produced a turnover. However, it would not surprise me to learn that a player turned one of those drills into a turnover in a **subsequent season** after I left the team.

I always emphasize picking up fumbles and running with them. Most years, we got two touchdowns from that. That happened with my JV team in 1994. The following year, after those JV players moved up to varsity, one was featured on the local *High School Sports Focus* TV program for picking up a fumble and running with it. I asked the player in question if our brief practice on that the previous year had anything to do with his picking up the ball. He confirmed that he would have fallen on it had it not been for our previous year emphasis on picking it up instead.

I have four books that contain nothing but football drills:

- *The American Football Coaches Guide Book to Championship Football Drills* by Jerry R. Tolley
- *American Football Coaches Association's Defensive Football Drills*
- *Football Drill Book* by Doug Mallory
- *The Complete Handbook of Winning Football Drills* by Donald Fuoss

Tolley's book, which came out in 1985, has no stripping drills whatsoever. Mallory's book, which came out in 1993, has four stripping drills. One, the Second-Man Strip Drill (page 142), is like the drill I described above. His others are

• Strip drill (page 140)	Strips receiver while he's catching
• Fumble Tackle (page 141)	Face-on-the-football form tackling
• Chase Drill (page 143)	Come-from-behind rip or swim through the ball while tackling with other arm

The AFCA book, which came out in 1996, has just one strip drill, the Clap (man coverage) Drill (page 94) which sounds like Mallory's Strip Drill. Fuoss's 1984 book has no stripping drills.

The book *Play Football the NFL* Way by Tom Bass is generally a narrative about offensive, defensive, and special teams position technique. But it contains many drills including one on stripping (page 320). Bass provides the best discussion I've found of stripping theory in pass-receiving situations. Among other things, Bass says the defensive back should attack the arm of the receiver on the same side as the pass. For example, if the pass is arriving on the receiver's left side, the db should attack the receiver's left arm to strip the ball. He recommends teaching in two steps: standing still, then at 3/4 speed.

Bass also makes a statement that is reminiscent of my one-rep theory. "Stripping the ball is as much mental as it is physical...each time a defensive back executes the drill properly he gets a mental picture of what he can do during a game to cause a receiver to drop a pass."

As you can see from this small sampling of drill books, the strip is a relatively **recent** innovation. As such, I think it is relatively undeveloped and thereby offers potential for coaches who are willing to devote some time to experimenting with better ways to strip and teach stripping.

Can stripping be raised to a high art?

It seems to me that innovative coaches who emphasized stripping might be able to raise it to a high art and thereby revolutionize football. Remember that passing was once considered an oddball maneuver perhaps similar to the way stripping is regarded now. Legend has it that Notre Dame's Gus Dorais and Knute Rockne perfected the forward pass on the beach in the summer of 1913 then used it to upset my alma mater, Army, which was good enough to be the consensus national champion a year later in 1914.

Actually, a *New York Times* account of the Army-Carlisle game of 1912, the year **before** the Notre Dame-Army passing game, said, "Both the Cadets and the Indians used the forward pass to great advantage."

The forward pass was made legal in 1906. Illinois coach Robert Zuppke said about 70,000 forward passes had been completed in games prior to the 1913 Army-Notre Dame game. I read somewhere that the forward pass was actually perfected at Washington University of St. Louis.

Whatever, my point is that football has been revolutionized in the past by things like the forward pass and the option. It could be revolutionized in the future by a coach who figured out how to strip the ball a much higher percentage of the time.

The theory of stripping

I have a theory. I have fooled with it in my practices but have never emphasized it the way a revolutionary innovator must. Here's the theory.

One ball carrier cannot prevent eleven defenders from taking the football away from him for long. If you simply gave a running back a football and put him in the middle of a field and told eleven defensive players to take the ball away from him, they would succeed in seconds.

Mirror image of fumble prevention

We all know how to teach fumble prevention. The ball carrier must carry the ball using four points of contact:

- his hand in an "eagle claw" on the front point of the ball
- his forearm pressing the ball against
- his ribs
- his bicep pressing the ball against his side.

If that's how to **prevent** stripping, then stripping is **undoing** one or more of those four points of contact.

Most players and coaches think of stripping as administering a sharp blow to the ball, usually downward but sometimes upward or a push from in front or behind. That works when the ball carrier does not expect it or when he fails to use proper carrying technique. But a blow to the ball is usually worthless when the ball carrier expects it.

Two mistakes

Current stripping techniques work many times. But I still think they fall far short of the potential. They are making two mistakes:

- trying for no more than an instant
- focusing on the ball.

I think the best chance of a strip is to make a **sustained effort** over one to three seconds, not an instantaneous slap. And I think the effort must be directed at the ball carrier's **arm**, not the ball. If you can get daylight between the ball and the ball carrier's ribs, the ball is yours for the taking. You can even take it without getting daylight if you can significantly reduce the pressure between the ball and the ball carrier's ribs.

I suggested the following technique to my junior varsity high school players one year:

> *There is a natural opening between the ball carrier's bicep and his ribs above the ball. Drive your arm in there bicep deep, then take off for the goal line. That's gets your leg strength and your arm*

strength working against the ball carrier's arm strength. The ball should come out. It may even come out into the tackler's arms so no one has to pick it up off the ground.

I can't tell you whether this works or doesn't work because none of my players ever tried it in a game.

Not even a sledge hammer

When the ball is carried properly, a downward blow drives the ball into the top of ball carrier's hip and hip pad. If the player was determined to hang onto the ball, even a sledge hammer blow in that direction would probably not dislodge it.

An **upward** blow runs into no protrusion like the hip bone or hip pad. But human biceps and forearm muscles produce a rather weak upward slap compared to the whole upper body explosion that can be delivered in a downward slap.

Longitudinal blows by a hand will not generally dislodge a tightly and properly held ball, but the same blow from a tackler's **helmet** often will. We have all seen many a fumble caused by a helmet blow on the ball-carrying hand or elbow.

The longitudinal blow from a defender's hand generally only works if the ball carrier does not see it coming and has a momentary lapse in the tightness of his grip on the ball.

Getting more time

OK, let's say the ball carrier's team is ahead, his coach has warned him that your team will be stripping, and he is calling conservative inside running plays only. How do you strip the ball? The problem is **time**. I said above that a group of eleven defenders should be able to take the ball away from a single ball carrier "in seconds." But where do you get the seconds needed to work the ball loose?

Normally, a tackle takes about one second from the time the ball carrier is hit until he hits the ground. It's tough to work the ball loose that fast. Fine. So the obvious solution is we have to make the tackle **last longer**. How do we do that?

The referees determine how much time we have to make the tackle. They blow the end-of-play whistle either when the ball carrier's body, other than his hands or feet, touches the ground, or when his forward progress is stopped. OK. So hold the son of a gun up and let him make just a little bit of forward progress for a couple of seconds while you work on getting the ball loose. Earlier in the book, I told how Campolindo did that to my freshman tight end on one play, although they did not get possession.

Now that I think about it, how could they **not** get possession when they had four seconds to work on the receiver with multiple defenders? I suspect they must not have been trying to strip the ball. If they **had** stripped it, they would have **won**. Unlike the subject of this chapter, Campo was ahead at the time.

Game thud tackles

Most coaches use thud tackling in scrimmages to prevent injuries. Thud tackling, in case you aren't familiar with the term, is tackling by **grabbing** the ball carrier, but not taking him to the ground.

Not taking him to the ground. That's one of those two things needed to keep the refs from blowing the dead-ball whistle. Thud tackling technique could be useful in **games**.

Thud tackling is seen by players and coaches as sort of half-hearted tackling. The guys on defense constantly whine about not being allowed to hit when thud is in effect.

That need not be the case. Thud can be a legitimate tackling technique for games as well. I am fortunate to have in my area one of the best high school football teams there is: DeLaSalle of Concord, CA. In many cases, their game tackles look like mass thud. The ball carrier from the opposing team runs into a mass of DeLaSalle tacklers and suddenly he is running sideways or backwards. Everyone is on their feet. They also happen to have hold of him and far outweigh him as a group. The DeLaSalle tacklers I saw were not trying to use the time they gained to strip the ball. They were content to put the guy in reverse.

I tell my tacklers to stay off the ground. My main reason has been that it keeps them from leaving their feet from too far away from the ball carrier, a common tackling mistake.

Run him sideways

The macho thing to do is to drive the ball carrier backwards. Impressive to be sure. But it rarely gets you the ball and it inspires a fast whistle by the officials. In this chapter, you are behind and on defense and desperate to prevent the opponent from getting to the take-a-knee point. Impressive "push-'em-back" hits, unless you can accumulate three of them in a row and force a punt, do not get you the ball.

If, instead of driving the ball carrier backward, you drive him sideways, even allowing a little forward progress as you go, you get the seconds you need to strip the ball. Here's a diagram:

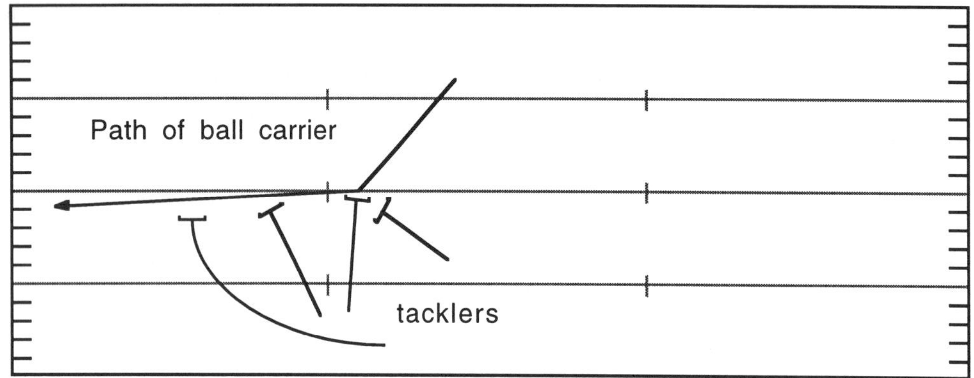

The basic idea here is that the ball carrier gets to the yard line unimpeded. But at the yard line, he is met by one or more defenders. Instead of driving him backward, they drive him toward the **sideline**, even permitting him to make a little forward progress along the way to prevent the official from whistling the play dead. They also hold the ball carrier **up** so he cannot get his knee down to get a dead ball whistle. While the defenders are moving the ball carrier sideways, they are stripping him of the ball.

Fourth-and-three game

What you emphasize, you achieve. One way to emphasize something is to create a competitive situation in practice where the normal rules of football are changed. Coaches do not have a monopoly on technique knowledge, especially when they are trying to pioneer a new technique. Players often figure out better ways to do things than the coaches know. To encourage the players to figure out how to strip better, you could play an intrasquad game where stripping is almost the **only** way to gain possession.

One way to do that would be to say that every down is fourth and three. Or to put it another way, you only get one down, but you only have to go three yards to get another. Requiring a gain of three yards forces the offense to run the kind of play you would see when a leading team has the ball near the end of a game.

The defense can focus on stopping the offense for a gain of less than three yards, or they can strip. You may need to adjust the number of downs allowed or the distance required for a first down to get the desired stripping effort.

In high school varsities and higher levels, coaches are reluctant to allow the kind of contact this game would involve. So at those levels, coaches might want to restrict it to spring practice, summer camp, or the earliest August practices. You could "make it interesting" by making the loser put away the equipment or some such.

It is important to enforce the rules about when to blow the play dead the way a referee would. I once was an assistant on a team where the coach scrimmaged every night and blew an ultra fast whistle "to prevent injuries." That practice came back to haunt us in a playoff game where the opposing team had been drilled to make a second effort when being tackled. We would have four or five tackles broken per play because our kids were used to the quick whistle and the opponent's kids were used to the opposite.

Scrums

In rugby, they often get in what is called a **scrum**. In a scrum, a bunch of players from each team push against one another. Inside running plays in football generally end up in a sort of scrum where several blockers and the ball carrier are pushing against four or five defensive linemen and linebackers.

This is prime time for the sustained, hold-him-up-and-work-on-his-arm stripping technique. Fortunately, it is also the typical type of play run by an offensive team which is ahead in its next-to-last series before the take-a-knee period. When my youth team stripped Napa three times in one game, it was during inside-running plays that turned into scrums.

Middle kick return scrums

I have also noticed that many middle kick returns end in scrums. I complained to my J.V. kickoff team many times in 1994 that they were not trying hard enough to get the ball in those kick return scrums—to no avail.

Remember that middle kick returns are typical of teams which are ahead late in the game. They want to run as much time off the clock as possible during the return and the middle return generally does that best.

Remember also that while trying to strip the ball on a **scrimmage down** may increase the chances that the opponent will get a **first down**, there is no such effect on a kick-return play because they have not yet set the chains. The first down will always be ten yards past the end of the return no matter how many yards the returner goes (outside the kickoff team's ten). The strip attempt may enable the ball carrier to get closer to the goal line. But late in a game where the returners are ahead, the goal line is a minor issue. The take-a-knee table pays no attention to field position, only to **down**, defense **timeouts**, and **time** remaining. So the kick return is a sort of free shot at stripping that gives no first-down advantage to the return team.

Of course, if you are behind near the end of a game, you will be kicking onside. Make sure your players go into the onside kick thinking not only get the ball, but also strip it if the receiving team gets it. In other words, it's not over just because the other guy got hold of it first.

Waiting for a punt takes too much time

The standard way of getting the ball when you are behind and on defense is to force the other team to punt. Jeez! That takes a long time! They will be in a slowdown. In four downs they can run about 2:00 off the clock.

The earlier the down, the more sense stripping makes. On fourth down, if they go for it, stopping them short of the first down is **equivalent** to a strip as far as possession goes. In *The Hidden Game of Football*, the authors assign point values to various turnovers and yardage gains based on computer analysis of hundreds of NFL games. They give minus four points to the offense on all first-, second-, and third-down turnovers. But they give zero points for fourth-down turnovers inside the opponent's 35 on a play that would not have gained a first down had the ball not been turned over. Why? Because on a play like that the defense would have gained possession **regardless** of the turnover.

Down and distance

Deciding whether to go for the strip or getting possession by forcing the offense to punt or turn the ball over on downs comes down to **which is most likely to get you the ball the soonest**. One issue is how likely is the offense to get a first down on this possession? How the game has gone so far give you one indication. Current down and distance give you a better one.

Four-down territory

Three-down territory is that part of the field where a team will generally punt on fourth down. **Four**-down territory is the part of the field where the offense will go for it on fourth down because they are close to your end zone that there is not enough room to move the ball very many yards by punting. The border between three- and four-down territory varies from level to level, from team-to-team. It is a function of how far your punter can punt.

Punts are risky plays because they can be blocked or result in bad snaps. The risk in generally offset by the fact that they move the ball far downfield. But when you are in the defense's half of the field, your punter's range often extends beyond the goal line.

Actually, you should not try to punt past the opponent's five-yard line because punting is not that accurate. If you try to do a coffin-corner punt that goes out inside the opponent's five, you will frequently kick it into the end zone resulting in a touchback, which brings the ball out to the 20. I would criticize a punter who kicked the ball out on the one because he came too close to it going into the end zone. I tell my punters to aim for the 5- to 10-yard line when that is within their range.

Generally, you stop punting on fourth down and start going for it when your punter's range would put a maximum-distance sideline punt inside the opponent's five-yard line.

The average **NFL** punt in 1995 was 41.8 yards. So the average NFL team hits four-down territory at about midfield.

The average major **college** punt in 1994 was 39.2 yards. So the average major college team hits four-down territory at about their opponent's 45-yard line.

I do not have stats on the **high school** average. But I figure it's about 30 yards. So they hit four-down territory at about their opponent's 35-yard line.

Most **youth** football teams are probably in four-down territory everywhere on the field. Most cannot punt far enough to warrant the risk of a bad snap or blocked punt. But some youth teams can punt just fine. They reach four-down territory at about their opponent's 25- to 30-yard line.

Of course, there is a point where you are too close to punt but **within your field-goal kicker's range**. If you are going to do a scrimmage kick within your field-goal kicker's range, it would be a field-goal attempt.

40% on first down, 60% on second,...

A football rule of thumb says that in **three-down** territory you must gain:

- **40%** of the yards needed for a first down on **first** down
- **60%** of the remaining yards needed for a first down on **second** down
- **100%** of the remaining yards needed for a first down on **third** down.

In **four-down** territory, the rule is:

- **40%** of the yards needed for a first down on **first** down
- **60%** of the remaining yards needed for a first down on **second** down
- **80%** of the remaining yards needed for a first down on **third** down
- **100%** of the remaining yards needed for a first down on **fourth** down.

The more the offense **falls behind** these rule-of-thumb milestones, the higher the probability that they will have to turn the ball over on fourth down. So the down when stripping makes the most sense is **first** down. That's when fourth down is most remote.

If they retain possession on their first-down play, see what their distance to a first now is. If they gained **less than 40%**, four yards normally, more if they had first and fifteen or some such, the probability that they will turn the ball over on fourth down goes **up**. So there would then be **less incentive to strip**.

If they gained **more than four yards**, the probability that they will get a first down on this series is higher so the **incentive to strip gets higher**. In other words, if they gained six yards on first down and only have four to go, you probably are **not** going to get a punt or turnover on downs this series. So if time is running out, **you'd better find another way to get the ball**, namely, stripping.

Two minutes left

Let's say there are 2:00 left. Your team has no timeouts. That means your opponent hits the take-a-knee point at about 1:35 if they get a first down (high school and college). That means you have **25 seconds to get possession—one play when your opponent is in a slowdown**. Let's further say that your opponent has second and four. Are you going to just try to hold them and force them to punt? It could work. If they don't get a first down, they'll have to punt or turn it over on downs around :30 left in the game.

But with only four yards to go, they're probably going to get the first on their third-down play which would be inside the take-a-knee period. If so, you lose.

In this situation, which is dire, you probably have a better chance of winning the game if you try to hold the ball carrier up for several seconds while you strip the ball than if you try to stop them short of a first down for three more plays.

I'll suggest a rule although I admit it's not as scientific as I'd like.

> *If the opponent can get to the take-a-knee period averaging less than three yards a carry, switch to a strip-at-all-costs mode.*

In other words, strip if your opponent has to go:

Down	Three-down territory	Four-down territory
First	• 9 or less yards	• 12 or less
Second	• 6 or less	• 9 or less
Third	• 3 or less	• 6 or less
Fourth		• 3 or less

I have seen many a defense try to strip the ball in the final minutes of a game in which they were trailing. But most teams I've seen in that situation did not even try to strip. And I suspect that those who **did** try devoted little or no practice to it.

I have often complained in baseball that bunting and sliding are relatively easy skills to master, but hardly anyone has because coaches act as if baseball players know how to bunt and slide **from birth**. Something similar is probably true of football stripping. More coaches have **asked** their defenses to strip the ball in the final minutes of a game than have **practiced** stripping or **taught** stripping technique.

Your clock-management assistant could show his yellow-colored panel when he wants the defense to got to an all-out stripping mode.

Strips result in touchdowns more often

A strip has a good chance of resulting in a touchdown on that same play. And even if it doesn't, your offense gets much better field position out of a strip than they do out of a punt. Punt-return touchdowns are rare. The average strip return probably goes more yards than the average punt return because the strip is **unexpected**. And successful drives are less likely after a punt than a strip because of the superior field position of the strip.

Trying hard to strip is the defense's equivalent of the Hail Mary pass. But I see an asymmetrical risk aversion among defensive coaches. **Offensive** coaches will throw a Hail Mary, even though many are intercepted. But **defensive** coaches will not try a stand-up strip tackle because it **might** result in the offense getting a first down.

When you are behind and approaching take-a-knee time, you **must get the ball**. Forcing a punt or turn over on downs can work, but it often does **not** work at all. And even when it does succeed in getting possession, it is often at a fatal cost in terms of field position and time lost.

Get the ball! Get it now! And get it here! In the window between about five minutes and two minutes left in the game, that means **strip it**.

Pass possible

It is extremely unlikely. But it is possible that an opponent which is leading and on offense may **pass** during their just-before-take-a-knee series. They may figure you won't be expecting it so it will work. They're right about you not expecting it. But if it happens, your defenders must get out of their normal bat-it-down mentality. They *must intercept the ball if at all possible.*

If the pass is **completed**, the **receiver should slide** as soon as he gets the first down. But unless this book becomes very popular and very accepted very fast, he probably will **not** be trained to do that. He will be in his normal "more" mindset and try to get more yards, thereby giving your defenders a chance to do a stand-him-up-and-strip tackle. And they **must**. Once this play is over, the other team is probably in take-a-knee period. If so, this is the ball game! This situation is the defensive equivalent of the offense's last-play-downfield-lateral situation. It's now or never, baby! Time to quit waiting for a punt.

I will again make the observation that I think offensive coaches and players are pretty well aware of what they need to do in the last minute of a game in which they trail. Offenses understand their risk-reward situation. But defenses do not. They are far too conservative. They have no defensive Hail Mary. But they need one no less than the offense. And the defense's Hail Mary is the stand-him-up-and-strip tackle.

Deliberately letting the other team score a touchdown

How can the defense get the ball?

- interception
- fumble recovery or strip
- punt
- blocked punt or bad snap not advanced for first down by kicking team
- turn over on downs
- free kick after safety
- kickoff after other team scores.

Look at that last one. Would you believe that some coaches and players, maybe just in bull sessions, suggest that it might be smart sometimes to let the other team score a touchdown as a way to get the ball back.

You would only do this if you were **down by one point**. You would do it when the opponent was **not yet in the take-a-knee period**.

If the opponent scores a touchdown, the clock stops as soon as the ball carrier crosses the goal line and stays stopped for the PAT. The opponent would certainly go for a **one-point conversion**. That puts them up by **eight**. Going for two and failing would leave them vulnerable to your scoring eight and thereby winning the game.

The clock restarts when a member of your team touches the kickoff.

If the other team is smart, they may kick **onside**.

Once you get the ball, you need to score a touchdown and a two-point conversion to tie, assuming the opponent was successful with their one-point PAT.

When would this be smart? When it was **the approach most likely to succeed**.

Obviously, if your defense was stopping the opponent normally during this game, it would make more sense to force a punt. If you were extremely good at stripping, that would be best. But I have never heard of such a team. An interception should be out of the question. In their next-to-last series, the opponent probably will not pass. If you have them pinned against their own goal line, trying to get a safety may be the best.

Deliberately letting the other team score a touchdown only makes sense when it seems more likely to succeed than any of the other alternatives. You probably should give your defense a chance to stop them on the second-from-last series before take-a-knee. But when you get into the **last series before take-a-knee**, it's time to consider this play. That would be around 3:00 to 2:00 in the NFL and 2:30 to 1:30 at lower levels.

20

Ahead on special teams

Kick return

The other team, which in this chapter we assume is trailing, will **onside kick** at the end of the game. You need your **hands team** on the field. A hands team is made up entirely of players who are used to carrying the ball, as opposed to linemen. I prefer to **always** use my hands team as my kick-return team. If *you are inside your take-a-knee period when the ball is kicked, your returner should get possession then* ***get to the ground****. He must* ***avoid being tackled*** *if possible.* The ball could be stripped during a tackle. There is no point in risking a turnover if field position is not important.

Once the kickoff is over, the ball can be safely snapped behind a line and the clock run out. *There is no benefit to the returner gaining yards unless you need another score to win, which you do* ***not*** *when you are ahead at the end of a game.*

1996 Florida-Florida State game

In the 1996 regular season Florida-Florida State game, Florida did an onside kick. But they kicked it hard and FSU's guys just stepped out of the way and let it go out of bounds.

I was impressed although I don't know how they knew to do that. I would be reluctant to teach the front line of a kick-return team to step aside for fear the kicking team might be able to recover the kick. In that game, however, FSU simply took possession of the ball where it went out of bounds and proceeded to run for a first down. With 1:09 remaining in the game and Florida having only one timeout remaining, FSU took a knee for the rest of the game and won 24-21. (My **worst-case** high school-college take-a-knee table says with first down and your opponent having one timeout, you can take a knee at 1:04.)

Do not throw yourself on the ground

Earlier in the game, I think the front line of the kick return team should make possession a priority, but **not** throw themselves on the ground after they have secured possession, as so many do. I tell my players, "Don't tackle yourself. That's what the other team is paid to do. If you field the ball cleanly while you are on your feet, go score a touchdown!" I have each of my front-line kick-return team members return onside kicks once or twice a week.

Also, I reject the notion that throwing yourself on the ground to secure a loose ball is more likely to result in recovery than grabbing the ball while you are still on your feet. Certainly if you do not get it when you first go to the ground, you are very **un**likely to chase it as well on your knees as on your feet.

Sometimes, when the opponent is nearby, fumble-recovery technique is the smarter way to go. But front-line kick-return players at all levels field balls cleanly while standing up, then throw themselves on the ground. If you are not yet in the last two minutes of the game, that seems dumb. I have always trained my front line to catch the ball and run straight ahead. We have gotten a number of great returns from that. And we never lost a possession because of that practice.

I actually think teaching all front-line kick-return players to fall on the ball all the time **reduces** the chances of gaining possession. The problem is that when you tell front-line guys to always fall on the ball, you are sort of telling your players to **panic** if the ball is kicked to them.

I teach the opposite. If it comes to you, catch it, and run for a touchdown. I wish I could put video of one of those returns in this book. They are funny because of the surprise on the kickoff team when the guy they expected to fall on the ball just grabs it and runs right at them. It's one of those plays that kind of sets a tone for the whole team. Our players are proud that the people who end up panicking on onside kicks are our opponents.

And I suspect it is unsettling to our opponents. Their whole careers in football they have seen the recipients of an onside kick panic and scramble madly for the ball. Indeed, that's what they, themselves, are trained to do. But not **this** team. "These guys grab the onside kick and run it straight down your throat like it's just another day at the office." When each and every one of your front-line guys has done it twice a week all season, it **is** just another "day at the office."

Kickoff

The kickoff is a dangerous play. *If you are ahead by four to eight points, you may want to kick **onside** to eliminate the possibility of a long return.* With that margin, you have no fear of a field goal.

The time remaining is a factor. If you have to turn the ball over with time remaining, you generally want to force the offense to run their **top-speed hurry-up**. If the field position resulting from an onside kick, around midfield, given the time remaining, would let them run a **slowdown** or even an **inbounds hurry-up**, and a deep kick that was well covered would force them into their top-speed hurry-up, you should probably kick deep. According to the graph in the slowdown chapter, *the correct time for an **onside** kick, even though you are **ahead**, is when the clock is down to **2:00 or less**.*

Remember also that you have an excellent chance to **recover** the kick. That would probably end the threat if you were close to the take-a-knee point. So your kickoff team should pursue **possession** with the same zeal when they are **ahead** as they would if they were **behind**.

*If you are ahead by **three or less**, you need to keep the receiving team **out of field-goal range**. Your best chance to do that is a **deep kick**.* The possibility of a long return is still a danger. A **deep squib kick** is probably best. The clock does not start until the receiving team touches the ball, but your main concern is avoiding the long return, not starting the clock as soon as possible. You want to delay the receiving team's touching the ball so your coverage has time to get to the returner.

If you are ahead by nine or more, your normal kickoff will be fine.

In the early eighties, the Raiders expected their kickoffs to have a hang time of 4.0 seconds. During that same era, Hall of Fame Vikings coach Bud Grant said his team had better than a 50-50 chance to recover their onside kick.

Pre-kickoff penalties

Normally, you kickoff from your own 40 in youth and high school football; your own 35 in college; and your own 30 in the NFL. But penalties before the kickoff can change that. A freshman head coach I worked for was previously a freshman assistant at another school. In one game there, he cursed the referee during halftime. "F*** you and f*** your crew!"

The referee dropped his yellow flag, picked it up, and dropped it again. When the team came out of the locker room for the second half, the referee walked off 15 yards to the team's 25-yard line then walked off half the distance to the team's 12.5-yard line. And that's where they kicked from.

Penalties can go the other way. A trailing team player may pull some dead-ball stunt after your team scores, thereby earning an unsportsmanlike penalty that will be enforced on the kickoff.

As your kickoff point moves closer to the other team's goal line, you may want to **switch to an onside kick**, because you are so far from the goal line you are defending. Plano East (Texas) head coach Scott Phillips kicks onside if the receiving team gets a 15-yard penalty before the kickoff. Or maybe if you do not normally kick deep, this might be the time to do it because your kicker can now reach the end zone for a **touchback**.

Sports Illustrated's NFL writer Paul Zimmerman asks,

> *When [coaches] get a 15-yard roughness penalty on an extra point or field goal, and they're kicking off from midfield, why don't they onside kick—every time? An onside kick's supposed to be 40 or 50 percent effective anyway. The downside risk is a loss of 15 yards of field position. The upside potential is the ball.*

Should you try to kick a field goal if penalties against your opponent bring your kickoff line within your kicker's field goal range? No. The rules do not allow you to score a field goal on any free kick other than a free kick following a fair catch, and then only in high school and the NFL.

Plano East (TX) vs. John Tyler, 12/3/94

Perhaps the most famous series of onside kicks in football history took place in the 1994 Texas high school playoffs. Plano East was down 41-17 with 3:03 left in the game. A lot of coaches would have used the remaining time to give their bench some playoff experience. Plano East coach Scott Phillips did not.

After receiving John Tyler's kickoff, he started his comeback with 2:56 remaining. Plano East drove down the field and scored. Their two-point conversion was good. 41-25.

Plano East kicked onside (grounder to the front line with a pop-up hop as it arrived) and recovered! They again drove down the field for a touchdown. This time their two-point conversion failed. 41-31.

They again kicked onside (same style onside kick) and again recovered the ball! Again they scored a touchdown. Again the two-point conversion failed. 41-37.

They kicked onside (same style) for a third time, and recovered again! Again they scored a touchdown, taking the **lead**: 43-41. Their extra point **kick** was good: 44-41.

Phillips did **not** consider another **onside** kick because:

- there was :26 left
- John Tyler had a great quarterback who could throw the long ball
- Tyler had timeouts left
- Phillips was only ahead by a field goal.

Coach Phillips considered what he calls a **pooch kick**—a high kick from the right hash mark across the field to the other team's 25-yard line. This gives the kickoff coverage time to arrive as the ball is descending. But John Tyler, having scouted Phillips' pooch kick, lined up in an anti-pooch-kick receiving formation. Here's a diagram of John Tyler's receiving team formation:

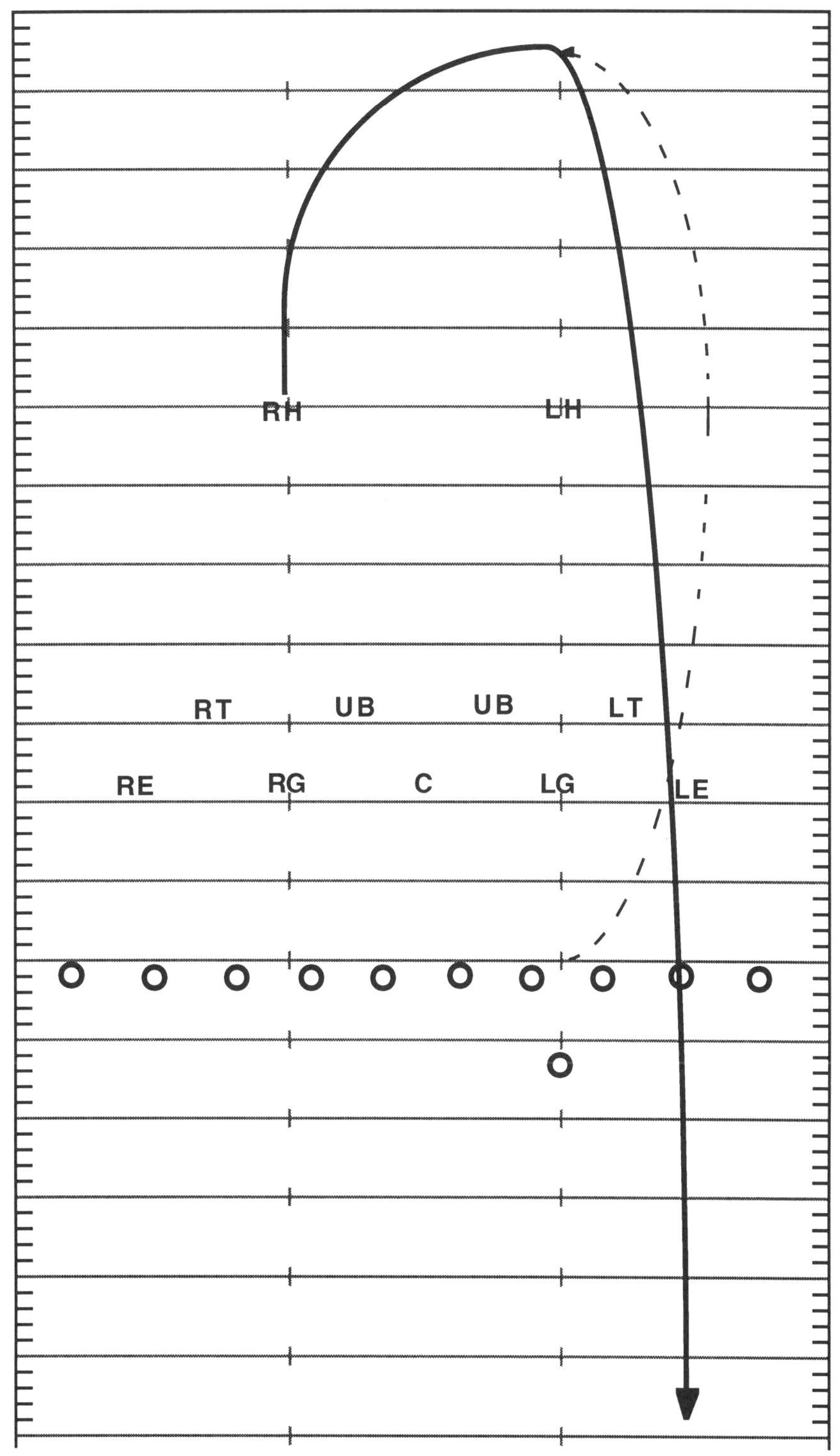

Plano East kicked deep down the right hash marks trying for a touchback. John Tyler's **left** halfback gave up on the ball and began to walk to the twenty-yard line where he assumed the ball would be placed after the touchback.

But the **right** halfback, Roderick Dunn, had begun walking backward while Plano East was waiting for the referee's ready-to-play signal. He was at the 18 when the ball was kicked. He sprinted to the other side of the field and made an over-the-shoulder catch of the kickoff at his own three-yard line on a dead run. He managed to avoid stepping on the goal line, got one good block, and he was gone. Touchdown. John Tyler won the game and went on to become state champions.

Roderick Dunn had extra incentive to score on the kickoff. He had fumbled two of Plano East's three onside kicks earlier in the quarter. He now plays football and runs track at Texas A&M. What Dunn did on that kick return showed remarkable smarts, courage, and athletic ability.

This sequence of events became nationally famous because of both its improbability and the impassioned call made by the television announcer who covered the game. He was beside himself with elation as Plano East made its comeback, and inconsolable when Dunn broke free for the winning score. The replay of the highlights of the last three minutes of the game, along with the call, ran on the network news programs.

One wonders if another onside kick or a pooch kick would have had a different result. I agree with Plano East's decision. The result was due to the great play made by Dunn, not to any clock-management blunder on Plano East's part.

Field goal

If you are ahead by eight or less, with time running out, you probably should **not** *kick in what would otherwise be a field-goal situation.* The danger of a bad snap or blocked kick and touchdown runback is too great.

I would not even run a fake field goal on the last play of a game if I were ahead. The long snap is always more dicey than a quarterback-under-center snap.

Do not let your team get into the mindset often voiced by TV announcers that the field goal is a "safe" play. Except for high school and NFL PAT kicks, all kicking plays are dangerous.

In the 1991 Notre Dame-Tennessee game, Notre Dame was ahead 31-17. With 14 seconds to go before the half, Notre Dame tried to add three points to their total with a field goal. It was blocked and run back 85 yards for a touchdown. Tennessee ultimately upset Notre Dame that day by a score of 35-34, thereby ending the Irish hopes of winning the national championship.

I do not question the decision to kick the field goal. It was the right thing to do. But I wonder if Notre Dame's players executed the play with as much concentration and effort as they would a normal "non-safe" play.

University of San Diego vs. St. Mary's, 11/12/77

San Diego is up 21-17 and has fourth down at the St. Mary's 28-yard line. What should San Diego do?

Their choices are:

- attempt a field goal
- go for the first down
- punt to the coffin corner
- take a safety.

Taking a **safety** can probably be ruled out on the grounds that the quarterback or punter would have too far to run (72 yards) and would likely be tackled short of the goal line—a disaster. Also, they already have better field position than they are likely to get after even a well-covered free kick from their own 20-yard line.

A **punt** can also be ruled out because, at best, it will go out of bounds around the five-yard line. That's only a 23-yard change in field position which would not warrant the risk of a blocked punt or bad snap. That leaves the field goal or first down.

If you attempt the field goal, three things can happen:

- kick is good

- kick fails (there should be no return from this distance)
- kick does not get off because blocked or bad snap.

If the kick does not get off, there could be two results:

- no return of the loose ball by St. Mary's
- St. Mary's advances the ball on the play.

If you go for a first down, two things can happen:

- get the first
- turn the ball over on downs.

In theory, you could fumble or throw an interception on the attempt to get the first, but the probability would probably be very remote because with this score, field position, and time remaining, USD would likely be conservative in its play calling.

What's at stake?

What's at stake here? If USD kicks a field goal, the score changes from 21-17 to 24-17. Is that an improvement?

Not much. With **either** score, St. Mary's has to score a **touchdown**. True, they also have to kick the extra point to tie if USD kicks the field goal. *The Official College Football Records Book* does not give PAT kick success rates for Division IAA schools like USD or St. Mary's. But the Division IA success rate for PAT kicks in 1977 was 90.8% and the Division II success rate was 87.4%. So let's interpolate that the success rate for Division IAA was halfway between the two or 89.1%.

That means the failure rate was 100% - 89.1% = 10.9%. So the sole benefit for USD of kicking that field goal is to enable them to take advantage of the 10.9% chance that St. Mary's will miss the extra point if and when they score a touchdown.

In theory, a successful USD field goal also prevents St. Mary's from tying the game with **two field goals**. But with only 1:43 left in the game before the USD field-goal attempt, two St. Mary's field goals are not a real threat.

If USD goes for the first down, and gets it, the game is over or almost over. If St. Mary's has no timeouts left, and USD can take eight seconds to get the first down, they have reached the take-a-knee point. If St. Mary's has any timeouts left, USD will need **two** first downs to reach take-a-knee.

If USD fails to get the first down, St. Mary's takes over first and ten at around their own 26-yard line with about 1:37 to go. That means they have to go 74 yards in 1:37 which requires a **top-speed, hurry-up pace**. That is, stopping the clock after every play. If they can stop the clock after every play, they can run about 16 plays and must therefore average 4.63 yards per play. If they fail to stop the clock after every single play or fail to average 4.63 yards per play (not per completion), the number of yards they must average will go up even higher.

How likely was St. Mary's to march 74 yards in 1:37? Well, stranger things have happened. But given that they had only scored 17 points in the previous 58:23, it seemed unlikely.

The problem with the field goal is that *whenever you attempt one, five things can happen and one of them is bad and three of them can be disastrous.*

- kick is good
- kick is no good but no return
- kick is short and returned
- kick is blocked

• snap is bad

Is the mere benefit of forcing St. Mary's to kick the PAT to tie worth risking disaster? I think not.

In the event, USD attempted the field goal. It was blocked by St. Mary's and run back 72 yards for the game-winning touchdown. I interviewed Kevin McGarry, the current head coach at USD. He was the long snapper and a defender for USD in the 1977 game, which was the final game of the season and of his playing career. McGarry said the snap and hold were good, but the protection broke down.

He said he would have gone for the first down if he were the coach, in large part because USD had completely dominated St. Mary's in the second half after being down 17-0 at halftime. He did not recall the specific yards to go on the play but remembers it was not close. He also agreed that the benefit of succeeding with the field goal when you are already up by four points was rather small considering the risk.

Let it roll, no matter the direction

When you are ahead in the final ten seconds or so of a game, and your field-goal attempt falls short, either because of lack of leg or a deflection, and the defense does not return it, let it roll. Let it roll even if it's going the wrong direction. Every second it rolls takes a second off the clock and the opposing offense is the one which will have possession when the whistle blows.

Premature celebration costs game

As Yogi Berra said, "**It ain't over till it's over**." And as I have said in this book, **the game does not end on the final gun or horn, it ends on the final whistle**. Some Defiance College (Division III) players learned that to their chagrin, and got themselves in the record books the wrong way.

On 10/30/93, on the **last play of the game**, Defiance was ahead of Thomas More College 18-16. Thomas More lined up at Defiance's six-yard line to attempt the winning field goal. Unfortunately, a Defiance player broke through and **blocked the kick**. The Defiance players celebrated. The player who blocked the kick turned toward the sideline with his arms up acknowledging the applause of his fans. However, he and his teammates forgot that a blocked field goal is a **live ball**. He also forgot that the game ends on the **whistle**, **not** the **horn**.

The blocked kick bounced up into the arms of Greg Stofko, Thomas More's holder. He ran it through the celebrating Defiance players for a touchdown. Thomas More won 24-18. Stofko's brother had been killed in a car accident the week before. He scored right in front of his mother and father.

Blocked field goals and punts are live balls at all levels. Under high school and NFL rules, blocking an extra-point kick ends the play, but in **college**, a blocked extra-point is also a live ball.

Either team can advance a blocked kick

In the 1994 Notre Dame-Michigan game, Notre Dame blocked a 29-yard field goal attempt. That's the **good** news for Notre Dame fans. The **bad** news was that Michigan's fullback Che Foster picked up the blocked kick and advanced it for a **first down**. Michigan went on to score a touchdown on that drive and beat Notre Dame 26-24 with a last-minute field goal.

I always tell my field-goal kicker and punter to deliberately kick at least one ball into the line in practice so both offense and defense can practice picking up a blocked kick and advancing it. **Possession** is predetermined by the fact that it is **fourth down**. So both the kicking team and the blocking teams should try to advance the ball. Falling on a blocked kick is one of the worst crimes one of my players can commit. The only exception would be where just securing possession wins the game.

I had a head coach who was adamantly opposed to my practicing what to do in the event of a blocked kick or bad snap. "I don't want to practice stuff I don't want to happen," he said. That's crazy.

In his book *The New Thinking Man's Guide to Pro Football, Sports Illustrated* football writer Paul Zimmerman says,

> *The ultimate mess-up in the kicking game, the fumbled snap or the snap that goes awry, has occasionally produced unhoped-for dividends—a touchdown off a field goal play. It's rehearsed—the Fire play.*
>
> *"I yell "Fire!' on a miscue," says Dallas holder Gary Hogeboom, who's also the backup quarterback. "Then I roll to my right and one guy goes short and another deep."*

Field-goal defense

It is common for the trailing team to attempt a field goal on the last play of the game if they are behind by three or less. Just as the **offense** must practice getting their field goal team onto the field as fast as possible, so must the field-goal **defense** do the same. You do **not** want to have to call timeout, as my opponent Campolindo did in 1996, thereby helping us to get lined up to beat them with a last-second field goal.

Even if the opponent is trailing by a field goal or less, you must be on the lookout for the **fake field goal**. This is especially true at the lower levels where field-goal success rates are lower.

If you have **timeouts** left, you should use them to "**ice**" the place-kicker. Can't hurt. Might help.

Leon Lett single-handedly, literally, loses Thanksgiving, 1993 game for Cowboys

On Thanksgiving day 1993, the Dallas Cowboys were leading the Miami Dolphins 14-13-with :15 left in the game. The Dolphins had the ball at the Cowboy 24 and lined up to kick what would be the game-winning field goal, a 41-yard attempt.

It was deflected, but went downfield. As such, it was returnable by the defense, like a punt. Cowboy defensive lineman, Leon Lett, for some reason, felt the need to go flying downfield and try to grab the ball. He was unsuccessful at gaining possession, but he did manage to **touch** the ball. Bad idea.

The Dolphins then recovered the ball at the Cowboy **one-yard line**. The clock was stopped until the snap because of the change of possession (Dolphins to Cowboy Lett and back to Dolphins). There were three seconds left in the game. The Dolphins again attempted a field goal, this time from the one, an 18-yarder, shorter than a PAT kick. It was good. The Dolphins won the game 16-14.

Everybody knows that members of a **punt**-receiving team should not touch the ball after it has gone beyond the neutral zone. They know that the ball is theirs if they don't touch it at all. But if they **do** touch it and fail to gain possession, the kicking team may then obtain possession and will have a first down even if the spot at which they recover the touched ball is not beyond the line they needed to gain for a first down.

What many people, including the pre-Thanksgiving, 1993 Leon Lett, do not know is that rule applies to "**scrimmage kicks**," not just punts. A scrimmage kick is a punt, field goal, or PAT kick—any kick which follows a snap. The other kind of kick is a "free kick," the most common example of which is the kickoff.

Here's the NFL rule that pertains to Lett's mistake:

> *When the kickers recover a legal kick from scrimmage after it has first been touched by the receiving team beyond the line, it is first-and-10 for the*

kicker's team or if it is recovered by the kickers in the receiver's end zone, it is a touchdown for the kickers. (NFL 9-1-6-Note)

As bad as Lett's mistake was, it was almost worse. Had the ball rolled one more yard into the end zone, the Dolphins would have had an instant game-winning touchdown because of Lett's ill-advised touching of the ball. Lett created a sort of **artificial muff** of the kick, thereby enabling the kicking team to recover the ball.

The pertinent **high school rule** is 6-2-4 and the pertinent **college rule** is 6-3-3.

You must teach your field goal defense that kicks that are blocked or deflected within the expanded neutral zone are the equivalent of punts when they go downfield. The expanded neutral zone is two yards in high school (NFICA 2-27-2) and three yards in college (NCAA 6-3-1b). The NFL does not use the phrase expanded neutral zone.

To put it in laymen's terms, you ignore any receiving team member's touching of a punt or field goal on the kicking team's side of the line of scrimmage or within two yards (in high school) or three yards (in college) on the receiving team's side. To state it roughly, a member of the kicking team cannot recover a ball because it was **deflected** by the receiving team. But he **can** recover a kick that is touched by a member of the receiving team **after the kick has gone downfield**.

The **receiving** team gets possession without having to do anything. But if a member of the receiving team touches the ball beyond the neutral zone in the NFL or expanded neutral zone at lower levels, a member of the **kicking** team may then recover (but not advance) it and the kicking team then has first-and-10. *So either get possession and fair catch or return the kick, including deflected field-goal attempts, or stay away from it.*

This is a classic example of a skill where just one repetition per season can probably save you from your own Leon Lett incident. Make a deflected field goal a standard **weekly** or **monthly** situation for your field-goal defense team to practice. I would also teach my **field-goal team** to take advantage of any Leon Lett-like behavior by our opponents.

Punt

*You generally do **not** want to punt if you are ahead near the end of a game*. The reason is that a punt is a very dangerous play. When you punt, four things can happen and three of them are **disastrous**:

- well covered punt with **little or no return**
- **long return**, maybe for a touchdown
- **blocked** punt, maybe picked up and run in for a touchdown
- **bad snap**, maybe picked up and run in for a touchdown.

If you turn the ball **over on downs**, the opponent gets **better field position** than if you punted well and prevented a return. But they almost never get a touchdown out of your fourth-down running play.

Whether you punt on fourth down when you are ahead is a function of several things:

- margin
- time remaining
- field position.

*You would **not** want to turn the ball **over on downs** at a field position that was **within the opponent's field-goal range** if you were ahead by **three or less points**.*

*You would **not** want to turn the ball **over on downs** if you were ahead by **eight or less points** and the other team had time to score a **touchdown** at an inbounds hurry-up or slowdown pace from the field position in question.*

*You would **not** want to turn the ball **over on downs** if you were ahead by **three or less points** and the other team had time to reach **field-goal kicking range** at an inbounds hurry-up or slowdown pace from the field position in question.*

You would ***not*** *want to punt if you were* ***ahead by three or more*** *and could kill the remaining game-clock time by* ***taking a safety***. Taking a safety lets you **free kick** from your twenty-yard line, a kick which will travel as far as **65 yards** from that twenty, depending upon your level. A **punt**, on the other hand, only travels about **40 yards** beyond the line of scrimmage, which may be inside your twenty-yard line.

You would ***not*** *want to punt if you were* ***ahead by one or two*** *and could kill the remaining game-clock time by running around in* ***fair*** *territory.*

You do ***not ever*** *punt if you are not confident that your line can protect the punter.*

Kansas City versus New England, 12/13/92

Kansas City had the ball and the lead 27-20 at their own 29-yard line on the last play of the game against New England. It was raining. They also had fourth down and 18 after a delay-of-game penalty. The clock was stopped until the snap because of the delay penalty. There were four seconds left in the game.

This play was memorialized in an NFL Films segment called "Rules of the Game" on the program *This is the NFL*. Here's what Kansas City head coach Marty Schottenheimer yelled out to his team,

> *Kick it and get it out of there. We're just gonna get the snap and kick the ball and go home.*

The Chiefs Kent Sullivan, an injury sub for the regular punter who had been hurt the week before, punted 59 yards and the balled rolled to the Patriots' 12-yard line. There, it was picked up by the Chiefs' Tracy Rogers, a lineman. Time ran out during the kick. Both teams and their coaches began to leave the field. Players from each team schmoozed and hugged at midfield. The public address announcer said,

> *The ball is downed. The game is over. Final score Chiefs, 27; Patriots, 20.*

Not so fast. Schottenheimer's brother Kurt, who was also special teams coordinator, walked up to the departing Marty.

Kurt: "That's a f****** foul, right?"
Marty: "What?"
Kurt: "We downed the ball!"

About that time the referees could be seen in the background giving stop-the-clock signals. The game was **not** over. Marty Schottenheimer spoke to the officials.

Marty: "Illegal touch. Another play. I understand the rule."

Quarterback Dave Krieg asks, "Why is that?"

Marty: "Because we touched the damn ball! We shouldna touched it."

As it turned out, no harm was done. New England was penalized five yards for a false start then their shotgun Hail Mary pass was easily intercepted on the untimed down, ending the game once and for all.

Point number one: *the lineman should not have touched the ball*. Had he let it roll, the Chiefs would have won the game on the punt. The rule is NFL 9-1-4. It says,

> *No player of the kickers may illegally touch a scrimmage kick before it has been touched by a receiver.*

Furthermore, NFL Rule 4-3-11 Exception (1) says,

> *If at the end of any period,...*
> *(b) If there is a foul by offense, there shall be no extension of the period.*
> ***Exception****: If offensive foul is (1) illegal touching of a kick,...the period may be extended by an untimed down, if defense so chooses.*

This rule does **not** apply to **high school**. In high school, it is "first touching" for a member of the kicking team to touch a scrimmage kick (punt or field goal) before the receiving team has touched it beyond the neutral zone (NFICA 6-2-5). The receiving team just gets the right to the ball at the spot of the first touching. But is not a "foul" *per se* in high school (NFICA 2-16-5). Only "fouls" create an untimed down (called an "extension of the period") in high school after a period has expired (NFICA 3-3-3).

It also does **not** apply in **college**. The college rule is essentially the same as the high school rule. (NCAA 3-2-3 and 6-3-2a)

Should have known the rule

Obviously, the Kansas City and New England coaches should have taught the rule well enough to avoid this mistake (New England players didn't violate the rule, but they were sufficiently ignorant of it that they, too, left the field) and the players should have learned it with or without the coaches' help. NFL Films asked 16 NFL head coaches about this rule. Only six got in right: Shula, Glanville, Levy, Marchibroda, Cowher, and Schottenheimer.

Kansas City's Rogers says he knew the rule. He just forgot momentarily.

Two responses come to mind. First, there were several Chiefs around the ball. They have to surround it to prevent a late pickup by the Patriots. One of Rogers' teammates could have reminded him to refrain from touching the ball. Second, knowing something, but forgetting in a game is usually caused by **not enough repetitions** in practice.

I don't know how many reps the Chiefs did of this situation before the game. But the typical football coach would probably do **none**, because it's such a rare situation. I would do one waste-time and one conserve-time punt per week in practice. You could do unusual situations like this once in pre-season or camp.

Only a dozen or so rules to learn

Most coaches and players would say you can't expect them to know every obscure rule in the book. I don't. But I **do** expect them to know every rule that pertains to their **job**.

Coaches should go through the entire rule book for their level with a felt-tipped pen. Mark each rule with the coach and position to which it applies. In the above example, you would put "ST" and "P" for "special teams" and "punt" team coaches and members next to NFL Rules 9-1-4 and 4-3-11. Then require those concerned to learn the rules that are marked with their team or position. Teach the few rules which the players have trouble with in practice.

Remember many of the rules in the rule book pertain **only to referees**, like spot-of-enforcement stuff. Neither coaches nor players need learn those rules. Some rules only apply to **coaches**, like the one that says only the head coach can talk to the officials.

Remember also that coaches and players **already know 90% to 95% of the rules** in the rule book from their many years of experience, like the rule that says you get four downs. Finally, platooning and **specialization** further limit the number of rules any given assistant coach or player must learn.

Whenever I coach, I make a list of "Often misunderstood rules." It's usually ten or twelve rules long. Those are the only ones I teach to my players. When you eliminate the rules for referees only, for coaches only, the rules for other positions, and the ones they already know, you are left with a very short list—a list short enough that **amateur** players at all levels should be required to know them. The idea that **professional** players and their coaches, making over $100,000 a year, can't be bothered to learn the ten or twenty obscure rules that apply to their position is ridiculous.

I recently ran into the father of a baseball player I had coached when he was six years old. The boy was now years older and had just played in a game where his rules knowledge saved him from making an unnecessary out. He was about to overtake and pass a teammate on the base path when he slammed on the brakes. When asked how he knew to do that, he said, "My tee-ball coach taught me."

In one of my youth football games, we attempted an onside kick, but the ball did not go ten yards. My players formed a tight half circle around it and followed it closely as it moved downfield. A member of the receiving team flew in and touched it, but did not get possession. We instantly pounced on it. The ref told me before the next play, "You're lucky your kids didn't touch it first." "Luck my foot," I told him. "We practice that exact situation every Tuesday. We call it the 'eight-yard kickoff.'"

We did not **intend** for the ball to go eight yards. But we knew that it sometimes happened and we made sure our kids were ready for it. Those kids were nine and ten.

Was Kansas City right to punt?

What about Kansas City's decision to punt at all? Rogers decision to pick up the ball was bad idea, but Schottenheimer's decision to punt was worse.

The Chiefs have fourth down and eighteen on their own 29 for the last play of the game. They are ahead by just seven points. On a punt play, you can have a **bad snap or blocked kick** which is often run in for a touchdown, especially from only 11 yards out (the approximate position where the punter would receive the long snap). It was **raining** heavily making the handling of the ball by the long snapper and punter more difficult than usual. The Kansas City punter was **not the regular punter**.

You could also have a **touchdown return**. Although in this case, New England had no one deep to return the kick. So I assume they made an **all-out block effort**—yet another reason to forget punting.

What were Marty Schottenhemier's alternatives? He could have run a **running play** or taken a **safety**. In the overview chapter, I gave the durations for various plays. Every type of play, except a dive or off-tackle play, lasts for four seconds, and dives and off-tackle plays sometimes last four seconds. In the take-a-knee chapter, you read that I say you can make the take-a-knee play last four seconds if you wait until you are about to be tackled before you drop.

A safety makes the score 27-22. New England still has to score a touchdown to win. If Kansas City can kill the clock with a punt, they can kill the clock with a safety. The Chiefs would **not** have to do the **free kick after the safety** unless the offense committed a foul during the safety. So the Patriots would never get possession, after the safety assuming the play took all the remaining time and was not accompanied by an offensive foul.

Go backwards

Since 29 yards is pretty far out, Kansas City would have wanted to run one to three go-backwards plays to get back to the 10 or 20 for a fourth-down safety play. Actually, they took a delay penalty as it was and were **still** out at the 29.

Kansas City had not reached take-a-knee unless you think you can run all four seconds off the clock with a prolonged take-a-knee. When they had first and ten, the Chiefs could have run the ball forward to gain a first down, thereby putting themselves inside the take-a-knee period.

But running forward risks two things: failure to get a first down or, horror of horrors, a strip. When you're up by more than two points, and within the quarterback-keep-sweep-slide period, which is :07 in the NFL, why not run **backward** instead of forward? There is **no risk of not succeeding** in going backwards. And there is **no risk of being stripped** because you can take-a-knee as soon as the bad guys get close.

I would **not** have used the **punt** formation and long snap to run a safety play because of the wet conditions and the substitute punter. Rather, I would have the quarterback take the snap under center run out the back of the end zone. Actually, I would have him slide immediately after the final gun while he was on his way to the end zone. Every step you take after the final gun is an unnecessary risk.

Don't touch a punt or field goal

If you punt when you are ahead, and the receiving team does not return or touch the punt, you should not touch it either, except to keep it out of the end zone. The clock is running while the ball rolls and while it lays there after it stops rolling. *You need to surround it to prevent a return-team member from making a* ***late pick up***. Herb Adderly scored a touchdown on a late pickup of a rolling punt once.

Punt times

In *The New Thinking Man's Guide to Pro Football*, Paul Zimmerman says,

> *I hear announcers say on TV, "This guy has a consistent five-second hang time, and sometimes he's up around six." Well that's just nonsense. Most of the hang times are in the high threes, the good punts will get into the fours, and in 1983 I saw only three punts that had a 5.0 or better hang time...two 5.0s and a 5.1, all by the Dolphin's Reggie Roby.*

Zimmerman says the Jets ball boy once set their punting machine at the maximum to see what the best hang time it could achieve was. The machine "punted" the ball from the back of one end zone to the middle of the opposite end zone—115 yards. The hang time was 6.5 seconds. Under special teams coach Joe Gardi, the New York Jets had the following punt time standards:

snap to punter	.7 seconds
catch to punt	1.3 seconds
total snap to punt	2.0 seconds
hang time	4.0 seconds
distance	40 or more yards

The Raiders in the early eighties had Ray Guy, the only punter ever drafted in the first round, and these standards:

snap to punter	.8 seconds
catch to punt	1.0 seconds
total snap to punt	1.8 seconds

The 'clock punt'

University of San Diego head coach Kevin McGarry says his team practices what he calls a "clock punt" once a week. **Offenses** are generally aware of the need to operate at different speeds. But **special teams** units generally only operate at one speed, and it is a hurry-up. McGarry punted once when he was ahead and found that his punt team got the kick off long before the end of the play clock. He now instructs his punt team to do a "clock punt" whenever they are in a time-wasting mode. A clock punt, simply, is one where the personal protector watches the play clock and does not say, "Ready!" until there are five seconds left. That way the punt is snapped close to the end of the 25-second play-clock period. Obviously, you should also have a similar "clock field goal" play. Letting the ball roll after it hits the ground is the second part of the "clock punt."

Quick kick

Quick kicks seem to have gone out with the single wing. I don't know why. The authors of *The Hidden Game of Football* wonder why, especially with the popularity of the shotgun formation. Paul Zimmerman of *Sports Illustrated* wonders why NFL teams run a draw play on third-and-25 when they could quick kick.

When I was a youth football coach, I always did what I called a **fourth-down quick kick**. That is, we lined up in our regular offensive formation as if we were going for it, then punted. Some years we were in a single wing which is more like a punt formation (no quarterback under center). But I also did it with a quarterback under center. We snapped the ball through the quarterback's legs to the fullback who punted. It was our best play of the day (net 50 yards) in one losing effort.

Here are the **advantages** of the quick kick:

- usually no return or fair catch because no one is deep to receive
- less chance of a blocked kick because the defense does not expect the kick
- longer net punt because no one deep to receive
- punter is not as far behind line of scrimmage as in regular punt formation so net punt is greater
- makes defense tentative on subsequent third downs.

Here are the **disadvantages** of the quick kick:

- give up one or more downs which might have resulted in a first-down play
- usually done by a player other than a punting specialist at high school and higher levels.

In the old days of football, it was common to quick kick on **first** down if you were inside your own twenty, **second** down inside your own forty, and on **third** down from your own forty to field-goal range. The word "quick" in the phrase "quick kick" refers to the fact that you are punting **before** the traditional down for doing so, fourth down.

The Hidden Game of Football authors say that if a quick kick went **five more net yards** than a traditional punt, it would be a good idea on third down and 15 or more yards to go and a breakeven idea on third and ten. My experience with it was that it went about **15** more yards at the ten-year old level. At higher levels, it would go even farther.

The Hidden Game... says Philadelphia's Randall Cunningham tried it twice in 1986. One was partially blocked and went only 15 yards. The other only went 39 yards.

The J.V. high school team where I coached in 1994 tried one. It was called back for illegal motion. The quarterback had to motion out but he did so without waiting one full second after everyone was set.

I suspect the problem with most quick kicks is **inadequate practice**. We did not have that problem with my youth teams where it was our only way to punt. We got about 15 minutes per week of quick kicking practice, which was enough to make us competent.

Toward the end of a half, a quick kick makes sense if you need a **little extra distance to get the ball out of field-goal range**. **The farther you have to go for a first down**, the more sense a quick kick makes. When you are **backed up** against your own goal line and must punt, a quick kick is safer than a regular punt, assuming equal protection. **The lower your level**, youth—high school—college, **the more sense the quick kick makes**.

The lack of quick kicks at all levels appears to be nothing more than fashion and coach timidity. Because of the high degree of job insecurity in football coaching, few coaches at any level have the guts to do what makes the most sense if they figure the fans, parents, administrators, owners, or media are not sophisticated enough to recognize the wisdom of the play.

Punt defense

If you are ahead and the current possession is likely to be the opponent's last, they should **not** punt, even though it is fourth down. If they line up in punt formation, it should be a **fake**. There is no point in your putting anyone back to return the punt. Indeed, trying to field the punt could result in a **muff** which could be disastrous.

Just play **defense** and try to stop them from gaining a first down. *If they actually do punt, stay away from it.* Blocking the punt would be good, but it is too difficult to play both defense and punt block at the same time. The danger is not the punt getting off but the opponent gaining the first down. Defense the punt formation the way you would defense a shotgun formation.

PAT guide

Here's one of those guides as to whether you should go for one or two after you take the lead with a touchdown. This one was in a newsletter from DigitalScout. I agree with the table when you are **ahead**. But as you'll see in the next chapter, I disagree with the standard one-or-two table in some cases when you are **behind**.

Margin after TD	Ahead
10	**kick**
9	**kick**
8	**kick**
7	**kick**
6	**kick**
5	**go for two**
4	**go for two**
3	**kick**
2	**kick**
1	**go for two**
0	**kick**

Analysis of the PAT guide

If you **tie** the game with a touchdown, should you go for one or two? One is usually a higher percentage play. One is **enough** to win. Obviously you go for one.

Up by one

Suppose you are **up by one** after your touchdown. The guide says to go for two. The benefit of that is a field goal by the other team ties, but does not win. The disadvantage of going for two is the lower probability of success. Failure to get the two points leaves you in a position where you can be beaten by a field goal, but so does a successful kick. So there is no downside whatsoever to going for two and failing. Therefore, you go for two. Here are the choices and consequences when you are up by one:

Action	post-PAT margin	consequence
kick good	2	opponent needs field goal to win
run/pass good	3	opponent needs field goal to tie
fail	1	opponent needs field goal to win

Up by two

Action	post-PAT margin	consequence
kick good	3	opponent needs field goal to tie
run/pass good	4	opponent needs touchdown to win
fail	2	opponent needs field goal to win

A successful two-point gives a great result, but it leaves you vulnerable to a field goal defeat if it fails. Go for the higher percentage kick to ensure you end up with nothing worse than having to go into overtime.

Up by three

Action	post-PAT margin	consequence
kick good	4	opponent needs touchdown to win
run/pass good	5	opponent needs touchdown to win
fail	3	opponent needs field goal to tie

There is no difference between succeeding with the one or two point attempt, but failure hurts. So pick the one least likely to fail, the kick.

Up by four

Action	post-PAT margin	consequence
kick good	5	opponent needs touchdown to win
run/pass good	6	opponent needs touchdown to win (PAT almost automatic)
fail	4	opponent needs touchdown to win

The best outcome if you succeed is the two-point conversion. Is the increased risk of failure worth the additional benefit? Yes, because failure leaves you in the same situation as if you had succeeded with a PAT kick. Go for two.

Up by five

Action	post-PAT margin	consequence
kick good	6	opponent needs touchdown to win (PAT almost automatic)
run/pass good	7	opponent needs touchdown to tie, 2-point PAT to win
fail	5	opponent needs touchdown to win

Again, a successful kick and a failure have the same result, so you might as well go for two, which gives you a significant advantage if successful.

Up by six

Action	post-PAT margin	consequence
kick good	7	opponent needs touchdown and 2-point PAT to win
run/pass good	8	opponent needs touchdown and 2-point PAT to tie
fail	6	opponent need touchdown to win (PAT almost automatic)

You want to avoid failure with these three results, so you pick the play least likely to fail, the kick.

Up by seven

Action	post-PAT margin	consequence
kick good	8	opponent needs touchdown and 2-point PAT to tie
run/pass good	9	opponent needs two scores to win
fail	7	opponent needs touchdown and 2-point PAT kick to win

Getting two puts you in great shape. But failing to convert leaves you vulnerable to a 2-point conversion loss. Kick.

Up by eight

Action	post-PAT margin	consequence
kick good	9	opponent needs two scores to win
run/pass good	10	opponent needs two scores to tie
fail	8	opponent needs touchdown and 2-point PAT to tie

Kick. The benefit of a successful two-point conversion is not worth the risk of a tie.

Up by nine

Action	post-PAT margin	consequence
kick good	10	opponent needs two scores and 2-point PAT to win
run/pass good	11	opponent needs two scores and 2-point PAT to tie
fail	9	opponent needs two scores to win

Kick so the opponent has to go for two.

Up by ten

Action	post-PAT margin	consequence
kick good	11	opponent needs two scores and 2-point PAT to tie
run/pass good	12	opponent needs two touchdowns to win (PAT almost automatic)
fail	10	opponent needs two scores and 2-point PAT to win

Kick. Going for two gets you a benefit but leaves you vulnerable to a loss.

In college, remember the danger of a PAT runback

The risk-reward ratio of a PAT attempt, either kick or two-point, is infinitely different in college than it is in high school or college. That's because failure by the offense to convert simply renders the ball **dead** in high school and the NFL. But in college, failure by the offense often leaves a **live** ball for the defense to run back for a two-point touchdown.

This unique rule can be an adjustment problem for coaches who are new to the college ranks as well as for players who have played under the high school rules for four to ten years in high school and youth football.

St. Mary's versus Davis, 9/28/91

On September 28, 1991 Saint Mary's College of California may have lost a heartbreaker because of the unique college rule. Saint Mary's was trailing the University of California at Davis 8-6 at Saint Mary's with 11:32 left in the fourth quarter when they got a touchdown making the score St. Mary's 12, Davis 8.

The standard PAT table says when a touchdown puts you ahead by four points, you go for two, and that's what St. Mary's did. Their two-point conversion pass was intercepted and run back for 100 yards scoring two points for Davis. The score was then St. Mary's 12, Davis 10. St. Mary's was unable to score on three subsequent possessions.

With 7:34 left in the game, Davis kicked a field goal and won the game 13-12.

Clock-management mistake?

Did St. Mary's make a clock-management mistake risking the PAT at all when they were ahead? No. You would not risk a PAT of either variety—one- or two-point—**if time had run out during the touchdown play** and you were only ahead by one or two points. But with 11:32 left, you cannot pass up the chance to score more points.

Should St. Mary's have gone for **one** instead of **two**? Yes, **if their success rate on the two-point conversion play was less than half their probability of success on the one-point play**. I do not know what their success ratio was on each type of PAT that season. But I **do** know there is little difference between being ahead by four, five, or six points. The opponent has to score a touchdown in all three cases.

You would also take into account **how the game had gone** up to that point in deciding whether to go for two. Going for two is generally a close call when you still expect additional possessions before the end of the game, because the typical two-point conversion success rate is almost precisely half the one-point conversion rate.

Wrong play?

Is it possible that St. Mary's was right to go for two, but picked the wrong play?

Certainly some plays have a higher probability of being returned for a touchdown than others, like pitches and flat passes. If your PAT-kicking team has a history of solid protection, good snaps, and sure-handed holds, the kick probably has a significantly lower chance of being run back for a two-point touchdown than **any** two-point conversion play.

You should always prefer plays with less danger of a touchdown runback when equally effective alternatives are available. Unfortunately, I have found wide plays are generally more successful in the goal-line area, so there may **not** be equally effective alternatives.

Two-ball drill

St. Mary's loss to Davis suggests it would be useful to practice your two-point conversion pass play with two balls. That is, always have a twelfth man who already has a ball standing behind the end zone. If a scout-team defender intercepts the pass, the PAT team can tackle **him**. But if the pass is **not** intercepted, the twelfth man always takes off through the end zone heading for the other end zone as if he had intercepted it. That way the PAT team gets in the habit of always going on defense once the pass is in the air.

When I was in the army, every time we captured an objective in war games, the enemy would counter attack. **Every time**. It taught us that you do not celebrate when you capture an objective, you immediately set up your defensive perimeter.

1995 Notre Dame–Texas game

In the 1995 Notre Dame-Texas game, Notre Dame blocked a Texas PAT kick, picked it up and returned it 98 yards for a two-point touchdown. No clock-management mistake, just an execution breakdown. Texas was down 17-13 when they lined up for the kick. Notre Dame went on to win 48-27.

Why not riskier ball handling?

This book is similar in nature to *The Hidden Game of Football* and *The New Thinking Man's Guide to Pro Football* or Bill James' books on baseball. That is, it is more analytical than the usual football book.

Those other books include several passages where the authors wonder why football coaches do one thing or fail to do something else. For example, in *The Hidden Game of Football*, authors Thorn, Carroll, and Palmer wonder why the popularity of the shotgun formation has not led to more **quick kicks**. In *The New Thinking Man's Guide…* Paul Zimmerman wondered why teams didn't use the **no-huddle** other than at the end of a half. (Since he wondered that in 1984, some teams **have** gone to a whole-game no-huddle.)

For my part, I wonder **why high school and NFL coaches don't use riskier ball handling on PAT plays**. You cannot tell from video of high school or NFL two-point conversion plays whether they are PATs or just regular plays from the two yard line. I can understand that in **college**, where the rules permit a two-point touchdown **runback** by the defense. But in high school and the NFL, the two-point conversion is a **unique situation**. The offense can score or fail to score, but the **defense cannot score** no matter what. In high school and the NFL, there is **no turnover risk**.

Given that fact, it seems to me that high school and NFL coaches could and should be running all sorts of dipsy-doodle plays. For one thing, the PAT seems a great time to run the **option**. Another normally risky play is the **throwback pass** where you run one way then throw all the way back to the corner of the other end zone.

You could do:

- multiple laterals
- blind passes like in basketball
- tailback passes
- double reverses

- single-wing spin series plays
- flicker handoffs (an old single-wing exchange in which the tailback ran into the line extending the ball behind his back for the wingback to grab and run around end)
- fumblerooskies (in high school, not the NFL)
- drop kicks
- single-wing buck-lateral plays
- jump passes (my 1996 single-wing team completed one in a tough pre-season scrimmage)
- run-pass options
- rugby plays
- you name it.

The drop kick would be for a fake two-point conversion and go for one in high school or NFL. In **youth** football, kicked PATs are often worth two points and run- or pass-PATs, only one. In youth football the drop kick would be for faking the one-point and going for two. High school and NFL two-point PATs ought to be occasions for the announcers to comment, "Here comes the crazy stuff."

Don't lose track of the objective, to win the game. Running the most creative razzle-dazzle play, and failing to score, does not advance the cause. Style points don't count.

If you are going to run one or more of these plays you must practice them and master their execution like any other football play. But there ought to be at least some difference in high school and NFL football games between the PAT, which is risk-free when it comes to turnovers, and other offensive plays, which carry the ever-present risk of a turnover which the opponent could convert to points. In fact, I see **no** difference whatsoever between PAT two-point conversion play calling and regular two- or three-yard-line non-PAT play-calling in high school and NFL games.

Also, last play of the game

Everything I just said about the high school and NFL two-point conversion play also applies to that other situation, in high school, college, and the NFL, where there is no meaning to turning the ball over to the defense: **the last play of a game in which you are trailing and have possession of the ball**. Cal's upset victory over Stanford using a five-lateral kick return in the 1982 Big Game is the classic example.

PAT defense

If you are still ahead after the opponent scores a touchdown, but only by one or two points, the PAT play will tie the game or give the lead to one side or the other. If you are ahead by one, you must be suspicious of any formation that appears to indicate that the opponent will go for a tie. *Your defense must emphasize preventing the loss rather than avoiding the tie.* From the trailing team's perspective, the **fake kick** would be an excellent play if they wanted to go for the win.

In college, if you are down by one or two after a touchdown on the final play of the game, you have the right to force the offense to run a PAT play (NCAA 8-3-2a), and you should. They should be smart enough to take a knee. But if they are not, your last hope is to block the kick or strip or intercept a two-point conversion attempt and run it back for a two-point touchdown.

21

Behind on special teams

Most coaches practice a two-minute drill for when they are behind on offense. A smaller number practice their four-minute drill for when they are ahead on offense. But hardly any coaches practice hurry-up and slow-down special teams. This chapter is about special teams plays when you are **behind** and need to save time.

Punt

Normally, when you punt and the other team does not catch the ball, you allow it to bounce and roll **as long as it's going in the direction you want**. This is a well-known football principle which almost does not have to be coached because players have seen it so often on TV.

But when you are behind in the final minutes of a game, **time becomes more precious than yards**. So you *down the ball as fast as you can regardless of the direction it's rolling*. I suggest you yell "Stop the clock!" and have your players yell it to each other when they practice this. You'll only need a couple of reps. But you have to practice it at least a little to plant the seed in their minds that **sometimes**, you don't let it roll.

A new high school rule for the 1997 season says the punting team can catch the punt **in the air** if no one from the receiving team is in a position to catch the ball. That would be the best way to conserve time.

Better idea, punt out of bounds

Here's a better idea, punt it out of bounds. I always tell my punters to punt it out of bounds unless I'm doing one of my "fourth-down quick kicks," in which case, there's nobody back to receive and we can kick straight down the field. When you punt out of bounds, the clock stops when the ball crosses the boundary. Or at least it's supposed to.

You should check to make sure. Also, punting out of bounds makes sure there is no damaging punt return.

Going for it on fourth-down

As I said above, when you are behind at the end of a game, field position is less important than time. **Possession** is also important. With the rare exception of a safety, you have to be in possession of the ball to get the winning score.

Punting gives up possession. So does that mean you never punt when you are behind near the end of a game? Let's think about it.

The purpose of a punt is to achieve a favorable field-position change. But in a clock-management situation, you need to remember the more-versus-enough principle. **Normally**, **more** yards are better than **fewer** yards. Normally, moving the ball toward the goal you are attacking, even in conjunction with a change of possession, is worthwhile. But there comes a time in a game when more yards are **worthless**.

*If your **current** possession is likely to be your **last**, you have to go for it on fourth down* because you must retain possession to have any chance to win. Telling which possession is your last is tricky.

Punted at 5:03 left; never got the ball back

In the 1994 Army-Navy Game, Navy was trailing 22-20 and had fourth and four at their own 30 with 5:03 left in the game. They punted, and **never got the ball back**. In hindsight, you can see they should have gone for the first down. But hindsight is not what this book is about. Can we draw a principle regarding how late in the game you switch from punting to going for it?

It's a function of how the game is going, how many points you need, your field goal kicker's range if three is enough, the wind, and so forth. So just put it in your memory banks that 5:03 left was **too late** in the game for Navy to have punted on fourth and four in 1994.

If it is earlier in the game, such that you believe you can regain possession by forcing the other team to punt, you should punt, but kick out of bounds or at least stop the ball from wasting time by rolling.

Remember, you should be in a time-conserving mode as soon as you fall behind in the game. If the punt is bouncing toward the goal you seek to cross at **high speed**, let it bounce. But if it's bouncing **sideways** or **slowly**, down it.

Fake punt or regular scrimmage play?

The fake punt is a great play. It should be done far more often. But toward the end of the game, when it is apparent to everyone in the stadium that you can no longer give up possession, it is silly to run a fake punt. The fake punt only makes sense when the opponent believes you are really going to punt.

In a 1996 game, where I was offensive coordinator, we were behind 10-0. Late in the game—about one minute left—we had fourth and long around our own 20. The head coach yelled "Punt team!" I immediately asked, "Fake punt?" "No" he said, and we punted. The other team never believed we were going to punt. They put no one deep and they reacted to the play as if they were sure we were faking it.

Once they saw the punt, they let it roll and just took a knee for the rest of the game. In fact, we should have gone for the first down on that fourth-down play. Our opponent knew it. But our head coach, for whatever reason, either wasn't thinking straight or decided there was no hope. When you're down 10-0 with less than a minute left, deep in your own territory, there **isn't** much hope. But stranger things have probably happened in the annals of football. As long as you have **any** hope, you do what you have to do to win.

Substitutions

In my warp-speed approach, I did not even want to waste time substituting for special teams. My kick-return team and my punt team deliberately used the same personnel as my offense. After our kickoff returner was tackled, we would immediately line up and run a play. Often the opposing team was engaged in some massive change of players as their kickoff team left and their defense came onto the field. Referees were sometimes chagrined to see that their usual practice of blowing the ready-to-play whistle while both teams were making post-kick substitutions was giving us an advantage because we would run a play within one or two seconds of the ready-to-play whistle while the other team was just arriving.

Against Benicia, my youth team pulled off a 43-yard pass play right after the kickoff. Benicia was so taken by surprise that they were still in their defensive huddle when we snapped the ball. That would have been OK. We had even practiced not politely waiting for the opponent to get ready. But we did **not** practice staying at the line of scrimmage on a **pass** play when there was no nearby opposition to block. Consequently, our entire offensive line ran to the defensive huddle to block and our pass was called back for **five ineligible receivers downfield**!

One of the biggest special-teams clock-management problems is getting the punt or field-goal team onto the field fast when time is running out. Why not use the offensive personnel for those two teams? Or at least hold the substitutions to an absolute minimum?

Charity unit?

Many coaches use the special teams as a sort of charity unit. It's a place to put guys who you'd like to give playing time, but who aren't good enough to make the offense or defense. On kickoff, kick return, and PAT kicks, that practice has few clock-management ramifications. But in punt and field-goal situations, it can cost you a game.

The relative weakness of the special-teams players is part of the problem, but the **main thing is simply the need to change personnel**. That would be a time problem even if you were replacing eleven Heisman Trophy winners with eleven more Heisman Trophy winners!

Buffalo's Jim Kelly said they ran a play every **18 to 20 seconds** in their no-huddle. My youth team's warp-speed could cut that to about **13 to 15 seconds**. In the 1997 Rose Bowl, Ohio State ran twelve plays in 1:21 or about **6.75 seconds** per play. But the authors of *The Hidden Game of Football* say it takes about **27 seconds** to get a punt or field goal team onto the field and snap the ball.

In his two-minute drill clinic in the 1990 *Coach of the Year Clinic Manual*, Grand Valley State coach Tom Beck said he can get his field goal team onto the field and kick within **15 seconds** as a result of practicing the move. Stanford's offensive coordinator Dana Bible says he can get his field-goal team out and snapping within **seventeen seconds** of the previous play end. Colorado head coach Rick Neuheisel says it takes **25 seconds** to get your field-goal team out, lined up, and snap; **15 seconds** if you got a first down on the previous play (moving the chains takes about ten seconds).

Putting in special personnel can cost you a game

The extra 7 to 14 seconds it takes you to make those personnel changes can cost you the game. Are the personnel changes **absolutely** necessary? Are you willing to lose a key regular season or playoff game because you could not get your field-goal team onto the field before the final gun? Are you willing to lose a crucial game because you had to run one less offensive play in order to leave the 27 seconds necessary for the field goal team to get onto the field?

In youth football, probably not. And maybe not in high school and the lower college levels. In youth football, my long snapper was my regular snapper (we ran the single wing) and my punter was my tailback, even though he was not the best pure punter. In higher levels of football, the long snapper is often a different person from the regular first-string center. Make the regular center also your long snapper if possible.

The place kicker is also often a guy who does not start on offense. For **long** kicks, you need the best long-distance kicker on the team, whether he starts on offense or not. But half the guys on the team can probably kick **short** field goals.

I have generally found that the best athlete on the team is the best **holder**. In fact, **only** the best athletes are even competent at it. Holding is the toughest job on the field-goal team. So I would have a guy like my first-string tailback hold in general. That happens to also be helpful in minimizing substitutions.

A strong argument can be made that a team ought to have a member of the starting offensive backfield who gets many practice and game reps at kicking short field goals and PATs.

Although there is never a great rush to kick an extra point (it is an untimed down), you could make this short-distance guy your PAT kicker. That would give him game experience and it would make for a simple, understandable command to be used by the coach in the last ten seconds of a game where you are three or less points behind and the **clock has not been stopped by the previous play**: "**PAT kick team!**" You don't want any confusion in such a situation.

Ideally, your offense personnel would also be your punt and field-goal team. In youth football, I did exactly that. I believe I could do it in high school as well, except for the likely need to substitute a long-distance place kicker for long-range field goals.

Fake-kick plays

There is an additional benefit to using your regular offense for punt and field goal teams: Fake-kick plays.

Number **one**, your **regular** offense can **execute a fake** punt or fake place-kick **better** than your special teams. Number **two**, the opposing defense will be **more afraid** of the fake if your number one offensive guys stay in the game. That will cut down any block-the-kick rush. The higher your level, the more it will screw up your opponent. They won't know what **defense** to call. They won't even know **which team** to send in. I saw that even in youth football.

We would punt out of our regular offensive formation with the same personnel. The **first** time, the opponents would figure we were going for it and send their defense in. We'd punt with nobody deep and it would roll an extra 15 yards. The **next** time they would again send in the defense, but they'd put one guy deep. What defense is that?

We'd punt again, only out of bounds. When the **third** fourth down came up, they were totally confused. This time they'd put their punt-return team in, their ends would penetrate like crazy to block the kick, and we'd trap them and run off tackle for the first down.

After that, their coaches would yell what I saw an NFL coach saying in one of those blooper videos: "Watch everything!"

Put yourself in your opponent's shoes

Think a bit more about the opponent's perspective on your punting and field-goal kicking with your regular offensive personnel. For one thing, you'll be ready to snap **immediately**.

Given the situation, the opposing defense will expect that you will change to punting or kicking team personnel and they will yell "Punt return!" or "Field goal defense!" to their bench. It takes a long time for the punt or field-goal teams to get on the field and lined up to snap. The same is true of their counterparts on the other side of the line of scrimmage. Furthermore, they are used to getting many seconds to make their changes.

If your guys are used to running a quick, no-personnel-change punt or field-goal play, and the other team is **not**, you get the same effect as the Bengals all-game no-huddle had on opposing defenses. Your special-teams opponents will not know whom to put in, what defense to run, or how to get them in fast enough even after they figure out which they want to do. In fact, there is a good chance that they will use a **timeout** if they have one. Then you'll have plenty of time to put in anyone you want.

If you substitute, hold down the number of subs

If you are going to substitute to punt, or place kick, try to hold the number of substitutes to a minimum. The fewer the subs, the faster you can get them lined up. The fewer the subs, the lower the probability of having too few or too many or the wrong personnel on the field. Many a last-ditch effort to run a play has dissolved into substitution confusion which ended only when the referee picked up the ball signaling the end of the game.

The regular center can probably be taught to **long snap**. An offensive back can probably be the **short-range place kicker and punter**. Another offensive back can probably learn to **hold**. The main problem that requires subs is the **wide receivers** on the field-goal team. In general, one would not expect them to do well at the tight-end and wing positions. A **spread-punt formation** could make use of wide receivers, although that would typically be additional incentive to punt out of bounds or run a fake-punt play.

If you substitute, practice doing it fast

Can you beat the 27 seconds *The Hidden Game of Football* says it takes to get a punt or field-goal kicking team onto the field and lined up? With practice, you can.

A lot depends on the coach in charge of the team in question. He has to recognize the need for the punt or field-goal team **in advance**. He then needs to gather the necessary players who are on the sideline. Typically, at the lower levels of football, other members of the special team will already be on the field playing offense.

The coach needs to have a chart or diagram that shows who is about to go **onto** the field, by jersey number, and who is about to come **off** the field. The players who need to go on the field should be "in the blocks" ready to bolt as soon as the dead-ball whistle is blown ending the previous play.

They are less of a problem than the players who need to get **off** the field. The players on the sideline have nothing else to think about. They are standing next to the coach in charge of sending them out. He can put them in a group as near to the line of scrimmage as possible and yell "Go!" at the whistle.

But the guys who need to come **off** have other things to think about. They are in the game trying desperately to gain yards. They often are unaware the down, distance, or the coach's intentions for the next play. The fact that they need to leave the field may come as a surprise to them.

It is especially hard for them to shift mental gears in an instant and remember whether they are on the special team in question. They may have trouble telling what team the coach wants on the field, let alone remembering whether they are **on** that team.

The trickiest part is making sure one player comes off for every player that goes on. The coach needs to see the right people come off. But if too few come off, he has to figure out **which player** mistakenly stayed out there. The more players you substitute, the harder that becomes. In fact, after about three players, it becomes **impossible** to tell who is in the wrong place if the number **on** does not equal the number **off**.

One of the subs going in should be captain of the subs in charge of getting the correct guys off the field. He should have a ***wrist plan*** *showing who goes on and who goes off and the alignment of the special team for the play in question. His wrist lists and diagram should be in jersey-number format.*

It is wise for the departing players to be required to go to a certain area segregated from the rest of the players on the sideline so any players in the wrong place can quickly be spotted.

Better ten than twelve

Whatever system you use should have a bias in favor of ending up with **ten** players rather than **twelve**. For example, you could select a player in advance who will be ordered off the field if you have too many men on the field. On the **punt** team, the **personal protector** is the best candidate. On **field goal**, it should be the **near wing**. Those are the positions you can do without most easily, especially when you have an eight-man line, which apparently you do or you wouldn't have to take another guy off the field. You should practice this emergency "get off the field" maneuver once or twice so the player in question doesn't hesitate in a game situation.

If you are a man short but do not have time to fix it, your field captain must make sure you have ***at least seven men on the line*** *before he calls for the snap.* Practice that, too.

Fake-field goal or fake punt

Fake-field goal and fake-punt plays can be very effective because of the element of **surprise**, the **unsound** nature of the opponent's special team when it comes to **defense**, and, in most cases, and **personnel mismatches**. But when the game situation makes it obvious that you are **not** doing a field goal or punt, lining up in a field goal or punt formation is **not** a good idea. If you **have to** go for it and everyone in the stadium knows it, line up in one of your regular offensive formations.

Scrimmage kick is not a 'safe' play

Again I want to make the point that you should **not** allow your players to believe the TV announcer line they've heard dozens of times: that field goals and punts are "safe" plays.

In the first quarter of the 1993 Notre Dame-Boston College game, Notre Dame tried to score first with a 47-yard field goal, but it was blocked and run back to the Notre Dame 15-yard line. Boston College was then successful in their field goal attempt. They later upset the 10-0 Notre Dame team on the last play of the game by a score of 41-39, thereby spoiling Notre Dame's national championship hopes.

There was nothing wrong with Notre Dame's decision to kick—as long as their kicker had a legitimate chance to succeed form 47-yards out. But there appears to have been a let-down executionwise on the Irish side. Kicking plays occur disproportionately in clock-management situations. Successful clock management requires preventing kicking team members from treating their duties less seriously than offensive and defensive players.

Onside kick

Whenever you need to score **twice** in a short period to win, the onside kick is virtually mandatory.

In his *Guide to Special Teams*, coach George Allen said,

> *...the outcome of an onside kick depends more on luck than on either skill or execution. The bounce of the ball has more influence on the result than any controlling factor...*

Allen ranks fourth (behind Lombardi, Madden, and Gibbs) on the all-time win percentage among NFL coaches with 100 or more victories. He invented the special teams coach, hiring Dick Vermiel to be the first one at the Los Angeles Rams in 1969.

In support of Allen, I recall no NFL team in my lifetime that was known as being good at onside kicks. However, I suspect a team can increase its success rate with the onside kick, especially at the lower levels of football.

Every kick

On my youth teams, I did onside kicks almost every time, regardless of the game situation. The first year I observed youth football, the opponents of my son's team ran about 20% of the kickoffs back for touchdowns. I decided I was not going to kick to the best returner if I ever became a youth coach.

My goal was only to **eliminate the return**. Youth kickers cannot kick very far to begin with, so the field position after an onside kick is about the same as on a well-covered "deep" kick. But to my surprise, we had great success recovering the kicks. We got about 30% of them one year and about 20% another.

15 minutes a week

On those youth teams, we practiced special teams 30 minutes per night three nights per week. There are six special teams so that works out to 15 minutes per team per week. Although that sounds like a brief period of time, it actually was enough to accomplish a lot if used efficiently.

The most successful strategy I found was a bit different from the usual onside kick. We found it best to put the ball on one hash mark and kick across the field to a spot outside the opposite hash mark. Furthermore, we kicked it **over** the first rank of the kick-return team. The usual onside kick goes **to** the front rank rather than over them. Here's a diagram:

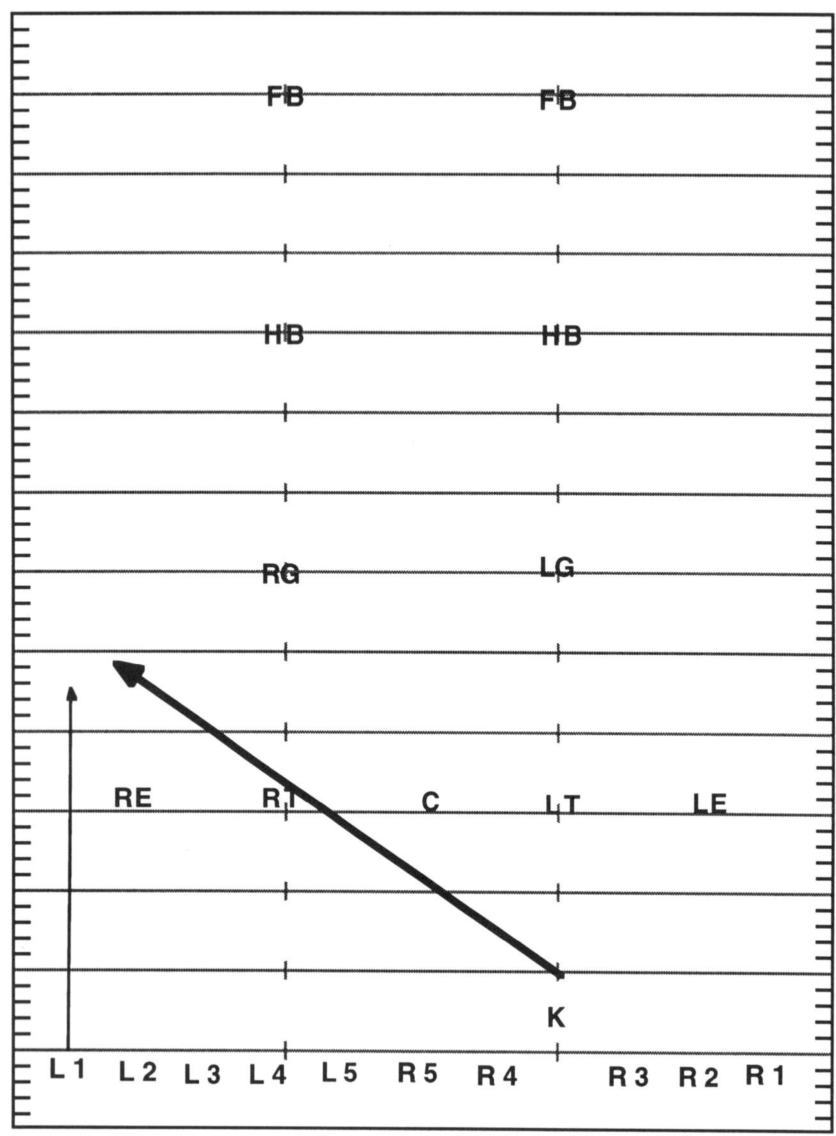

Like a pass

This approach to the onside kick is pass-like. The kicker on the right hash is the "quarterback." The intended "receiver" is the left end (L1) on the kickoff team. Although all other members of the kickoff team are "eligible" and other players like L2 or L3 sometimes recover the kick.

I hasten to add that the kickoff team may **not** catch the ball **in the air** in high school. I have had arguments with high-school coaches over that. You can look it up. NFICA Rule 6-1-5:

> *Any kicking team member may recover a free kick if it has* ***both touched the ground and*** *gone beyond the plane of R's free kick line [ten yards]. [emphasis added]*

So in high school, the "pass" from the kicker to L1 or whomever is **at least a one-hopper**.

In college and the NFL, you **can** catch the ball in the air (NCAA 6-1-3, NFL 6-2-4). I saw it happen at a St. Mary's College game a couple of years ago.

Block onside kick

Another type of kick that I believe should work great is what I call the block onside kick. I say "should" because I was never able to get it to work well. But the reason seemed to be a lack of discipline rather than defect in the play.

You can**not** block the kick returner who is waiting for a **fly** ball. That would be **interference**.

But what if the kick is **not** a fly ball? Then you can block anybody you want, including the guy who is trying to get possession of the ball.

So why not kick a **grounder** diagonally from the right hash to the return team's right end (who is on the kickoff team's extreme left)? The ball will take a while to get there because of its diagonal course. Your kickoff guys, on the other hand, are **not** on a diagonal course. They are running full speed right at the right end. How about assigning two of them to knock him into next week? I nominate L2 and L3 for the job. L1 and L4 will concern themselves with recovering the ball. Here's a diagram:

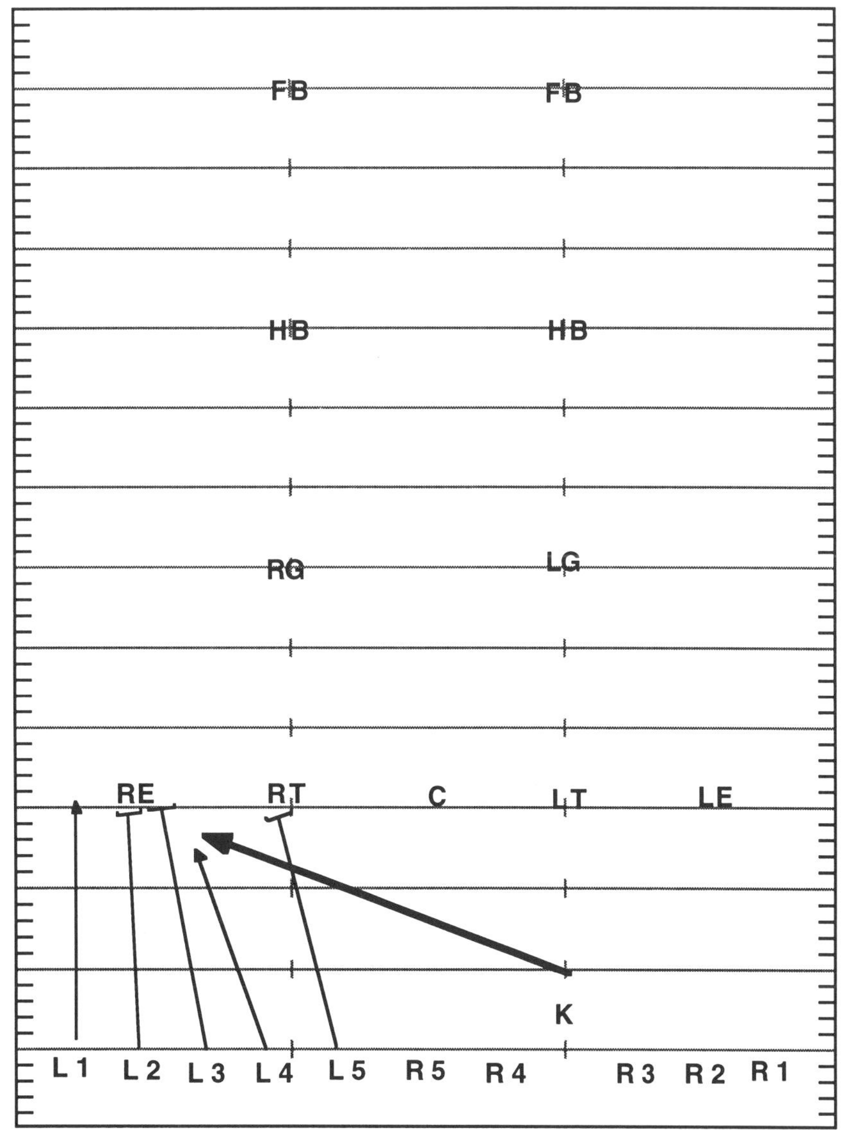

I don't know how you could stop this. The right end on the receiving team is going to be hit by two full speed blockers before the ball arrives. The right tackle is blocked by one guy. Two kickoff team guys, L1 and L4 are free to recover the ball as soon as it goes ten yards or is touched by a member of the receiving team.

The ball should be kicked above its middle. It will typically bounce low along the ground for about 15 yards then pop up ten or fifteen feet into the air. The pop is usually the third bounce. The right end can't catch it. He's taking inventory of his body parts. The right tackle is busy, plus he's not at ground zero. But the kickoff team has two guys there. Actually, they could have **ten** if they wanted. The kick **return** team cannot change their alignment much because the kickoff team can kick to any open space and only needs one guy there to recover the ball.

In practice, we found that the right end goes paranoid. He knows the blockers are coming. He knows the ball is coming. He knows the ball is supposed to be his priority. But it ain't.

The problem I have had is it is extremely difficult to get L2 and L3 to stick to blocking. They want to recover the ball!

The early eighties Vikings designated one guy to bat the ball—6'5" defensive lineman Randy Holloway, and one to catch it—wideout Terry LeCount. That went four for four at one stretch with LeCount recovering all four. In one game against the Vikings, 6'5" Charger Kellen Winslow said "I was getting ready to catch the ball and somebody jumped me." If the kick is a grounder, "jumping" or blocking the receiver is legal.

Starting the kickoff team

The way you **start** the kickoff team is important. Your goal should be to have the members of the kickoff team at full speed one yard behind the kickoff yard line when the kicker's foot hits the ball. To get to full speed, they need to start about seven to ten yards back. When do they start?

You have to fiddle with it. I always had the kicker signal "Go!" by dropping his arm. He then waits the appropriate amount of time before kicking. He learns by trial and error what that interval is. I or another coach stands as line judge in practice. The kicker and the kicker alone is responsible for offside. The tacklers are told to take off full speed without regard to the kick. They are not to even look at the ball until after it is kicked. If they are offside, the kicker is at fault. He needs to learn to time his yell and kick correctly.

Some players are faster than others. My kickoff teams generally have most players at seven yards back and one or two at eight or nine yards back. They deeper ones are the guys who went offside when they started at seven yards. That is, they are the faster players on the kickoff team.

Two balls

Sometimes, onside kicks are returned for touchdowns. I was on a youth chain gang in 1991 when that happened. The kick bounced off a receive team member—back toward the kicking team. They ran right past it. They seemed to think they could not touch it for some reason. They can and they should have. A member of the kick return team ran through the kickoff team and picked it up behind them. If anyone had been assigned safety duties, he was not doing his job.

It happens at higher levels, too. In the 1990 Navy-Notre Dame game, Navy kicked onside. Todd Lyght caught the ball and returned it 53 yards for a touchdown.

You should practice the onside kick with **two balls and twelve men** to make sure the kickoff team safety does his job. Let the onside kickoff unfold normally. Then, as the ball carrier is about to go down, have the twelfth man who is already carrying the second ball run onto the field as if the original kick returner had stayed up and broken through. Do this **every time** to teach the safeties on the kickoff team to get into the habit of taking their job seriously.

Kick return

You will generally get a deep kickoff when you are behind. If the kickoff is the **last play of the game**, you should have a **trick return** and the ball carriers should be ready to **lateral** if they can go no farther.

Otherwise, just do your regular return. The game clock will stop at the end of the kick return so you don't need to get out of bounds.

Punt return

If it is the last play of the game, the other team is not going to punt on fourth and whatever. Or at least they shouldn't. The danger of a block, bad snap, or touchdown return is too great. (Kansas City did it in a game I told about earlier in the book.)

If they **line up in a punt formation** for the last play of the game, it is most likely to deliberately **take a safety**, if they are ahead by more than two. If they line up in regular formation on fourth down when they are ahead by more than two it is also likely to be a deliberate taking of a safety. This is especially true when there are about ten to fifteen seconds left in the game and they are inside their own twenty.

You should have your fastest defenders lined up on each side of the offensive formation. *They must strip the ball at all costs.* Here's a diagram:

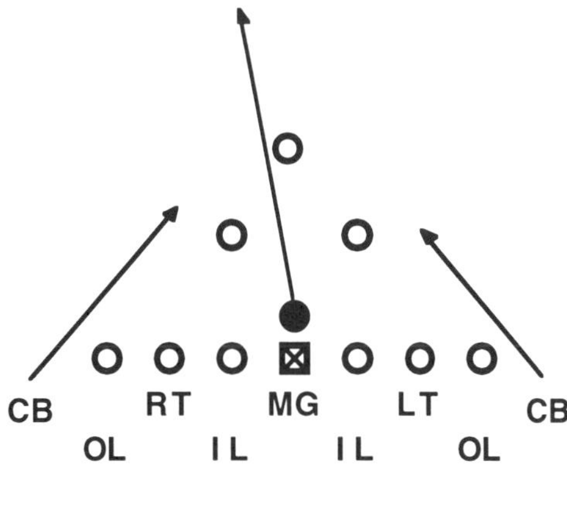

There is no specific best formation. If you get too stop-the-safety oriented in your defensive alignment, the offense may go for the first down, and get it.

Behind by two or less

Of course, if the opposing team is leading by two or less, they almost certainly will not **deliberately** take a safety. But if they are on their own two-yard line or some such, you may be able to inflict an **involuntary safety**. Also, in this case, if the offense cannot make the fourth-down play last until time runs out, they had better **punt**. You should have one guy back but make an all-out effort to block. The punter will be restricted by the end line. And you probably have a better chance of blocking the punt than of returning it.

If they get the punt off, your returner must catch it and return it or, in high school or the NFL, make a **fair catch**. If he can make a fair catch in field-goal range, and you are behind by three or less points, he should do so.

Remember that a fair-caught kick can be free kicked for a field goal during an untimed down in high school and the NFL. That is, you can fair catch the ball, even after time runs out, then free kick from the yard line at which you made the fair catch. A free kick is like a kickoff, not a scrimmage-kick field goal. The tee or hold is at the line of scrimmage and the opposing team must stay at least ten yards away until after the kick just like in a kickoff. The kicking team can request that the ball be placed anywhere they want between the hashes.

Because it is a free kick, your place-kicker's **range is extended by at least seven yards**. He also can take a longer run, like a kickoff, which should boost power if not accuracy. And there is no snap or blocking commotion, so the success rate should be higher than normal. Your team should practice this kick once or twice, mainly so they do not get a delay penalty asking you what the heck you're talking about when you try to do it for the first time in a game.

If you believe you have little chance of blocking the punt, and the offense is deep in their own territory with a lead of three or less, you may want to do as some teams have and put **three returners back** to maximize the possibility of a fair catch to set up the free-kick field goal.

When to attempt a fair-catch field goal

In general, when you fair catch a kick, you want to try to drive down the field and score a touchdown. Attempting a free-kick field goal after a fair catch should only be done when it's a better idea than a touchdown drive. When is that?

Touchdown drives take **more time** than field goals. If you have little time, like ten seconds left in the half, the free-kick field goal will probably be the better approach. There is also the issue of **enough**. If three points is enough to win, and you are well within your kicker's range, and there is little or no time for the opponent to come back and retake the lead, it's a no-brainer.

Is there any **danger** to a free-kick field goal? Yes. The kick can be **returned** if the field goal is not good. In **high school** it can be returned if it does not make it to the goal line. High school kicks that cross the goal line are touchbacks. In the **NFL** it can be returned if it does not go out the back of the end zone.

Your kicker's range is part of the equation. But a shank is always a possibility. Keep in mind that no matter how far the kicker can kick, it still has to be **accurate**. So the range you are interested in is the through-the-uprights-consistently range, not the raw distance your kicker can free kick.

There is no danger of a bad snap, bad hold, or blocked kick. Just a return danger. The kick must be covered if it is returnable.

Bears versus Packers, 11/3/68

In 1968, the Bears and Packers were tied at 10. Packer Donny Anderson punted from his own five-yard line. Chicago's Cecil Turner fair caught the punt at the Packer 43 stopping the clock with :32 left in the game. Bears' placekicker Mac Percival then did a 43-yard free-kick field goal which was good. Chicago won 13-10.

Normal field position

If the other team lines up in punt formation with less than fifteen seconds left in the game, in a normal field position, they are probably **not** going to punt. But you have to have someone back to receive just in case.

Your returner must score on the play or stop the clock before it runs out. He can**not** dance away from the ball and let it roll. The punt team could refrain from touching it until after the final gun, in which case, you lose. *If the ball is punted, the returner must catch it, even if he has to do so on a dead run.* If he runs out of room to run after time has run out, he must **lateral**.

PAT guide

Over the years, I have seen many guides to whether you should go for one or two after a touchdown. Here's DigitalScout's version.

Margin after TD	Behind
10	**go for two**
9	*go for two*
8	*kick*
7	**kick**
6	*either*
5	**go for two**
4	*kick*
3	**kick**
2	*go for two*
1	*kick*
0	**kick**

I have often wondered what the basis for these guides was. I was especially intrigued by the notion that these were taken as gospel without any explanation or discussion. I have put the ones I agree with in **bold** and the ones I think are questionable in *italics*.

Analysis of the PAT guide

If you **tie** the game with a touchdown, should you go for one or two? One is usually a higher percentage play. One is **enough** to win. Obviously you go for one.

Down by one

Suppose you are **down by one** after your touchdown? The guide says to go for the tie. Did Ara Parseghian write this guide? Why not go for the win?

Seems to me that you would make the decision on which to go for based on the criteria I discussed in the "Tie or win" chapter. I would be inclined to **kick during the first three quarters** of the game, but **go for two in the last quarter**. If I thought the overtime procedure gave **me** an advantage, I would kick and thereby tie. If I thought the overtime procedure gave my **opponent** an advantage, I would go for the win now. In the **NFL**, I would go for the win in the fourth quarter on the grounds that I **might never get the ball in overtime**.

Of course, the success rate of your one- and two-point conversion teams is a key factor in the decision. The PAT guides that are given out by football equipment vendors assume certain success probabilities for each play. Those probabilities might apply to the college and pro levels. But high school and youth coaches frequently cannot count on their PAT kicking unit. Here are the pro and college success rates:

Level	year	kick	two-point
NFL	1995	96.0%	38.5%
NFL	1994	94%	51.0%
NCAA Division I-A	1994	93.4%	41.3%
NCAA Division II	1994	85.0%	43.9%

Here are the choices and consequences when you are behind by one:

Action	post-PAT margin	consequence
kick good	0	you need field goal to win or overtime
run/pass good	1	opponent needs field goal to win
fail	-1	you need field goal to win

Down by two

Action	post-PAT margin	consequence
kick good	-1	you need field goal to win

run/pass good	0	you need field goal to win or overtime
fail	-2	you need field goal to win

Since the win consequence of all three possible outcomes is the same, you should choose the one **most likely to succeed**: the **kick**. Then a subsequent field goal gives you victory. In the **fourth quarter**, you need to go for two and tie because you may not get another chance.

Down by three

Action	post-PAT margin	consequence
kick good	-2	you need field goal to win
run/pass good	-1	you need field goal to win
fail	-3	you need field goal to tie, touchdown to win

There is no advantage to **succeeding** with the **2-point** conversion. But there is a big disadvantage to failing, which is more likely to happen on a two-point conversion. Kick.

Down by four

Action	post-PAT margin	consequence
kick good	-3	you need field goal to tie, touchdown to win
run/pass good	-2	you need field goal to win
fail	-4	you need touchdown to win

The best outcome if you succeed is the two-point conversion. Is the increased risk of failure worth the additional benefit? The only benefit of a successful kick is the opportunity to tie. If you want to avoid a tie, you should go for two.

Down by five

Action	post-PAT margin	consequence
kick good	-4	you need touchdown to win
run/pass good	-3	you need field goal to tie, touchdown to win
fail	-5	you need touchdown to win

If you want to **win**, all three outcomes are the same, but the kick has the highest probability of success. If you are willing to settle for a tie, going for two has a better outcome, and failure leaves you in the same position as success on a kick. So go for two.

Down by six

Action	post-PAT margin	consequence
kick good	-5	you need touchdown to win
run/pass good	-4	you need touchdown to win
fail	-6	you need touchdown and PAT kick to win

The outcomes here are essentially the same. PAT kicks are pretty certain. There is no benefit of going for two and little disadvantage to failing. So you should pick the one most likely to succeed, the kick.

Down by seven

Action	post-PAT margin	consequence
kick good	-6	you need touchdown and PAT kick to win
run/pass good	-5	you need touchdown to win
fail	-7	you need touchdown and PAT kick to tie

The scoring of one or two has about the same consequence. But the consequence of **failing**, which is more likely in the two-point conversion, is bad. So avoid failing. Kick.

Down by eight

Action	post-PAT margin	consequence
kick good	-7	you need touchdown and 2-point PAT to win
run/pass good	-6	you need touchdown and PAT kick to win
fail	-8	you need touchdown and 2-point PAT to tie

In this situation, you either need a **two-point** conversion **now or later**. If you get it now, you can win with another touchdown and PAT kick. If your PAT kick is good, you need to score another touchdown and go for two. Sounds like a toss-up to me.

Down by nine

Action	post-PAT margin	consequence
kick good	-8	you need touchdown and 2-point PAT to tie
run/pass good	-7	you need touchdown and 2-point PAT to win
fail	-9	you need two scores to win or tie

If you want to win, not tie, you go for two. If you are willing to tie, go for one.

Down by ten

Action	post-PAT margin	consequence
kick good	-9	you need two scores to win or tie
run/pass good	-8	you need touchdown and 2-point PAT to tie
fail	-10	you need two scores to win or tie

Gotta go for two. Otherwise you need to score twice. That's tough to do.
Here's **my** "PAT guide" for trailing teams:

Margin after TD	Inside take-a-knee period	Pre-take-a-knee period
-10	go for two	go for two
-9	kick for tie, go for two to win	kick for tie, go for two to win
-8	either	either
-7	kick	kick
-6	kick	kick
-5	go for two	go for two
-4	go for two	**kick**
-3	kick	kick
-2	go for two	**kick**
-1	go for two*	**kick**
0	kick	kick

* In college or high school, if you believe the **overtime rules** favor your team, you should **kick** the PAT to tie the game. In the NFL, sending the game into overtime puts you at the mercy of the coin toss. If you lose the toss, you may never get possession again. If your defense has been stopping the opponent consistently, losing the toss is not that big a deal. I put the choices that are different when you are not yet in take-a-knee in **bold face**.

PAT defense when you are behind

You should expect the opponent to go for the number of points dictated by the standard PAT guide shown above. They may go for two via a fake-place kick. Since you are already behind, there is no way to win the game in high school or the NFL. However, in **college**, it is possible to pick up a loose ball or interception and run it back for a score.

However, success by the offense on the PAT—either one or two points—could make your comeback harder by increasing the margin :

- above three—field goal no longer enough
- above seven—touchdown and PAT kick no longer enough
- above eight—one score no longer enough.

Other than looking for the two-point play when indicated by the guide, there is no clock-management aspect to PAT defense. It is an untimed down.

Field goal or touchdown?

Sometimes, the decision to go for a field goal or a touchdown is a no brainer dictated by the game situation. For example, if you are down by two and on the opponent's ten yard line with fourth down and four seconds left and the clock stopped until the snap, you kick the field goal. But what if it's not so clear-cut?

Super Bowl III

Super Bowl III, 1/12/69, was the most famous one ever played. Jets quarterback Joe Namath guaranteed victory, then his AFL Jets defeated the NFL's Colts and changed the face of pro football forever. The NFL had not previously lost to an AFL team and the NFL claimed to be a superior league. In that game, then-Colts coach Don Shula made a possible clock-management mistake that has been little discussed.

With about 2:26 left, Shula was down 16-7 in the fourth quarter. He had fourth and five at the Jets 19. Should he have gone for the touchdown or field goal?

He needed a touchdown **and** a field goal to win, with a successful onside kick in between given the time remaining in the game.

Scoring a touchdown from the 19 in one play is difficult. Getting even a first down on fourth and five in the Red Zone is tough. The field goal would have been a 36-yarder. I do not have the success rates from 1969 for NFL field-goal kickers. But in 1995, the San Francisco 49ers' opponents were 9 of 11 from 30 to 39 yards—an 82% success rate.

The field-goal success rate was probably lower in 1969, but it still had to be higher than the from-19-yards-out touchdown rate. It would appear that Shula should have taken the 75% or so field goal and gone for the touchdown on his last drive **after** his team had recovered the onside kick. If you are going to go for the first down or touchdown in this situation, I would think a **fake field goal** would have a much better chance of success than a regular play. There were some other pertinent factors. The Colts had tried two field goals earlier in the game and missed them both—one from the same 19-yard line. Shula may have felt that his field-goal unit was unreliable that day and that he therefore had to score **two touchdowns** to win.

I do not know the Colts' 1969 fourth-down conversion rate, but earlier in the fourth quarter they had successfully converted fourth-and-10 at their own twenty.

Backup quarterback Earl Morrall had played most of the game because Hall of Famer Johnny Unitas had a sore elbow. But Unitas had come in late in the fourth quarter and led the Colts to their first touchdown. The Colts then recovered an onside kick and seemed to be on a roll as Unitas again led the team down the field. It may be that Shula felt it was necessary to maintain that emotional state by showing confidence in Unitas.

Obviously, even a successful field goal would not have had much chance of changing the outcome of the game. They would still have to recover the onside kick and drive half the length of the field for a touchdown.

As you know, the fourth-down conversion failed and the Colts turned the ball over on downs. The Jets subsequently got a first down but, after two delay-of-game penalties, had to punt. The Colts ran two more plays but were unable to score as the game ended.

When you have to score twice, go for the most probable score on the first fourth down.

22

Football clock-management practice plan

You need to practice your clock-management skills and dealing with all possible situations. Just one rep can be enough to cause the player(s) in question to make the right choice if and when they encounter that situation.

Just two or three reps of taking a safety

In 1993, I practiced taking a safety. We only did two or three reps. And we never took a safety that year. But the **following** year, we won two games by taking a safety. I was not the head coach that year. The guy who **was** the head coach did not ever practice taking a safety. I was the special-teams coach.

But many of my players from the previous year were on the team. And when we needed to run the play, they remembered it from the previous year. I can only imagine what they would have done had we told the kids **for the first time** during the final two minutes of the first game we won by taking a safety. We would have told a player, "Go tell the quarterback to run out the back of our own end zone. Tell him to delay stepping out until just before he is about to be tackled."

The messenger would say, "What!?" Then when he got to the quarterback, the players on the field would figure, "The messenger really screwed this one up. It's fourth down. We'd better punt."

Jonesboro (AR) High School's wide-ranging game-day eve practice schedule

In the May/June 1997 *Scholastic Coach & Athletic Director*, Jim DeVazier, defensive coordinator of Jonesboro (AR) High School wrote about an interesting, wide-ranging day-before-the-game practice schedule which, in part, covers an extraordinary number of clock-management situations. This might more accurately be described as a rehearsal. Here's a summary:

1. Normal kick return
2. Five offensive plays against scout team
3. Normal punt
4. Three defensive plays against scout offense
5. Normal punt return
6. Five offensive play ending in touchdown
7. PAT kick
8. Normal kickoff
9. Three defensive plays against scout offense no-huddle
10. Third-down long count, or other special situation
11. Punt block or trick return
12. Three offensive plays
13. Fake punt
14. Three offensive plays ending in touchdown
15. Two-point conversion
16. Onside kickoff
17. Goal-line defense against scout offense
18. PAT defense against scout offense
19. Goal-line offense
20. Deliberately take a safety
21. Free kickoff after taking a safety
22. Three defensive plays with substitutes
23. Return of long field-goal attempt by scout team
24. Punt from inside own ten-yard line
25. Quick kick from inside own ten
26. Fair catch punt from scout team out of their end zone
27. Hustle free kick field goal team out to free kick field goal after fair catch
28. Three nickel defense plays against scout offense
29. Two-minute drill
30. Field-goal unit hustles out to kick with clock running
31. Onside kick return
32. Two offensive take-a-knee plays

I really like this approach. But I think it should go farther. You should be doing **individual** and **group** periods on other days. And those do not easily fit this format. But when you get to **team** period, this format or a variation of it could be used every day of the week.

'Chance cards'

In the game of Monopoly, you have Chance cards which confront you with various situations. Your football practices could use the "Chance card" concept. Make a list of all the situations that you want your team to be able to handle. Put them on 3 x 5 cards. Then get at least one rep of each during the season. As you go through the stack of cards, put the ones you've done in the "finished" box.

When to practice clock management

Coaches either ignore clock management (especially below the high school varsity level) or they devote one or two days per week to it. Grand Valley State coach Tom Beck said, "We practice our two-minute offense every **Thursday and Friday**." In spring practice and early in the season, he practices **without a defense**. They gradually bring in the defense over the season.

Kevin Reilly, the Aberdeen (MD) High School coach who runs the "Bingo!" transition offense, says he practices that no-huddle offense **every day**. Tom Muhs of Westhampton Beach (NY) High School said he spends 10 minutes **every day** practicing his trips no-huddle offense. I agree with Reilly and Muh: every day.

Peter Moe of Washburn (ND) High School practices the no-huddle in a thud scrimmage for an extended period of time on **Mondays**. On **Tuesdays** and **Wednesdays**, he calls it on a **surprise** basis during regular offense practice. On **Thursdays**, they run it for another extended period against air.

How to practice clock management

Richard Strack, the freshman coach at Colonia (NJ) High School, said in his 4/97 *Scholastic Coach and Athletic Director* article that he introduces the no-huddle without a defense. I sort of had to do that in 1993. I only had 20 kids and they were rarely all present and 100%. So we ran eleven on six or some such.

During practice when a defense is used, Strack stands behind the defense and yells "Me!" just before he signals the play. That tells the defense not to look and the offense to look.

Necessary equipment

Football practice schedules should have a section marked "equipment needed" for each drill. Here's the "equipment needed" for clock-management practice:

- chains
- down marker
- whistle
- yellow flag
- play clock
- game clock
- score indicator
- pace panels (green, yellow, red, checkered) and timeouts-remaining indicator.

My impression is that few teams have a scoreboard at their practice field—unless they are an AstroTurf team and practice at their game field. I suspect a statistical study would find that coaches with **AstroTurf game fields** do a **better job of clock management** than grass-field coaches. The reason is that grass-game-field coaches are afraid to practice on their game field because they don't want to hurt the grass.

You should have a scoreboard (with score, time remaining, timeouts, etc.) at your practice field if at all possible. How can you do that?

- Move the old scoreboard to the practice field when you get a new game field scoreboard.
- Get an old scoreboard from another team that's replaced theirs.
- Arrange things so you can see the game field scoreboard from your practice field and turn the game field scoreboard on.
- Put your game field scoreboard on a swivel so you can turn it to face the practice field.
- Buy the cheapest new scoreboard you can find for the practice field.
- Make an old-time second-hand-style game clock and have a manager or off-duty player operate it by hand.
- Project a digital countdown clock up on the wall or some such with an opaque projector or computer projector.
- To hell with the doggone grass! Get your darned team ready. Practice on the game field and turn the game clock on.

At the very least, get your chains and down marker out, two stop watches, and a manager or player who will play referee. That's sort of what Stanford does.

I cite the lack of the above equipment at the vast majority of football practices even up to the college level as evidence of my claim that clock management is an underdeveloped aspect of football. Few coaches would deny their field goal kicker a goal post or their linemen a sled. Why do so many expect their players to learn clock management without giving them a chance to practice with a clock?

Personnel assignments for clock-management practice

Players can learn a lot by playing various roles during clock-management practice. Here's what I suggest:

• clock operator	quarterback, defensive captain
• referee	running back, quarterback, linebacker
• line judges	wide receivers, defensive ends or outside linebackers
• chain gang	running back, linebacker
• down marker	tight ends, strong safety

Of course, you need to rotate the first- and second-string guys between the various official positions and their regular positions on offense and defense. Having the players play these roles will teach them clock-management rules, the need to think about where the chains are when running with the ball or making a tackle, the need to stay in bounds or get out of bounds, and so forth. You can have managers do all this stuff. But they don't need to learn anything. Your players do.

Using video games for coach practice

Video games like *Madden '97* or *College Football USA 97* enable you to practice many aspects of game clock management without having your players present. *Madden '97* has a 25- and 40-second play clock and appears to be coordinated with the official NFL rules for realism. I rented these games and a Super Nintendo player at my local Blockbuster store to test them for this book. It's a tough job but somebody had to do it.

A disadvantage of the video games is they may not have all your plays or formations. Furthermore, the success rates for each play versus each defense which are programmed into the game may vary from your actual success rate in games.

Think of it as a simulator

Some may balk at using kid games to prepare a football team. First, I'll remind you that football itself is a kid game. Besides, you're already going to Toys R Us to pick up your Magna Doodle®. You might as well get a few football video games while you're there.

Second, I will point out that computer **simulators** are extremely popular and extremely effective for training professionals from tank drivers to pilots to astronauts, as well as to train those who must make decisions under time pressure like business executives, 911 operators, and admirals and generals participating in computerized war games.

You could pay someone to design a computer clock-management training program just for you. But it would cost a mint and would probably be inferior in many ways to the cheap games available in toy stores.

Toy designers are amazingly clever at holding down costs, plus they have the economies of scale that result from mass production. I recall a TV variety show when I was a kid. They had a production number in which dozens of dancers were wearing hats with blinking lights. The emcee explained that they had asked their engineers to design such a flashing-light hat, only to be told the cost would be prohibitive. So where did they get the hats? An executive found them in a nearby toy store.

Some variation in games

The defense in *Madden 97* gets five seconds to choose a defense. That's an unrealistic restriction.

You can choose the length of the quarters including. In *Madden '97*, you can choose quarters of three, five, ten, or fifteen minutes. *College Football USA* lets you choose game lengths of 20, 40 or 60 minutes. By selecting the shortest quarter or game length available you get to focus on end-of-half time-remaining situations.

A quarterly magazine, *Sports Video Games*, rates many football video games. Their Spring '97 issue reviews the following football video games:

Play Station
- Madden '97
- NFL Gameday
- NFL Gameday '97
- NFL Quarterback Club '97

Saturn
- NFL '97
- Quarterback Attack

There are other games and other machines. These just happen to be the ones this magazine has rated. I will not give their ratings because that might violate their copyright. Suffice it to say that they liked *NFL Gameday '97* a lot and were not impressed by *NFL '97*, which is Dolphins coach Jimmy Johnson's game. Ignore the coach whose name is on the game. The programmers are what matters.

College versions best for non-pro coaches

Youth, high school, and college coaches should use one of the **college** video games because the rules are the same or as close as you can get in a commercially available video game. They even have all 111 major college stadiums built in, for wind and other weather conditions I presume. Only NFL coaches should use the NFL games because their play clock and rules are different and that will screw up lower level coaches.

Use only as situation generator and scoreboard clock

Do **not** use the video games as they were designed. That is, don't play the darned things like they're intended audience plays them. Many aspects of the video games are unrealistic and a distraction. Rather use them just as football **situation generators**.

That is, use the game to give you a score, time remaining, field position, hash position, as well as occasional injuries and penalties. The video games do a great job of simulating a play clock and game clock as well as play results and unplanned events like injuries and penalties. They also have timeouts.

However, their play selection is very unrealistic and a skill you should not waste time learning. They offer a bunch of formations. You are to select a formation, then a play from their diagrams. Forget that. Rather make a rough translation table from their play book to yours. Then convert each play that you want to use to keystrokes. For example, in *College Football USA*, you run a triple option to the left out of the wishbone formation by pushing A then down arrow then A. The wishbone happens to be in the first set of diagrams you see and is labeled A. The down arrow scrolls you to a set of plays in which triple option left is also labeled A.

You would create your own playbook using the best equivalent play in the video game then ascertain and write down the keystrokes needed to run the formation and plays you want. When you practice, the offensive coordinator could say "wishbone triple option left" to an assistant who would quickly hit A down arrow A on the game controller.

If you try to use the game's own plays the way it is designed to beat the computer or a human opponent, you'll waste a lot of time learning the game's play book. Also, you really cannot run a top-speed hurry-up, one of the most important things you want to practice, using a video game, if you try to look at the many diagrams to select your next play. It takes too long to scroll and scrutinize each diagram.

As you play, the game will run its plays, which may be different from yours. But it will keep on generating various results and hash and field positions, all the while running the play and game clocks according to the rules.

Do not control the players

Some games give you the option of controlling one or more players during the play. You can't do that in games as a coach so turn it off in the video game when it's optional.

Turn on:

- injury generator
- penalty generator
- substitution option
- audible option (when your quarterback is participating in your video game)

Games typically offer options like weather and endurance. Turn them on. They add realism. If you have a weather report for your upcoming game, duplicate it.

Video your computer session

Video your play calling session on the computer. Evaluate it and look for ways to improve just as you do with film of your players.

Computer not necessary

Colorado head coach Rick Neuheisel does an off-field simulation with his quarterbacks. He makes a game board that looks like a football field and puts a pin where the ball is. He generates the various situations while his quarterbacks take turns making decisions. Neuheisel's two-minute drill relies on quarterback audibles. Off-duty quarterbacks keep the clock, keep track of the timeouts, and yell and try to distract the quarterbacks. His simulation was described briefly in the 1996 *Coach of the Year Clinic Manual*.

Use this book to make your practice schedule

Sit down with this book and your practice calendar for the year. As you go through the book, mark the date you want to practice something in the margin of the book and write the page number on the practice calendar on the day you want to put it in. Remember, I put the various principles in italics so you only need look for stuff in italics to get a list of things to teach.

23

Rules related to clock management

Youth football rules

Youth football generally adopts the high school rule book because there are many refs around who can officiate games that follow high school rules. But local youth football programs often **modify** the rules. For example, there are **minimum-play rules** which have clock-management implications. One of the reasons I ran the 70-to-80-plays-a-game, warp-speed, no-huddle offense in youth football was to minimize the percentage of plays my weakest players were on the field.

Another example, I found through trial and error that the 10-1 defense was the best one at the lower levels of youth football—and I so wrote in my two books on youth football. But many readers contacted me to say the 10-1 was **illegal** in their league. Some did not allow lining up in the gap (I told them to go to eight-foot splits on offense).

Apparently I was not the first coach to figure out that the 10-1 worked great in youth football. The leagues where it was illegal were probably dominated at one time by a 10-1 coach. In typical youth sports fashion, the incompetent opposing coaches ran crying to the league officials and outlawed the defense they couldn't stop.

Because they typically play four sequential games on the same field on the same day, youth football leagues and/or the officials often modify the rules to prevent delaying subsequent games. So in youth football, you need to ascertain what rule book they are following and what modifications, if any, they have made to it.

High school rules

Some freshman and junior varsity high school games which are played sequentially on the same field use modified clock rules to avoid delaying the start of the varsity game.

College rules

I presume most college coaches are sufficiently professional that they know the rules. When I called Arizona State coach Bruce Snyder to ask for his comments on my slowdown chapter, his secretary said he could not come to the phone because the entire staff was taking a test on football rules.

However, there may be some college coaches who have overlooked a clock-related rule or two. And I find that many youth and high school coaches get fouled up because of all the college and pro games they watch on TV. At youth and high school games, I often hear parents and opposing coaches protesting officials' calls with such comments as "In the grasp!" or "Uncatchable!" or "He got back in time!" Those are college or pro rules which do not apply to high school.

NFL rules

The NFL is obviously the most sophisticated form of football. Pro coaches have tried the hardest to get around the rules. Accordingly, the NFL competition committee has tried the hardest to **prevent** these most sophisticated coaches from getting around the rules. That creates an interesting opportunity. If you study the NFL rules, you will find little relatively unknown clock rules. These odd rules, which are **not** in the high school or NCAA rule books, could be used as a book of tricks—at least where sportsmanship or ethics are not an issue.

So I analyze the NFL rules in this book not so much to teach NFL coaches, but to point out to lower level coaches the differences between the rules they see on TV and the rules that apply to their games, and also to suggest that the NFL-only rules are a list of tricks that have been outlawed at that level, but which have not yet been outlawed at the lower levels, and therefore may suggest smart tactics.

High school, NCAA, and NFL rules are the same in most cases. But there are exceptions. It would be a good idea for high school and youth officials to give the table below to their game-clock operators the same way they give their public address announcers a diagram of the referees' hand signals.

Here is when the game clock starts in the various situations.

Clock starts...

Kickoff	**HS & NCAA**: When touched except that touches by the kicking team don't count if the ball has not gone at least ten yards (NFICA 4-1-a & 4-3, NCAA 3-2-5) **NFL**: When kicked (4-3-2) except during the last two minutes of a half in which case the rule is the same as HS and NCAA (NFL 4-3-2-2)
Start of even-numbered quarter	Snap (NFICA 4-1b, NCAA 3-2-5a, NFL 4-3-2)
Official's timeout	Ready-to-play signal (if previous play not incomplete, out of bounds, etc.). (NFICA 4-2a, NCAA 3-2-5-a-2 or 3 or 6 or 7 or 9 or 10, NFL 4-3-2-5)
First down	**HS, NCAA, & NFL**: Ready-to-play signal (NFICA 4-3b, NCAA 3-2-5-1, NFL 4-3-2-5)
Penalty enforcement	Ready-to-play signal (NFICA 4-2b, NCAA 3-2-5a-4, NFL 4-3-2-5) (The clock does not run at all during PATs or after a quarter has ended on downs that are replayed because of a penalty.)
Team timeout	Snap (NFICA 4-2b-1,NCAA 3-2-5a,NFL 4-3-2)
Inadvertent whistle	Ready-to-play signal (NFICA 4-2c, NCAA 3-2-5a-5, NFL 4-3-2-5)
Ball out of bounds	**HS&NCAA**: Snap (NFICA 4-3a,NCAA 3-2-5) **NFL**: Ready-to-play signal except during the last two minutes of the first half and the last five minutes of the game, in which case the clock starts on the snap. (NFL 4-3-2-3)
Free kick after safety	**HS & NCAA**: When touched except that touches by the kicking team don't count if the ball has not gone at least ten yards (NFICA 4-1-2a & 3-4-1a, NCAA 3-2-5) **NFL**: When kicked (11-4-3, 4-3-2) except during the last two minutes of a half in which case the rule is the same as HS and NCAA (NFL 4-3-2-2)
Touchback	Snap (NFICA 3-4-3d, NCAA 8-6-2 & 3-2-5, NFL 11-6-4 & 4-3-2)

Incomplete pass	Snap (NFICA 3-4-3e, NCAA 3-3-2a-5 & 3-2-5, NFL 4-3-1e & 4-3-2)
Attempted illegal consumption of time	Snap (NFICA 3-4-3h, NCAA 3-4-3, NFL 4-3-9)
Delay-of-game penalty	Snap (NFICA 3-4-3i,NCAA3-2-5a-4,NFL4-3-2)
Two-minute warning	**NFL**: Snap (NFL 4-3-2)
Change of possession	Snap

Clock stops

End-of-play whistle with penalty flag	NFICA 4-4-a, NCAA 3-2-6 & 3-3-2a-3, NFL 4-3-1d
Timeout	NFICA 4-4-b, NCAA 3-2-6, NFL 4-3-3
End of quarter	NFICA 4-4-d, NCAA 3-2-6, NFL 4-3-1h
Ball goes out of bounds	NFICA 4-4-e
Incomplete pass	NFICA 4-4-f
Score	NFICA 4-4-g
Fair catch	NFICA 4-4-h
Inadvertent whistle	NFICA 4-4-i
Two-minute warning	NFL 4-3-1g

Kickoff

Some people think the clock starts on a kickoff when the ref blows the ready-to-play whistle. No. In high school and college, the clock operator must wait until the ball is touched (not counting the "touch" by the kicker's foot). That's also the NFL rule for the last two minutes of the first half and the last five minutes of the game. Otherwise, in the NFL, the clock starts on the kick.

One of the referees will almost invariably remind the clock operator to start the clock, by making a circle with his arm, when the receiving-team member touches the ball. But the clock operator should try to start on the touching itself, not the official's signal.

In rare cases, a member of the kicking team will touch the ball first. If the ball has gone ten yards before a member of the kicking team touches it, the clock starts on the touch by the member of the kicking team. But if a kicking team member touches it **before** it goes ten yards and before a member of the receiving team touches it—almost invariably on a botched onside kick—the clock does **not** start.

Even-numbered quarters

If the second or fourth quarter starts with a snap as opposed to a kick, the clock starts on the snap. It is possible, by coincidence, for an even-numbered quarter to start with a kick, if the last play of the previous quarter was a score. All odd-numbered quarters start with kickoffs.

Official's time out

Official's time outs are called for things like injuries or equipment problems. It may be unseemly, but a team that is running out of time must line up to snap the ball before the end of an injury time out so as not to lose time between the ready-to-play whistle and the snap.

First down

The gaining of a first down only stops the clock temporarily until the chains are moved and the referee gives the ready-to-play signal.

Penalties

The clock does not start until the snap after a delay-of-game penalty for obvious reasons. If it did, the team that was leading near the end of a half would deliberately get multiple delay-of-game penalties to run out the clock. Teams often do deliberately take **one** delay-of-game penalty. But that is to make sure they get every single second of the play clock off the game clock and it is only done where field position means little or nothing to the offending team.

On all other penalties, the ref throws a flag during or after the play. If the play is in progress when the flag is thrown, the clock continues to run. But as soon as the play-over whistle is blown, the refs will signal stop the clock by waving both hands across each other above their head.

The refs will then signal the infraction to the sidelines and audience, discuss the penalty with each other and with the innocent team captain, and either enforce the penalty or indicate that it has been declined. They will then move the chains and change the down indicator as required by the penalty, if it was accepted, or by the play, if the penalty was declined. During all this time, the game clock is stopped. As soon as the refs are done with all this housekeeping, they will give the signal to start both the play clock and the game clock. A team that is running out of time must line up during the penalty housekeeping ready to snap the ball as soon as the ready-to-play whistle is blown. Otherwise, precious seconds will be lost.

Inadvertent whistle

Refs sometimes accidentally blow the whistle. When they do, they have to stop the clock and explain what happened to everyone. When they are done, they start both the game clock and play clock with a ready-to-play whistle. If you are trying to save time, get ready to snap during this period and snap as soon as the ready-to-play whistle is blown.

Ball out of bounds

The clock should stop when the ball goes out of bounds. That is generally when it is carried out by a runner. But it also means when it is thrown, kicked, or fumbled out of bounds. Whenever the ball crosses the sidelines or end line, the clock stops, assuming it was running to begin with. Players whose teams want to save time must get out of bounds before they are tackled. Make sure your players remember that the object is not to get out of bounds *per se*. Some may run out of bounds when they are in no danger of being tackled!

In high school and college, the clock that is stopped by the ball going out of bounds does not restart until the subsequent snap. That's also true in the NFL during the last two minutes of the first half and the last five minutes of the game. Otherwise in the NFL, the game clock starts on the ref's ready-to-play signal after an out-of-bounds.

After a safety

When a safety occurs, the clock is stopped. Safeties are followed by free kicks from the 20-yard line of the team that gave up the safety. A free kick is either a place kick, drop kick, or punt. The high school and college clock does not start until the ball is touched the same as on a kickoff. In the NFL, it starts on the kick unless it is in the last two minutes of the first half or the final five minutes of the game, in which case the rule is the same as in high school and college.

Touchback

College and pro players can run kickoffs out of the end zone. High school players can**not**. It is also a touchback when

- a punt goes into the end zone (NFICA 8-5-3a-1)
- an unsuccessful field goal crosses the goal line (NFICA 8-5-3a-2)
- a kick is muffed by the receiving team and the ball then goes into the end zone (This is the same as the kick going into the end zone without having been touched by the receiving team. A muff does not change the situation but a catch followed by a fumble would be entirely different.) (NFICA 8-5-3b)
- a muff or fumble by one team which goes into and out the back or side of the end zone their opponent is defending or is recovered by that opponent in the end zone they are defending. (NFICA 8-5-3c)
- an interception in the end zone or where the interceptor's momentum carries him into the end zone which is not run out and the interceptor chooses to down the ball rather than run out of the end zone (NFICA 8-5-3d)

The clock stops for a touchback when the ball crosses the goal line and touches the ground or is downed by a player. It restarts when the team that acquires possession snaps. You can tell the officials to place the ball anywhere between the hashes after a touchback.

Illegal consumption of time

The most common illegal consumption of time is getting up off the pile slowly. When a referee judges that has happened, he stops the clock and can restart it on the subsequent snap. The referee administers a delay-of-game penalty in addition. (NFICA 3-6-3, NCAA 3-4-3, NFL 4-3-10)

Score

When a touchdown, safety, or field goal is scored, the clock stops. Extra points are untimed. That is, the clock does not run during a try for the extra point.

Fair catch

The fair catch is interesting. The clock does not **start** until the ball is touched on a kickoff. But it also **stops** on a fair catch. So a fair catch on a kickoff would result in a kickoff where the clock never started at all. It is little known, but the receiving team has the option of doing a field goal attempt, as a free kick, after a fair catch, in high school and the pros. (NFICA 6-5-4, NFL 10-1-6a) College does not have that rule.

If you received a kick at a spot close enough to the opponent's goal post to be within your place kicker's range, you could then try to kick a field goal. The great thing about this is **the other team has to stay at least ten yards away**, just like on a kickoff. They cannot line up like usual a ball width away from your line and try to block the kick.

Two-minute warning

In the NFL, there is a two-minute warning which stops the clock until the next snap before the end of each half. There is also a two-minute warning in high school and college football, but it does **not** stop the clock. Rather the referee just quietly tells each coach that there are two minutes or less remaining the first dead-ball opportunity after the two-minute mark is reached.

Index